EARTH SYSTEM LAW

Written by leading experts, this open access book provides the first comprehensive and critical exploration of earth system law.

Environmental law, as it stands, does not meet the challenge of governing the many complex planetary transformations of the Anthropocene. Earth system law marks a new legal paradigm – replacing the fragmented, human-centred, state-based approach with an integrated, Earth-centred approach to planetary governance, purpose-built for our turbulent epoch.

The book offers innovative proposals for legal principles, actors, institutions, and ethics designed to safeguard the stability and integrity of Earth's life-support systems. It also delivers the first full stocktake of the earth system law framework and its scholarship, coupled with a forward-looking research and implementation agenda.

Earth System Law is for all those who are frustrated by the persistent inability of environmental law to address the interconnected governance challenges of the Anthropocene – and for those ready to help shape the next legal frontier. Researchers, students, practitioners and policy-makers alike will find here both the vision and the tools to rethink law for a human-dominated planet.

Earth System Law

Governing Planetary Transformations in the Anthropocene

Edited by
Louis J Kotzé

•HART•
OXFORD • LONDON • NEW YORK • NEW DELHI • SYDNEY

HART PUBLISHING

Bloomsbury Publishing Plc

Kemp House, Chawley Park, Cumnor Hill, Oxford, OX2 9PH, UK

1385 Broadway, New York, NY 10018, USA

Bloomsbury Publishing Ireland Limited, 29 Earlsfort Terrace, Dublin 2, D02 AY28, Ireland

HART PUBLISHING, the Hart/Stag logo, BLOOMSBURY and the Diana logo are trademarks of Bloomsbury Publishing Plc

First published in Great Britain 2026

A catalogue record for this book is available from the British Library.

A catalogue record for this book is available from the Library of Congress.

ISBN: HB: 978-1-50999-466-3
ePDF: 978-1-50999-468-7
ePub: 978-1-50999-467-0

Typeset by Compuscript Ltd, Shannon

For product safety related questions contact productsafety@bloomsbury.com

To find out more about our authors and books visit www.hartpublishing.co.uk. Here you will find extracts, author information, details of forthcoming events and the option to sign up for our newsletters.

BLOOMSBURY
OPEN ACCESS

An ebook edition of this book is available open access on bloomsburycollections.com. Open access was funded by the Bloomsbury Open Collections Library Collective.

Bloomsbury Open Collections is a collective-action approach to funding open access books that allows select authors to publish their books open access at no cost to them. Through this model, we make open access publication available to a wider range of authors by spreading the cost across multiple organizations, while providing additional benefits to participating libraries. The aim is to engage a more diverse set of authors and bring their work to a wider global audience.

More details, including how to participate and a list of contributing libraries, are available from http://www.bloomsbury.com/bloomsbury-open-collections.

Für Erich und Sabine Zweckberger

FOREWORD

It is a profound honour and pleasure to introduce *Earth System Law: Governing Planetary Transformations in the Anthropocene*, a timely and visionary book edited by Louis J Kotzé with contributions from luminaries across multiple disciplines. As Earth enters an era of unprecedented disruption of its biophysical systems at the hands of human systems, this collection serves as a call to reimagine the very foundations of law, to design a legal regime operating *for*, and not merely *in*, the Anthropocene. I am confident that this book will inspire scholars, practitioners, policy-makers, and students alike to think more boldly about the role of law in stewarding our shared planetary home.

A new vision of this scope is much needed. Consider that formal legal systems date back at least 4000 years. Over that span of millennia, legal institutions have proven remarkably adaptive in responding to the relentless march of social and technological change. Change has been a constant for law. Except in one important respect: one assurance legal systems throughout history and around the world enjoyed over those millennia was a stable Earth system. To be sure, Nature has presented many challenges to humans in the form of floods, storms, droughts, wildfires and other natural conditions, and law responded innovatively over the centuries. But law could put the Earth system in the background, knowing it was the dependable canvas on which Nature's varied images were painted. The weather changed; the climate system did not. Law had to deal only with changes in the weather.

Indeed, to the extent that law has paid much attention at all to the Earth system, it has until recently been primarily to enable the extraction and destruction of natural resources needed to support humanity's ever-expanding global social and economic footprint. Mining law is about mining minerals. Oil and gas law is about extracting oil and gas. Water law is about withdrawing water from lakes, rivers, and aquifers. Eventually, however, the vastness and intensity of human impacts on global resources, and the resilience with which legal systems facilitated them, led to the emergence of the field of environmental law. As the impacts on nature piled up and became more visible in polluted rivers and declining biodiversity, public sentiment demanded that Nature be protected for its own sake, not just for humans. Law responded, first with conservation and then through regulation. Only in the last 100 years, though – a mere blip in the history of legal systems – can it be said that the formal legal regime of environmental law formed and then proliferated.

This shift from enabling harms to Nature to preventing them made environmental law one of the most ambitious normative projects of modern governance: a body of doctrines, institutions, and principles designed to mediate the relationship between human societies and the 'natural world'. It has generated treaties, regulatory regimes, judicial decrees, and an extensive scholarly literature, all searching for ways to manage that relationship. The underlying mediative logic of environmental law is that, through *self-restraint* in the form of conservation of resources (eg, national parks) and *self-regulation* in the form of regulatory constraints on actions harming resources (eg, pollution control laws), it is possible to moderate and repair humanity's impacts on Nature. The trick, however, is to not restrain and regulate human activity too much, lest economic engines fail under the weight of law, or too little, lest ecosystems suffer extreme injury, but rather to get the so-called 'sustainability' balance between humans and Nature 'just right'.

Alas, the 'Goldilocks' logic of environmental law has turned out to be a fairy tale. It accomplished much good, to be sure, but as it clung harder and longer to the sustainability balance for its organising principle, environmental law itself became unsustainable. Less pollution is still some pollution; fewer trees cut is still some trees cut; less water dammed is still some water dammed; fewer species driven to extinction is still some driven to extinction; and the list goes on. Well intended and progressive at its founding, environmental law ultimately missed the forest for the trees. It is, of course, necessary to keep track of pollution, trees, water, species, and all the other *parts* of the Earth system that show up on the canvas as Nature. But the relentless accumulation of pressure on all the parts has begun to disrupt *the system*. The canvas is tearing.

Indeed, the paradox is that, at the very moment of environmental law's greatest sophistication and global reach, the Earth system itself is nonetheless undergoing accelerating destabilisation. Biodiversity loss continues at rates widely described as a Sixth Mass Extinction event. Climate change has moved from computer models to lived reality, marked by intensifying extreme weather events, sea-level rise, and ecosystem disruption. Plastics and other novel pollutants have permeated even the most remote environments, from deep oceans to human bloodstreams. These crises are not isolated; they are deeply interconnected manifestations of systemic disruption.

Environmental law has not succeeded in slowing, let alone reversing, the trajectory of this planetary degradation. Change is needed. Is environmental law up to the task? After all, environmental law has experimented, with great success, in the past to take on new challenges. Its institutions have designed liability rules, information-based and market-based programmes, technology-based regulations, vast licensing programmes, and a long list of other innovations to keep pace with new challenges. But these were all just different ways of tuning the dials of self-restraint and self-regulation to keep the sustainability balance 'just right'. With the Earth system itself moving out of balance, however, continuing with environmental law's dial-tweaking Goldilocks project would be utter folly. Environmental law didn't stop the aggregating harms in time to avert Earth system disruption, so why believe that more dial tweaking will? In short, environmental law will always be *necessary*, but it is no longer *sufficient*.

The emergence of 'earth system law' as a distinct legal design concept thus marks a moment of both reckoning and possibility, and this edited book's exposition on the coalescing field arrives in that context of urgency. No one could better lead the effort to take stock of the field's roots, current form, and future promise than editor Louis J Kotzé. In 2019, Kotzé and Rakhyun E Kim, also a contributor to this book, published an article in the *Earth System Governance Journal* with the ambitious goal of envisioning a 'new overarching legal phenomenon that, more than environmental law (among others) comprehensively accommodates and encapsulates the juridical aspects of earth system governance'. They laid out an accompanying research agenda for what they christened earth system law, the fruits of which appear as chapters in this book penned by an impressive international team of scholars.

The looming question that these and other earth system law theorists and practitioners face is obvious: How is this not simply more dial tweaking with a new label on the dials and a claim of paradigm change? The contributions herein take that question head on. Not to steal their thunder, but rather as encouragement for reading beyond this foreword, three overarching themes in this respect are revealed by the very name which Kotzé and Kim used to mark the project:

Earth: Environmental law was hamstrung by its name from the start. The term 'environment' does not imply an obvious scope or scale. The environment could refer to air, water, forests, or other specific resources, or everything. An environment could be anything from a small pond to an ocean. This indeterminacy permitted, if not encouraged, environmental law to follow reductionist paths dividing the law into media-specific (air, water, land) and object-specific (plastics, species, waste) silos. Referring to the environment also promotes a dualist perspective separating Nature from humans, as if 'the environment' is some external entity which the law is to manage.

It was a bold move for Kotzé and Kim to frame a new legal regime around the Earth, plain and simple. The Earth encompasses all environments, *and* all humans. Leading with that as the opening word for this new field of law makes it clear just how big the challenge truly is. The law can, of course, take on the Earth in parts, but earth system law reminds us to begin and end by asking how what the law does with respect to any part affects the Earth holistically.

System: The United States Endangered Species Act, considered a model for nations around the globe, professes in its statement of purposes to be intended to conserve the ecosystems upon which imperiled species depend for their survival. The word 'ecosystem' never appears again in the statute. Rather, the underlying design of the statute is based on a static equilibrium model of Nature: if the threat to a species can be identified, remove the threat and the species will recover. Fifty years after its enactment, we now know the law that should have been enacted would have been the Endangered Ecosystem Act, and that recovering species nearing extinction is a long, expensive, complicated challenge. Yet this is the pattern that much of environmental law followed, and inertia and path dependency prevented meaningful updating to keep pace with what science increasingly revealed about the complex dynamics of the Earth.

Cleverly, Kotzé and Kim avoided repeating that mistake. After all, they could have named the project 'earth law'. By inserting 'system' following Earth, they insisted that the 'law' component *from the start* recognises the Earth as a system of complex adaptive systems. It is brimming with non-linear dynamics, feedback loops, tipping points, and deep uncertainty. On top of that is the complexity of social systems affecting the earth system. Expecting the highly interconnected social-ecological systems that dot the Earth at innumerable scales to 'behave' in the way a law says they must, is a fool's errand.

Law: With the 'earth system' firmly anchored as their subject, Kotzé and Kim positioned 'earth system law' as informed by two larger projects. Earth system *science* provides the underlying understanding of and fluency in the Earth's complex dynamics. Earth system *governance*, forged by Frank Biermann and others as a distinct governance theory, envisions designing institutions, public and private, around that complex earth system. The point of this book, however, is that for earth system governance to leverage knowledge from earth system science and put governance into action, will require some amount of *law*. Yet scholars and practitioners in science and governance disciplines all too often identify problems and solutions and then turn to law to 'make it so', as if law is simply a collection of levers that can be thrown to make change happen in predictable and straightforward manners. But law is the product of legal systems that are vastly complex and adaptive in their own right. To be blunt, making law to 'make it so' is hard.

By isolating law within the larger project of earth system governance, therefore, this book allows the contributors to draw on the interdisciplinary insights of earth system science and governance disciplines while seeking to realign legal thinking with the realities of a dynamic, interconnected planet. Adopting the earth system itself as the relevant unit of legal analysis has profound implications, requiring law to grapple with earth system complexity, not avoid it. This demands a move from reactive regulation to anticipatory and precautionary approaches. Effective institutional structures must be polycentric, involving multiple actors across scales, from local communities to international institutions. Ultimately, the shift from 'environmental' to 'earth system' will require reconfiguring legal norms, including extending recognition and rights to non-human entities and future generations.

The daunting challenge of designing a complex legal system for engaging the complex earth system is not lost on the contributors to this book. The research agenda Kotzé and Kim laid out in 2019 produced this impressive body of work, but earth system law is not presented herein as being in final design blueprint form. Quite the opposite: the contributors are explicit that it remains an evolving, contested, and pluralistic framework. This frank openness is not a weakness but a strength. It allows for, even asks for, diverse perspectives, interdisciplinary engagement, and continuous adaptation. Embracing this generative approach, the authors explore new legal principles, such as those grounded in ecological reflexivity and intergenerational justice. They interrogate existing bedrock principles, including precaution, prevention, and 'polluter pays', revealing both their limitations and the potential values they could extend to earth system law. Alternative worldviews, including Indigenous and feminist perspectives, challenge dominant assumptions about human–Nature relations. Institutional and practical dimensions of legal transformation, from courts and regulatory bodies to novel actors such as scientific institutions and even cultural media like film, are investigated. In short, earth system law is not just a new label on old dials. It is a new kind of equipment altogether.

There are, of course, reasons for caution. As several contributors note, conceptual innovation alone does not guarantee practical impact. Legal systems are deeply embedded in political, economic, and social structures. Without corresponding shifts in these domains, even the most compelling legal ideas may fall flat, or even backfire. There is a risk that new frameworks could be co-opted or diluted, reproducing the very dynamics they seek to overcome.

Yet these reasons for caution should not diminish the significance of the endeavour proposed herein. The history of environmental law itself reminds us that transformative ideas often begin at the margins before reshaping mainstream practice. Concepts such as precaution and intergenerational equity were once novel and contested; today they are central to legal discourse. Earth system law may well follow a similar trajectory. In this respect, the value of this book lies not only in its specific arguments but primarily in its broader contribution to legal imagination. It expands the horizon of what law can be and what it can do, challenging the reader to think beyond established categories and to envision legal systems that are commensurate with the realities of the Anthropocene.

For scholars and practitioners of environmental law, the earth system law project thus offers both a challenge and an invitation. The challenge is to confront the limitations of familiar frameworks, environmental law in particular, and to acknowledge that law itself has contributed to severe earth system harm. This is not an easy task, particularly for a discipline that has long positioned itself as a force for environmental protection.

Yet this breadth and depth of critical reflection is necessary if law is to remain relevant in a rapidly changing world. Taken together, the contributors to this book thus also have delivered an invitation, asking lawyers and others to participate in the co-creation of this new legal paradigm. This environmental lawyer gladly accepts their invitation. Henceforth, I am an earth system lawyer!

JB Ruhl
David Daniels Allen Distinguished Chair in Law,
Vanderbilt University Law School, United States

ACKNOWLEDGEMENTS

A collected book is much more than the sum of its parts. It can only come about when a group of people who share some common curiosity come together to further explore that curiosity. This is what we set out to do almost three years ago when we decided to write a book about earth system law. The 'we' at the heart of this effort is a group of scholars who are curious about what it means to be human in the world we live in; how the rules, institutions and actors we construct and empower shape our lived realities and those of the more-than-human world; and how we could live better lives collectively, more carefully, caringly, and humbly in the Anthropocene.

The earth system law community has become a dynamic, diverse, and energetic one; we come from different disciplines and often disagree, as you will see in this book. But we are very much united around our passion to explore alternatives to the legal status quo, how the world is shaped by law, how the world shapes the law, and ways to do law and legal scholarship differently, and hopefully, more appropriately for the tumultuous epoch we live in. I am deeply grateful to all the wonderful authors who have contributed to this book, and who have so generously shared their time, experience, perspectives, and knowledge. While some of us collaborate in the Earth System Governance Project and its Taskforce on Earth System Law, we have also made new friends along the way; a delightfully enriching co-creative experience that also reflects in the diverse chapters in the book.

I could well imagine that some academic publishers might think twice before committing to a project like this one. Why support the publication of research that raises more questions than it offers answers, deliberately breaks away from mainstream environmental law scholarship and its burgeoning enterprise, and with recommendations that might only partially be realised in practice? Why invest in a vision? These are legitimate questions, but they did not deter Hart Publishing from supporting us in the exemplary way that this exceptional academic publisher is very well known for. Our sincerest thanks to the entire team at Hart Publishing – Sasha Jawed, Roberta Bassi and Linda Goss – for their commitment, support, and outstanding professionalism throughout. A special word of thanks also to Joanne Choulerton; the one copy editor that every book should have. We are particularly delighted, and grateful, that this book is available open access through the Bloomsbury Open Collections initiative. Thanks to Bloomsbury for its incredible generosity and investment in science.

A special word of thanks to the wonderful JB Ruhl for his deeply honest, personal and reflective foreword that sets the scene for this book. Much of what we know about law and complex systems, law as a complex system, and law's possibilities and limitations in the Anthropocene, derives from the path-breaking work he has done over the years.

We hope you will enjoy reading this book as much as we enjoyed writing it. Our creative journey was not uncomplicated, uncontested or predetermined; it was a delightfully disruptive struggle with ourselves, with the law, and the world order that the law shapes and is shaped by. If you find it equally disruptive, we will have succeeded in our project.

Louis J Kotzé

CONTENTS

LIST OF CONTRIBUTORS

J Michael Angstadt is Associate Professor of Environmental Studies (Law & Policy) at Colorado College, United States of America.

Frank Biermann is Professor of Global Sustainability Governance at Utrecht University, the Netherlands, and the founding chair of the Earth System Governance Project.

Emille Boulot is a Lecturer at the Law School of the University of Tasmania, Australia.

Peter D Burdon is Professor of Law at Adelaide University, Australia.

Louise du Toit is a Lecturer in Law at the University of Southampton, United Kingdom.

Geoffrey Garver is Research Associate and Course Lecturer at McGill University, Canada.

Işık Girgiç is a Post-doctoral Researcher in Law and Planetary Transformations at the Law Group, Wageningen University and Research, the Netherlands.

Frederic Hanusch is Professor of Planetary Change and Politics at Justus Liebig University Giessen, Germany.

Cameron Holley is Professor at the School of Law, Society and Criminology at University of New South Wales Law & Justice, and a Deputy Director of the University of New South Wales Institute for Climate Risk and Response, Australia.

Rakhyun E Kim is Associate Professor of Earth System Governance at the Copernicus Institute of Sustainable Development, Utrecht University, the Netherlands.

Louis J Kotzé is Chair of the Law Group and Professor of Law at Wageningen University and Research, the Netherlands, and Extraordinary Professor of Law at Stellenbosch University, South Africa.

Michael C Leach is Assistant Professor in the Department of Public Law and Governance at Tilburg Law School, the Netherlands.

Michelle Lim is Associate Professor in the Yong Pung How School of Law, Singapore Management University, Singapore, and the UNESCO Chair in Sustainability Law Futures.

Laura Mai is Endowed Professorship for Climate Law and Society, University of Bern, Switzerland.

Benoit Mayer is Professor of Climate Law at the University of Reading, United Kingdom.

Karen Morrow is Professor of Environmental Law at Swansea University, United Kingdom.

Samantha Moyo is Adjunct Lecturer and a PhD candidate at the University of Cape Town, South Africa.

Benjamin J Richardson is Professor of Environmental Law at the Faculty of Law, University of Tasmania, Australia.

Shaun Sellers is President of the Canadian Society for Ecological Economics, Canada.

Clifford Shearing is Professor Emeritus at the University of Cape Town, South Africa.

Iván D Vargas Roncancio is Assistant Professor in the Department of Social Sciences at York University, Canada.

Rosalind Warner is College Professor of Political Science at Okanagan College, Canada.

PART I

Origins and Conceptual Development

1

Earth System Law for the Anthropocene

LOUIS J KOTZÉ, J MICHAEL ANGSTADT, RAKHYUN E KIM, IŞIK GİRGİÇ AND FRANK BIERMANN

I. Introduction

Law is central to society; consciously made by people to delimit the boundaries within which acceptable and unacceptable human behaviour is allowed to happen. As a social construct, law is what (some) people wish it to be. Law is neither neutral nor decoupled from other social institutions that operate in society. Law instead reflects, is shaped by (and shapes), the Zeitgeist, its politics, economics, cultural and religious beliefs and practices, the fantastical whims of flamboyant politicians, the destructive oppression of dictators, and sometimes, the hope of new beginnings. Law is, in essence: 'enmeshed in assemblages reflecting the materio-semiotic affects (and affectivity) of institutional, constitutional, historical, national and international narratives, architectures, bodies of text, conceptual formations, patterns of coercion and facilitation and other modes of normative organization and juridical praxis'.[1]

As a formidable tool of social organisation, law is purposefully designed to achieve certain goals: most famously order and justice, but also human 'growth', 'development' and 'progress' through the enabling processes and institutions that it sets up.[2] The corporation, a mere (but immensely powerful) fiction that law creates and to which it affords legal personhood and rights, is one example, suggesting how law determines who is a person and who is not, and what this 'legal person' can and cannot do. Setting aside for the moment the deeper concern about the adverse impacts on the planet caused by legally sanctioned corporate actions,[3] the corporation is only one of many instances where law activates, enables

[1] A Grear, 'Legal Imaginaries and the Anthropocene: "Of" and "For"' (2020) 31 *Law and Critique* 351, 352.

[2] LJ Kotzé, and S Adelman, 'Environmental Law and the Unsustainability of Sustainable Development: A Tale of Disenchantment and of Hope' (2023) 34 *Law and Critique* 227.

[3] Eg, P Dauvergne, *Will Big Business Destroy our Planet?* (Cambridge, Polity Press, 2018).

and emboldens the destructive and unjust drivers of a selectively privileging, exploitative and predatory world order that is broadly characterised by the term 'Anthropocene'.

Although it has become a contested notion,[4] and rightly so, the Anthropocene usefully depicts a period in Earth's geological history where (some) humans have become as powerful as meteorites and volcanoes, capable of 'shaping the lifeworld of the planet itself',[5] dislodging planetary equilibrium, and deepening the existential crisis of a highly differential vulnerable living order.[6] The assumption, therefore, that law is always 'good', protective and caring, is mediated by concerns revolving on law's complicity (alongside other social institutions with which it is intertwined – such as politics and economics) in creating and maintaining the conditions that are propelling the planet into the Anthropocene epoch.

In what arguably ranks as one of her most incisive publications, Anna Grear contrasts the 'dominant imaginary underlying "law of the Anthropocene"' with an imaginary reaching towards "law/s for the Anthropocene"'.[7] Her contrast specifically reflects upon law's 'existing [Anthropocene-based] imaginary of quasi-disembodiment and an alternative [future] imaginary of embodiment';[8] in other words, what law currently *is in the Anthropocene* and what law could, or more precisely, *should be(come) for the Anthropocene*. Her distinction between 'law of' and 'law for' is much deeper (and complex) than meets the eye. Its important temporal inflection, first and foremost, foregrounds the reality that a specific type of law exists that has been crafted, shaped and embedded in social systems across the globe by the many actors, institutions, processes, values and worldviews, among many other law 'creators' and influences on law-creation that have given and continue to give rise to the Anthropocene.[9] As mentioned earlier, this type of law is not necessarily as 'good' as what one imagines it to be. More importantly though, Grear's temporal inflection also opens up the possibility of there being an entirely 'new' *law for the Anthropocene*, including new ways to look at law, to understand, reinterpret or overhaul law's role in society, and ultimately, to reimagine law, its objectives, ethics, actors, agents, process – its very fabric, as it were – to enable the entire living order to live better lives in and with the Anthropocene.

[4] Eg, D Haraway, *Staying with the Trouble: Making Kin in the Chthulucene* (Durham NC, Duke University Press, 2016).

[5] A Grear, 'Deconstructing *Anthropos*: A Critical Legal Reflection on "Anthropocentric" Law and Anthropocene "Humanity"' (2015) 26 *Law and Critique* 225, 226.

[6] LJ Kotzé, 'The Anthropocene, Earth System Vulnerability and Socio-ecological Injustice in an Age of Human Rights' (2019) 10 *Journal of Human Rights and the Environment* 62.

[7] Grear (n 1) 351.

[8] ibid.

[9] Elsewhere, Grear notes that 'the actors at the heart of Anthropocene origins and the origins of the international legal order were an identifiable, highly selective, group of dominant humans', especially apparent in the vestiges of colonialism and colonial powers that have been instrumental in creating the ongoing uneven world order. A Grear (n 5), 230. See also Mayer, Chapter 13 in this book.

II. Law *of* the Anthropocene

Over the years, several scholars have become increasingly concerned, frustrated even, by *law of the Anthropocene*'s questionable legacy and ongoing complicity in co-creating the Anthropocene, including its inability to effectively mediate the Anthropocene's deepening planetary crisis.[10] Considerable criticism has been levelled especially against environmental law, that body of law which is supposed to protect the planet's life sustaining systems. *Environmental law of the Anthropocene*, to return to Grear's imagery, has been criticised for being too state-centric, relying as it predominantly does on the nation state and its formal governance apparatus and an increasingly outdated – and therefore ineffective – United Nations system. It is now clear that many states, thoroughly lobbied as they are by corporate and other interest groups, do not always have the best interests of the environment, and sustainability more generally, at heart.

Multilateralism and its erstwhile grandeur are in steady decline in several domains ranging from humanitarian efforts, human rights protection, prevention of armed conflict, and in the environmental protection domain. While Ukraine is being devastated, preliminary plans that are backed by the most powerful nation in the world, fantastical and hypothetical as they (still) are, have already been drawn up to turn Gaza into an exotic oceanfront destination for the world's super rich. The absurdness of such a proposal is overshadowed only by the appallingly brutal refusal to recognise the dire plight of millions of displaced people that have nothing to go back to, let alone them having the capacity to contemplate how to permanently vacate their destroyed lands to make way for mansions, swimming pools, manicured golf courses, and ice rinks in the desert. In many other parts of the world, millions of people continue to starve, as hope for better living conditions fades away amidst the unwashed realities of thirsty, filthy, homeless, climate-impacted lives. Meanwhile states' agreement to work towards the 'beginning of the end' of the fossil fuel era have been met by relieved negotiators (and representatives of the fossil fuel industry) at the end of the 28th climate Conference of the Parties in Dubai.[11] This, despite sound evidence that it might already be far too late to halt the most severe impacts of climate change even if the world somehow manages to transition to net zero economies *tomorrow*.[12] Agreeing

[10] See for a range of perspectives, P Burdon and J Martel (eds), *The Routledge Handbook of Law and the Anthropocene* (Abingdon-on-Thames, Routledge, 2023); LJ Kotzé (ed), *Environmental Law and Governance for the Anthropocene* (Oxford, Hart Publishing, 2017).

[11] https://unfccc.int/news/cop28-agreement-signals-beginning-of-the-end-of-the-fossil-fuel-era.

[12] Eg IPCC, 'Summary for Policymakers' in *Climate Change 2023: Synthesis Report. Contribution of Working Groups I, II and III to the Sixth Assessment Report of the Intergovernmental Panel on Climate Change* [Core Writing Team, H Lee and J Romero (eds)] (IPCC, Geneva, Switzerland, 2023) pp 1–34.

on the 'beginning of the end' of fossil fuels during a global climate governance meeting held in one of the world's largest oil producing countries that is chaired by the CEO of Abu Dhabi National Oil Company, without taking any meaningful action to actually end the world's considerable – and growing – fossil fuel appetite as soon as possible, sets the bar so low (and possibly deliberately so) that anything else slightly more ambitious agreed upon in future could be considered a major victory in tackling climate change. This is yet another win for the sort of incrementalism and low ambition that now increasingly characterises the international legal and political order.

Numerous commentators have also pointed to the ongoing concern over environmental law's anthropocentrism; how environmental law very effectively manages to prioritise human concerns at the cost of all other life forms by subjugating non-humans in an instrumentalised and ultimately, predatory, way to 'resources' that feed human 'development', 'progress' and 'growth'.[13] A general conclusion is that 'it is intensely problematic that the human subject stands at the centre of the juridical order as its only true agent and beneficiary'.[14] Apart from some instances where 'rights of nature' movements are slowly prying open stubbornly sturdy Cartesian divides and breaking down legally constructed hierarchies and structures of historical and ongoing domination and mastery, and searching for ways to nurture relationality, *the human* is still law's preferential referent and privileged subject. The trite view that we are masters of the planet, and not part of it, and that we have the right to use, exploit and shape the planetary system and its 'resources' to our will,[15] is one that has become so deeply embedded in law that any other juridical configuration, including one that places non-humans on equal legal footing with humans, is seen as 'radical', 'revolutionary' and 'innovative'; and therefore virtually impossible to achieve. Moreover, because they are characterised thus, such juridical configurations remain at the marginal peripheries of the debate. Deepening frustration about law's inability to embrace and protect all of the living order, including non-humans, is reflected in a simple question: if law is able and willing to enthusiastically and without reservation afford a fictitious entity such as a corporation the same legal status, rights and standing that a human being has, why can it not also do so for other non-human living entities such as those often referred to collectively as 'nature'?

Another overarching concern about *law of the Anthropocene* is that it has been created based on assumptions deriving from a relatively stable, predictable and harmonious Holocene epoch.[16] This is especially true for environmental law

[13] Eg P Burdon, 'The Earth Community and Ecological Jurisprudence' (2013) 3(5) *Oñati Socio-Legal Series* 815–37.

[14] Grear (n 5) 225.

[15] Vividly explicated, among other ongoing projects, by the powerful movement that promotes solar geoengineering. See for a critique, F Biermann and others, 'Solar Geoengineering: The Case for an International Non-use Agreement' (2022) 13 *WIREs Climate Change* e754.

[16] The Holocene is the current geological epoch, beginning after the last major ice age (Pleistocene) ended, characterised by a relatively stable climate, and encompassing the entire span of human recorded history and civilisation.

that is criticised for its reductionist tendency to focus on specific, localised environmental 'problems' without recognising that these problems are very much interconnected within one earth system and that they manifest on a planetary scale even if they are sometimes very localised.[17] Environmental law, bound and circumscribed as it is by sovereign state borders, as well as environmental law's narrow focus on defined problem domains, thus loses sight of the bigger picture, often ignoring the fact that biodiversity, climate, water and soil governance, to name but a few, must be addressed collectively in order to achieve a net positive result and to avoid problem shifting.[18] The question is: is the *environment*, or should it be, the sole concern of *(environmental) law for the Anthropocene*? Or should *law for the Anthropocene* be more attentive to discarding a reductionist focus on the 'environment' in favour of holistically focusing on a planet-wide earth system as an intertwined governable domain, or as some put it, the 'planetary commons'?[19]

A similar discussion is taking place in political science circles with some pointing to the much-needed paradigm shift that must move from 'environmental' policy and governance to more expansive notions of 'earth system' governance; a paradigm shift that is already happening to some extent.[20] Earth system governance marks a shift of focus from a narrowly defined, nation-state-oriented 'environmental governance' paradigm to a more expansive understanding of multi-level and multi-actor governance that is emerging on the back of a deeper appreciation of planet Earth as an interlinked system characterised by a telecoupled network of interacting social-ecological relations. Unlike traditional conceptualisations of fragmented, linear, state-driven environmental governance approaches, earth system governance offers an innovative earth system-focused framework for governing complex, interlinked, multi-scalar governance challenges arising from a continuously transforming earth system. In broad terms, earth system governance encapsulates the sum of formal and informal rule systems and actor networks at all levels of human society that are set up to influence the co-evolution of social-ecological systems

[17] LJ Kotzé and RE Kim, 'Towards Planetary Nexus Governance in the Anthropocene: An Earth System Law Perspective' (2022) 13 *Global Policy* 86.

[18] Eg RE Kim and H van Asselt, 'Global Governance: Problem Shifting in the Anthropocene and the Limits of International Law' in E Morgera and K Kulovesi (eds), *Research Handbook on International Law and Natural Resources* (Cheltenham, Edward Elgar Publishing, 2016) 473. See also I Girgiç, RE Kim, F Biermann, and H van Asselt, 'Clustering as a Solution to Environmental Problem Shifting? The Case of the Basel–Rotterdam–Stockholm Synergies Process' (2025) *Global Environmental Politics* 1; AV Adipudi, RE Kim, and F Biermann, 'The Potential Negative Impact of the UNFCCC: An Analysis of Sectoral, Geographical, and Temporal Problem Shifts from Climate Policies and Measures in 25 Industrialized Countries' (2025) 95 *Global Environmental Change* 103075; AV Adipudi and RE Kim, 'The Latent Net Effectiveness of Institutional Complexes: A Heuristic Model' (2024) 382 *Philosophical Transactions of the Royal Society A* 20230161.

[19] J Rockström et al, 'The Planetary Commons: A New Paradigm for Safeguarding Earth-regulating Systems in the Anthropocene' (2024) 121 *Proceedings of the National Academy of Science* e2301531121.

[20] F Biermann, 'The Future of "Environmental" Policy in the Anthropocene: Time for a Paradigm Shift' (2020) 30 *Environmental Politics* 61.

at the planetary level in ways that secure sustainability and planetary resilience, now and in future.[21]

A holistic systems focus would foreground complexity (of law *and* the earth system) by recognising the combination and interplay of hyperconnectivity, nonlinear dynamics, directional change, and emergent properties of the earth system.[22] It also acknowledges that ecological dynamism is an inherent characteristic of an interconnected, unpredictable, and complex earth system, while emphasising the need to embrace ecological reflexivity that prioritises the need for precaution and foresight to anticipate future transformations in the face of uncertainty. Such a predictive and anticipatory approach stands in stark contrast to environmental law's reactive, incremental nature.

III. Earth System Law *for* the Anthropocene

These are some of the general considerations, concerns and frustrations that prompted a group of lawyers and political scientists who are active in the Earth System Governance Project,[23] the largest global community of scholars focusing on the social dimensions of planetary transformations, to start thinking about new imaginaries of *law for the Anthropocene*. We came up with the term 'earth system law', which was introduced and expanded upon in a 2019 publication.[24] Earth system law was meant to offer a framework to identify and craft legal interventions to more effectively deal with the social dimensions of earth system transformations. As a framework, it is therefore particularly suited to better understanding earth system change, its planetary wide social-ecological impacts and, more importantly, how law and legal actors should govern these impacts through law, legal institutions and processes.

Of course, earth system law was and still is not the only effort to rethink *law for the Anthropocene*. Examples of other proposals are 'earth-centred law',[25] or 'planetary boundaries law'.[26] Yet, the one advantage that earth system law as a new conceptual framework had over other proposals was that it could draw upon the strengths and build on the momentum of the Earth System Governance Project.

[21] F Biermann, '"Earth System Governance" as a Crosscutting Theme of Global Change Research' (2007) 17 *Global Environmental Change* 326; F Biermann, *Earth System Governance: World Politics in the Anthropocene* (Cambridge MA, MIT Press, 2014).

[22] JB Ruhl et al, 'Harnessing Legal Complexity' (2017) 355 *Science* 1377.

[23] https://www.earthsystemgovernance.org/.

[24] LJ Kotzé and RE Kim, 'Earth System Law: The Juridical Dimensions of Earth System Governance' (2019) 1 *Earth System Governance* 100003.

[25] K Bosselmann, 'Shifting the Legal Paradigm: Earth-centered Law and Governance' in P Magalhães et al (eds), *The Safe Operating Space Treaty: A New Approach to Managing our Use of the Earth System* (Cambridge, Cambridge Scholars Publishing, 2016).

[26] G Chapron and others, 'Bolster Legal Boundaries to Stay Within Planetary Boundaries' (2017) 1 *Nature Ecology and Evolution* 0086.

Many, if not most, of the concerns and issues that the earth system governance agenda seeks to address are similar to those noted above with respect to *law of the Anthropocene*. Although it has been crafted mostly in the political science domain, the earth system governance framework offers an analogous framework for lawyers to think about ways to fashion *law for the Anthropocene*. It is therefore fair to say that earth system law, as a legal concept, had the benefit of rooting itself in a fairly well-established political science-centred framework, and could draw, as it continues to do, on the rich related worlds of political science and interdisciplinary sustainability sciences operating in the earth system governance domain. In this sense, earth system law offers an opportunity for legal and political science scholars to jointly engage with efforts that attempt to reshape law in the image of the earth system.

As Chapter two in this book explains,[27] however, there is (still) no standardised definition of earth system law. One could argue that there should not necessarily be one standard definition that is universally endorsed, although some scholars disagree.[28] While some common understanding of the basic tenets of earth system law is obviously useful, being caught in a definitional straitjacket significantly limits its potential for conceptual growth and maturation over time, while shutting out richly diverse perspectives and contributions from a larger community of stakeholders. Insisting on a formalised unitary definition might ultimately also inhibit the creation of a shared epistemic framework that enables and enhances collaborative intradisciplinary and interdisciplinary research and co-learning that go hand in hand with transdisciplinary stakeholder engagement to allow for a clearer understanding of what makes law more sensitive and responsive to earth system governance challenges.[29] Moreover, a key feature of earth system law is that it deliberately militates against the statism, rigidity, inherent conservatism and homogeneity that characterise *law of the Anthropocene*. If it is unable to be continuously sculpted by the views, positionalities, contributions and lived realities of its co-creators, then the earth system law project runs the risk of falling into the same trap that *law of the Anthropocene* is already irretrievably deeply engulfed in.

One objective of this book is to bring us a step closer to co-creating an understanding of what earth system law is, and what it could become, while also revealing its potential to inform efforts that must shape *law for the Anthropocene*. Generally speaking, earth system law is arguably better understood in terms of what it aims to do than what it essentially is. To the extent that it represents a vision of *law for the Anthropocene*, earth system law essentially urges a critical reflection upon law in an earth system context, thereby attempting to disrupt the foundational assumptions of *law of the Anthropocene*, and the latter's

[27] Kotzé, Angstadt and Kim, Chapter 2 in this book.
[28] See, for a summary of these views, ibid.
[29] LJ Kotzé and others, 'Earth System Law: Exploring New Frontiers in Legal Science' (2022) 11 *Earth System Governance* 100126.

(in)ability to govern complex social-ecological transformations, as described above.[30] This paradigm shift includes considering how law could better respond to earth system transformations caused by, among other things, climate change, and how law must transform itself to better govern the social-ecological aspects of earth system transformations. In such a view, earth system law is not necessarily intended to be a new autonomous body of law, such as human rights law, although it could be in time. It is rather a new way of thinking about the role, purpose, objectives and design of law that specifically draws on the earth system context for the purpose of governing transformations in the Anthropocene. Just like earth system governance is not simply about global environmental politics,[31] earth system law is intended to be a more generically applicable framework that spans the entire spectrum of law that is relevant for responding to earth system transformations.[32]

While earth system law is a work in progress that continuously endeavours to articulate its identity, boundaries, and role as a scholarly movement and roadmap for decision-makers,[33] the concept is gaining traction. This is evident from the increasing number of publications focusing on this concept and that are canvassed in Chapter two of this book, as well as the centrality and expansion of this focus area in the wider Earth System Governance Project and its specialised Taskforce on Earth System Law.[34] Also outside of the Earth System Governance community, earth system law is becoming an increasingly popular notion that offers a framing of law for the Anthropocene and law's role in governing earth system transformations in the Anthropocene. This is evident in the growing number of law journals that publish research on earth system law, including among others, *Transnational Environmental Law, Review of European, Comparative and International Environmental Law*, and *Law and Critique*.

IV. The Journeys of Earth System Law

This book traces the many journeys of earth system law, including its origins and conceptual development; ongoing attempts to define itself and to construct its identity; and visions of possible destinations where the journey might lead to. In doing so, all chapters attempt to reveal a deeper understanding of what earth system law is or could be(come); while identifying, constructing and interrogating

[30] JC Gellers, 'Earth System Law and the Legal Status of Non-Humans in the Anthropocene' (2021) 7 *Earth System Governance* 100083.

[31] Biermann (n 20).

[32] RE Kim, C Blanchard, LJ Kotzé, 'Law, Systems, and Planet Earth: Editorial' (2022) 11 *Earth System Governance* 100127.

[33] M Leach, 'Seeking 'Systems' in Earth System Law: Boundaries, Identity, and Purpose in an Emergent Field' (2023) 15 *Earth System Governance* 100162.

[34] See, Kotzé, Angstadt and Kim, Chapter 2 in this book.

new legal principles, concepts, ethics, actors, and institutions that continuously shape earth system law for the Anthropocene.[35]

Each chapter is ultimately concerned with initiating and stimulating new thinking about the role of law and legal science in social, epistemic, and broader governance spaces and processes that must address earth system transformations and promote sustainability. Central to such an effort is our aim to push the boundaries of law and of legal thinking by opening up new, and in some instances critically self-reflective, epistemic spaces for juridical imagination in innovative ways that go well beyond, and that challenge, the stifling confines of *law of the Anthropocene* imaginaries. Some of these efforts also include thought experiments.[36] The overall exploratory approach therefore throughout the book rejects the prevailing 'closed' epistemologies of law that have been shaped in the context of *law of the Anthropocene*, and instead embraces a creative, forward looking and innovative re-imagination of *law for the Anthropocene*.

A. Origins and Conceptual Development

Earlier parts of this chapter briefly reflected upon the origins of earth system law, the rationale behind its innovation, the context that supported its conceptual development, and some of its broader ambitions. Louis J Kotzé, J Michael Angstadt and Rakhyun E Kim take this discussion several steps further in Chapter two by engaging in a deep-dive analysis of the emerging scholarship on earth system law. The chapter offers a stocktake of earth system law scholarship as it has developed over the past five years, and investigates the prevailing critique of earth system law, while also looking ahead to propose a future research agenda that is informed by key findings of this assessment. Collectively considered, the analysis offers insights into both the potential of earth system law as a discursive-epistemic framework and as a new legal paradigm that is intertwined with earth system governance, while also serving as a critical self-reflection upon the merits of this new paradigm as well as its shortcomings.

When earth system law was introduced in 2019, it was broadly framed as a 'new legal phenomenon' that 'accommodates and encapsulates all juridical aspects of earth system governance, including a new research agenda that is able to respond to the unique epistemic, ontological and normative characteristics, demands and nature of earth system governance in the Anthropocene'.[37] The open-endedness of this description was deliberate: first to avoid a situation where the innovative – and above all creative, multi-perspectival and critical – development of a new concept

[35] To accurately represent the voices of authors of each chapter, some parts in this section are based on summaries written by the authors of each of the chapters. All these contributions are acknowledged with gratitude.

[36] Eg, Leach, Chapter 4; Hanusch, Chapter 15 of this book.

[37] Kotzé and Kim (n 24).

could be constrained by the confines of a predetermined definition, as explained above; and perhaps less obviously, but in retrospect increasingly plausibly, that its proponents were themselves unsure whether earth system law is a new body of law, a legal framework, an imaginary and/or an approach.

The task of further sculpting its definitional curves was thus articulated as being the responsibility of future endeavours. This decision had both benefits and drawbacks, as Chapter two shows. While creative (mostly legal but also political science) minds could run with this new idea and flesh it out as they wished in rich and diverse ways in numerous contexts within the broader outlines of the original proposal, some commentators cautioned that lack of a clearer definition inhibited the concept's plausibility, its autonomy and ultimately its discursive impact and ability to penetrate debates concerned with shaping *law for the Anthropocene*. Moreover, ambiguity also raises questions about earth system law's practical application, how it can move from theory to practice, as it were, and how it could become a scientific and policy-oriented framework to make the actual, much-needed changes happen. Despite such ambiguity, though, Chapter two also illustrates how subsequent studies have shown how earth system law could be practically relevant and how it already influences, and in future could inform, the development of law in niche areas such as water law, climate law and biodiversity law.

An important conclusion in Chapter two is that an increasing number of academics are engaging in earth system law scholarship, notably oriented around three frames that affirm and elaborate the three 'dimensions' of potential research proposed in the foundational earth system law publication: analysis of law and legal regulation in the Anthropocene; normative consideration of earth system governance and possible legal pathways to promote desired objectives; and prescriptive attention to how existing law should be transformed to advance these objectives.

B. Resituating Law and Legal Principles in Relation to Planet Earth

Several chapters in this book focus on legal principles. This is unsurprising: principles are often seen as the foundation of law. 'Legal principles' are as endemic to law – to the institution of law, its architecture, its constitution, ie *law's language* – as the notions of 'human rights', 'constitutions' or 'justice' are.

In Chapter three, Louis J Kotzé and Louise du Toit broadly set the scene for the other chapters in this Part that critique law and its principles in an earth system context. The chapter reflects, first in general terms, on the debate concerning law and legal principles, including why legal principles are important for law and governance, and why and how principles could play an important role in attuning law towards an Earth-centred approach. It takes the discussion further by also canvassing reasons for adopting new, more innovative, and possibly more radical legal principles, or at least new approaches to designing legal principles for the purpose of governing social-ecological relations in the Anthropocene. A main finding is that earth system law offers a unique opportunity to think about a new set of legal principles for the Anthropocene alongside the earth system metaphor and the complex contemporary governance challenges emanating from a complex earth system.

The chapter shows that principles, including the principles of precaution, prevention, polluter pays, and sustainable development, emerged in the twentieth century and have evolved to play a central role in national, regional, and international environmental law regimes. Accepting that environmental law has largely failed to restrain human activity and address socio-ecological decline, the chapter evaluates the ineffectiveness of environmental law's principles in addressing earth system destruction. The chapter focuses on principles due to their unique juridical characteristics, including their inherent flexibility and ability to influence legal reasoning and legal development, and thus reflects on the role that legal principles could play in aligning law with a more Earth-centred approach. While not all principles have necessarily become undesirable or inadequate, there is a convincing argument in support of discarding those principles that have become outdated, reimagining new principles for environmental law, and exploring more progressive principles that are beginning to emerge, including more 'radical' principles. Situating the discussion within the context of earth system law, which provides a useful framework for this exercise, the chapter identifies three specific categories of earth system law principles (functional, architectural and ethical), and proposes a selection of new *legal principles for the Anthropocene* that have the potential to guide better responses to the unprecedented challenges of the Anthropocene.

While Chapter three inherently assumes that new legal principles are necessary and should be adopted, and even proposes some new candidate legal principles, Michael C Leach follows a more careful and critical approach in his analysis in Chapter four. He ponders, namely, what contextual conditions would be necessary for earth system-inspired principles to ever become recognised as principles of international law. Guided by an objective of this book to imagine how earth system law principles might shape the adaptation or re-orienting of law around the concept of the 'earth system', his chapter adopts a historical gaze to situate the project within a wider discussion about how international law changes and where its principles come from. By looking at the origins and evolution of three major principles from international environmental law, namely the polluter pays principle, the prevention principle, and the precautionary principle, it reveals that international legal principles are birthed at moments when jurists, diplomats, judges and arbitrators need normative reference points to guide their decision-making in the face of new problems that complicate the ordinary and practical concerns of state actors and international organisations.

Furthermore, the original meanings and purposes of international legal principles can and do change over time as the demands for whatever optimising benefits they bring also change and as they are put to multiple new uses. Departing from these considerations, Leach argues that for earth system-inspired norms to ever become principles of international law, it would be necessary that international legal actors, especially states, willingly orient themselves towards something resembling the concept of the 'earth system' for which they would require such principles to guide their future decision-making and dispute resolution. In other words, one should expect earth system principles like those proposed in this book to emerge on the global stage as legal instruments only if and when demand for them arises as a result of an a priori shift in the international political and legal order to an earth system orientation. Until such a demand arises, thinking about new principles might be an interesting academic exercise – but it is unlikely to have any meaningful practical impact.

Emille Boulot, Laura Mai, and Shaun Sellers confirm in Chapter five the centrality of legal principles in efforts to shape environmental law doctrine and jurisprudence and in crystallising paradigms that characterise and demarcate environmental law as a distinct field of legal expertise. Like Kotzé and Du Toit in Chapter three, they accept that international environmental law and its principles have failed to arrest dramatic social-ecological decline. They ask: Does earth system law need to set out 'better' principles in terms of re-designed, updated and revised normative substance to respond to the Anthropocene's crises? Or is it necessary to re-think the legal forms, strategies and techniques which we mobilise in scholarly efforts? Like Leach, they are more critical of simply accepting the argument that we need new legal principles for the Anthropocene, and that designing new principles would somehow 'solve law's problems' in the context of a new geological epoch. The authors instead alert us to the oft-neglected fact that the emergence of new principles is a much more nuanced and delicate process that is itself contingent on and shaped by several considerations such as demand for them (as Leach argues), and a thorough consideration of the social, political and economic contexts that prevent the sort of transformations that principles need to drive. Chapter five thus foregrounds the necessity to carefully reflect on the interweaving of law with the global economy and the processes of change required to shift away from harmful lifeways. There is a subtle but important warning here: relying on legal principles as the primary legal technique for transformation has the potential to re-inscribe current legal tendencies that prioritise economic over socio-ecological interests; sustain structural injustices of colonialism between the global South and North; and maintain claims to universalism and concomitant forms of epistemic exclusion.

Boulot, Mai and Sellers instead present a critical approach that they term 'being de-principled' as a strategic practice which allows one to resist the urge to follow the mainstream disciplinary conception of law as a normative phenomenon with an internal order, a hierarchical structure and a pre-defined purpose – as something that can simply be reconfigured abstractly through scholarly discourse. By being de-principled, Chapter five centres practices which allow one to *think and do law differently*. Becoming de-principled means rendering law more open to plural ways of knowing, doing and relating and becoming attuned to how law is both socially and materially imagined, produced, sustained and, at times, allowed to wither away. Their intervention is specifically addressed to emerging earth system law scholarship in the hope that it assists in the ongoing development of a theory of change within this scholarship.

C. Alternative Worldviews and New Ethics Shaping Earth System Law

Karen Morrow launches this Part of the book's focus on the need for law to embrace alternative worldviews and new ethics within the context of the earth system law framework. She argues in Chapter six for the adoption of a new, relational ethic to ground the human–Earth relationship. Like several other chapters, this one also shows how the Anthropocene necessitates a profound re-consideration of the role of human agency as both the cause of and response to shifts away from the Holocene. Morrow argues that the exploitative and hierarchical relationship between humanity and the environment, clearly evident in the post-enlightenment paradigm of mastery, has ill-served the planet, its life forms and much of humanity. The more profound shift that is required is positioned as a form of relational, feminist theory-based ethics of care. Morrow suggests that the main contours of such an ethic in this context comprise responsibility, relationality and responsiveness. Collectively these require a much more demanding incarnation of harm prevention and a fuller embrace of an ethics of care that nurtures self-restraint and humility, rather than succumbing to the illusion of mastery and its accompanying hubris.

Can the idea of 'territories of life' help us move towards *law for the Anthropocene*? In some places, Indigenous or local communities are maintaining 'territories of life' where they exercise self-governance that provides for community well-being while conserving sustaining and sustainable ecosystems. In many territories of life, nonhuman life and the territory itself are viewed not as property, but as kin with legal agency. 'Territories of life', and everything that goes with this impulse, starkly contrasts with dominant legal systems worldwide that support human mastery over non-human beings and other vulnerable humans. Moreover, dominant legal systems, fully represented by *law of the Anthropocene*, empower capitalist and neo-colonial industrialism, trade, and foreign investment, whereby remote owners or decision-makers exploit faraway ecosystems and people. Consequently, as they fall prey to law's predatory instrumentalism, many life systems and people are sacrificed to profit and growth, without respecting critical ecological relationalities or ensuring ecological justice. In Chapter seven, Geoffrey Garver and Iván D Vargas Roncancio delve into the idea of 'territories of life', as a counter-narrative to the prevailing *law of the Anthropocene* paradigm. They explore how the conceptual development of earth system law and related approaches could be guided by a long-term vision of Earth made up of 'territories of life' with a plurality of life-enhancing, place-based legal systems. They suggest the creation of umbrella territories of life and life-enhancing legal systems that reach the global level. Importantly, realising this long-term vision for earth system law will require strong commitment to eco-cultural restoration; non-hierarchical power sharing and dialogue among peoples from a plurality of knowledge traditions; moving past the pervasive growth-insistent economic paradigm; a re-emergence of the commons; and a strong focus on territorial care that enhances all life instead of concentrating only on utilitarian human desires.

Several '-scenes' are emerging in scientific and other discourses: obviously Anthropocene, but also Capitalocene, Chthulucene and Plasticene. In Chapter eight, Michelle Lim invokes the recently coined Enshittocene, which explains the phenomenon by which digital platforms (such as X / Twitter) become 'bad' for both users and advertisers, ultimately resulting in the platform's demise. In this view, we now live in the Enshittocene, which also references characteristics of the Anthropocene: while the Enshittocene characterises the degradation of online life, the Anthropocene characterises the degradation of planetary life – of the planet itself. Lim argues that 'enshittification' of the online space thus stems from the same neoliberal ideology that has wrought social-ecological destruction across the planet. The question is: How can earth system law, and the novel principles, concepts, values and imaginaries that it inspires, be protected from the corrupting factors of neoliberalism? The question stimulates a conversation around the pitfalls and opportunities for earth system law as it strives to develop new legal principles, concepts, processes and actors in the face of inevitable confrontations with neoliberalism and its many filthy stains. Lim explores the possibilities of 'stain-guarding' earth system law, as it were, by focusing on the neoliberal principle of sustainable development, a principle that has been abducted by, and assimilated into, the powers of free-market capitalism. Her chapter recalls what sustainable development was meant to be and contrasts this with the predatory, destructive principle it has become, thus highlighting the processes of enshittification well beyond the digital sphere. Essentially, an exploration of enshittification of sustainable development facilitates stain-guarding of similar aspirations of equity alongside multigenerational and multispecies flourishing set out in earth system law.

The deeper critique of *law of the Anthropocene* that permeates this Part of the book continues in Chapter nine. Rosalind Warner focuses here on the role of metaphors in shaping international environmental law. Although they are also legal concepts, metaphors like property, sovereignty, and public trust, she argues, are central to the imaginary of *law of the Anthropocene*, shaping legal subjectivity, agency, and the ethical scope of human/non-human relationships. The chapter situates international environmental law within the broader concept of the social imaginary: a set of underlying cultural prototypes and framings that influence our understanding of the natural world and legitimise social discourses and practices. Dominant legal metaphors, particularly those inherited from Western jurisprudence, construct nature as an object of ownership and instrumentality, limiting law's ability to care for ecological systems. These metaphors underpin treaties, regulations, and doctrines, reinforcing and permitting individual and sovereign rights while subordinating collective claims and obligations. Even doctrines like the public trust, which aim to safeguard shared resources, often fall short due to their interpretation within the logic of property and sovereignty, prioritising present interests over those of future generations, and human interests above non-human interests. Thinking about *law for the Anthropocene*, Warner explores the transformative potential of kinship as a possible foundational metaphor for earth system law. Kinship aligns with Indigenous worldviews as well as certain strands of Western theory and articulates human–nature relationships in terms of mutual obligation, intergenerational relations, and intrinsic value, rather than reductionist ownership. It allows for nature's legal subjectivity and moral agency, thus envisioning law as a vehicle for planetary care and regeneration rather than exploitation. By reframing ethical relationships in terms of family and relations, kinship potentially offers a promising foundation for the transformational agenda of earth system law, particularly in relation to legal practices and policies oriented toward protecting and restoring the planetary community in the Anthropocene.

In Chapter ten, the final chapter of this Part, Peter D Burdon focuses on ecological integrity and asks whether ecological integrity is suitable as a foundational ethical principle for earth system law and its project of aligning legal systems with the earth system. Can ecological integrity, or its recent iteration as biosphere integrity, provide guidance for governing complex planetary systems while remaining responsive to local realities? Burdon argues that earth system law, in its quest to govern complex planetary systems, requires principles that can operate on a global scale while remaining responsive to local realities. Ecological integrity presents an intriguing, but not unproblematic, candidate for such a principle. Tracing ecological integrity's intellectual origins from early wilderness ethics reveals problematic connections to untenable notions of purity, wilderness, and civilisational progress – an attachment that is incompatible with Anthropocene realities. Moreover, ecological integrity measures local ecosystem health, while the Anthropocene requires planetary-level thinking. The chapter then examines biosphere integrity as a proposed alternative, particularly through the planetary boundaries framework. However, biosphere integrity also reproduces similar concerns, remaining trapped in idealist discourse that abstracts from reality while staying silent on the material causes of the Anthropocene rupture. The retention of 'integrity' itself proves problematic, carrying inescapable historical baggage. Beyond critiquing specific concepts, the chapter develops a methodology for examining potential earth system law principles, questioning whether earth system law itself might fall into idealist traps. Burdon argues that the Anthropocene demands analytical modes grounded in material conditions and real human existence rather than abstract representations. By critically examining ecological and biosphere integrity through this materialist lens, the analysis illuminates fundamental challenges in developing earth system law principles that truly respond to planetary complexity, opening new pathways for thinking about ecological integrity that engage with earth system science while avoiding environmental legal scholarship's pervasive idealism.

D. Earth System Lawyering: In Search of New Actors, Architectures and Institutions

Contemplating the conceptual contours, normative foundations, principles and ethics of earth system law is one thing. Thinking about how to translate these into more practical terms, how to operationalise earth system law, or at least thinking about scenarios how it could play out, as it were, is quite another. The chapters in the penultimate Part of the book concern themselves with the latter point: thinking about some of the key considerations that are critical for earth system *lawyering*. How can we reimagine architectures, actors and institutions that will be instrumental in shaping earth system law?

Re-thinking law for the Anthropocene using the earth system governance framework requires an architecture that supports systems thinking and the marshalling of various legal fields, other disciplines, and multiple stakeholders to better understand and formulate responses to the Anthropocene's complex governance challenges. This point has been made in several chapters. Cameron Holley, Clifford Shearing and Samantha Moyo specifically point in Chapter eleven to the critical necessity of a principle to shape this architecture. They argue that a constitutive conception of governance can shape a new paradigm of legal analysis, design and implementation. The chapter consequently recognises and builds upon a well-established critique of regulatory scholarship that has drawn attention to the failure to attend to the constitutive features of regulatory tools. Law, in the light of this critique, must be understood not simply as a set of rule-based directions for ordering relationships between objects within a field, but also as constituting the objects and the field itself. The chapter seeks to remedy this neglect in relation to the regulation of anthropogenic impacts on planetary boundaries by considering the possibility of earth system law adopting a constitutive conception of regulation as a foundational principle. A constitutive conception of regulation argues that 'reality' is not simply given but rather must be understood as socially constructed. Law, say the authors, constitutes the realities it seeks to regulate, through processes of social construction that have consistently produced inequitable power relations. The chapter discusses how a constitutive conception of earth system law can focus attention on governance spaces and foreground interdisciplinary experience and empirical observation, rather than a priori knowledge. Under this principle, governance institutions, actors and providers will be required to understand how polycentric governance spaces have been constituted and shaped by multiple processes and actors. The chapter also explores the strengths, weaknesses, and implications of a constitutive principle, including how it can guide earth system law to influence a wider range of social and legal orders, while also appreciating and responding to the fact that other legal, political, social and economic processes can influence how earth system law operates.

Much of what makes up the idea of earth system law differs significantly from many dominant environmental law practices. This means that efforts to advance an earth system law agenda will require reimagining contemporary understandings of how courts, legal actors, and juridical systems engage with environmental law and with one another. Such efforts will also demand fundamental transformation of existing environmental law frameworks and judicial institutions in ways that strive to advance the rationale and objectives of earth system law. To date, imagining these transformations has mostly been a theoretical exercise. However, as J Michael Angstadt argues in Chapter twelve, theoretical legal frameworks must eventually also be mapped onto real-world courts, tribunals, and other institutional architectures, implemented by their personnel, and contoured by their procedures and resources. Thus, courts, other legal and quasi-judicial institutions, and the actors that shape these institutions, will eventually shape how fully and effectively earth system law can be operationalised. Chapter twelve focuses more generally on how we can begin to adapt institutional architectures to the legal transition advocated by earth system law. More specifically, it explores adaptations that may be required to equip courts and related environmental law institutions to pursue earth system law objectives. Angstadt shows that much of the existing scholarship emphasises 'the here', or dominant environmental law approaches (*law of the Anthropocene*). Simultaneously, many earth system law accounts theorise 'the frontier', or ideal transformations (*law for the Anthropocene*). The chapter highlights and emphasises the interstitial 'near frontier', where existing institutions and actors can undertake transformative work to pursue and operationalise earth system law objectives. The analysis draws specific attention to how we might reimagine institutions in 'the near frontier' and examines potential structural determinants of systemic change. It does so by specifically evaluating the prospect of courts as sites of bottom-up, systemic transformation to earth system law. The chapter also illustrates some of these pathways of institutional transformation by highlighting models of novel cognisance, jurisdiction, and disposition found within domestic courts. Angstadt shows that many of these earth system law precepts are already viable.

Much of the literature on earth system law discusses what it could entail. This is also evident from several chapters in this book and specifically the analysis in Chapter two. In Chapter thirteen, Benoit Mayer extends the debate by interrogating the identity of earth system law-makers. He argues that national, international, and scientific institutions could all conceivably play a role in the making of earth system law. Among these three types of institutions, the earth system law literature tends to promote the role of scientific institutions and international law-making while often discounting the importance of national political processes. This chapter argues that each type of institution may have a legitimate role to play in earth system law-making and that a balance needs to be struck between these three types of institutions. While scientific institutions must inform earth system law-making, they cannot legitimately make the value-based decisions required for the development of earth system law. Conversely, while international institutions are instrumental in addressing collective action issues, they might lack the legitimacy to decide how environmental protection is to be achieved. The chapter consequently suggests the need for earth system law to develop a principle akin to subsidiarity to determine the competence of each institution regarding the protection of the planet. According to this principle, each type of institution should only act if and insofar as it has a comparative advantage over other types of institutions.

Although it may not seem obvious at first glance, cinema has more to do with earth system law than one would have expected. In Chapter fourteen, Benjamin J Richardson argues that film can shape *law for the Anthropocene*. A core element and objective of earth system law, after all, is pursuing novel strategies and identifying and empowering actors to innovatively govern the social dimensions of earth system transformations. A wholly underexplored domain in law and governance literature, as Richardson notes, is documentary and fiction films dealing with environmental subjects, such as climate change, citizen protests and wildlife conservation. He delves into the richly colourful world of cinema to reveal how this medium could impact the processes by which law reform *for the Anthropocene* might ensue within the context of earth system law. Film is a seminal part of popular culture that contributes to the representation of environmental issues and audiences' understanding of environmental problems. Because of the cultural significance of film, and its potential to influence social change, it is important that those interested in earth system law consider how environmental cinema may shape the processes by which law reform might ensue. Whether the natural world is the subject of fiction movies or critical documentaries, these forms of environmental cinema can, by entertaining and educating the public, make them more aware of neglected environmental issues. Film also has limitations, however, such as when it is used to manipulate the public via corporate 'greenwashing' or government propaganda. Overall, though, cinema must be recognised as being highly relevant to the processes of social change to support the journey to earth system law, and, more broadly, the journey of social transformation for sustainability that earth system law aspires to facilitate.

Thought experiments are potentially powerful impulses that can sometimes be realised and put into practice over time under favourable conditions. The final chapter in this book is dedicated to a thought experiment that challenges our (human) understanding of time in relation to planetary time, including how earth system law could more fully embrace an expanded understanding of time that is commensurate with the multi-generational and deep-time characteristics of the Anthropocene. Frederic Hanusch argues in Chapter fifteen that the project of earth system law must explicitly embrace temporality in order to govern conflicts that arise when human timescales collide with planetary timescales. Building on the spatial ideal of cosmopolitanism, he introduces a corresponding temporal principle *chronopolitanism*, which seeks equal opportunities and well-being for all regardless of the temporal conditions into which humans and more-than-humans are born or live. The chapter traces historical phases of 'temporal contestation', ranging from Enlightenment historical consciousness and geological deep time, through post-War extractivist futurism and the Great Acceleration, to the more recent and ongoing clash between scientific climate timescales and 'retrotopian' politics. Hanusch develops a temporalised, but tangible, vision of earth system law by focusing on: the process of environmental impact assessment, which must be extended to explicitly evaluate long-term, intergenerational effects; governing freshwater withdrawals with temporal thresholds to prevent subsidence and ecological depletion; and cultivating temporal maturity and literacy so that people and institutions can align social rhythms with Earth's rhythms. Finally, the chapter advances the United Times thought experiment: a complementary organisation to the United Nations with a Secretariat, a General Assembly, and an International Court of Temporal Justice. The United Times is based on a chrono-political ideal to propose an institutional basis capable of dealing equitably with the temporal interactions between societies and the planet. This thought experiment shows how legal architectures might mediate between short-term interests and long-term planetary habitability, and how education and 'time design' principles could structure temporal governance. A key insight is that integrating temporal principles into earth system law is essential in order to mitigate temporal conflicts and to sustain planetary habitability over deep time.

V. Earth System Law Destinations

This introductory chapter has so far reflected upon the origins and journeys of earth system law, elucidated as these are by the rich, and at times provocative, chapters in this book. In this final section, we look ahead in an attempt to trace some of the possible *destinations* of earth system law.[38] It is not so much an effort to define a concrete point which the earth system law project is, or should be, heading towards, or an effort that definitively declares what earth system law is

[38] The content in this section also draws on key outcomes and messages formulated during an international symposium titled, *Exploring New Frontiers in Earth System Law: From Theory to Practice*, held on 12 and 13 November 2025, and jointly organised by Wageningen University and Research, Utrecht University (the Netherlands) and Colorado College (US).

and what it should do next. 'Destinations' for us are more about the process of getting there than the actual 'there'. The complex process of 'getting there' can inform efforts to trace the broader contours of earth system law's destinations, speculative and abstract as they may still be. Several chapters in this book have explored parts of the journeys that might lead us to the destinations of earth system law.

In what follows, we propose some of the next steps that could inform the evolution of *earth system law for the Anthropocene*, reaffirming the pluralistic, multifarious, evolving and contested nature of emergent earth system law scholarship. We see at least three thematic clusters that may orient a new generation of earth system law research towards solutions- and practice-related inquiry.

First, researchers and practitioners are increasingly attentive to how goals of accountability, justice and rights can better align with the complexity of a dynamic earth system. Second, analysts of earth system law who are researching and pursuing a path-to-practice agenda have affirmed the need to examine its plural and polycentric approaches, and to develop new methodologies that can engage this complexity. Finally, in exploring how to realise earth system law's transformative potential, researchers have affirmed the need to re-think the institutions, actors, agents, and jurisdiction that will connect the framework's normative aspiration to practice. In anticipation of a new phase of earth system law research and future practice-oriented dialogue, this section explores each of these emergent emphases in turn.

A. Accountability, Justice, and Rights in an Evolving Earth System Law Context

This book and recent dialogues underscore the continued value of interrogating how questions of accountability, justice and rights have been, and should be, operationalised across existing and emergent contexts in an evolving earth system. Given the close connections between the earth system law framework and the broader Earth System Governance Project, the alignment in conceptual emphases between this community's Science and Implementation Plan[39] and earth system law's research foci is unsurprising. Nevertheless, earth system law's distinct attention to how legal frameworks and institutions may advance these objectives provides a valuable foundation from which to interrogate the normative contours of law's desired elements.

Recent earth system law examinations of accountability, justice, and rights underscore the need to consider new ontological and epistemological orientations,

[39] Earth System Governance Project. *Earth System Governance. Science and Implementation Plan of the Earth System Governance Project* (2018), https://www.earthsystemgovernance.org/wp-content/uploads/2018/11/Earth-System-Governance-Science-Plan-2018.pdf.

such as considerations of kinship,[40] ecological integrity,[41] and relational framings,[42] and the ways that formulations of law can become more attentive to 'territories of life'.[43] An earth system law orientation to the broad, normative objectives of accountability and justice also invites simultaneous consideration of questions that foreground complementary themes of agency and architecture – including which existing legal principles may be seen as resonant with earth system law's desired elements,[44] and what new legal principles may be required to realise its ideals.[45] Collectively, these contributions highlight that earth system law continues to provide a foundation for novel inquiry alongside broader earth system governance analyses.

As earth system law researchers continue to explore the practice-relevant dimensions of these emphases, multiple novel themes emerge. In one, ongoing work suggests value in further interrogating how earth system law is operationalised *across scales* and exploring how the broad objectives of a planetary legal framework can be made resonant in regional, national and subnational institutions and legal engagements.[46] Additionally, a path-to-practice research agenda could explore how earth system law can operationalise considerations of justice and rights *within regimes*, for instance property law[47] and water governance,[48] while still acknowledging the interconnected character of the earth system and attendant legal responses. Further, recent discourse accentuates a solutions-oriented interest in further engaging questions of *knowledge and power*, interrogating what forms of knowledge are presently embraced in 'legal' venues and what new forms of knowledge could better support law in engaging with pressing planetary challenges and transformations. Finally, while future research can further promote justice, accountability, and rights in an earth system context, it can also facilitate identifying earth system law *blockages*: 'inhibitory provisions' that appear across scales and contexts and may impede further development of earth system law. Mapping such constraints is essential for understanding how law is shaped by the legacies of the Holocene and where transformation towards an adaptive, planetary disposition will require deliberate intervention.

[40] Warner, Chapter 9 in this book.
[41] Burdon, Chapter 10 in this book.
[42] Morrow, Chapter 6 in this book.
[43] Garver and Vargas Roncancio, Chapter 7 in this book.
[44] Kotzé and Du Toit, Chapter 3 in this book.
[45] Leach, Chapter 4 in this book.
[46] A Buser, 'Earth System Litigation: Potential Contributions of Rights-Based Biodiversity Litigation to Developing the Contours of Earth System Law' (*Exploring New Frontiers in Earth System Law: From Theory to Practice*, Wageningen, 2025).
[47] A Calo, 'Confronting Property Regimes to Facilitate Earth System Law' (*Exploring New Frontiers in Earth System Law: From Theory to Practice*, Wageningen, 2025).
[48] M Augustijn, E Alblas, and A Richter, 'Catching Up with Drought in Historically Wet Regions: Pathways for Law and Governance' (*Exploring New Frontiers in Earth System Law: From Theory to Practice*, Wageningen, 2025).

B. Plural, Polycentric, and Methodological Developments in an Evolving Planetary Legal Order

This book and recent conversations also indicate significant interest in further exploring the plural and polycentric frameworks that characterise dominant legal approaches – and that could contribute to the realisation of earth system law ideals. Indeed, the earth system law framework was initially motivated, in large measure, by such complexity: acknowledgment of rapidly changing planetary dynamics,[49] the need for governance frameworks to accommodate this reality,[50] and structural deficits in the legal capacity to meaningfully engage these challenges.[51]

However, as the intervening years following the initial proposal of the earth system law framework demonstrate, the contextual conditions that demanded this approach have further evolved. Acknowledging this complexity and dynamism has led earth system law researchers to emphasise two interrelated areas of inquiry: the plural and polycentric foundations of an evolving planetary legal order; and the methodological approaches that can support analysis of this reality.

As researchers seek to understand an evolving planetary legal order, their work affirms the dynamic nature of challenges at the intersection of planetary and socio-political realities. Earth system and planetary boundaries assessments continue to evolve as existing domains further approach or exceed threshold points and novel scientific understandings refine insights into systems dynamics.[52] Simultaneously, social and political realities are dynamic. For instance, recent discussions have underscored the effects of ongoing geopolitical trends, including polarisation, militarisation, and foundational tensions surrounding the stability of the rule of law.[53] These trends challenge earth system governance, broadly, and the emergence of a planetary legal framework, specifically, by constraining cooperation, eroding trust and reshaping conditions under which legal innovations can be advanced and implemented.

Additionally, recent earth system law assessments indicate value in further interrogating the legal complexities posed by emergent challenges. Some affirm the increasing salience of new modes of governance such as plurilateral institutions and algorithmic data-driven regulation, of novel technologies such as artificial intelligence,[54] and planetary-scale geoengineering,[55] and of global focusing events

[49] Potsdam Institute for Climate Impact Research, Planetary Boundaries Science (PB Science), *Planetary Health Check 2025*, https://www.planetaryhealthcheck.org.

[50] F Biermann, '"Earth System Governance" as a Crosscutting Theme of Global Change Research' (2007) 17 *Global Environmental Change* 326.

[51] Kotzé and Kim (n 24).

[52] Potsdam Institute for Climate Impact Research (n 49).

[53] A Ettinger and A Collins, 'Trumpism and the Rejection of Global Climate Governance' (2025) 39 *International Relations* 76.

[54] JC Gellers, 'Emerging Technologies and Earth System Governance in the Anthropocene' (2022) 14 *Earth System Governance* 100157.

[55] Biermann and others (n 15).

such as pandemics or financial crises within the dominant capitalist system. While earth system law has long urged consideration of such challenges, these prospects were not fully realised in the way the earth system law framework was initially articulated. Collectively, these and other evolving contextual conditions emphasise the need for future earth system law research to truly engage with and articulate law for a 'no-analog' future characterised by polycentricity, evolution, and differential change across contexts.

The plural, polycentric, and evolving nature of an emergent planetary legal framework presents complexity that can both challenge analysis and provide multiple opportunities for fruitful inquiry. Therefore, recent earth system law efforts suggest a keen interest in further interrogating and elaborating the epistemological and ontological positions that can support this research,[56] and exploring the methodological approaches – including quantitative, qualitative, and participatory – that can guide such research efforts. By directing attention to these important questions of research design, scholars can better navigate the complexity inherent in this area and support an ambitious and practice-oriented new phase of earth system law research.

First, while earth system law scholars have embraced constructive critique from within regarding the extent and nature of this new framework,[57] more clarity regarding the contours of earth system law and its emphases can facilitate new synergies with other legal discourses, particularly progressive and critical approaches. Because the boundaries of earth system law have remained conceptually porous,[58] much of earth system law's first generation of scholarship maintained an inward disposition, seeking to elaborate its contours, emphases, and distinctions from existing frameworks. Now it is time to consider how a new generation of scholarship might direct attention outward, to opportunities for conceptual synergy with other frameworks and approaches.[59]

Second, the question arises how earth system law may incorporate insights of theories that can further aid in exploring law's role in governing planetary transformations. While such an emphasis is not novel,[60] scholars have been exploring numerous theories and approaches that could be relevant, including transnational legal pluralism, legal geography, telecoupling approaches, decolonial scholarship, and queer theory. Such examinations could support earth system

[56] Eg, M Klimke and C Zengerling, 'How to Operationalize Earth System Law Research? Conceptual, Methodological and Practical Options' (*Exploring New Frontiers in Earth System Law: From Theory to Practice*, Wageningen, 2025).

[57] As detailed in L du Toit, 'Assessing the State of Earth System Law' (*Exploring New Frontiers in Earth System Law: From Theory to Practice*, Wageningen, 2025).

[58] Kotzé, Angstadt, and Kim, Chapter 2 in this book.

[59] See, eg, R Talenti, 'Bridging Earth System Law and Critical Legal Scholarships: Synthesising a Counter-Hegemonic Legal Paradigm' (*Exploring New Frontiers in Earth System Law: From Theory to Practice*, Wageningen, 2025).

[60] J Auz, 'The Political Eology of Earth System Law: Outlining a Lex Capitalocenae' (2022) 40 *Wisconsin International Law Journal* 217.

law analysis, for instance, by demarcating what is and is not considered 'law' in an earth system law framework. This effort could also clarify the emphases of science and scholarship, creating a coherent research agenda that directs earth system law's theoretical work towards practice-relevance. In addition to leveraging generative and discursive power by aligning the earth system framework with compatible efforts, such an approach may also add additional ontological, epistemological, and axiological frameworks that can support emergent practice-oriented analyses.

C. Institutions, Actors, Agents, and Jurisdictions of a Solutions-oriented Earth System Law Approach

Extensive scholarly engagement with earth system law's theoretical, normative, and analytical dimensions has provided a valuable foundation from which to pursue solutions-oriented and practice-relevant research.[61] Existing efforts to interrogate earth system law's transformative potential reflect engagement with conceptual emphases that may promote coherence among future research projects: the configurations of architecture and agency that can enact earth system law,[62] the anticipatory and imaginative character that can inflect a planetary legal framework,[63] and the adaptive and reflexive elements that must characterise future legal developments.[64] As earth system law scholarship matures, its analysts increasingly examine the institutions, actors, agents, and jurisdictions that may support the transformations that the framework advocates.

While these examinations can explore idealised or hypothetical institutions, a new chapter of earth system law research increasingly explores institutions, actors, and agents across jurisdictions, seeking indicia of existing and emergent planetary legal transformations. These indicia are often implicit and uneven, yet they reveal how law, across multiple regions, legal cultures, and scales, has begun to acknowledge ecological interdependence, planetary complexity, and the inadequacy of isolated or fragmented regulatory approaches. Identifying such developments can not only illustrate promising approaches to systemic legal thinking and facilitate the circulation of best practices, but also signal where future research and reform efforts might most productively concentrate.

[61] Kotzé, Angstadt, and Kim, Chapter 2 of this book; L du Toit, 'Assessing the State of Earth System Law' (*Exploring New Frontiers in Earth System Law: From Theory to Practice*, Wageningen, 2025).

[62] Benoit Mayer, Chapter 13 of this book.

[63] A Gupta and C Macchi, 'Anticipatory Governance of the Global Commons to Avoid Future Harm: Exploring the Relevance of Earth System Law' (*Exploring New Frontiers in Earth System Law: From Theory to Practice*, Wageningen, 2025).

[64] JB Ruhl, 'Earth's Re-domination of Human Systems' (*Exploring New Frontiers in Earth System Law: From Theory to Practice*, Wageningen, 2025).

The interstitial space between law's existing formulations and the transformative orientation of earth system law thus becomes a critical site of inquiry: a vantage point from which researchers can observe where the law is starting to move, how these shifts are taken up, and what they imply for the next steps in the evolution of earth system law.

One set of such indicia appears in the substantive and preambular texts of international and domestic instruments that increasingly recognise the interconnected nature of the earth system. Several treaties, constitutional provisions, and other legal texts now reference concepts such as ecosystem integrity, planetary crises, and intergenerational justice. The Paris Agreement, for instance, emphasises the 'integrity of all ecosystems' and situates climate action within a broader constellation of social and ecological concerns; the Kunming–Montreal Global Biodiversity Framework frames biodiversity, climate and pollution as interlinked planetary challenges that demand integrated responses; and the Biodiversity Beyond National Jurisdiction Agreement is grounded in an understanding of the ocean as a connected, dynamic system whose conservation requires cumulative and system-wide impact assessment.[65] The Sustainable Development Goals likewise gesture towards such a systemic orientation by linking environmental stability with social and economic well-being, although their architecture tends to disperse ecological concerns across separate goals rather than embed planetary integrity as an organising principle.[66] Domestic legislation and constitutional provisions in South Africa, New Zealand, and Ecuador similarly articulate relational and systemic understandings of environmental protection that extend beyond sectoral or project-based approaches. While often couched in aspirational or interpretive language, these textual developments increasingly guide administrative and judicial interpretation, thereby functioning as quiet, yet significant, pathways for a more earth system-attuned legal reasoning.

Litigation and judicial review present another, and particularly striking, set of indicia. Courts and tribunals are increasingly confronted with claims that expose the cross-sectoral and long-term nature of environmental harm, prompting shifts in how legal obligations are interpreted and applied. Examples include the German Constitutional Court's reasoning on biodiversity and intergenerational protection;[67] climate cases in Italy, Kenya and Pakistan addressing the social-ecological dimensions of displacement linked to emergency and

[65] See generally J Mossop and D Freestone (eds), *The Agreement on Marine Biodiversity of Areas Beyond National Jurisdiction: Commentary and Analysis* (Oxford, Oxford University Press, 2025).

[66] LJ Kotzé and others, 'Planetary Integrity' in F Biermann, T Hickmann, and CA Sénit (eds), *The Political Impact of Sustainable Development Goals: Transforming Governance Through Global Goals?* (Cambridge, Cambridge University Press, 2022).

[67] A Buser, 'Earth System Litigation: Potential Contributions of Rights-Based Biodiversity Litigation to Developing the Contours of Earth System Law' (*Exploring New Frontiers in Earth System Law: From Theory to Practice*, Wageningen, 2025).

adaptation measures;[68] and constitutional case law in Colombia recognising ecosystems as legal subjects and articulating biocultural rights rooted in the ties between communities and their territories.[69] Advisory proceedings before international courts and tribunals, such as the recent pronouncement of the International Court of Justice on the climate obligations of states and the advisory opinion of the International Tribunal for the Law of the Sea connecting ocean and climate protection, further reveal how environmental obligations are increasingly interpreted in light of integrated, systemic conditions rather than isolated issue areas. While research can beneficially explore the prospects of current efforts, earth system law ideals will also need to resonate in other, more focused, scales and settings. Therefore, exploring litigation in numerous venues and legal cultures can meaningfully inform earth system law's emergent prescriptions.

A further set of indicia emerges in the institutional frameworks through which legal authority is organised, including judicial, quasi-judicial, regulatory, administrative, and multilateral decision-making bodies. Across these settings, questions of mandate, jurisdiction,[70] accountability, and coordination increasingly reveal points of friction and adaptation to complex and systemic risks. Together, these indicate how institutional design and practice may evolve in the solutions-oriented direction envisioned by earth system law, and suggest ongoing scholarly interest in interrogating how an evolving planetary legal framework can best advance these ideals.

VI. Conclusion

In this introductory chapter we have sought to make out a case in support of continuing our efforts to co-create a new legal paradigm for the Anthropocene. The project of earth system law is ongoing, shaped by different voices and perspectives, changing contexts, and evolving agendas, among many other fluid impulses. Importantly, as a new framework to think about *law for the Anthropocene*, earth system law is not a panacea for all of law's ills in this new epoch. It certainly will not magically offer an instantaneous answer to the many questions bedevilling the ambitions of earth system governance and the role of law in this effort. But, as we have argued in this chapter, and as the rich contributions in this book show,

[68] M Scott, 'Justice Sector Institutions and Environmental Human Mobility: Towards an Anthropocene Legal Praxis' (*Exploring New Frontiers in Earth System Law: From Theory to Practice*, Wageningen, 2025).

[69] E Macpherson, J Torres Ventura and F Clavijo Ospina, 'Constitutional Law, Ecosystems, and Indigenous Peoples in Colombia: Biocultural Rights and Legal Subjects' (2022) 9 *Transnational Environmental Law* 521–40.

[70] JM Angstadt, 'Seeking "Earth System Jurisdiction": Insights from Specialist Courts' (*Exploring New Frontiers in Earth System Law: From Theory to Practice*, Wageningen, 2025).

humanity cannot continue its present path of planetary destruction. We need to change course. To the extent that law is a social institution to help us do precisely that, we should continue with our efforts to look for alternatives to the status quo. As a framework that fundamentally and critically challenges the foundational assumptions of *law of the Anthropocene*, earth system law holds out promise to help shape the contours and content of *law for the Anthropocene*.

2

The Evolution of Earth System Law: New Pathways for Legal Innovation

LOUIS J KOTZÉ, J MICHAEL ANGSTADT AND RAKHYUN E KIM

I. Introduction

Is environmental law, as a discipline and field of expertise, and a set of specialised norms aimed at environmental protection, still able to effectively respond to the planetary crisis of the Anthropocene? Or does the Anthropocene, and the qualitatively 'new' living environment that this trope represents, require a fresh look at environmental law, its achievements, underlying ethics, objectives, and foundational building blocks? More importantly, does the Anthropocene require a different legal paradigm that could guide the development of a new generation of laws that contribute to ensure, alongside other social institutions, a realistic prospect for all present and future life to flourish on a critically ill planet? If so, what could this new legal paradigm for the Anthropocene look like?

These are some of the key questions that inspired the original proposition of earth system law.[1] Many acknowledge the inability of environmental law to drive the type of structural transformations that are required to confront the planetary crisis, and the limitations of the debilitating epistemic closures apparent in environmental law discourse, including a lack of 'radical', innovative and future-oriented interdisciplinary thinking that is arguably necessary to live in and with the Anthropocene.[2] Motivated by these observations, the proponents of earth system law thought it presented a useful alternative framework to environmental law, and law more generally, to be able to operate more effectively in the Anthropocene.

Five years after the original proposal was published, it is now an opportune moment to critically reflect on the development of earth system law as a domain of

[1] LJ Kotzé and RE Kim, 'Earth System Law: The Juridical Dimensions of Earth System Governance' (2019) 1 *Earth System Governance* 100003.

[2] LJ Kotzé (ed), *Environmental Law and Governance for the Anthropocene* (Oxford, Hart Publishing, 2017).

scientific enquiry. Has the concept been taken up by others? Has it been expanded in other possible directions? In which contexts has it been applied? What are the main points of criticism levelled against earth system law? How does its current manifestation compare to the original proposition? What has its impact been on policy and broader science domains? And what are the key elements of a future earth system law research agenda?

This chapter broadly reflects on these questions by offering a deep dive into the emerging scholarship on earth system law. In doing so, it offers a stocktake of earth system law scholarship as it has developed over the past five years, while at the same time looking ahead to propose a future research agenda that is informed by key findings of this assessment. Collectively considered, the analysis offers insights into the potential of earth system law both as a discursive-epistemic framework and as a new legal paradigm that is intertwined with earth system governance, while also serving as a critical self-reflection on the merits of this new paradigm, its shortcomings, and advances.

In terms of methodology, to identify relevant publications, we conducted a literature search in the Scopus database using the term 'earth system law' in the title, abstract, and keywords. We also supplemented this search with a more general Google Scholar search to identify chapters and books that are not included in Scopus. The results comprise approximately 120 publications. For the sake of completeness, we also draw on the chapters written for this book. Those publications that only indirectly focus on or mention earth system law in passing were not considered.

Following this introduction, we first summarise the original proposition and then look at how this proposition has subsequently been expanded. The next section focuses on the mainstream critique of earth system law, while the final section sketches a future research agenda.

II. The Original Proposition

Earth system law was initially proposed as a response to the existence of a so-called 'Anthropocene gap'[3] in relation to law and legal science's undefined and underexplored role in earth system governance. This epistemic 'gap' broadly reflected upon the difficulties in crafting appropriate legal responses to earth system transformations. The steady growth of earth system science on the one hand,[4] and earth system governance research on the other,[5] marked a 'planetary

[3] V Galaz, *Global Environmental Governance, Technology and Politics* (Cheltenham, Edward Elgar Publishing, 2014).

[4] W Steffen, 'The Emergence and Evolution of Earth System Science' (2020) 1 *Nature Reviews Earth and Environment* 54.

[5] F Biermann, *Earth System Governance: World Politics in the Anthropocene* (Cambridge MA, MIT Press, 2014).

turn' in sustainability governance discourse, and it set the scene and created opportunities to start thinking about 'environmental' change in planetary or earth system terms.[6]

The 'planetary turn' suggested that the earth system, and more specifically earth system transformations, are characterised by high levels of uncertainty; functional interdependence of various elements and processes; myriad human and non-human interactions and interdependence; and unprecedented degrees of anthropogenically induced harm. The planetary context of the Anthropocene, as it were, vividly illuminated environmental law's disappointing achievements in governing human behaviour in relation to the earth system;[7] the governance challenges that a complex earth system creates simply seemed too overwhelming for environmental law to deal with.[8]

A different legal response is required that aligns with evolving earth system thinking in the natural and social sciences: one that could offer alternatives, and possibly solutions, to environmental law's shortcomings. Earth system law was accordingly proposed as a 'new legal phenomenon' that 'accommodates and encapsulates all juridical aspects of earth system governance, including a new research agenda that is able to respond to the unique epistemic, ontological and normative characteristics, demands and nature of earth system governance in the Anthropocene'.[9]

The central referent 'earth system' law was deliberate insofar as it suggested something broader and more encapsulating, and possibly deeper and more radical, than 'environmental' law. While related concepts such as 'ecological' or 'planetary' law similarly call for a fundamental rethinking of law for the Anthropocene, the notion of 'earth system' law was distinctive in emphasising the systemic and interconnected nature of planetary processes. It also explicitly situated this legal reimagination within the Earth System Governance Network's broader research agenda and its Science and Implementation Plan.[10] Moreover, as the title of the original 2019 paper suggests, the earth system law framework was intended as a first attempt to explicitly explore the *legal* dimensions, aspects and concerns of this predominantly political science-oriented network, and to offer lawyers an entry point into discussions about what law's contribution to earth system governance is or could be.

The original paper did not offer a standardised definition of earth system law. The concept was instead framed, and elaborated to some extent, in more descriptive

[6] F Biermann, 'The Future of "Environmental" Policy in the Anthropocene: Time for a Paradigm Shift' (2021) 30 *Environmental Politics* 61.

[7] Kotzé and Kim (n 1); LJ Kotzé, 'The Transnationalization of Environmental Constitutionalism' in V Heyvaert and L-A Duvic-Paoli (eds), *Research Handbook on Transnational Environmental Law* (Cheltenham, Edward Elgar Publishing, 2020) 159.

[8] RE Kim and K Bosselmann, 'International Environmental Law in the Anthropocene: Towards a Purposive System of Multilateral Environmental Agreements' (2013) 2 *Transnational Environmental Law* 285.

[9] Kotzé and Kim (n 1).

[10] S Burch and others, *Earth System Governance: Science and Implementation Plan of the Earth System Governance Project* (Earth System Governance Project, Utrecht 2018).

terms by reflecting on five key concerns explicating the shortcomings of environmental law. These included environmental law's inability to drive deep structural reforms; its state-centrism and proclivity to shut out polycentric forms of governance; its structurally embedded anthropocentrism that is complicit in exacerbating the vulnerability of the living order; its assumptions of Holocene stability that have become outdated in an unpredictable Anthropocene context; and its reductionism that focuses on 'the environment' instead of a holistic, all-encompassing, intertwined and complex earth system consisting of many 'environments' of which humans are an integral part.

Earth system law was accordingly loosely described as a reimagined vision of law that is *not* any of the foregoing, namely, law that must: keep humanity from crossing planetary boundaries and achieve deep structural social change; elevate and meaningfully facilitate polycentric forms of governance; fully embrace all present and future earth system constituents, including humans and non-humans; discard outdated assumptions of Holocene stability and respond to complexity, instability and unpredictability; and embrace an earth system approach as a 'fully functioning complex adaptive system of earth system law that adaptively manages other complexly adaptive natural and social systems'.[11] This idea built on work conceptualising law as a complex adaptive system.[12]

The original proposal then briefly sketched what it called a 'conceptual progression' of earth system law.[13] It used international environmental law as an illustrative example, among many others that could have been used.[14] This description was based on two axes: (i) the regulatory object of law, ie, 'environmental', 'ecological' and 'earth' along the one axis; and (ii) the geographical or jurisdictional scope of law, ie, 'international', 'global/ transnational' and 'planetary', along the other. It was indicated that some of this progression is already happening, as is evident in the rise of ecological law (especially rights of nature), and the discourse on global or transnational environmental law, that includes state and non-state actors and different forms of norms, operating interdependently across different geographical levels and jurisdictional categories.

A research agenda mapping future research trajectories was also proposed, linking these to the Earth System Governance Network's Science and Implementation Plan (2018),[15] and further identifying three broader dimensions by which to organise earth system law research, ie, analytical, normative, and prescriptive/transformative.[16] These include: understanding the science of

[11] Kotzé and Kim (n 1).

[12] RE Kim and Mackey, 'International Environmental Law as a Complex Adaptive System' (2014) 14 *International Environmental Agreements: Politics, Law and Economics* 5; JB Ruhl and R Craig, '4 °C' (2021) 106 *Minnesota Law Review* 191.

[13] Kotzé and Kim (n 1) 6.

[14] LJ Kotzé and RE Kim, 'Towards Planetary Nexus Governance in the Anthropocene: An Earth System Law Perspective' (2022) 13 *Global Policy* 86.

[15] Burch and others (n 10).

[16] Kotzé and Kim (n 1).

law for understanding the structure, content, processes, and institutions of legal systems (analytical); exploring and addressing a set of normative considerations of earth system governance, eg, how law could best steer and orchestrate the actions of multiple actors on different scales to respond to Anthropocene challenges; and how the prescriptive nature of law could be used to drive social transformations. These three dimensions were elaborated in some detail in a subsequent publication that critiqued the shortcomings of international environmental law, arguing that analytically, international environmental law and its lawyers are unable to fully understand and respond to the complex governance challenges arising from a complex earth system. Normatively, international environmental law has failed to provide appropriate norms to prevent humans from encroaching on earth system limits. In a transformative sense, international environmental law has not been sufficiently ambitious to achieve the type of radical transformations necessary to ensure planetary integrity and socio-ecological justice.[17]

In sum, the original proposal was deliberately idealistic and conceptually ambitious, intended to provoke debate and inspire new directions in legal thought. It was, by design, more a conceptual starting point than a detailed blueprint. Yet, as subsequent work has shown, the framework carries both practical relevance and considerable potential to inform how legal systems might evolve in response to global environmental change. Earth system law was conceived as a new approach to thinking about and organising law in the context of the Anthropocene; an analytical and normative paradigm for enabling legally-driven societal transformations at the pace, scale and depth that planetary crises demand. Importantly, earth system law was never meant to denote a discrete body of law, such as human rights or trade law, but rather to offer a way of re-envisioning law as an integral component of an interconnected earth system.[18]

III. Expansion of the Original Proposal and Emerging Themes

How was the proposition of earth system law received by the scientific community, and how has the original proposal been engaged with and given new form, content and meaning? Rather predictably, most of the engagement with earth system law has been occurring within the Earth System Governance Network community and has been driven principally by the Network's Taskforce on Earth System Law, the majority of whom are lawyers, but also includes political scientists and scholars

[17] LJ Kotzé, 'Earth System Law for the Anthropocene: Rethinking Environmental Law Alongside the Earth System Metaphor' (2020) 11 *Transnational Legal Theory* 75.

[18] P Magalhães, 'Common Interest, Concern or Heritage? The Commons as a Structural Support for an Earth System Law' in T Cadman, M Hurlbert and AC Simonelli (eds), *Earth System Law: Standing on the Precipice of the Anthropocene* (Abingdon-on-Thames, Routledge, 2022).

working in other (mostly social science) disciplines.[19] Since 2019, there have been two collected milestone publications focusing on earth system law.

The first was a special issue in the journal *Earth System Governance* titled 'Earth System Law: Towards a New Legal Paradigm for the Anthropocene'.[20] It was an initiative of the Taskforce leadership at that moment, Louis J Kotzé, Rakhyun E Kim, and Catherine Blanchard. Their editorial places the concept in a broader context, acknowledging that it draws on previous work on ecological, planetary, and systems approaches to law.[21] This collection contained nine articles focusing on: the transformative potential of earth system law and how such transformation could play out in practice;[22] a re-examination of the legal status of non-human beings through the lens of earth system law;[23] a critique of the logic, aspirations and assumptions of earth system law and what these mean for an effort to reconfigure Earth, its subjects and the law;[24] a critique of the siloed and ineffective international legal regime governing fossil fuels, through the lens of earth system law;[25] earth system law as a tool to address gaps in governance that arise from the mismatch between the global hydrological cycle and dispersed regulatory architecture across institutions and geographic regions;[26] earth system law as the basis to critique law's short-term horizon and inability to secure the basic needs of future people, while arguing for a new form of international human rights law that is better able to protect the rights of future generations;[27] developing a new justice model for earth system law around the idea of socio-ecological justice;[28] proposals for international environmental law to embrace an earth system perspective and therefore to remain relevant in the Anthropocene;[29] and earth system law as a shared epistemic framework to enable and enhance collaborative

[19] Earth System Governance Network, 'Research Taskforce on Earth System Law', https://www.earthsystemgovernance.org/research/taskforce-on-earth-system-law/#:~:text=The%20Task%20Force%20on%20Earth%20System%20Law%20is%20composed%20of,within%20an%20Earth%20System%20context.

[20] Earth System Governance https://www.sciencedirect.com/special-issue/10ZQL018KHP.

[21] RE Kim, C Blanchard, and LJ Kotzé, 'Law, Systems, and Planet Earth: Editorial' (2022) 11 *Earth System Governance* 100127.

[22] L Mai and E Boulot, 'Harnessing the Transformative Potential of Earth System Law: From Theory to Practice' (2021) 7 *Earth System Governance* 100103.

[23] JC Gellers, 'Earth System Law and the Legal Status of Non-Humans in the Anthropocene' (2021) 7 *Earth System Governance* 100083.

[24] MC Petersmann, 'Sympoietic Thinking and Earth System Law: The Earth, Its Subjects and the Law' (2021) 9 *Earth System Governance* 100114.

[25] H van Asselt, 'Governing Fossil Fuel Production in the Age of Climate Disruption: Towards an International Law of "Leaving It in the Ground"' (2021) 9 *Earth System Governance* 100118.

[26] H Ahlström and others, 'An Earth System Law Perspective on Governing Social-Hydrological Systems in the Anthropocene' (2021) 10 *Earth System Governance* 100120.

[27] N van Dijk, 'From Exacerbating the Anthropocene's Problems to Intergenerational Justice: An Analysis of the Communication Procedure of the Human Rights Treaty System' (2021) 10 *Earth System Governance* 100123.

[28] K Pope, M Bonatti and S Sieber, 'The What, Who and How of Socio-Ecological Justice: Tailoring a New Justice Model for Earth System Law' (2021) 10 *Earth System Governance 100124.*

[29] L du Toit and LJ Kotzé, 'Reimagining International Environmental Law for the Anthropocene: An Earth System Law Perspective' (2022) 11 *Earth System Governance* 100132.

intradisciplinary and interdisciplinary research and co-learning that go hand in hand with transdisciplinary stakeholder engagement.[30]

The second publication appeared in 2022 in edited book form and is titled *Earth System Law: Standing on the Precipice of the Anthropocene*.[31] It was a bottom-up initiative of a few members of the Earth System Law Taskforce. The book deals with the conceptual contours of earth system law, and its analytical, normative and transformative dimensions. Topics include, among others, a focus on international relations;[32] the interplay between science and law for sustainability;[33] ecological approaches and rights of nature;[34] new ethics for law in the Anthropocene;[35] a proposal for earth system justice grounded in earth system law;[36] and the commons as a basis for earth system law.[37]

Looking beyond these two more organised initiatives, an increasing number of academics are engaging in earth system law scholarship. While acknowledging the emergent nature of this body of research, we nevertheless perceive several existing frames that have oriented many early analyses. These frames, as detailed below, largely affirm and elaborate the three 'dimensions' of potential research proposed in the foundational earth system law publication: (1) analysis of law and legal regulation in the Anthropocene; (2) normative consideration of earth system governance and possible legal pathways to promote desired objectives; and (3) prescriptive attention to how existing law should be transformed to advance these objectives.

A. Analysis of Legal Regulation in the Anthropocene and Earth System Law

Several contributions have supported a sweeping reconsideration of law and regulation in the Anthropocene. These contributions largely reflect and affirm central emphases of the Earth System Governance Network community: exploring implications of diverse governance responses to accelerating change; considering interlinked social, political, and environmental pressures; and

[30] LJ Kotzé and others, 'Earth System Law: Exploring New Frontiers in Legal Science' (2022) 11 *Earth System Governance* 100126.
[31] Magalhães (n 18).
[32] JM Angstadt, 'International Relations and the Analytical Foundations of Earth System Law' in Cadman, Hurlbert and Simonelli (n 18).
[33] E Fernández Fernández, 'An Earth System Science-Based Perspective: A Foundational Feature of Earth System Law' in Cadman, Hurlbert and Simonelli (n 18).
[34] A Bleby, 'Rights of Nature as an Expression of Earth System Law' in Cadman, Hurlbert and Simonelli (n 18).
[35] R Warner, 'The Ethical Place of the Non-Human World in Earth System Law: Pathways of Transformation' in Cadman, Hurlbert and Simonelli (n 18).
[36] M Nyke, 'A Framework of Earth System Justice in the Earth System's Legal Context' in Cadman, Hurlbert and Simonelli (n 18).
[37] Magalhães (n 18).

identifying responses to inequality within the Anthropocene.[38] As earth system law researchers map these considerations onto existing legal frameworks, three clusters of analytical emphasis predominate: (1) the foundations and deficits of law as a point of departure for earth system law; (2) law and governance's engagement with the unique challenges of the Anthropocene; and (3) attributes and contributions of key legal institutions and actors.

The first broad cluster of scholarship considers how existing legal frameworks both undergird and impede earth system law. As these works acknowledge, legal frameworks offer a point of departure for new approaches while simultaneously reifying many key structural challenges. Accordingly, researchers assess how the desired objectives of earth system law interface with more conventional environmental law considerations across scope and scale. One such group of publications possesses a systemic emphasis, and critiques the overarching architecture of law. For instance, Kotzé and Kim[39] highlight that international environmental law has failed to achieve broad structural reforms that meaningfully address a problematic foregrounding of states, human interests, and a historical Holocene stability. These broad concerns are carried forward in various other publications that urge: a discontinuation of international environmental law in its dominant form; a reorientation of international environmental law that more explicitly and ambitiously engages with Anthropocene demands for polycentrism, holism, and acknowledgment of complexity;[40] and consideration of dominant legal systems' failure to meaningfully acknowledge human–nonhuman relations as intrinsic to contemporary governance challenges.[41]

Alongside these more systemic analyses, additional works illustrate how dominant approaches have neglected specific earth system challenges. For instance, publications emphasise the need to create architectures that better address: the global character and intricate contributions of oceans to earth system processes;[42] the necessary magnitude and nature of rights-based reforms required to realise climate justice;[43] and the resources and practices required to secure human rights and usher in a transition to more sustainable corporate practices.[44] Researchers similarly explore the implications of key international environmental law principles, advocating, for instance: an approach to state sovereignty that can better steward natural resources and address the climate crisis;[45] a reimagination of sustainable

[38] Earth System Governance Network (n 19).

[39] Kotzé and Kim (n 1).

[40] Du Toit and Kotzé (n 29).

[41] Petersmann (n 24).

[42] TB Rudolph and others, 'A Transition to Sustainable Ocean Governance' (2020) 11 *Nature Communications* 3600.

[43] S Adelman, 'Human Rights in Pursuit of Climate Justice' (2020) 38 *Wisconsin International Law Journal* 171.

[44] B Sjåfjell, 'Sustainable Value Creation within Planetary Boundaries – Reforming Corporate Purpose and Duties of the Corporate Board' (2020) 12 *Sustainability* 6245.

[45] T Olsen, *A Critical Perspective on the Principle of State Sovereignty Over Natural Resources and Its Role in Hindering the Effective Regulation of Climate Change at the International Stage* (Master's thesis, UiT Norges Arktiske Universitet, 2023).

development that could more meaningfully promote resilience and respect;[46] and an ecological constitution that could help to codify these and other environmental principles.[47]

Another cluster of analytical scholarship explicitly explores how existing legal frameworks have engaged with the unprecedented challenges posed by the Anthropocene. Early publications highlight the nature and degree of legal responses that are required. Among these works, one recurrent theme is the notion of complexity. For instance, Galaz highlights temporal complexity by highlighting the multiple time scales on which Anthropocene challenges and responses are unfolding, and underscoring the governance challenges that these realities present.[48] Elsewhere, Scobie emphasises scalar complexity, underscoring the multiple spatial scales on which legal frameworks structure the rights and obligations of human and more-than-human interests.[49] Other researchers further develop the theme of spatial complexity, noting the varying degrees of nuance and precision in how the planetary boundaries have been defined and operationalised;[50] and the multiple scales on which planetary boundaries insight can be operationalised, ecosystem restoration pursued, and governance mechanisms structured.[51]

These early assessments of legal engagement with Anthropocene challenges that also touch on aspects of earth system law have collectively urged more reflexive examination of legal frameworks' necessary attributes. Kotzé has underscored the foundational role of law in structuring socio-ecological relations, affirming the need for a more 'fit for purpose' legal architecture,[52] also exploring options that could include a more directly responsive environmental constitutional approach.[53] Likewise, researchers highlight perceived barriers within existing environmental law that may impede a departure from dominant responses. For instance, researchers highlight a need to: acknowledge the more active role that law will

[46] A Cardesa-Salzmann and E Cocciolo, 'Global Governance, Sustainability and the Earth System: Critical Reflections on the Role of Global Law' (2019) 8 *Transnational Environmental Law* 437.

[47] L Collins, *The Ecological Constitution: Reframing Environmental Law* (Abingdon-on-Thames, Routledge 2021).

[48] V Galaz, 'Introduction' in V Galaz (ed), *Global Challenges, Governance, and Complexity* (Cheltenham, Edward Elgar Publishing, 2019) 1–14.

[49] M Scobie, 'Treaty Preambles and the Environmental Justice Gap' (2021) 12 *Global Policy* 273, 276.

[50] F Biermann and RE Kim, 'The Boundaries of the Planetary Boundary Framework: A Critical Appraisal of Approaches to Define a "Safe Operating Space" for Humanity' (2020) 45 *Annual Review of Environment and Resources* 497; RE Kim and LJ Kotzé, 'Planetary Boundaries at the Intersection of Earth System Law, Science and Governance: A State-of-the-Art Review' (2021) 30 *Review of European, Comparative and International Environmental Law* 3.

[51] O Bertolami and F Francisco, 'A Digital Contract for Restoration of the Earth System Mediated by a Planetary Boundary Exchange Unit' (2022) 9 *The Anthropocene Review* 462.

[52] LJ Kotzé, 'Earth System Law for the Anthropocene: Rethinking Environmental Law Alongside the Earth System Metaphor' (2020) 11 *Transnational Legal Theory* 75, 77.

[53] LJ Kotzé, 'The Transnationalization of Environmental Constitutionalism' in V Heyvaert and L-A Duvic-Paoli (eds), *Research Handbook on Transnational Environmental Law* (Cheltenham, Edward Elgar Publishing, 2020).

likely play in addressing irreversible Anthropocene transformations;[54] reimagine the legal education curriculum;[55] and embrace a more reflexive, generative, and change-oriented approach to legal practice.[56]

A further cluster of analytical scholarship explores the legal actors who are engaged in promoting law and regulation in the Anthropocene. These works echo broader earth system governance attention to such actors and the varying configurations and collaborations that shape their agency in addressing Anthropocene challenges.[57] Numerous initial works explore judges and courts as participants in Anthropocene governance. For instance, some research papers have considered the judiciary's engagement with climate litigation. These works have broadly underscored courts' engagement in a transnational matrix of climate litigation that transcends their function as domestic decisional institutions and suggests their role as innovative actors in Anthropocene governance.[58] This broad conclusion is further amplified through attention to individual decisions, including the German *Neubauer et al v Germany* case[59] and 'future generations' lawsuits.[60] Nevertheless, additional publications explore the ordering and configuration of discourse and exchange. These, including an analysis of the epistemic communities that research environmental courts, similarly affirm the need to further explore the diverse actors that will direct an earth system law response.[61]

B. Normative Consideration of Earth System Law

Another growing body of literature explores new ethics, ontologies, and frameworks for justice. This normative orientation inflects the emergent earth system law frame with an imaginative disposition, supporting consideration of the tenets that could best support the realisation of its objectives. While broad in scope, this normative scholarship has foregrounded three complementary considerations: human rights and experiences in earth system law; the potential to support mutually beneficial human and non-human interactions; and opportunities to de-centre human considerations in Earth's legal frameworks.

[54] Kim, Blanchard and Kotzé (n 21).

[55] J Liljeblad, 'Integrating the Anthropocene in Legal Education: Considerations for Asia' (2022) 9 *Asian Journal of Law and Society* 207.

[56] L Mai, 'The "Question of Possibilities" as a Leitmotif for Re-imagining Law for the "Anthropocene"' (2022) 13 *Global Policy* 49, 53–55.

[57] M Betsill, T Benney and A Gerlak (eds), *Agency in Earth System Governance* (Cambridge, Cambridge University Press, 2020).

[58] LJ Kotzé and others, 'Courts, Climate Litigation and the Evolution of Earth System Law' (2024) 15 *Global Policy* 5.

[59] BVerfG, 24 March 2021, 1 BvR 2656/18, 1 BvR 78/20, 1 BvR 96/20, 1 BvR 288/20; LJ Kotzé, 'Neubauer et al. versus Germany: Planetary Climate Litigation for the Anthropocene?' (2021) 22 *German Law Journal* 1423.

[60] Van Dijk (n 27).

[61] JM Angstadt and M Schink, 'Specialist Environmental Courts and Tribunals: A Systematic Literature Review and Case for Earth System Governance Analysis' (2023) 18 *Earth System Governance* 100192.

In this space, many researchers have emphasised the importance of exploring human rights, responsibilities, and realities within an imagined earth system law. Some highlight the close relationship between social inequality, exceedance of planetary boundaries, and the potential for rights frameworks to better mediate and defuse these tensions.[62] Elsewhere, researchers explore the cosmology of *buen vivir* as a potential approach to better mediate social justice, human development, and related ecological considerations.[63] Collectively, these frameworks highlight the need to foreground human equity considerations, even as new legal responses seek to transcend a fundamentally anthropocentric orientation.

Additional contributions to normative scholarship complement this sensitivity to human rights by exploring opportunities for earth system law to structure mutually-beneficial human, more-than-human, and non-human interactions. For example, Lawrence[64] highlights how representation and justice can be conceptualised to benefit both nature and future human generations; and others explore socio-ecological justice as a frame by which to balance the intrinsic value of human and non-human actors, across space and time.[65] Others explore rights of nature as a framework that could support earth system law's development by foregrounding human obligations in response to environmental pressures;[66] and centring the interlinkage of cultural and biological diversity by foregrounding considerations of 'bioculturality'.[67]

A further body of research emphasises the need to de-centre human interests within an earth system law framework. These responses, grounded in an acknowledgment that most existing legal approaches pursue environmental protection by regulating human engagement, explore the prospect of more equitable and expansive legal understandings and ontological orientations.[68] Some authors pursue this objective by broadly considering how law structures relations, whether by reimagining normativity,[69] or by considering how interdependence could provide a principle for broadening the scope and orientation of law.[70] Others explicitly

[62] J Ensor and E Hoddy, 'Securing the Social Foundation: A Rights-Based Approach to Planetary Boundaries' (2020) *Earth System Governance* 100086.

[63] LJ Kotzé and S Adelman, 'Environmental Law and the Unsustainability of Sustainable Development: A Tale of Disenchantment and of Hope' (2023) 34 *Law and Critique* 227. *Buen Vivir* is an alternative development model gaining popularity in South America. Originating from indigenous cultures, it emphasises harmony with nature as key to the well-being of the community.

[64] P Lawrence, 'Justifying Representation of Future Generations and Nature: Contradictory or Mutually Supporting Values?' (2022) 11 *Transnational Environmental Law* 553.

[65] Pope, Bonatti and Sieber (n 28).

[66] A Bleby, 'Rights of Nature as a Response to the Anthropocene' (2020) 48 *University of Western Australia Law Review* 33.

[67] P Wesche, 'Rights of Nature in Practice: A Case Study on the Impacts of the Colombian Atrato River Decision' (2021) 33 *Journal of Environmental Law* 531, 539–40.

[68] E Boulot and J Sterlin, 'Steps towards a Legal Ontological Turn: Proposals for Law's Place beyond the Human' (2022) 11 *Transnational Environmental Law* 13.

[69] N Buitendag, 'Can Norms Bridge Boundaries? Systems Theory's Challenge to Eco-Theology and Earth System Law' (2023) 79 *HTS Theological Studies* 8587.

[70] T Bartolomei, 'From Globalisation to Planetarisation: The Principle of Interdependence as a Vector for a New Law of the Earth: The Lex Anthropocenae' (2023) 14 *Religions* 1176.

highlight certain non-human entities, including those occasioned through technological advances, and consider how earth system law could provide a mechanism to more fully represent these interests.[71] Altogether, existing normative explorations highlight the need for expansive, imaginative thinking as researchers begin to draw upon earth system law to prescribe legal responses.

C. Prescriptive Attention to Earth System Law Transformations

Finally, an emergent body of literature adopts a more transformative posture, advocating responses that may be seen as desirable or necessary to realise a regulatory environment premised on an earth system law approach. But how might law bridge what can appear a considerable gap between present-day institutions and those envisioned by earth system law analysts? This question is garnering increasing attention from scholars who are: foregrounding the theory-to-practice considerations that will ultimately determine the effect and regulatory impact of earth system law;[72] exploring transformative pathways to earth system law;[73] and highlighting the interactive and coupled human–environment interactions, across spatial scales, that will, in many ways, dictate its success.[74]

One way that emergent research has explored this challenge is by examining opportunities to leverage inter- and trans-disciplinary insights. These efforts emphasise that operationalising earth system law will require a more integrative approach across discourses and disciplines. In many ways, moving beyond dominant environmental law approaches will require instantiating the insights of earth system law within specific regimes, such as water law.[75] Simultaneously, its insights will need to infiltrate legal spaces less frequently conceived in environmental terms, including corporate regulation.[76] To do so, earth system law must broadly embrace insights and approaches from the humanistic, social, and natural sciences. For instance, researchers note the benefits to be realised from the broader embrace of: cinema,[77] ethics,[78] and earth system science.[79]

[71] J Gellers, 'Earth System Law and the Legal Status of Non-Humans in the Anthropocene' (2021) 7 *Earth System Governance* 100083.

[72] Mai and Boulot (n 22).

[73] Angstadt, Chapter 12 in this book.

[74] L du Toit, G Porras and LJ Kotzé, 'Guiding Environmental Law's Transformation into Earth System Law through the Telecoupling Framework' (2021) 30 *European Energy and Environmental Law Review* 104.

[75] G Porras, 'Integrating the Mexican Water Law into the Earth System Law Perspective' in Cadman, Hurlbert and Simonelli (n 18).

[76] Sjåfjell (n 44).

[77] Richardson, Chapter 14 in this book.

[78] Morrow, Chapter 6 in this book.

[79] G Porras and J Ciesielczuk, 'De la Ciencia del Sistema Tierra al Derecho del Sistema Tierra: Permitiendo un Nuevo Paradigma Jurídico para el Antropoceno' (2024) 9 *Derecho Global. Estudios sobre Derecho y Justicia* 283.

Likewise, they must engage deeply with the structures that mediate legal theories, relations, and practice, including: sustainability indicators,[80] relational structures,[81] and understandings of kinship.[82] Finally, and crucially, earth system law must meaningfully incorporate historically marginalised considerations to avoid reproducing the harms realised by dominant environmental law approaches. These include relational approaches that could situate human needs within more holistic, ecological understandings of place and space.[83]

The emergent explorations of earth system law's transformative potential have bifurcated in interesting and complementary ways. One group of researchers considers how the frame might inform thinking about specific environmental regimes within the context of broader earth system interactions. This more confined approach has been particularly manifest within efforts to identify equitable legal responses to the climate system, including by exploring regulatory architectures that could more holistically and effectively support a net-zero transition,[84] and constraining fossil fuel production.[85] Similar attention has explored the hydrosphere, whereby researchers have sought more inclusive and prospective assessment of freshwater governance;[86] riverine ecosystems and potential governance insights from ecological law;[87] and oceans governance,[88] especially as inflected by emergent technological and regulatory approaches.[89] Other regimes provide similarly useful analytical foundations. These include natural resources,[90] biodiversity,[91] and urban environments.[92]

An additional group of researchers explores how earth system law should inform and inflect specific legal constructs. For instance, one effort considers how a proposed Global Pact for the Environment could be structured to

[80] J Ellis and D Edmonds, 'Coming to Terms with the SDGs: A Perspective from Legal Scholarship' (2023) 36 *Leiden Journal of International Law* 251.

[81] Lim, Chapter 8 in this book.

[82] Warner, Chapter 9 in this book.

[83] Garver and Vargas Roncancio, Chapter 7 in this book.

[84] A Burke, 'An Architecture for a Net Zero World: Global Climate Governance beyond the Epoch of Failure' (2022) 13 *Global Policy* 24.

[85] van Asselt (n 25).

[86] Ahlström and others (n 26).

[87] Garver and Vargas Roncancio, Chapter 7 in this book.

[88] M Bender, R Bustamante and K Leonard, 'Living in Relationship with the Ocean to Transform Governance in the UN Ocean Decade' (2022) 20 *PLoS Biology* 3001828.

[89] K Bakker, 'Smart Oceans: Artificial Intelligence and Marine Protected Area Governance' (2022) 13 *Earth System Governance* 100141.

[90] P Dobner and J Finkeldey, 'Natural Resources and the Tipping Points of Political Power – A Research Agenda' (2022) 14 *Sustainability* 14721.

[91] E Colombo, 'A Paper Tiger in the Fog of Governance: Norway's Riddle in Biodiversity Matters' (2024) 33 *Review of European, Comparative and International Environmental Law* 109.

[92] LJ Kotzé, 'Cities, the Anthropocene and Earth System Law' in H Aust and J Nijman (eds), *Research Handbook on International Law and Cities* (Cheltenham, Edward Elgar Publishing, 2021).

foreground the considerations of earth system law;[93] and another explores how an 'Earth Trusteeship' model could help to cohere fragmented treaty and regulatory architectures within the United Nations system.[94] Another example is how earth system law could offer the legal framework for reconstructing the notion of the global commons into an all-embracing 'planetary commons' approach that includes not only areas lying beyond national jurisdictions, but all of Earth's critical biophysical systems that require protection.[95]

Similar scholarship critiques elements of the Energy Charter Treaty, suggesting how it might better navigate regulatory fragmentation that has limited the effect of other environmental trade agreements;[96] and explores the United Nations programme on Harmony with Nature as a framework with potential to both transform and reify components of responses to global environmental change.[97]

A further, broad grouping of prescriptive scholarship explores how earth system law should be operationalised when structuring environmental principles and frameworks. While acknowledging the grounded, practice-based origins of many existing environmental principles,[98] emergent research valuably examines what attributes emergent structures should emphasise.[99] Examples include examination of how a potential *Grundnorm* of planetary integrity could reorient international environmental law;[100] how emphasising a concept of acceptance within international instruments might foreground relational and equitable considerations;[101] and how the planetary boundaries might be understood to emphasise justice when allocating obligations and resources.[102] Collectively, this emergent analysis underscores that earth system law is fundamentally motivated by a desire to explore law's potential contributions to earth system governance, yet also valuable and adept at considering its more focused impacts, implications, and instantiations for (environmental) law more generally.

[93] D Kumar, 'An Analysis of Earth System Approach to the Global Pact for the Environment' (2021) *Global Environmental Law Annual* 145.

[94] J Sobion, *Earth Trusteeship: A Framework for a More Effective Approach to International Environmental Law and Governance* (PhD thesis, University of Auckland, 2023).

[95] J Rockström and others, 'The Planetary Commons: A New Paradigm for Safeguarding Earth-Regulating Systems in the Anthropocene' (2024) 121 *Proceedings of the National Academy of Sciences* e2301531121.

[96] E Cocciolo and L Reins, 'A Critical Review of the Energy Charter Treaty from an Earth System Law Perspective' (2025) 14(1) *Transnational Environmental Law* 94.

[97] J Schmidt, 'Of Kin and System: Rights of Nature and the UN Search for Earth Jurisprudence' (2022) 47 *Transactions of the Institute of British Geographers* 820.

[98] Leach, Chapter 4 in this book.

[99] Kotzé and Du Toit, Chapter 3 in this book.

[100] RE Kim and K Bosselmann, 'Operationalizing Sustainable Development: Ecological Integrity as a Grundnorm of International Law' (2015) 24 *Review of European, Comparative and International Environmental Law* 194; Kotzé and Kim (n 14).

[101] J Bendik-Keymer, 'Acceptance Governance' (2023) 16 *Earth System Governance* 100170.

[102] J Gupta et al, 'Earth System Boundaries and Earth System Justice: Sharing the Ecospace' (2024) 33(7) *Environmental Politics* 1286.

IV. The Main Streams of Critique

As noted above, the inclusive nature of earth system law discourse has generated diverse interpretations and analytical emphases. The earliest earth system law publication invited broad imagination of what legal responses in the Anthropocene could and should mean,[103] rather than pre-defining the earth system law frame. Owing to this expansiveness and the provocative nature of its central effort to reimagine mainstream environmental law, a vigorous debate has emerged. Participants have raised important and valuable questions about the applications and implications of earth system law's various conceptions.

In a first body of critique, scholars suggest that the expansiveness of earth system law as a conceptual frame can present both opportunities and challenges. For instance, some suggest that the emergent, open nature of the earth system law frame has enabled outcomes including: an implicit specificity of purpose and coherence of precepts that have not yet formed;[104] and a generalised response to international environmental law which is itself highly diverse and difficult to cohesively characterise.[105] Given the structuring effect of early earth system law scholarship, it will be critical to explicitly consider these broad-level considerations as earth system law research enters its next half-decade.

Elsewhere, and relatedly, researchers express discomfort with some of the implicit tenets of earth system law. At the broadest level, these include a perceived disposition to accept the normative desirability of aligning legal structures with those of the earth system;[106] and the potential for unintentionally reproducing anthropocentrism by addressing planetary forces through legal measures.[107] Elsewhere, scholars highlight the potential that emphasising the Anthropocene and other overarching analytical frames could unintentionally exclude essential, critical consideration of power imbalances and differentiation.[108] With many of these potential risks flowing from the tendency of an earth system approach to centre planetary-scale engagements,[109] authors suggest a need to simultaneously acknowledge more granular and relational considerations of justice and inequality.[110] Many of these critiques appear to amplify important earth system

[103] Kotzé and Kim (n 1).

[104] M Leach, 'Seeking "Systems" in Earth System Law: Boundaries, Identity, and Purpose in an Emergent Field' (2023) 15 *Earth System Governance* 100162.

[105] G Stenseke Arup, 'Tankar om en proaktiv miljörättsvetenskap: En kritisk analys av Earth System Law' (2023) 1 *Nordisk miljörättslig tidskrift* 7.

[106] M Leach, 'Negotiating the Descriptive–Normative Frontier of Complexity Research in the Anthropocene' (2021) 9 *Frontiers in Physics* 665727.

[107] A Grear, 'International Law, Legal Anthropocentrism, and Facing the Planetary' in V Chapaux, F Mégret and U Natarajan (eds), *The Routledge Handbook of International Law and Anthropocentrism* (Abingdon-on-Thames, Routledge, 2023).

[108] J Auz, 'The Political Ecology of Earth System Law: Outlining a Lex Capitalocenae' (2022) 40 *Wisconsin International Law Journal* 217.

[109] Hanusch, Chapter 15 in this book.

[110] Petersmann (n 24).

governance dialogues about: avoiding inadvertent reproduction of inequalities and colonial structures;[111] and centring equity and social justice within dialogues about sustainability transformations.[112] Therefore, as noted below, we affirm and advocate ongoing attention to applied, decentralised, and critical dimensions in emergent and proposed earth system law scholarship.

V. Future Research Agenda

The 2019 research agenda for earth system law laid a critical foundation but left numerous questions unanswered and critiques to be addressed. As the field evolves, several key areas require focused attention to deepen its relevance and impact. These priorities not only address conceptual gaps but also aim to make earth system law a useful transformative legal framework that is fit for purpose in the Anthropocene.

First, earth system law scholarship must extend beyond its predominant focus on international environmental law to encompass other branches of law, and *law* (as a social phenomenon) more generally. Achieving planetary-scale integrity and justice requires legal frameworks that integrate across fields such as trade, human rights, and energy law, not only at the international level, but also at urban, domestic and regional levels. Advancing international environmental law alone, regardless of its sophistication, will be insufficient. Instead, earth system law should serve as a point of convergence for various legal domains, fostering synergy between multiple governance levels, legal actors, and disciplines. While some progress has been made in areas like human rights and energy law, most earth system law scholarship has focused narrowly on international environmental law, leaving critical intersections underexplored.

Second, the development of earth system law must embrace interdisciplinary, transdisciplinary and empirical approaches.[113] Law is not merely a set of enforceable rules but a system that functions through societal compliance and practice. Understanding how law works in context requires collaboration across disciplines, such as sociology, political science, and earth system science, to illuminate its mechanisms and impacts. Moreover, making earth system law effective necessitates transdisciplinary engagement with practitioners, policy-makers, and affected communities. This collaborative approach ensures that earth system law reflects ground realities and fosters legal processes that are inclusive, functional, and adaptable.

[111] M Jackson, 'Response to Commentary: Probing the Politics of Plurality, Inclusion, and Diversity in the Earth System Governance Project' (2023) 113 *Annals of the American Association of Geographers* e-vii.

[112] Earth System Governance Project's Science and Implementation Plan (n 10).

[113] Kotzé and others (n 30).

Third, earth system law must address the implications of planetary tipping points and treat the Anthropocene as more than a rhetorical device. The Earth as a complex adaptive system is now crossing critical thresholds, demanding a rethinking of legal systems in order to anticipate and mitigate unprecedented challenges. This involves preparing legal frameworks to navigate political instability and technological solutions increasingly framed as emergencies.[114] The law's role in turbulent times will be paramount, requiring it to balance the urgency of action with principles of equity, justice, and sustainability.

Finally, there must be dedicated efforts to explore the policy implications of earth system law. Theoretical advancements must translate into practical governance tools. This requires empirical research on concrete cases where earth system law principles or approaches have been applied, evaluating their transformative potential and limitations. By building a robust evidence base, earth system law can strengthen its contribution to the science–policy interface and provide actionable insights for addressing the complex challenges of the Anthropocene.

Through these focused efforts, earth system law can evolve into a multidimensional framework that bridges theory and practice, responds to the Anthropocene's systemic risks, and advances justice and sustainability across governance levels.

VI. Conclusion

Earth system law scholarship has gained significant traction in recent years, as evidenced by growing references and analyses on platforms such as Google Scholar and Scopus. This development highlights the expanding interest and contributions in this field, showcasing its relevance and applicability in contemporary academic discourse.

The concept of earth system law emerged as a means to explore the legal dimensions of earth system governance, which itself is a relatively new paradigm for guiding societies in the Anthropocene. It aims to address the complexities of preventing, mitigating, and adapting to earth system transformations from a planetary perspective. In this context, earth system law serves as a multifaceted framework: analytically, it aids in understanding the promises and limitations of law in the Anthropocene; transformatively, it provides guidance for evolving legal systems to better address planetary challenges; and normatively, it engages with the justice dimensions inherent in these transformations.

This emerging field has been further developed and enriched by a growing community of scholars. Their work has broadened the scope of earth system law,

[114] RE Kim, 'Taming Gaia 2.0: Earth System Law in the Ruptured Anthropocene' (2022) 9(3) *The Anthropocene Review* 411; Ruhl and Craig (n 12).

both in empirical focus and theoretical orientation, contributing to its evolution as a robust field of inquiry.

Despite these advancements, earth system law remains a work in progress. This book contributes to the ongoing dialogue by advancing the principles and theoretical foundations, and application domains of earth system law, further enriching the scholarly debate and its application in addressing global challenges.

PART II

Resituating Law and Legal Principles in Relation to Planet Earth

3

Law, Legal Principles and Planet Earth

LOUIS J KOTZÉ AND LOUISE DU TOIT

I. Introduction

Legal principles are 'far more widely in evidence in environmental law than in any other field of law'.[1] The principles of sustainable development, polluter pays, prevention, precaution, public participation, access to information and access to justice, to name just a few, have evolved over the course of half a century to form a central pillar of contemporary international, regional and domestic environmental law regimes.[2] These principles 'articulate collective aspirations that play an important role over the longer term', and they help to frame discussions about the future development of environmental law.[3] To this end, environmental law principles often have no immediate effect; they are instead focused on shaping 'attitudinal regularities', with the possibility to influence, over time, 'behavioural regularities' of a more prescriptive nature.[4]

Environmental law principles are, furthermore, central to the adjudication efforts of courts all over the world that use them to interpret, apply and develop environmental law, and to resolve legal conflicts.[5] They play a central role in guiding decisions and actions of policy-makers, and those practically engaged in environmental governance. Imparting something more profound about the rules they undergird, and in line with the role of legal principles more generally, environmental law principles reveal the deeper, often hidden, essence of environmental law and its core ethics and values, thus reflecting environmental law's 'way of being and appearing, its physiognomy, its soul or spirit'.[6]

[1] N de Sadeleer, *Environmental Principles: From Political Slogans to Legal Rules* (Oxford, Oxford University Press, 2002) 1.

[2] E Scotford, *Environmental Principles and the Evolution of Environmental Law* (Oxford, Hart Publishing, 2017) 1.

[3] D Bodansky, *The Art and Craft of International Environmental Law* (Cambridge MA, Harvard University Press, 2010) 200.

[4] ibid 199–200.

[5] E Fisher, 'Precaution, Precaution Everywhere: Developing a 'Common Understanding' of the Precautionary Principle in the European Community' (2002) 9 *Maastricht Journal of European and Comparative Law* 89.

[6] G Alpa, 'General Principles of Law' (1994) 1 *Annual Survey of International and Comparative Law* 1, 2.

These principles have been the darling of scholars for decades, with many lauding their contribution to shaping environmental law and influencing environmental governance.[7] But a recent critical strand of scholarship questions whether many of the principles are in fact able and still *appropriate* to continue mediating increasingly severe human impacts on the earth system in the light of the Anthropocene trope.[8] This trope's haunting visions of a looming Sixth Mass Extinction event,[9] and of fast-approaching planetary boundaries, suggest that environmental law, as a key social regulatory institution, is not suitably configured to confront *Anthropos* and its assumed telluric force.[10] Although not all humans are equally responsible for causing the events that are exacerbating the planetary crisis,[11] the Anthropocene trope reveals *Anthropos* as 'a veritable Prometheus Unbound',[12] while at once illuminating the complicity of environmental law in ongoing failed efforts to restrain human activity and to address the Anthropocene's crisis of human hierarchy and socio-ecological decline. Because environmental law's principles are key foundational building blocks of environmental law, at least some of them are guilty by association in environmental law's unsuccessful efforts to restrain *Anthropos*, as we argue below.

On the back of such a realisation, Richardson has suggested that environmental law's 'relative lack of success warrants new principles and methods … Better principles to guide the redesign of our environmental decrees and standards are necessary'.[13] Robinson similarly believes that 'human society needs to guide its adaptation by recognising a new set of legal principles' for environmental law that reflects 'deep norms that can guide a new epoch of environment–society relations'.[14] He says these could be fashioned around 'evolved norms' inherent in

[7] D Bodansky, J Brunnée and E Hey (eds), *The Oxford Handbook of International Environmental Law* (Oxford, Oxford University Press, 2007) Part V: 'Key Concepts', 531–724; P Sands and J Peel, *Principles of International Environmental Law*, 4th edn (Cambridge, Cambridge University Press, 2018) 197–251; J Verschuuren, *Principles of Environmental Law: The Ideal of Sustainable Development and the Role of Principles of International, European, and National Environmental Law* (Baden-Baden, Nomos, 2003).

[8] J Verschuuren, 'The Role of Sustainable Development and the Associated Principles of Environmental Law and Governance in the Anthropocene' in LJ Kotzé (ed), *Environmental Law and Governance for the Anthropocene* (Oxford, Hart Publishing, 2017) 1–29.

[9] There have been five previous 'mass extinction events' in which more than 75% of known species became extinct within a short period of time. The first occurred around 444 million years ago at the end of the Ordovician period, and the last 65 million years ago at the end of the Cretaceous period, https://ourworldindata.org/mass-extinctions.

[10] J Viñuales, 'Organisation of the Anthropocene in Our Hands?' (2018) 1 *International Legal Theory and Practice* 1–81; D French and LJ Kotzé (eds), *Research Handbook on Law, Governance and Planetary Boundaries* (Cheltenham, Edward Elgar Publishing, 2021).

[11] LJ Kotzé, 'The Anthropocene, Earth System Vulnerability and Socio-Ecological Injustice in an Age of Human Rights' (2019) 10 *Journal of Human Rights and the Environment* 62.

[12] de Sadeleer (n 1) 14.

[13] B Richardson, *A Damp Squib: Environmental Law from a Human Evolutionary Perspective* (Osgoode Hall Law School Research Paper Series, 2011) 30–31.

[14] N Robinson, 'Fundamental Principles of Law for the Anthropocene?' (2014) 44 *Environmental Policy and Law* 1, 13.

human nature, such as cooperation, resilience, foresight, sufficiency, happiness and justice.[15]

Building on such suggestions, we aim to start a conversation about the need for new and/or reimagined legal principles for the purpose of governing human behaviour in the Anthropocene. We do not suggest that all the principles of environmental law are or have become undesirable, ineffective or insufficient for the Anthropocene. Some, such as the precautionary principle, have led to positive transformations of law, and to changing human behaviour in favour of environmental outcomes. These could be maintained and strengthened going forward. But there is also a convincing argument in support of reimagining new principles, discarding some that are outdated or even inappropriate, exploring more progressive principles that are already tentatively emerging in some instances, and considering more 'radical' principles that law, lawyers and legal systems have not yet been adventurous enough to embrace.

We situate the discussion within the context of earth system law, the focus of this book. Acting as a new context and framework for thinking about law in and for the Anthropocene, earth system law embraces a systems perspective that is anchored in the Anthropocene's planetary context, a perspective that is also arguably better attuned to the new regulatory realities, normative and transformative demands, and ethical and analytical implications, of the Anthropocene trope.[16] We argue that earth system law offers a unique opportunity to think about new legal principles for the Anthropocene epoch alongside the earth system metaphor and the complex contemporary governance challenges (political, economical, ethical and otherwise) emanating from a complex earth system.

Our argument is based on two assumptions. First, law is a living and ever-changing phenomenon that can and must continuously adapt to new circumstances and realities. As a result, 'a legal system may well shift from one set of principles to another over time'.[17] Second, legal principles are 'special' norms that lie at the core of a body of law. Because they are reflective of its essence or core identity, and because they offer a roadmap for the future development of law, distilling a set of principles would be a useful first step toward thinking about the design, nature and purpose of new legal approaches in and for the Anthropocene. While Leach,[18] and Boulot, Mai and Sellers,[19] correctly argue that one should not over-estimate their usefulness and overstate the need to reimagine existing principles and create new ones, we believe there is also merit in already starting a debate on what type of principles we might want to develop once we have a deeper understanding of

[15] ibid 18–24.

[16] LJ Kotzé and RE Kim, 'Earth System Law: The Juridical Dimensions of Earth System Governance' (2019) 1 *Earth System Governance* 100003, 1.

[17] Verschuuren (n 7) 37.

[18] Leach, Chapter 4 in this book.

[19] Boulot, Mai and Sellers, Chapter 5 in this book.

the contexts and histories within which principles emerge and their potential for concrete transformation.

Section II below summarises what legal principles are, what they mean at their core, why they are necessary, and how they contribute to law's coherence, integrity and functions. Section III takes stock of some existing environmental law principles and highlights their inability to respond to complex earth system governance challenges. Section IV discusses why we need new earth system law-oriented principles for the Anthropocene. As a contribution to what will hopefully evolve into an ongoing debate, the final section (as in some other chapters in this book) proposes a few possible 'new' legal principles for earth system law that might be more fit for purpose in the Anthropocene.

II. A Matter of Principles

The literature on legal principles is vast and impossible to condense here in any meaningful way.[20] We can only offer a snapshot of the many extant views on legal principles in order to briefly reveal the essential meaning, role and essence of principles within the bigger scheme of juridical things.

Reflecting on the essence of principles and their use in legal reasoning in his famous (and much critiqued)[21] essay on legal positivism in which he differentiates between rules, principles, and policies, Dworkin says the difference between rules and principles is a logical distinction: 'Both sets of standards point to particular decisions about legal obligation in particular circumstances, but they differ in the character of the direction they give. Rules are applicable in an all-or-nothing fashion'; while principles 'do not set out legal consequences that follow automatically when the conditions provided are met'.[22] So, as 'axioms of the legal system', principles steer in a certain direction without prescribing a specific course of action.[23]

Legal principles are 'norms commanding that something [usually stated in the positive legal rule] be realized to the highest degree that is actually and legally possible'.[24] Principles also express moral values:

> there is no rule that does not correspond to a principle, and there is no principle that does not connect to a value. The principle is the *medium* in which we find a moral opening to the value and a practical opening to the rule.[25]

[20] R Alexy, *Recht, Vernunft, Diskurs: Studien zur Rechtsphilosophie*, 2nd edn (Berlin, Suhrkamp, 2016) 177–212.

[21] L Alexander and K Kress, 'Against Legal Principles' (1997) 82 *Iowa Law Review* 739–86.

[22] R Dworkin, 'The Model of Rules' (1967) 35 *University of Chicago Law Review* 14, 25.

[23] G Zagrebelsky, 'Ronald Dworkin's Principle Based Constitutionalism: An Italian Point of View' (2003) 4 *International Journal of Constitutional Law* 621, 629.

[24] R Alexy, 'On the Structure of Legal Principles' (2000) 13 *Ratio Juris* 294, 295.

[25] Zagrebelsky (n 23) 632.

This means that a legal principle is 'a standard that is to be observed, not because it will advance or secure an economic, political, or social situation deemed desirable, but because it is a requirement of justice or fairness or some other dimension of morality'.[26]

The objectives that principles pursue are therefore often grounded in moral considerations (or, as Fuller says, in a 'morality of aspiration').[27] The moral qualities of legal principles are thought to derive from some underlying ideal. An ideal is

> a value that is explicit, implicit, or latent in the law, or the public and moral culture of a society or group, that usually cannot be fully realized, and that partly transcends contingent, historical formulations, and implementations in terms of rules and principles.[28]

The moral foundation of a legal principle that derives from an underlying ideal, in turn, expresses or promotes some sort of collective ethic: 'law by principles inevitably involves an "ethicalization"'.[29] An example in this respect is the principles generally enshrined in human rights law.[30]

Legal principles are seen to derive their legitimacy from within themselves in the sense that they are often 'external to law-making institutions, though law-making institutions may develop principles by specifying them in rules and applying them to concrete situations'.[31] Legal principles are therefore not necessarily dependent on a legislature or other law-making authority to create them: 'principles as such precede law-making. They are already present in the legal system, sometimes waiting to be discovered'.[32] Conversely though, principles are capable of influencing the creation of legal rules; they offer an underlying justification of legal rules, while the abstract and aspirational aspects of principles are elaborated, applied and operationalised in specific legal rules.[33] In other words, for a principle to have effect, it must often be 'concretised' by a legislature, an administrative body, or a court, for example.[34]

Legal principles are by their very nature vague, abstract, indeterminate and flexible, which make them particularly suitable to incorporate general goals and values into more precise legal rules.[35] Their vagueness also means that principles

[26] Dworkin (n 22) 23; see also R Dworkin, *Taking Rights Seriously* (Cambridge MA, Harvard University Press, 1977).

[27] L Fuller, *The Morality of Law* (New Haven CT, Yale University Press, 1969) 5–6.

[28] Verschuuren (n 7) 37.

[29] Zagrebelsky (n 23) 631.

[30] C Gearty, *Principles of Human Rights Adjudication* (Oxford, Oxford University Press, 2004). The author lists respect for civil liberties, legality and human dignity as the core principles of human rights law.

[31] H Gribnau, 'Not Argued From but Prayed To: Who's Afraid of Legal Principles?' (2014) 12 *eJournal of Tax Research* 185, 191.

[32] ibid 198.

[33] ibid 187.

[34] Zagrebelsky (n 23) 631.

[35] J Raz, 'Legal Principles and the Limits of Law' (1972) 81 *Yale Law Journal* 823, 841.

are evolutionary and could be progressively given more concrete form, content and meaning, if desired.[36] Generally speaking, they have the ability to adapt with and to whatever issue they should address, and therefore can change if they become inappropriate, obsolete, or even offensive. This is because their origin also lies 'in a sense of appropriateness developed in the [legal] profession and the public over time. Their continued power depends upon this sense of appropriateness being sustained'.[37]

Their appropriateness is determined

> by grappling with a whole set of shifting, developing and interacting standards (themselves principles rather than rules) about institutional responsibility, statutory interpretation, the persuasive force of various sorts of precedent, the relation of all these to contemporary moral practices, and hosts of other such standards.[38]

It is their flexibility and malleability that render legal principles possibly the most likely candidate to react to and to shape-shift in tandem with an ever-changing reality, and in doing so, to transform the legal system itself.

Raz suggests that legal principles have several objectives, ranging from less to more invasive.[39] While not a closed list, principles act as grounds for interpreting laws (and other principles): 'There is a very strong presumption in most legal systems that … an interpretation which makes a law conform to a principle is to be preferred to one which does not'.[40] In doing so, legal principles contribute to the coherence and systematisation of a legal system,[41] and thus perform a constitutive task.[42] Principles also act as grounds for extending or modifying laws. Principles could be grounds for particular exceptions to law, notably in those instances where applying a specific law would offend certain principles. Principles could also serve as grounds for making new laws to the extent that they often form the basis of political and policy processes, which has a steering effect on law development processes. Some commentators add that legal principles act to justify legal rules, and resolve conflict among legal rules,[43] and they often work to enhance the normative power of legal rules.[44]

Legal principles have the same meaning and fulfil similar roles in the environmental law domain. In her thoroughgoing account of environmental law principles, Scotford argues that environmental law principles play an important role in developing legal reasoning, while they facilitate 'steps in the evolution of legal doctrine'.[45] They are 'significant and highly charged concepts for scholars

[36] de Sadeleer (n 1) 1.
[37] Dworkin (n 22) 41.
[38] ibid.
[39] Raz (n 35) 839–42.
[40] ibid 839.
[41] Gribnau (n 31) 198.
[42] Zagrebelsky (n 23) 636.
[43] Alexander and Kress (n 21) 748.
[44] Verschuuren (n 7) 39–40.
[45] Scotford (n 2) 2.

in thinking about the nature of environmental law as a discipline', thus carrying 'high hopes' for scholars by 'relating not simply to the roles and impact of environmental principles in legal reasoning, but also to the coherent structure and legitimacy of environmental law as a subject'.[46] In the environmental protection domain specifically:

> The complexities of this task [environmental protection] suggest that it cannot be achieved by clear and precise legal rules applicable in all circumstances. Rather, it requires general norms, i.e. principles, that may serve as the basis for more specific and differentiated rules in particular legal areas, cases and situations … By allowing for a wide range of meanings, principles are more suitable to meet the task than specific and detailed rules.[47]

At a practical level, environmental law principles 'bridge the gap between the highly abstract ideal and the very concrete substantive and procedural legal rules [of environmental law]'.[48] Environmental law principles could offer possible solutions to conflicts arising within a socio-ecological setting, providing tools for interpretation, balancing of interests, and guidance for the resolution of disputes. And even if environmental law principles do not always prescribe and proscribe particular behaviour in the same way that binding environmental legal rules do, some of these principles have persuasive authority that also derives from moral obligations. Bodanksy and van Asselt argue, to the extent that general principles of international environmental law do not have a legal basis, they must be justified on other grounds, for example because 'they are viewed as substantively correct'.[49] In addition, environmental law principles 'can be seen as the link between ideals and duties, between the morality of aspiration and the morality of duty, between values and rules';[50] or, as Beyerlin says, they are 'twilight norms' which have some sort of relative normativity.[51]

The current set of environmental law principles include, among others: the preventive principle; the principle of rectification at source; the precautionary principle; the polluter pays principle; the integration principle; the principle of sustainable development and its associated principles of inter and intra-generational equity; the principle of environmental impact assessment; procedural principles related to access to information, access to justice and public participation; the no-harm principle; the principle of common but differentiated responsibilities and respective capabilities; the principle of cooperation; the principle of fair and

[46] ibid.

[47] L Paradell-Trius, 'Principles of International Environmental Law: An Overview' (2000) 9 *Review of European, Comparative and International Environmental Law* 93, 93.

[48] Verschuuren (n 7) 37.

[49] D Bodansky and H van Asselt, *The Art and Craft of International Environmental Law*, 2nd edn (Oxford, Oxford University Press, 2024) 290.

[50] Verschuuren (n 7) 25.

[51] U Beyerlin, 'Different Types of Norms in International Environmental Law: Policies, Principles, and Rules' in Bodansky, Brunnée and Hey (eds), *The Oxford Handbook of International Environmental Law* (n 7) 426.

equitable benefit sharing; the free, prior and informed consent principle; the principle of common heritage and common concern of humankind; and the principle of state sovereignty over natural resources.

III. Environmental Law's Principles

At the most basic level, our social institutions (including law and its principles), and the processes that these institutions create, shape and drive,

> even though they likely produce little that may be regarded as a direct stratigraphic signal, are eminently worth investigating for their impact on Earth System processes, as variations in their operation certainly act to strongly amplify, diminish or otherwise modulate key Earth System characters such as carbon emissions and forest cover.[52]

While human-made law is part of the social system and is squarely focused on facilitating human self-regulation, the earth system is also self-regulatory and has its own set of laws, colloquially known as the 'laws of nature'. While the laws of nature do not follow the laws of humans, the laws of nature are increasingly being impacted by human laws to the extent that human laws facilitate the type of human activities that alter the earth system and which, as a result, are leaving a distinct stratigraphic imprint on the biosphere that manifests in the Anthropocene epoch.

The laws of human-self regulation, of which environmental law is an important part, are now interfering with the self-regulation of the earth system, propelling, as they do, some privileged humans to the top of the living order's hierarchy and pushing the earth system into an unknown state that is becoming unconducive to all life everywhere, now and in the future. Human laws are thus contributing to transforming, very rapidly, humans into geological agents:[53]

> Human self-regulation, however conceived, is but a small part of a bigger whole. But that part is becoming more disruptive of the broader self-regulatory system of the biosphere, the Earth system. This is an important reason why the social construct that we call law can no longer be understood in the way it is learnt, transmitted and practised today.[54]

This unsettling reality is evident when viewed through the lens of the planetary boundaries, which 'define the safe operating space for humanity with respect to the Earth system and [that] are associated with the planet's biophysical subsystems or processes'.[55] If these boundaries are crossed, the chance of maintaining the

[52] J Zalasiewicz and others, 'Petrifying Earth Processes: The Stratigraphic Imprint of Key Earth System Parameters in the Anthropocene' (2017) 34 *Theory, Culture and Society* 83, 96.

[53] N Oreskes, 'The Scientific Consensus on Climate Change: How Do We Know We're Not Wrong?' in JFC Dimento and P Doughman (eds), *Climate Change: What It Means for Us, Our Children, and Our Grandchildren* (Cambridge MA, MIT Press, 2007) 65, 93.

[54] J Viñuales, 'Two Layers of Self-Regulation' (2020) 11 *Transnational Legal Theory* 16, 16.

[55] J Rockström and others, 'A Safe Operating Space for Humanity' (2009) 461 *Nature* 472, 472; W Steffen and others, 'Planetary Boundaries: Guiding Human Development on a Changing Planet' (2015) 347 *Science* 1259855.

relatively stable Holocene-like state necessary for human existence significantly diminishes as we step closer to 'dangerous levels', or where applicable, 'tipping points' in earth system processes.[56] While the planetary boundaries define the biophysical limits within which human actions must remain, law (and specifically environmental law), must ideally provide the 'legal boundaries that prevent human activities from reaching and breaching planetary boundaries'.[57] These legal boundaries must ultimately ensure that 'human action does not disrupt the homeostatic power of life on the Earth system'; while law must be 'designed specifically to enable life's ability to self-regulate itself'.[58]

Environmental law has been unable to accomplish the foregoing in any meaningful way; or at least to effectively contribute to the larger global governance effort aimed at restraining humans:

> We should not be misled by [environmental law's] occasional triumphs, such as the accelerated phasing out of atmospheric ozone-depleting chemicals, the rescue of iconic species from the brink of extinction, or the international rhetoric about 'sustainable development' as environmental law's guiding objective. At most, we could concede that environmental law has 'succeeded' in mitigating what would be a direr prognosis.[59]

One might go further and even suggest that environmental law is deeply implicated in facilitating human mastery over the earth system, its biophysical processes, and its vulnerable co-constituents; it has helped create the Anthropocene by empowering humans to 'become a geological factor by their activities';[60] it is unable to prevent, mitigate and rectify earth system harm; and it is unable to comprehensively facilitate adaptation to a changing earth system.[61] We see this in the way that environmental law has been unable to constrain the agents of geological change at the heart of the Great Acceleration's exponentially growing human enterprise – an enterprise that is characterised by unrestrained population growth, predatory corporate destruction, extractivism, primary energy use, paper and plastic production, and transportation, among many others. This perpetual growth and consumption and the accompanying environmental destruction have been supported by (fossil fuel) capitalism, and by the liberal capitalist-oriented legal frameworks that enable pro-growth economies to flourish.[62]

[56] K Richardson and others, 'Earth beyond Six of Nine Planetary Boundaries' (2023) 9(37) *Science Advances* eadh2458, 2.

[57] G Chapron, 'Bolster Legal Boundaries to Stay within Planetary Boundaries' (2017) 1 *Nature Ecology and Evolution* 1, 1.

[58] Viñuales (n 54) 28.

[59] Richardson (n 13) 6.

[60] Zalasiewicz and others (n 52) 87.

[61] LJ Kotzé and RE Kim, 'Exploring the Analytical, Normative and Transformative Dimensions of Earth System Law' (2020) 50 *Environmental Policy and Law* 457.

[62] A Malm, *Fossil Capital: The Rise of Steam Power and the Roots of Global Warming* (London, Verso Publishing, 2016); N Klein, *This Changes Everything: Capitalism vs. the Climate* (London, Penguin, 2015); JW Moore (ed), *Anthropocene or Capitalocene? Nature, History and the Crisis of Capitalism* (Binghamton NY, PM Press, 2016).

In the main, and although there are exceptions, environmental law continues to offer minimalist alternatives that are facilitated through its mantra principle of sustainable development. At its core, the essence of the principle of sustainable development is to balance social, economic and environmental concerns in a politically appeasing way.[63] Sustainable development has been instrumental in keeping environmental protection on the international political agenda as a concern rhetorically shared and endlessly restated by states and their corporations, while it very explicitly must not be allowed to inhibit socio-economic development.[64] For example, the Preamble to the United Nations Framework Convention on Climate Change (UNFCCC) provides that 'responses to climate change should be coordinated with social and economic development in an integrated manner with a view to avoiding adverse impacts on the latter'.[65] To achieve this objective, the principle of sustainable development is deliberately vague, and its threshold of achievement is not set very high; it must merely balance interests, not pursue planetary integrity or any other form of meaningful earth system protection.[66]

While the intention might have been different at the time of its conception, sustainable development, in its present form, is not a socio-ecologically protective principle.[67] It remains an elusive ideal that should be achieved through discretionary, non-interventionist, and politically inoffensive global governance strategies such as the Sustainable Development Goals (SDGs).[68] This most recent liberal embodiment of environmental law's core principle is intrinsically incapable of comprehensively addressing socio-ecological vulnerability. From a planetary integrity point of view, the SDGs' most laudable achievement is probably that they facilitate some general agreement on the need to take collective action to promote 'development' in broad terms over several years.[69] Yet, by 'balancing' social, environmental and economic concerns, the SDGs continue to merely facilitate (political, often corporate-driven) compromises. They do not endeavour to radically change the status quo, thus at once also conveniently avoiding trickier

[63] See Lim, Chapter 8 in this book.

[64] Principle 1 of the Rio Declaration on Environment and Development of 1992 cements environmental law's anthropocentric, socio-economic development–biased ontology, and the idea that humans are environmental law's privileged subject by proclaiming that 'Human beings are at the centre of concerns for sustainable development': Rio Declaration on Environment and Development (June 1992) 31 ILM 874.

[65] United Nations Framework Convention on Climate Change (UNFCCC) (adopted 9 May 1992) 31 ILM 849.

[66] LJ Kotzé and S Adelman, 'Environmental Law and the Unsustainability of Sustainable Development: A Tale of Disenchantment and of Hope' (2023) 34 *Law and Critique* 227.

[67] S Adelman, 'The Sustainable Development Goals, Anthropocentrism and Neoliberalism' in D French and LJ Kotzé (eds), *Sustainable Development Goals: Law, Theory and Implementation* (Cheltenham, Edward Elgar Publishing, 2018) 15–40.

[68] United Nations General Assembly, *Transforming our World: The 2030 Agenda for Sustainable Development*, UNGA Res 70/1 (21 October 2015).

[69] Y Zeng, 'Environmental Destruction Not Avoided by the Sustainable Development Goals' (2020) 3 *Nature Sustainability* 795, 795.

conversations about the need to maintain planetary integrity, which could be far more disruptive to the status quo.[70]

A critical reflection on sustainable development offers a useful opportunity to also briefly evaluate some of the other principles of environmental law that derive from or relate to sustainable development. After all, it is quite possible that '[t]he current interest in the principles of international environmental law stems to a large extent from a need to define and give content to the notion of sustainable development'.[71] With few exceptions, other principles of environmental law that operate within the realm of sustainable development are equally non-offensive, politically appeasing and biased towards promoting neoliberal economic development for the benefit of a privileged few.

For example, the polluter pays principle has been unable to guide the creation of ambitious anti-pollution laws that can prevent corporations, many of which have now morphed into powerful 'private sector *quasi-states*',[72] from causing pollution and profiting therefrom. In only one case – the *Trail Smelter* arbitration[73] – has an international adjudicatory body awarded compensation for transboundary pollution.[74] The inability of public trusteeship principles to shape the attitudes and behaviour of states that destroy their natural resources and the livelihoods of Indigenous people in the name of economic development, is another continuing worrying trend. One observes this with the principle of sovereignty over natural resources. The Brazilian government's ravaging of the Amazon rainforest to promote agriculture is a case in point,[75] where the principle of sovereignty over natural resources is explicitly used to justify ecological destruction in pursuit of striking a misguided, and economically biased, imbalance between environmental, social and economic considerations. It should now be evident that the principle of state sovereignty over natural resources is simply a manifestation of law's socio-ecologically destructive right to property, which has transformed the intellectual basis of international law from natural law and morality towards one

[70] LJ Kotzé, 'Planetary Integrity' in F Biermann, T Hickmann and CA Sénit (eds), *The Political Impact of the Sustainable Development Goals: Transforming Governance Through Global Goals?* (Cambridge, Cambridge University Press, 2022) 140–71.

[71] Paradell-Trius (n 47) 93.

[72] A Grear, 'Towards "Climate Justice"? A Critical Reflection on Legal Subjectivity and Climate Injustice: Warning Signals, Patterned Hierarchies, Directions for Future Law and Policy' (2014) 5 *Journal of Human Rights and the Environment* 103, 108.

[73] *Trail Smelter Case (United States v Canada)*, Award 16 April 1938 and 11 March 1941, reported in (1939) 33 *American Journal of International Law* 182 and (1941) 35 *American Journal of International Law* 684.

[74] Compensation for transboundary damage was also awarded by the International Court of Justice in *Certain Activities Carried Out by Nicaragua in the Border Area (Nicaragua v Costa Rica), Compensation* [2018] ICJ Reports 15 – however, this case was not concerned with pollution: AE Boyle and C Redgwell, *Birnie, Boyle & Redgwell's International Law and the Environment*, 4th edn (Oxford, Oxford University Press, 2021) 236.

[75] EJDL Pereira and others, 'Brazilian Policy and Agribusiness Damage the Amazon Rainforest' (2020) 92 *Land Use Policy* 1–6.

embracing instead a destructive form of positivism and national economic and political self-interest.[76] Populist rhetorical labels such as 'America First', or 'Make America Great Again', are examples of a worrying trend that seeks to abscond from global climate obligations and responsibilities when political expediency so demands in support of sovereignty.[77]

But there are some exceptions to the general negative trend, although they remain few and far between. One example is the precautionary principle that has arguably played an important role in the relative success of the global ozone law and governance regime. Amid uncertainty over the causes and extent of ozone depletion, and before evidence of harm due to ozone depletion had actually materialised, the global community concluded the Vienna Convention[78] and Montreal Protocol,[79] in which parties explicitly agreed to take precautionary measures to control and eliminate emissions of substances that could potentially deplete the ozone layer. Due to the conclusion of these agreements, the ozone layer is recovering and the global ozone regime has even had climate co-benefits.[80] While several factors have played a role in the success of the ozone regime, including its adaptiveness and provision for developing countries,[81] it is clear that taking a precautionary approach led to these agreements being concluded in time to avoid dangerous socio-ecological harms.

In sum, while there are exceptions, the bulk of environmental law's principles have not been able to significantly influence the transactions that lead to earth system destruction. They have mostly masked the negative externalities caused by these transactions because, as a key part of environmental law, they have been 'organised as an additional layer specifically designed not to interfere with the possibility of continuing the transaction'.[82] Linked to this interim conclusion, is the lack of a mechanism to resolve conflicts between principles. For example, it is not clear how tension between the 'right' to sustainable development provided for under the climate change regime would be balanced against the prevention principle, or how the tension between sovereign rights over biological resources and the precautionary principle would be resolved.

[76] MR Islam, 'History of the North-South Divide in International Law: Colonial Discourses, Sovereignty, and Self-Determination' in S Allam (ed), *International Environmental Law and the Global South* (Cambridge, Cambridge University Press, 2015) 23, 26.

[77] S Collins, 'America First: The Trump Effect on Climate Change Policy' in J Pereira and A Saramango (eds), *Non-Human Nature in World Politics: Theory and Practice* (Heidelberg, Springer, 2020).

[78] Vienna Convention for the Protection of the Ozone Layer (adopted 22 March 1985), 1513 UNTS 323.

[79] Montreal Protocol on Substances that Deplete the Ozone Layer (adopted 16 September 1987), 1522 UNTS 3.

[80] R Goyal, 'Reduction in Surface Climate Change Achieved by the 1987 Montreal Protocol' (2019) 14 *Environmental Research Letters* 124041.

[81] L du Toit, 'Stratospheric Ozone Depletion' in D French and LJ Kotzé (eds), *Research Handbook on Law, Governance and Planetary Boundaries* (Cheltenham, Edward Elgar Publishing, 2021).

[82] Viñuales (n 10) 31.

IV. Legal Principles for the Anthropocene

The planetary crisis of the Anthropocene requires us to 'de-familiarise' ourselves and our laws, as Webster and Mai say, 'from Holocene orthodoxies and develop new legal forms, strategies and technologies that can help navigate Anthropocene realities'.[83] Earth system law is a continuous imaginative epistemic process and the result of ongoing efforts to confront concerns that are increasingly being raised in relation to law's continued suitability for the Anthropocene.[84] It offers a new legal form, strategy or frame by which to think about the sort of laws we would need for the Anthropocene, including thinking about possible new legal principles, and reimagining or strengthening existing principles. As a new legal imaginary that is more fit for purpose in the Anthropocene, earth system law is aimed at: facilitating interdisciplinary analysis and co-learning alongside an earth system perspective to better understand and formulate regulatory responses for the type of complex governance challenges emanating from a complex earth system; offering the basis to design more appropriate norms that are able to restrain human behaviour and avoid transgression of earth system limits; and providing innovative options for more ambitious legal reforms that can achieve meaningful transformations in pursuit of planetary integrity and socio-ecological justice.

These objectives of earth system law also characterise its analytical, normative and transformative dimensions.[85] The normative and transformative dimensions of earth system law are especially apposite for the purpose of commencing a debate about new legal principles for the Anthropocene, as such a debate will be a critical first step in the continuous norm development process that must drive meaningful transformations. Moreover, earth system law, with its focus, inter alia, on adaptiveness, provides a useful framework for considering new principles – which are by their nature flexible – that are better suited to current challenges.

Our assumption is that whatever new principles are developed within the context of earth system law, they must at least be able to answer to one or more of the following imperatives: be congruent with, and be able to respond to, the new Anthropocene reality and the new geological power of *Anthropos*, including the differentiated vulnerabilities that arise in the Anthropocene; go well beyond the hitherto simplified understanding of environmental concerns and instead be fully based on and respond to the myriad unique governance challenges emanating from a complex earth system; and inaugurate a new planetary ethic for the

[83] E Webster and L Mai, 'Transnational Environmental Law in the Anthropocene' (2020) 11(1/2) *Transnational Legal Theory* 1, 10; see also L Mai, '(Transnational) Law for the Anthropocene: Revisiting Jessup's Move from "What?" to "How?"' (2020) 11(1/2) *Transnational Legal Theory* 105.

[84] See Kotzé, Angstadt and Kim, Chapter 2 in this book.

[85] LJ Kotzé and RE Kim, 'Exploring the Analytical, Normative and Transformative Dimensions of Earth System Law' (2021) 50(6) *Environmental Policy and Law* 457.

Anthropocene. These three minimum imperatives translate into three broader (possibly overlapping in some instances) categories of earth system law principles: functional, architectural and ethical.

Identifying specific principles within each of these categories is, at least for now, an intuitive conceptual exercise that requires creative out-of-the-box thinking, among other things, and it could be informed by the initial proposal concerning the conceptual development of earth system law. The 2019 paper that introduced earth system law[86] offered a framework describing the conceptual and regulatory changes required to eventually progress from 'international environmental law' to a form of 'planetary earth law'. The framework is based on two core considerations in the conceptual progression towards earth system law. These two axes include: (i) the regulatory object of law – 'environmental', 'ecological' and 'earth' – along the one axis; and (ii) the geographical or jurisdictional scope of law – 'international', 'global/ transnational' and 'planetary' – along the other. The conceptual progression, as it were, from environmental law to earth system law shown in Table 1 below usefully illustrates the re-imaginative progression that would be required to identify possible candidate principles in the functional, architectural and ethical categories.

Table 1 A conceptual framework of earth system law along two selected dimensions for illustrative purposes. The framework identifies nine different developmental stages of earth system law ranging from international environmental law to planetary earth law[87]

	Environmental law	**Ecological law**	**Earth law**
International law	Human-centred regulation of transboundary harm based on state sovereignty	Nature-centred environmental protection in a state-centric system	Earth-centred respect for the community of all life in a state-centric system
Global or transnational law	Human-centred environmental protection through transnational legal processes involving state and non-state actors	Nature-centred environmental protection in a transnational setting involving state and non-state actors	Earth-centred sustainability governance in a transnational setting involving state and non-state actors
Planetary law	Human-centred recognition of environmental limits from a planetary perspective	Nature-centred environmental protection from a planetary perspective	Earth system-centred law for governance by and for all living beings from a planetary systems perspective

[86] Kotzé and Kim (n 16).
[87] ibid.

A preliminary proposal outlining some possible candidate principles within these three categories could include:

Table 2 Proposed functional, architectural and ethical principles for earth system law

Functional Principles	Architectural Principles	Ethical Principles
Restraint	Complexity	Sufficiency
Restoration	Temporality	Humility
Reflexivity	Spatiality	Integrity
Transformability	Interconnectivity	Solidarity
Respect (possibly overlapping with ethical principles)	Reciprocity	Inter-speciesism
Responsibility (possibly overlapping with ethical principles)	Polycentricity	Happiness

While considerably more research will have to be done to elaborate each of these categories and their specific principles, we briefly describe in the following what these principles might mean. Against consumerism and over-consumption, restraint requires avoiding exploitation and unnecessary consumption of natural resources and of resources and products more broadly. Restoration requires that ecosystems be returned to their former states or, where this is not possible, that they be healed as far as possible.[88] Reflexivity refers to the capacity of institutions, amongst others, to reflect, evaluate and change what is not working.[89] Transformability relates to 'the capacity to create a fundamentally new system when ecological, social, and political conditions make the existing system untenable'.[90] Respect entails having regard for ecosystems, and all humans and all living non-human beings, and treating others in the same way one would like to be treated oneself. Related to this, responsibility envisages care for and protection of Earth's ecological and human components and becoming stewards of the earth system.[91]

Complexity recognises that the earth system is a complex adaptive system that consists of numerous components that may, and often do, interact in unpredictable ways.[92] Temporality relates to time, recognising the differing human and geological timescales and that law must discard its reliance on political

[88] B Richardson, 'The Emerging Age of Ecological Restoration Law' (2016) 25 *Review of European, Comparative and Inyternational Environmental Law* 277.

[89] J Dryzek, 'Institutions for the Anthropocene: Governance in a Changing Earth System' (2014) 46 *British Journal of Political Science* 937, 942.

[90] B Walker and B Salt, *Resilience Thinking: Sustaining Ecosystems and People in a Changing World* (Washington DC, Island Press, 2006) 62.

[91] W Steffen, 'The Anthropocene: From Global Change to Planetary Stewardship' (2011) 40 *AMBIO* 739.

[92] W Steffen and others (ed), *Global Change and the Earth System: A Planet Under Pressure* (Heidelberg, Springer, 2004).

time-frames and instead embrace an understanding of present time and 'deep' (past and future) time.[93] Spatiality is concerned with global spatial unevenness and how different living beings are differentially situated on the planet and in the earth system, and how this situatedness positively and/or negatively impacts everyone and everything. Interconnectivity entails recognising interconnections between different earth system components and processes, including between humans and non-human beings and present and future generations. Reciprocity contrasts with self-serving exploitation, domination and accumulation and is concerned with cooperation, exchange and mutual support.[94] Polycentricity relates to systems involving 'multiple governing authorities at differing scales'.[95]

A sense of sufficiency is also relevant. Indeed, '[r]ecognizing abundance rather than scarcity undermines an economy that thrives by creating unmet desires. Gratitude cultivates an ethic of fullness, but the economy needs emptiness'.[96] Humility will be important in regard to overcoming dualist conceptions that see humans as having 'mastered' nature.[97] Humility is also relevant in relation to the continuing human desire to explore and exploit less easily accessible areas such as the deep seabed and space and to interfere with the earth system's natural functioning, such as in the case of solar-geoengineering.[98] Integrity relates to acting with honesty and in accordance with moral values, and acknowledging that all life has integrity that must be respected.[99] Solidarity, or unity, arises from sharing common interests and objectives. Inter-speciesism relates to the idea that humans have an innate tendency to seek connections with nature and other forms of life,[100] demanding, as such a view does, new expansive and imaginative visions of inter-species justice, which must be fostered.[101] Happiness is connected to sufficiency or abundance and relates to being content and experiencing a sense of well-being, which contrasts with the sense of inadequacy and discontentment that drives consumerism and over-consumption.

Some of these principles are already reflected to a greater or lesser extent in international and national legal instruments (both binding and non-binding). Although their emergence is still tentative at best, the fact that some principles already manifest in some form or another signals a gradual opening up of societal,

[93] B Richardson, *Time and Environmental Law: Telling Nature's Time* (Cambridge, Cambridge University Press, 2017). See also Hanusch, Chapter 15 in this book.

[94] RW Kimmerer, *Braiding Sweetgrass: Indigenous Wisdom, Scientific Knowledge and the Teachings of Plants* (London, Penguin, 2020).

[95] E Ostrom, 'Coping with Tragedies of the Commons' (1999) 2 *Annual Review of Political Science* 493, 528.

[96] ibid 111.

[97] S Adelman, 'Epistemologies of Mastery' in A Grear and LJ Kotzé (eds), *Research Handbook on Human Rights and the Environment* (Cheltenham, Edward Elgar Publishing, 2015).

[98] C Hamilton, 'Geoengineering and the Politics of Science' (2014) 70(3) *Bulletin of the Atomic Scientists* 17.

[99] See Burdon, Chapter 10 in this book.

[100] K Rogers, 'Biophilia Hypothesis', *Encyclopaedia Britannica*, https://www.britannica.com/science/biophilia-hypothesis.

[101] M Matevia, 'Justice for All: Revisiting the Prospects for a Biocommunitarian Theory of Interspecies Justice' (2016) 19(3) *Journal of International Wildlife Law & Policy* 189.

epistemic and legal closures to entertain more radical alternative earth system law-oriented principles that could form the foundation of a new framing for law in the Anthropocene.

For example, the non-binding but United Nations-endorsed World Charter for Nature[102] gives effect to interconnectivity and inter-speciesism in its recognition that humankind 'is a part of nature and [that] life depends on the uninterrupted functioning of natural systems'. More recent multilateral environmental agreements (MEAs) possibly also reflect interconnectivity. For example, the 2023 Agreement under the United Nations Convention on the Law of the Sea on the Conservation and Sustainable Use of Marine Biological Diversity of Areas Beyond National Jurisdiction (BBNJ Agreement)[103] recognises that biodiversity loss and degradation of ocean ecosystems are 'due, in particular, to climate change impacts on marine ecosystems, such as warming and ocean deoxygenation, as well as ocean acidification, pollution, including plastic pollution, and unsustainable use'.[104] This provision goes further than those contained in earlier MEAs in recognising interconnected issues and impacts. Although an integrity-oriented approach is very much absent from the daily politics and governance of global climate change, the 2015 Paris Agreement includes a cursory note on the importance of 'ensuring the integrity of all ecosystems, including oceans, and the protection of biodiversity, recognized by some cultures as Mother Earth, and not[es] the importance for some of the concept of "climate justice"'.[105]

The BBNJ Agreement's Preamble reflects the Parties' desire to 'act as stewards of the ocean in areas beyond national jurisdiction on behalf of present and future generations by protecting, caring for and ensuring responsible use of the marine environment'.[106] Against calls for planetary or biosphere stewardship,[107] this seems to be one of the first references to environmental stewardship in an MEA. References to 'protecting' and 'caring for' in the BBNJ Agreement's Preamble also go further than more neutral and detached references to 'conservation' and 'sustainable use' in earlier MEAs such as the Convention on Biological Diversity.[108]

The World Charter for Nature affirms the importance of respect, recognising that '[e]very form of life is unique, warranting respect regardless of its worth to [humankind]' and that '[n]ature shall be respected and its essential processes shall not be impaired'. The Charter also emphasises restraint and regeneration,

[102] United Nations General Assembly, World Charter for Nature (adopted 29 October 1982).
[103] Agreement under the United Nations Convention on the Law of the Sea on the Conservation and Sustainable Use of Marine Biological Diversity of Areas Beyond National Jurisdiction (adopted 20 September 2023).
[104] ibid Preamble.
[105] Paris Agreement, UN Doc FCCC/CP/2015/L.9/Rev/1 (adopted 12 December 2015), Preamble.
[106] BBNJ Agreement (n 102).
[107] J Rockström and others, 'The Planetary Commons: A New Paradigm for Safeguarding Earth-Regulating Systems in the Anthropocene' (2024) 121 *Proceedings of the National Academy of Sciences* e2301531121.
[108] Convention on Biological Diversity (5 June 1992) 31 ILM 818.

providing that '[n]atural resources shall not be wasted, but used with a restraint appropriate to the principles set forth in the … Charter [including that] [l]iving resources shall not be utilized in excess of their natural capacity for regeneration'.

It is arguably also relevant that explicit references to the sovereign right of states to exploit their own resources, as contained in earlier MEAs, including the 1992 UNFCCC,[109] the 2001 Stockholm Convention on Persistent Organic Pollutants,[110] as well as the (non-binding) Rio Declaration on Environment and Development,[111] are absent from the more recent Paris Agreement and BBNJ Agreement.

At a domestic level, some of the principles proposed above are also reflected in the national laws of countries such as Ecuador and Bolivia. The Ecuadorian Constitution explicitly recognises, in Article 71, the rights of nature, or *Pacha Mama*, to 'integral respect for its existence and for the maintenance and regeneration of its life cycles, structure, functions and evolutionary processes'.[112] Bolivia's Law of the Rights of Mother Earth,[113] inter alia, requires the state to

> ensure the necessary conditions in order that the diverse living systems of Mother Earth may absorb damage, adapt to shocks, and regenerate without significantly altering their structural and functional characteristics, recognizing that living systems are limited in their ability to regenerate, and that humans are limited in their ability to undo their actions.[114]

This principle, notably, also reflects systems thinking. The law further recognises, in Article 7.6, Mother Earth's 'right to timely and effective restoration of living systems affected by human activities directly or indirectly'. These principles would arguably act as a counter to the focal principle of environmental law, namely sustainable development, which has enabled continual extractivism and growth, as we have argued above.

Beyond the legal sphere, the limits of growth and gross domestic product (GDP) are being recognised, and other indicators based on happiness and well-being are being identified as increasingly relevant for humanity and the Earth, including by intergovernmental organisations and think tanks.[115] Furthermore, in 2011, the United Nations General Assembly (UNGA) adopted a resolution, titled 'Happiness: Towards a Holistic Approach to Development',[116] which invites Member States to develop measures that 'better capture the importance

[109] United Nations Framework Convention on Climate Change (n 65).

[110] Stockholm Convention on Persistent Organic Pollutants (adopted 22 May 2001), 40 ILM 532.

[111] Rio Declaration on Environment and Development (n 64).

[112] Constitution of the Republic of Ecuador (2008).

[113] Republic of Bolivia, 'Law 071 of the Rights of Mother Earth' (December 2010).

[114] On the right to regeneration, see also Klein (n 62) ch 13.

[115] This can be seen in the development of indices and reports such as the *World Happiness Report*, https://worldhappiness.report/data/, *Happy Planet Index*, https://hotorcool.org/hc-projects/happy-planet-index/, and Organisation for Economic Co-operation and Development, *Better Life Index*, https://www.oecdbetterlifeindex.org/.

[116] United Nations General Assembly, *Happiness: Towards a Holistic Approach to Development*, UNGA Res 65/309 (25 August 2011).

of the pursuit of happiness and well-being in development with a view to guiding their public policies'. The UNGA also proclaimed an 'International Day of Happiness' in 2012.[117] At the national level, the Kingdom of Bhutan has gone further by developing the Gross National Happiness (GNH) Index, which is used to assess Bhutan's progress and is intended to influence policy-making and planning. In addition to assessing more traditional socio-economic indicators such as health, education and living standards, the GNH Index also evaluates psychological well-being, community vitality, ecological diversity and resilience, and time use, among others.[118] These initiatives are unsystematic and aspirational rather than legally enforceable. Yet, the recognition by the UNGA that 'the gross domestic product indicator by nature was not designed to and does not adequately reflect the happiness and well-being of people in a country',[119] and by the Organisation for Economic Co-operation and Development (OECD), that '[t]here is more to life than the cold numbers of GDP and economic statistics',[120] is promising.

V. Conclusion

For environmental law and its principles, the core governance dilemma of the Anthropocene and its fast-approaching planetary boundaries is a straightforward but acute one: we have been creating unambitious and reactive legal interventions in the image of the Holocene epoch and its context of predictability, accommodative harmony, relative stability and perceived limitless resources that we thought could sustain the highly differentiated and selectively privileging human development enterprise forever. Holocene environmental law and its principles have served the purpose of the Great Acceleration and its Industrial Revolution well by pursuing environmental protection only insofar as it does not offend socio-economic progress for a privileged minority of the world's states and some of its people. This, in turn, is leading to a false sense of security and business-as-usual path-dependency, a lack of regulatory ambition, and even a sense of failure and hopelessness. Meanwhile, 'the unjustified inertia continues without explanation, let alone justification'.[121] It is also clear that the environmental law-making process has been influenced by the capitalist context, evidenced, inter alia, by the role of

[117] United Nations General Assembly, *International Day of Happiness*, UNGA Res 66/281 (12 July 2012).

[118] Oxford Poverty and Human Development Initiative, *Gross National Happiness*, https://ophi.org.uk/gross-national-happiness; see also Constitution of the Kingdom of Bhutan (2008).

[119] United Nations General Assembly (n 115).

[120] Organisation for Economic Co-operation and Development (n 114).

[121] J Bendik-Keymer, *Involving Anthroponomy in the Anthropocene: On Decoloniality* (Abingdon-on-Thames, Routledge, 2020) 6.

fossil fuel corporations and some states in climate change negotiations, which has at times resulted in weakened outcomes.[122]

As we are transitioning into the Anthropocene epoch, it is becoming increasingly evident that environmental law and many of its existing principles are unable to tackle, head on, the numerous complex and intertwined governance challenges that are emerging from within an equally complex and intertwined earth system context. Our analysis has endeavoured to show that we need a new way of thinking about law and its principles for the purpose of the Anthropocene. Earth system law presents such a framework and therewith also an opportunity to engage in wholesale legal reforms over time. We have argued that legal principles, because of their unique nature, objectives and functions, are a useful starting point to begin (re)shaping the foundations of a new legal paradigm for the Anthropocene.

We have proposed a non-exhaustive set of principles that might 'help trigger new normative and ethical thinking',[123] which could guide humanity to use its geological power more carefully and sparingly. And perhaps they might 'stimulate transformational thinking, to enable us to better integrate into the Earth System', and

> enable the Anthropocene to symbolize hope rather than despair, and enable a practical and reflective response to the geological transformations under way, as the Earth evolves towards a novel state with no precedent on this or any other planet that we are aware of.[124]

The evolution of earth system law and its principles will be fraught with challenges and will solicit pushbacks on several fronts from politicians, corporations, positivists and others. But such opposition to creative and urgent legal innovation should never be a reason to abandon any endeavour that aims to make better and more effective laws to govern a planetary society that is increasingly in peril.

[122] J Kluger, 'There Are More Fossil Fuel Lobbyists than Ever at COP28', https://time.com/6342799/fossil-fuel-lobbyists-cop28/; E Masood and J Tollefson, 'COP26 Hasn't Solved the Problem: Scientists React to UN Climate Deal' (2021) 599 *Nature* 355. The presence of fossil fuel lobbyists at COPs under the UNFCCC increased from 503 in 2021, to 636 in 2022, to 2456 in 2023.

[123] Zalasiewicz et al (n 52) 98.

[124] ibid.

4

(Past) Reflections on the (Future) Origins of Earth System Law Principles

MICHAEL C LEACH

I. Introduction

Legal principles are a special kind of purpose- and goal-oriented norm that inspires and guides the interpretation of legal rules.[1] Asking questions about principles invites discussions about ideal 'oughts' that have not yet been relativised to actual legal possibilities; therefore it is entirely appropriate for earth system law scholars at this moment to be contemplating the normative scaffolding that could guide and inspire their imaginative work.[2] However, one must be cautious about how prescriptive this imaginative work can be in practice. The relationship between legal principles and the legal orders that they shape and within which they reside is ambiguous and messy. As we in this present book imagine how to use 'principles', among other things, to guide the adaptation or re-orienting of law around the concept of the 'earth system' in the future, it behoves us to pay close attention to what legal principles are and how they work in practice so that we can better situate this task within a larger discussion about how law changes in the first place.

Further building on the analysis in Chapter three,[3] this chapter puzzles over the question of where legal principles come from. The invitation I offer here is to turn our gaze backwards instead of forwards to enquire how norms come to be principles in law, so that we can better understand how and when earth system law principles might take root as law in the future. The historical record shows that legal principles in practice do not emerge in international law through scholarly

[1] RS Summers, 'Two Types of Substantive Reasons: The Core of a Theory of Common-Law Justification' (1978) 63 *Cornell Law Review* 707; N MacCormick, 'Argumentation and interpretation in law' (1993) 6 *Ratio Iuris* 16, 17.

[2] R Alexy, 'On the Structure of Legal Principles' (2000) 13 *Ratio Juris* 294, 300.

[3] See Kotzé and Du Toit, Chapter 3 in this book.

introspection. Rather, they are birthed at moments when there is sufficient demand from legal actors for some optimising benefit that a norm can provide as a 'principle' for a novel and contextually-specific decision-making dilemma that those actors are facing. Whatever meanings these norms have when jurists first declare them to be principles, they change over time as the demands for their optimising benefits change and as they are put to multiple new, and not always synchronous, uses.[4] Given that, this chapter ponders what conditions would be necessary for earth system law norms to ever become principles of international law, and how constant and coherent one should expect any such principles to remain if and when that happens.

The chapter will limit its discussion to international law for the principal reason that earth system law scholars, in their critiques of international environmental law, often imply that the international domain is a natural home for imagining earth system law.[5] Inspired by the work of Nicolas de Sadeleer, the chapter will look at the origin stories of three international environmental law principles – namely, the polluter pays principle, the prevention principle, and the precautionary principle – to demonstrate how it is that principles like these came to be in international law.[6] Doing so will demonstrate that principles like these emerge when jurists, diplomats and/ or judges and arbitrators need normative reference points to guide their decision-making in the face of new problems that complicate the ordinary and practical concerns of state actors and international organisations. With this in mind, earth system law scholars who are curious about how or when earth system-inspired principles might ever become instruments of law should also consider the range and type of legal problems that states and other international legal actors would have to face such that they would demand earth system law principles to facilitate their collective decision-making.

II. Legal Principles and Earth System Law

The question 'where do principles come from?' is not one that has animated much empirical inquiry over the years. Legal scholars have been more concerned with questions about how to define what principles are, what their legal effects are and whether or not they have legal consequences akin to 'rules'.[7] In part, this

[4] IJ Gassama, 'The Incoherence and Functional Incompetence of International Law: Toward a New Paradigm of Human Relationship' (2013) 37 *Fordham International Law Journal* 53; O Pedersen, 'Modest Pragmatic Lessons for a Diverse and Incoherent Environmental Law' (2013) 33 *Oxford Journal of Legal Studies* 103; H Friberg-Fernros and D Brommesson, 'The Responsibility to Protect – an Incoherent Doctrine?' (2013) 50 *International Politics* 600; J Ohlin, 'In Praise of Jus Cogens' Conceptual Incoherence' (2018) 63 *McGill Law Journal* 701.

[5] LJ Kotzé, 'Earth System Law for the Anthropocene' (2019) 11 *Sustainability* 6796. See also Kotzé, Angstadt and Kim, Chapter 2 in this book.

[6] N de Sadeleer, *Environmental Principles: From Political Slogans to Legal Rules* (Oxford, Oxford University Press, 2020).

[7] *North Sea Continental Shelf Case (Federal Republic of Germany v Denmark; Federal Republic of Germany v Netherlands)* (1969) ICJ Rep 3, para 37, 20 February 1969.

is because the ambit of the legal effects of principles is ambiguously wide, ranging from vague or even empty goal statements to harder-edged quasi-legislative mechanisms that can impose obligations on international actors, especially when principles have been recognised by courts as reflecting customary rules of international law.[8]

At their most general, principles can be understood as ideal statements that set forth reasons for the existence of obligations that are prescribed by rules.[9] Whereas principles are abstract and general and invite subjective interpretation when invoked, rules are (in theory) more certain and specific, requiring relatively less subjective input when they are applied. Principles are often thought of as foundations or pillars upon which a legal order rests and from which its effects radiate.[10] When they speak to higher values, principles can also shield law-makers who invoke them when they are faced with painful policy choices that might impose significant economic or social costs.[11]

Rules typically entail an obligation that consequences will follow when certain conditions are met. As a matter of logic, therefore, a legal order abhors any conflict between two or more rules, requiring courts to interpret their relative validity and meanings in order to choose one that will prevail over the other. Principles, on the other hand, are axiological foundations upon which rules are made and thus can be treated as more suggestive than obligatory. Unlike rules, when two principles collide both can be equally valid, requiring the jurist to weigh their relative merits against one another.[12] Robert Alexy once described principles as having a supportive function in moments when rules clash whereby an overarching principle can be brought to bear to resolve the question of which rule should prevail. This function makes them akin to 'optimisation commands', not necessarily determining the outcome of the rule clash, but rather calling for 'something [to] be realised to the highest degree that is actually and legally possible'.[13]

All of this raises the question of why some scholars interested in developing a new field of law around the concept of the earth system would be interested in elaborating *principles* rather than *rules* to give this new field its substance. One cannot assume that pre-determining or imagining new legal principles will necessarily do this, especially if one harbours dreams of earth system law one day operating on the international stage. This is because legal principles in international law have rarely been created to do this field-constructing work. Looking at the historical record, it does not seem to be accurate to describe principles as

[8] P Sands and J Peel, *Principles of International Environmental Law*, 4th edn (Cambridge, Cambridge University Press 2018).

[9] JC Hage, *Reasoning with Rules. An Essay on Legal Reasoning and Its Underlying Logic* (Alphen aan den Rijn, Kluwer Academic Publishers, 1997) 67.

[10] H Avila, *Theory of Legal Principles* (Heidelberg, Springer, 2007) 44.

[11] BD Goldstein, 'The Precautionary Principle and Scientific Research Are Not Antithetical' (1999) 107(12) *Environmental Health Perspectives* A594.

[12] R Dworkin, *Taking Rights Seriously* (London, Duckworth & Co Ltd, 1991).

[13] Alexy (n 2) 295.

things that are typically dreamed up by scholars from the outset to achieve this grand purpose. Rather, they have emerged when states, international lawyers, negotiators, diplomats, and policy-makers interacting in international fora are confronted with novel problems for which they need new normative language and a new optimisation function to assist their future decision-making.

III. Principles of International Environmental Law

The field of international environmental law is still very young. Sands and Peel argue that, in the absence of any universal, governing legal instrument of general application for international environmental law, principles and general rules instead have had to be distilled over the years from 'tens of thousands of acts adopted at the national, bilateral, subregional, regional and global levels'.[14] It was only two decades ago that arbitrators in the *Iron Rhine Railway* decision about a rail route between the Netherlands, Belgium and Germany first described a set of 'principles of international environmental law'. The arbitrators expressed consternation about the persistence of 'considerable debate as to what, within the field of environmental law, constitutes "rules" or "principles"; what is "soft law"; and which environmental treaty law or principles have contributed to the development of customary international law'.[15]

In the years since *Iron Rhine*, jurists have continued trying to coherently articulate the principles of international environmental law as they have arisen in treaties and international acts or custom. Many of these have emerged as reactions to global events or new scientific evidence as states looked for ways to protect their access to natural resources that were threatened by the actions of others.[16] Other principles were forged from court and arbitration judgments to resolve novel international disputes, the most famous being the *Trail Smelter* case about air pollution between Canada and the United States, when arbitrators inferred a general principle of 'prevention' to negate any inherent right of states to use their territories in ways that were known to cause damage to other states.[17] Running parallel to these developments was the signing of a number of international treaties that incorporated versions of these international environmental law principles to guide agreements on how to prevent the over-exploitation of natural resources and shared uses of territory.

These piecemeal instances were complemented by a series of United Nations (UN)-organised global meetings that concluded with formal declarations of sets

[14] Sands and Peel (n 8) 141.

[15] *The Iron Rhine (Ijzeren Rijn) Railway* arbitration (*Belgium v Netherlands*) Award of 24 May 2005, Permanent Court of Arbitration Award Series, XXVII RIAA pp 35–125, para 58.

[16] Sands and Peel (n 8) 22.

[17] *Trail Smelter Case (United States v Canada)*, III RIAA pp 1905–1982 (Award 16 April 1938 and 11 March 1941) (final decision).

of general international environmental law principles. The first such meeting was somewhat unusual for the UN to host, since the environment is not mentioned in the UN Charter as part of its mandate. Over time, though, environmental concerns came to be recognised as part of the expanding mandate of the UN to engage with the collective social, cultural, economic, and humanitarian problems of the world, and different agencies of the UN have gradually incorporated the environment into their agendas. This process started as early as 1949 with the United Nations Conference on the Conservation and Utilization of Resources (UNCCUR). Shortly thereafter, the first General Assembly resolutions on environmental topics were passed in the 1950s in the form of expressions of concern over the effects of nuclear radiation, which laid the foundations for the 1963 Test Ban Treaty.[18] The 1950s and 1960s also saw increasing efforts by states to draft treaties to control and regulate interventions to prevent marine oil pollution and over-fishing, like the 1959 Antarctic Treaty,[19] and the 1972 Oslo Dumping Convention,[20] or river-specific treaties, like that of the Mosel (Moselle)[21] or the Rhine.[22]

By the 1970s, the UN had become aware that a new, if sporadic, international rule framework for environmental concerns was slowly evolving, and this inspired it to organise conferences to give it more cohesion. The first was the 1968 Biosphere Conference,[23] followed by the 1972 Stockholm Conference on the Human Environment,[24] and then the 1992 Rio Conference on Environment and Development.[25] It was at the Stockholm Conference where delegates made the first attempt to articulate a set of 26 principles for international environmental law. This list of principles was the outcome of protracted negotiation and compromise between different state interests, and while they did not have the same binding effect as rules agreed upon in treaties, their pronouncement was nevertheless significant for the normative scaffolding it built, upon which any further normative organisation of international environmental law could be developed. After the 1972 Stockholm Conference and upon a request from the General Assembly, the newly created UN Environment Programme (UNEP) in 1978 composed a set of draft 'Principles of Conduct in the Field of the Environment for the Guidance of States in the Conservation and Harmonious Utilization of Natural Resources

[18] Treaty Banning Nuclear Weapon Tests in the Atmosphere, in Outer Space and Under Water (adopted 5 August 1963, entered into force 10 October 1963) 480 UNTS 43.

[19] Antarctic Treaty (adopted 1 December 1959, entered into force 23 June 1961) 402 UNTS 71.

[20] Convention for the Prevention of Marine Pollution by Dumping from Ships and Aircraft (adopted 15 February 1972, entered into force 7 April 1974) 11 ILM 262.

[21] Protocol concerning the establishment of an International Commission to Protect the Mosel against Pollution (adopted 20 December 1961, entered into force 1 July 1962) 940 UNTS 211.

[22] Berne Convention on the International Commission for the Protection of the Rhine against Pollution (adopted 29 April 1963, entered into force 1 May 1965) 994 UNTS 3.

[23] The formal title was the 'Intergovernmental Conference of Experts on the Scientific Basis for Rational Use and Conservation of the Resources of the Biosphere'.

[24] Report of the UN Conference on the Human Environment, UN Doc A/CONF.48/14.

[25] Rio Declaration on Environment and Development, Annexed to the Report of the United Nations Conference on Environment and Development (3–14 June Rio de Janeiro). UN Doc A/CONF.151/26 (Vol 1), 12 August 1992.

Shared by Two or More States'. A few years later, the 1981 Programme for the Development and Periodic Review of Environmental Law would propose a further set of principles to guide the UNEP's work for the next decade in developing regional and soft-law international environmental law instruments. A year later, the UN General Assembly adopted the World Charter for Nature in 1982, which also had a set of 'principles of conservation by which all human conduct affecting nature is to be guided and judged'.[26]

By the time of the 1992 Rio Conference, international environmental law had evolved with the signing of a number of environmental treaties, judgments in arbitration and court cases, and a number of statements of principles as outcomes of international conferences. Organised in the wake of the end of the Cold War, the overall goal of the Rio Conference was to construct an overarching strategy for international environmental law and policy that addressed the challenge of striking a balance between environmental protection and economic development. As with the Stockholm Conference, Rio ended with a declaration that included a list of 27 (non-binding) principles to guide future cooperation and to develop 'international law in the field of sustainable development'. For the most part, these principles were not innovations but re-statements of principles that had already been proposed earlier and elsewhere. The only genuinely new principle in the collection was that of 'common but differentiated responsibility', found in Principle 7 and repeated in Article 3(1) of the UN Framework Convention on Climate Change (UNFCCC) signed at the same time.[27] This innovation was a recognition that the shared common cause of tackling climate change did not neatly map onto the differing historical records of cumulative contributions to climate change. The challenge of achieving agreement on this principle at the Rio Conference presaged a brewing conflict between states about how to balance past responsibility and future commitment to tackling climate change.[28]

The three decades that followed Rio have not been a fertile period for new international environmental law principles. Instead, it has been mostly a time of consolidation of the principled framework that Rio and the UNFCCC consolidated.[29] This period is generally characterised by an increasing number of international conferences and treaties that built upon that principled scaffolding, most notably the 1997 Kyoto Protocol,[30] but also several others including

[26] World Charter for Nature, UNGA Res. 37/7, 28 October 1982.

[27] Paris Agreement to the United Nations Framework Convention on Climate Change (adopted 12 December 2015, entered into force 4 November 2016) 3156 UNTS 79.

[28] L Rajamani, 'Common but Differentiated Responsibility and Climate Change' (2000) 120 *Review of European, Comparative and International Environmental Law* 120.

[29] S Bernstein, 'The Absence of Great Power Responsibility in Global Environmental Politics' (2020) 8 *European Journal of International Relations* 24; LE Suskind and ZA Hamid, *Environmental Diplomacy: Negotiating More Effective Global Agreements* (Oxford, Oxford University Press, 2015).

[30] Kyoto Protocol to the United Nations Framework Convention on Climate Change (adopted 10 December 1997, entered into force 16 February 2005) 2303 UNTS 162.

the 2013 Minamata Convention on Mercury,[31] the 2015 Paris Agreement on Climate Change, and the 2023 Agreement on Marine Biodiversity of Areas Beyond National Jurisdiction.[32] The period was also characterised by new kinds of litigation as states brought cases to international tribunals to test the contours of this new legal field. The most notable instances of this were a number of landmark International Court of Justice (ICJ) cases like *Gabčikovo-Nagymaros*,[33] *Pulp Mills*,[34] and the *Whaling*[35] cases. Other tribunals were also issuing significant judgments in the same period, citing environmental rules and principles, like the World Trade Organization (WTO) panels and the WTO Appellate Body,[36] the International Tribunal for the Law of the Sea (ITLOS),[37] the Permanent Court of Arbitration (PCA)[38] and International Centre for Settlement of Investment Disputes (ICSID),[39] and regional human rights bodies like the European,[40] and Inter-American[41] courts of human rights.

This brief history, while superficial, demonstrates one important feature of international environmental law principles, which is that they emerged over past decades in a relatively piecemeal fashion when legal actors needed them to help resolve disputes and address collective concerns. It also suggests a certain pattern of international disputes forcing tribunals to come up with new principles to resolve novel legal problems, delegates at international conferences and treaty negotiations then proclaiming them formally as general principles, followed by further litigation as courts and tribunals fleshed out their meanings and effects.

The ongoing project to conceive of new earth system law principles, including also efforts in this book, is a part of that story as well. In a way, earth system law as a scholarly field has taken root in a lot of frustration that this evolving principled framework for international environmental law has not gone far

[31] Minamata Convention on Mercury (adopted 10 October 2013, entered into force 16 August 2017) 3202 UNTS 1.

[32] Agreement under the United Nations Convention on the Law of the Sea on the conservation and sustainable use of marine biological diversity of areas beyond national jurisdiction (adopted 19 June 2023, not yet in force) UN Doc A/CONF.232/2023/4.

[33] *Gabčikovo-Nagymaros Project (Hungary v Slovakia)*, Judgment, Merits, [1997] ICJ Rep 7.

[34] *Pulp Mills on the River Uruguay (Argentina v Uruguay)*, Order, Provisional Measures, [2006] ICJ Rep 113.

[35] *Whaling in the Antarctic (Australia v Japan; New Zealand intervening)*, Judgment, [2014] ICJ Rep 226.

[36] For example, *United States – Import Prohibition of Shrimps and Certain Shrimp Products* (1998) WTO Doc WT/DS58/AB/R (98-000) (12 October 1998).

[37] For example, *Southern Bluefin Tuna (New Zealand v Japan; Australia v Japan)* (Provisional Measures) (1999) ITLOS Nos 3 & 4; *MOX Plant (Ireland v United Kingdom)* (Provisional Measures) (2001) ITLOS No 10.

[38] Notably the *Iron Rhine* case (n 15).

[39] For example, *Burlington Resources Inc v Republic of Ecuador* (2017) ICSID Case No ARB/08/5.

[40] For example, *Tătar v Romania*, Application no 67021/01, ECtHR, 27 January 2009.

[41] For example, Inter-American Court of Human Rights, Advisory Opinion OC-23/17 Requested by the Republic of Colombia 'The Environment and Human Rights' Series A No 23 (15 November 2017).

enough or is not moving fast enough to effectively guide and facilitate collective action around an Earth-focused framework of governance, cooperation and responsibility.[42] This book, in a way, is an articulation of a kind of demand for earth system law principles. However, while several contributions here consider the contents of earth system law principles that could offer better solutions than international environmental law principles are currently able to do, it is worth delving a bit more into the socio-political origins of specific international environmental law principles so as to invite further questions about what future conditions would be necessary for earth system law norms to ever emerge one day as international legal principles.

A. The Polluter Pays Principle

The first example examined here is the polluter pays principle, whose name indicates its purpose, namely, to address the problem of determining who should cover the costs of cleaning up pollution. In a recent request for public consultation on the polluter pays principle, the European Union (EU)'s Commissioner for Environment, Oceans and Fisheries, Virginias Sinkevičius, declared that:

> The polluter pays principle is fair and simple: it requires polluters to bear the cost of the pollution they cause. Correct application of the principle provides incentives to avoid damaging the environment and makes polluters responsible for cleaning up. When it is not properly applied, the bill for environmental damage caused by polluters too often ends up being paid for by citizens and weighs heavily on public funds.[43]

While the Commissioner's rhetoric suggests that the principle is relatively self-evident, its origin story was hardly 'simple'. It began as an economic theory in the 1920s about the efficient allocation of pollution costs that was later picked up and converted into an international law principle half a century later when certain states needed help with managing their trade relations. Although its 'polluter pays' name implies that its main function is to assign liability for environmental damage, this was not exactly its original purpose. Indeed, when it first emerged in the 1970s there was no need for a new liability principle in international law. One had already existed for 30 years by that point, ever since the *Trail Smelter* arbitration award, which ordered Canada to compensate the United States for damage caused by air pollution. Instead, the polluter pays principle was introduced in the 1970s to address the novel problem of how to reconcile trade imbalances caused by trading partner states using different domestic

[42] See, Kotzé, Angstadt and Kim, Chapter 2 in this book.

[43] Directorate-General for Environment, 'Zero Pollution: Commission Consults Citizens and Stakeholders on the "Polluter Pays" Principle' (European Commission 2023) online at: https://environment.ec.europa.eu/news/zero-pollution-commission-consults-citizens-and-stakeholders-polluter-pays-principle-2023-05-12_en#:~:text=The%20polluter%20pays%20principle%20is,of%20the%20pollution%20they%20cause.

mechanisms like subsidies to deal with the pollution that certain facilities in their domestic economies were producing.

Demand for a principle like polluter pays arose out of a specific collective action problem at the confluence of two different trends prevalent in the 1970s and 1980s: the growth of international free trade and the increasing scientific awareness of global environmental deterioration caused by the economic activities of (certain) humans over centuries. This moment was the start of a very fertile era for bi-lateral and multi-lateral free trade agreements, such as the North American Free Trade Agreement (NAFTA), Mercosur, and the European Community (since 1993, the EU), a process that would really take off a decade later in the 1990s. The absence of international agreements between countries that were pursuing different policies to allocate, absorb, or counteract the costs of industrial and other kinds of pollution was complicating the ability of peer states to trade with one another on a balanced footing.[44] Much of this rested on the recognition that pollution and environmental damage caused by economic development carried costs, and how states dealt with these costs affected their competitiveness on the international stage.

This framing of the economic costs of environmental protection dated back to the theories of efficient allocation of pollution costs developed by the British economist Arthur Cecil Pigou in the early 1920s.[45] Pigou's primary concern was that market prices often did not incorporate the external costs of pollution caused by economic production, and he argued that this created distortions that would encourage economies to generate inefficient and unsustainable mixes of polluting and non-polluting activities and services. Pigou's solution to this problem was either for producers to internalise those costs in their prices or for states to impose taxes corresponding to the economic value of the externalised environmental damage. In the 1970s and '80s, though, some states were doing something different by giving assistance to domestic industries to clean up the pollution they were causing. For some of their trading partners, this looked like an uncompetitive subsidy that was anathema to free trade. This critical viewpoint caught on and created a demand for a general principle that states should not use pollution subsidies to give a competitive edge for their producers in international markets.[46]

The first international forum where the polluter pays principle was proposed to serve this purpose was the Organisation for Economic Co-operation and Development (OECD). The relative simplicity of the principle that polluters – not states – should pay to clean up the pollution they cause made sense to the OECD's mostly liberal, democratic, free marketeer, capitalist Member States that were willing and eager to collectively adopt the same standards to make trade easier

[44] S Gaines, 'The Polluter-Pays Principle: From Economic Equity to Environmental Ethos' (1991) 26 463 *Texas International Law Journal Texas International Law Journal* 465, 465.

[45] AC Pigou, *The Economics of Welfare* (London, Macmillan & Co, 1920).

[46] Gaines (n 44) 470.

amongst them.[47] The polluter pays principle made its first appearance in the 1972 OECD Council Recommendation on Guiding Principles concerning International Aspects of Environmental Policies. This Recommendation defined it as meaning that 'the polluter should bear the expenses of carrying out the [pollution control] measures decided by public authorities to ensure that the environment is in an acceptable state'. The Recommendation then advised states 'not to assist the polluters in bearing the costs of pollution control whether by means of subsidies, tax or advantages'.[48]

It was not long before the polluter pays principle began to appear in other international venues. The year after the OECD Recommendation was published, the European Community (as it then was) transposed the polluter pays principle as Principle 5 of its 'Principles of a Community Environment Policy', which read in part:

> The cost of preventing and eliminating nuisances must in principle be borne by the polluter. However, there may be certain exceptions and special arrangements, in particular for transitional periods, provided that they cause no significant distortion to international trade and investment.[49]

Transplanting the polluter pays principle in this way was relatively easy to do, since all European Community members were also members of the OECD, and this new principle quickly became part of a larger policy approach of the EC, and the EU that followed, to standardise rules around state aid to polluting industries among its Member States.[50] A decade later it was enshrined in Article 130r (later Article 174) of the Single European Act of 1986.[51] From that point forward it was up to the Commission, the Member States, and the courts to hammer out what its precise contours were over subsequent years, because while, conceptually, the polluter pays principle is uncomplicated, contentious questions remained about it, like who should be deemed a 'polluter' or for what and how they should be obliged to 'pay'.[52] Even though such questions remained open and were contested in European courts, this did not prevent the principle from being applied to areas of law beyond trade. Secondary legislation in the EU has given the polluter pays principle further concrete manifestation in the form of hard rules and policy guidance to incentivise polluters to reduce their own pollution in the fields of waste,[53]

[47] ibid.

[48] OECD Guiding Principles Concerning International Economic Aspects of Environmental Policies, 11 ILM 1172 (1972).

[49] Declaration of the Council of the European Communities and of the representatives of the Governments of the Member States meeting in the Council of 22 November 1973 on the programme of action of the European Communities on the environment [1973] OJ C 112/6.

[50] European Commission, Fourth Report on Competition Policy, Brussels-Luxembourg 1975, no 181.

[51] Art 130r, Single European Act [1987] OJ L 169/11.

[52] Gaines (n 44) 472.

[53] OECD, 'Recommendation Concerning the Application of the PPP to Accidental Pollution' OECD/LEGAL/0251 (1989).

water management,[54] landfills,[55] and invasive alien species,[56] but also general ones on environmental liability.[57]

With each adaptation, though, the principle's meaning and uses evolved. In its current form it is used in reference to multiple things: the importance of accounting for all real costs of goods in managing markets; the importance of avoiding distortions and imbalances in resource use and market competition; the importance of holding entities liable for damage to the environment; and the importance of allocating responsibility for costs of environmental protection. The multifaceted utility and conceptual expansion of the principle have come at some cost to its coherence, however. Even though the uses of the principle in these areas share the same broad goal of internalising previously externalised costs, preventing competition distortions, and remedying pollution damage, some observers have noted how these different applications do not necessarily work well or always help one another.[58] In 2021, the European Court of Auditors published a report on the polluter pays principle concluding that its coverage and application in EU environmental policies was incomplete and inconsistent.[59] Thus, if the quote from Commissioner Sinkevičius at the start of this section sounded confident about how important the principle is to EU law, in a way it is because of this importance that efforts to better understand it continue. Coherent or not, this robust formalisation of the polluter pays principle in the European Community/EU's legal framework has provided a concrete example to inspire other international agreements. By the late 1980s and early 1990s, different versions of it began to appear in several international and multilateral treaties and agreements, in both binding[60] and non-binding formats,[61] although, as de Sadeleer cautions, in practice its acknowledgement outside of the OECD and EU law is still relatively rare.[62]

[54] Directive 2000/60/EC of the European Parliament and of the Council of 23 October 2000 establishing a framework for Community action in the field of water policy, [2000] OJ L 327/1–73, Art 9(1).

[55] Council Directive 1999/31/EC of 26 April 1999 on the landfill of waste, [1999] OJ L 182/1–19, Art 10.

[56] Regulation 1143/2014 of the European Parliament and of the Council of 22 October 2014 on the Prevention and Management of the Introduction and Spread of Invasive Alien Species, [2014] OJ L 317/35–55, Art 21.

[57] Directive 2004/35/EC of the European Parliament and of the Council of 21 April 2004 on environmental liability with regard to the prevention and remedying of environmental damage, Art 1 and Recitals (2) and (18) in the Preamble.

[58] de Sadeleer (n 6) 42.

[59] European Court of Auditors, *Special Report 12/2021: The Polluter Pays Principle: Inconsistent Application Across EU Environmental Policies and Actions* (Luxembourg, European Court of Auditors, 2021) 5.

[60] Eg Art 2(1) of the 1991 Convention on the Protection of the Alps (signed at Salzburg, 7 November 1991, entered into force 6 March 1995); Art 73 of the 1992 Porto Agreement to establish the European Economic Area (EEA) (signed in Oporto on 2 May 1992, entered into force 1 January 1994).

[61] Eg, 1992 Helsinki Convention on the Transboundary Effects of Industrial Accidents (signed at Helsinki on 17 March 1992, entered into force 19 April 2000); United Nations, Agenda 21, United Nations Conference on Environment & Development (Rio de Janeiro 1992).

[62] de Sadeleer (n 6) 31.

B. The Principle of Prevention

The second principle reviewed here is the principle of prevention. If the story of the polluter pays principle took root in the needs of states to manage their expanding trade relations, the prevention principle is rooted in more traditional concerns about state responsibilities to one another. As knowledge of the environment and state capacity to cause or facilitate environmental harm to other states has grown over the years, so too has the need for rules to prevent environmental harm grown in turn. The basic normative rationale behind the principle of prevention is that environmental damage and pollution should be prevented (usually at source), and/ or that avoiding environmental damage is better than repairing it after the fact.[63] In international law, it is invoked to justify obligations on states to ensure that their actions do not cause significant environmental transboundary harm beyond their jurisdiction or control. While this may sound uncontroversial, it is worth considering how much a principle like this is at odds with another fundamental and deeply embedded principle of international law, namely state sovereignty.

'Sovereignty' speaks to a default setting in international law whereby any state is presumed to have the authority to do what it likes within its own borders. Sovereignty lies at the core of the international state system that functions on the basis of formal equality between states and their commitment to mutual non-interference.[64] International law recognises that it is possible to restrict this state autonomy and authority, but only when a state expressly surrenders it by binding itself in treaties with other states, or by tacitly consenting to restrictions by participating in an international system that is structured around common rules of international conduct,[65] such as 'good faith' or 'abuse of rights' or 'due diligence'[66] that have long restricted how states make use of their own territories vis-à-vis others.[67] A principle like prevention can be understood to be one of those norms that exists in international law to constrain one state's sovereignty for the sake of the well-being of others. However, how much a state's freedom should be constrained to prevent damage to others has long been a contentious question.

This tension between the principles of prevention and sovereignty is on full display in Principle 2 of the 1992 Rio Declaration, which Sands et al have given the elaborate label of: 'Sovereignty over Natural Resources and the Responsibility Not

[63] L Duvic-Paoli, 'Fighting Plastics with Environmental Principles? The Relevance of the Prevention Principle in the Global Governance of Plastics' (2020) 114 *American Journal of International Law Unbound* 195.

[64] United Nations Charter (1945) XV UNCIO 355, Art 2(1).

[65] *SS Lotus Case (France v Turkey)* [1927] PCIJ Series A No 10, Judgment of 7 September 1927; S Beaulac, 'The *Lotus* Case in Context: Sovereignty, Westphalia, Vattel, and Positivism' in S Allen (ed), *The Oxford Handbook of Jurisdiction in International Law* (Oxford, Oxford University Press, 2019).

[66] *Pulp Mills* (n 34) para 101.

[67] Sands and Peel (n 8) 125.

to Cause Damage to the Environment of Other States or to Areas Beyond National Jurisdiction'.[68] Principle 2 reads:

> States have, in accordance with the Charter of the United Nations and the principles of international law, the sovereign right to exploit their own resources pursuant to their own environmental and developmental policies, and the responsibility to ensure that activities within their jurisdiction or control do not cause damage to the environment of other States or of areas beyond the limits of national jurisdiction.

Like the polluter pays principle, the principle of prevention has evolved as international tribunals arbitrating disputes between states on matters of transboundary environmental damage have invoked it to prescribe ever more detailed obligations about how states should act to prevent causing harm to one another. In the *Gabčikovo-Nagymaros*,[69] *Iron Rhine*,[70] *Pulp Mills*[71] and *Indus Waters*[72] cases, both the ICJ and arbitration panels recognised the 'duty of prevention' as a 'principle' of law that takes the form of a state obligation to take appropriate regulatory, administrative and other measures to prevent damage to other states, as well as to be required to be vigilant, to take early preventative action and, if possible, even before any damage occurs.

Whenever states, treaties, or judicial and arbitral bodies have invoked the principle of prevention to declare a duty on states to protect other states from environmental damage originating from their territories, it has elicited relatively little controversy. When the principle is invoked to prevent states from damaging 'the environment' in general, though, especially when it comes to a state's sovereign right to exploit its own natural resources, it has been much more contentious. A mere half a century ago in the post-WWII period of decolonisation and national self-determination, the idea that international law might prevent a state from exploiting its natural resources to maximise its development potential seemed antithetical to the spirit of the times. One can see this adherence to the sovereign rights of both new and older states in the new world order in a 1952 UN General Assembly resolution that declared as a blanket principle that 'the right of peoples freely to use and exploit their natural wealth and resources is inherent in their sovereignty and is in accordance with the Purposes and Principles of the Charter of the United Nations'.[73]

Twenty years later, though, in the lead-up to the Stockholm Conference in 1972, one sees some disruption in this international consensus as serious consideration was given to restricting state sovereignty over how states used their territories and natural resources for the sake of the global environment.

[68] ibid 212.
[69] *Gabčikovo-Nagymaros* (n 33) para 140.
[70] *Iron Rhine* (n 15) paras 55 and 222.
[71] *Pulp Mills* (n 34) para 104.
[72] *Indus Waters Kishenganga Arbitration (Pakistan v India)* Partial Award, ICGJ 476 (PCA, 18 February 2013), XXXI RIAA pp 1–358, para 449.
[73] UNGA Res 626 (1952) 20 Supp 18.

At the time, environmental policy scholars saw sovereignty as being a major impediment to achieving international cooperation on the environment and they complained about a world system based on 'the logic of a divided and competitive world composed of nations, grossly and inexorably unalike and unequal, and obsessed by the illusion of sovereignty'.[74] Such critiques were on the agendas of the Preparatory Committee of the Stockholm Conference, whose members vigorously debated whether or not sovereignty was an absolute right of states.[75] Some delegations wanted to limit sovereignty in order to protect the global environment. Others, like natural resource-rich Canada, tried navigating an awkward middle ground by proposing that protecting the environment should be simultaneously a sovereign duty as well as a right of states.[76] Still others, like one group of nine newly de-colonised African states, advocated for the untrammelled sovereign right of states to control the exploitation of their own resources, especially vis-à-vis foreign companies.[77]

In the end, the final consensus on the principle of prevention achieved at the conference was extremely fragile compared to any other of the principles negotiated there. When it was ultimately incorporated into the conference declaration as Principle 21, the only form that it could take that could gather sufficient agreement was one that tacked very closely to the principle of sovereignty:

> States have the sovereign right to exploit their own resources pursuant to their own environmental policies, and the responsibility to ensure that activities within their jurisdiction or control do not cause damage to the environment of other States or of areas beyond the limits of national jurisdiction.

This principle, as stated, is remarkable given the overall grain of the conference, whose final declaration asserted the existence of a supra-national 'human environment' that needed to be preserved and improved on for the benefit of all.[78] The most generous interpretation of Principle 21 would be to see it as a constraint on sovereignty, but one could hardly celebrate it as a sea change in international law. Little had changed two decades later by the time of the 1992 Rio Conference, when delegates generally expressed as little enthusiasm as their predecessors for revisiting the question of restricting sovereignty.[79] As such, the principle was only assigned aspirational perambulatory status in the final text of the UNFCCC that was signed at the same time.

[74] LK Caldwell, 'Defense of Earth in a Divided World' (1972) 35 *Journal of Environmental Health* 228, 230.

[75] LB Sohn, 'The Stockholm Declaration on the Human Environment' (1973) 14 *Harvard International Law Journal* 423, 488.

[76] ibid 488.

[77] ibid; CC Joyner, 'Stockholm in Retrospect: Progress in the International Law of Environment' (1974) 136 *World Affairs* 347, 356.

[78] Sohn (n 75) 491.

[79] JD Kovar, 'A Short Guide to the Rio Declaration' (1993) 4 *Colorado Journal of International Environmental Law and Policy* 119, 125.

If this account of states jealously guarding their sovereignty and pushing back on the principle of prevention suggests that the principle was doomed from the outset, the story did not end there. In the decades since Stockholm and Rio, there has been growing recognition not only of there being a (vaguely defined) transnational 'environment' that states might have a shared duty to protect, but also that the global climate is undergoing enormous and deleterious changes. Island states vulnerable to rising sea levels in recent years have taken the lead in trying to revive the discussion and push for an expansion of the scope of the principle of prevention to better encompass this collective responsibility. In 2022, for instance, Vanuatu circulated a draft UNGA Resolution to request an Advisory Opinion by the ICJ to confirm the obligations of states to take action to ensure the protection of the climate system.[80] In July 2025, the ICJ issued its *Advisory Opinion on the Obligations of States in Respect of Climate Change*.[81] The Advisory Opinion confirms that states have binding obligations to prevent significant climate-induced harms, to cooperate internationally, and to uphold fundamental rights in the face of escalating climate risks.

Furthermore, courts and arbitration panels have been more willing than states to expand the principle to include protecting the global climate system within its ambit. Much of this work is currently happening domestically, where some courts have found binding obligations on states to protect the global environment and climate, such as in the Dutch *Urgenda* case;[82] or the Colombian constitutional court's decision in the *Atrato River* case, which cited 'prevention' as a principle in international law that has as its goal the avoidance of environmental damage in general.[83] However, in other jurisdictions courts have been less willing to interpret the principle of prevention so expansively, so there is still no general consensus on how far its normative ambit should reach.[84] It is still very much an open question whether or not the principle has evolved in such a way that states today should be presumed to have inherent obligations under international law to protect the global environment or to mitigate climate

[80] Draft Resolution: Request for an Advisory Opinion of the International Court of Justice on the Obligations of States in Respect of Climate Change' referenced in L Duvic-Paoli and M Gervasi, 'Harm to the Global Commons on Trial: The Role of the Prevention Principle in International Climate Adjudication' (2022) 32 *Review of European, Comparative & International Environmental Law* 226.

[81] International Court of Justice, Advisory Opinion: *Obligations of States in Respect of Climate Change*, 23 July 2025, https://www.icj-cij.org/sites/default/files/case-related/187/187-20250723-adv-01-00-en.pdf.

[82] *State of the Netherlands v Urgenda Foundation* Supreme Court of the Netherlands, ECLI:NL:HR:2019:2007, 20 December 2019, para 5.7.5.

[83] *Atrato River case*, Judgment T-622/16, Constitutional Court of Colombia (16 November 2016) para 7.34.

[84] *Greenpeace Nordic Association and Nature & Youth v Norway's Ministry of Petroleum and Energy*, Oslo District Court, Judgment of 4 January 2018; *Plan B Earth and Others v United Kingdom*, ECtHR, Application 35057/22 (application refused); *ASBL Klimaatzaak v Belgium*, Tribunal de premiére instance francophone de Bruxelles, Section Civile 2015/4585/A, judgment of 17 June 2021.

change.[85] Some international treaties, like the UNFCCC and the Convention on Biological Diversity, display at least some consensus among states that supra-national environmental concerns exist for which there is a collective interest to protect and preserve. Thus, at the very least the idea is no longer controversial that states might be obliged to trade with one another under a shared appreciation of a need to preserve and protect a transnational and borderless 'environment'. Nevertheless, in the slow-moving timescale of legal normative evolution in international law, the contours of how far law should prevent states from harming that collective good is still being worked out.

C. The Precautionary Principle

The third principle of interest here is the precautionary principle. Whereas the polluter pays principle and principle of prevention were both created to help states resolve specific kinds of problems about their inter-relations, the precautionary principle engages with a quite different kind of problem of what legal and policy actors should do when they are confronted with situations of scientific uncertainty.[86] Sometimes the principle manifests as a common-sense norm that cautions states to protect the environment from risky and uncertain human activities. At other times, though, its use can be quite technical, especially when it is relied upon to identify the scope of permissible action that states may take when they are faced with situations where some kind of action is necessary or desirable but whose environmental outcomes are uncertain. It is in this latter sense that the principle engages questions about expert calculations and interpretations of acceptable risk, uncertainty and the weight of evidence in public policy.[87]

The precautionary principle first emerged in the 1980s amid increasing public awareness of environmental danger and climate change as well as of the limitations of science in understanding and predicting the scale and degree of the changes that were afoot. The new field of climate science was revealing the scale of damage caused by many generations of (particular) humans, while also revealing how uncertain scientific knowledge of this newly unfamiliar changing world was.[88] The first planetary-scale shock of this realisation probably came in the form of the 'ozone hole' crisis of the mid-1980s, which was so stunning that it spurred the signing of the 1987 Montreal Convention.[89] Observations of planetary-scale

[85] B Mayer, 'International Advisory Proceedings on Climate Change' (2023) 44 *Michigan Journal of International Law* 41, 75.

[86] Sands and Peel (n 8) 230.

[87] MD Adams, 'The Precautionary Principle and the Rhetoric Behind It' (2002) 5 *Journal of Risk Research* 301, 307.

[88] W Steffen, *Global Change and the Earth System: A Planet Under Pressure* (Heidelberg, Springer 2004).

[89] WW Kellogg, 'Mankind's Impact on Climate: The Evolution of an Awareness' (1987) 10 *Climate Change* 113.

environmental damage and grim models of climate change futures were also being published around the same time, though they were not as obviously attributed to any specific agent or source of contamination or pollution. It was certain that something very worrying was afoot, but it was also unnerving that there was no way to know for sure how bad things were, or were going to become. This epistemological ambivalence created a legal problem for which the precautionary principle was enlisted to help states determine what activities should be permissible when their future effects on this increasingly grim reality were uncertain. This was especially problematic when the science was pointing to future transnational environmental change and damage on a scale far beyond the capacity of any private or government entity to indemnify.

The precautionary principle became an international principle in response to a need to facilitate this kind of decision-making and to help governments legitimise proactive policies that they might choose to impose to protect against *possible* future harms. It also legitimised states to go beyond a scope of action that limited them to preventing only harms that were known to be foreseeable or those that were probable or likely.[90] This was no small feat. The countries that would first promote the precautionary principle all had legal orders structured to correct for actions known to have caused (past) environmental damage through tort compensation regimes. They were also constrained in different ways by politics and principles of administrative law that limited their ability to take administrative actions that could impinge on or harm the interests of some segments of society to instances where anticipated damage was demonstrably likely. By permitting action in the face of merely *possible* future harms, the precautionary principle provided a normative basis to both sidestep constraints and permit more aggressive preventative action. The arrival of this principle on the international legal stage seemed to signal a major shift, so much so that when it first emerged as a legal principle, commentators at the time even wondered aloud whether it was a harbinger of a new kind of legal revolution.[91]

It is perhaps unsurprising that the first international agreements to make explicit reference to the precautionary principle were international maritime treaties, given how chronically poor the present state of knowledge of marine ecosystems is (only about 26 per cent of the ocean floor has been mapped to date, for instance).[92] The principle was first articulated in the 1987 Ministerial

[90] PH Martin, '"If You Don't Know How to Fix It, Please Stop Breaking It!" The Precautionary Principle and Climate Change' (1997) 2 *Foundations of Science* 263, 276.

[91] H Hohmann, *Precautionary Legal Duties and Principles of Modern International Environmental Law: The Precautionary Principle: International Environmental Law Between Exploitation and Protection* (London, Graham and Trotman, 1994).

[92] Seabed 2030, 'Seabed 2030 announces latest progress on World Hydrography Day' (21 June 2024) online at: https://seabed2030.org/2024/06/21/seabed-2030-announces-latest-progress-on-world-hydrography-day/.

Declaration of the Second International Conference on the Protection of the North Sea,[93] which in its Preamble states that:

> [I]n order to protect the North Sea from possibly damaging effects of the most dangerous substances, a precautionary approach is necessary which may require action to control inputs of such substances even before a causal link has been established by absolutely clear scientific evidence.[94]

This formal recognition of the precautionary principle in the Declaration was a major negotiation goal of the West German delegation, who had come to the conference wanting to transplant a legal mechanism into it from West German law called the *Vorsorgeprinzip*.[95] When deciding what to do with the environment, West German law- and policy-makers had faced similar knowledge problems like those that were glaringly evident at the conference, especially in the pages of the 'Quality Status Report' prepared for it that had compiled scientific contributions from each of the participating states. While the contributions were unanimous in their concern about the general health of the North Sea, their compilation into one report revealed a confusing and disconcerting plurality and inconsistency of methodologies, factual knowledge, and even terminology among them.[96] Conference delegates ultimately adopted the precautionary principle and incorporated it into the conference declaration because it offered a straightforward way to coordinate their shared use of the North Sea on a collectively cautious footing.

Although that particular conference was a relatively minor event in the history of international environmental law, the epistemological anxiety that drove its adoption of the precautionary principle can also be seen as part of broader developments in global environmental policy discourses at the time. These were particularly charged by very new and terrifying concerns like the hole in the ozone layer and 'acid rain' that were mainstreaming the politically contentious idea that the planetary 'environment' did not have an unlimited capacity to absorb pollution caused by human activities.[97] As such, it was not long before the principle made another appearance in international law a year later, this time in Article 2.2(b) of the 1985 Vienna Convention for the Protection of the Ozone Layer, which called for adoption of

> appropriate legislative or administrative measures … to control, limit, reduce or prevent human activities under their jurisdiction or control should it be found that these

[93] *Ministerial Declaration of the Second International Conference on the Protection of the North Sea* (adopted 24/25 November 1987) (1988) 27 ILM 838.

[94] ibid. Later in the text at Article C9 it also declared that: 'If the state of knowledge is insufficient, a strict limitation on emissions of pollutants at source should be imposed for safety reasons'.

[95] S Boehmer-Christiansen, 'The Precautionary Principle in Germany – Enabling Government' in T O'Riordan and J Cameron (eds), *Interpreting the Precautionary Principle* (London, Cameron May, 1994).

[96] 'Quality Status of the North Sea: A Report by the Scientific and Technical Working Group' (Second International North Sea Conference 1987), cited in PC Reid, 'The Work of the North Sea Task Force' 5 *International Journal of Estaurine and Coastal Law* 80.

[97] VR Ramanathan, 'Greenhouse Theory of Climate Change: A Test by an Inadvertent Global Experiment' (1988) 240 *Science* 293.

> activities have or are likely to have adverse effects resulting from modification or likely modification of the ozone layer.[98]

Four years after the 1988 entry into force of the Ozone Layer Convention, the precautionary principle was enshrined in the 1992 Rio Convention Declaration in the form of Principle 15:

> In order to protect the environment, the precautionary approach shall be widely applied by States according to their capabilities. Where there are threats of serious or irreversible damage, lack of full scientific certainty shall be not used as a reason for postponing cost-effective measures to prevent environmental degradation.

There are a number of notable differences between this version of the principle and that in the 1987 North Sea Conference Declaration and the Vienna Convention. The first is a tacit acknowledgement that some countries might be better placed than others to manage the costs of precaution ('according to their capabilities'); second is that the principle should be limited only to 'threats of serious or irreversible damage'; and third is that the principle should guide future preventive action to be 'cost-effective'. Such language reveals how, even after only four years, the precautionary principle was already contested and facing pushback from states, and it is not difficult to read between the lines to imagine what cleavages must have divided delegates around the Rio negotiation tables for them to settle on its final terminology.

Such cleavages were less of a concern in the EU, however. That same year its Member States signed the Maastricht Treaty, Article 130r(2) of which combined the polluter pays, preventive and precautionary principles in one bold statement:

> Community policy on the environment shall aim at a high level of protection taking into account the diversity of situations in the various regions of the Community. It shall be based on the precautionary principle and on the principles that preventative action should be taken, that environmental damage should as a priority be rectified at source and that the polluter should pay.

A few years later, the 1997 resurgence of BSE ('mad cow disease') and the 1999 Belgian dioxin food crisis provided the first opportunities to demonstrate the extent of the commitment enshrined in Article 130r, which the Commission confirmed by expressly articulating in a policy response to both crises that 'where appropriate, the precautionary principle will be applied in risk management decisions'.[99] However, if the Commission's professed commitment to the precautionary principle was unambiguous, the same could not be said about

[98] Vienna Convention for the Protection of the Ozone Layer (adopted 22 March 1985, entered into force on 22 September 1988) 1513 UNTS 324.

[99] Commission of the European Communities, *White Paper on Food Safety* COM (99) 719 final. See also Commission of the European Communities, *Commission Green Paper – General Principles of Food Law in the European Union* COM (97) 176 final.

how it should apply the principle in ways that could balance protecting public health and the environment with protecting the EU's internal market and its external trade profile.[100] This became increasingly challenging for European lawyers as the principle was applied to an ever-increasing and diverse range of policy areas overlapping with environmental and public health, such as: telecommunications, agriculture, food services and production, animal welfare, pharmaceuticals, new technologies, product safety, waste, chemicals, among others.[101]

As seen with the other principles above, once declared and encased in legal instruments, the precautionary principle also became a focal point for clashes both at negotiating tables and in courtrooms in the decade that followed. While almost every international environmental treaty or declaration signed since the 1990s has included some version of the precautionary principle in its terms, it has sparked a number of legal disputes, the most notable being a trade dispute between the United States and the EU over topics related to environmental health and safety, such as greenhouse gases, livestock hormones, chemicals, and genetically modified organisms.[102] This 'transatlantic schism'[103] bubbled to the surface in WTO disputes between the two over the EU's ban on US beef imports treated with hormones, which the US blamed in part on the EU hiding behind the smokescreen of the precautionary principle to pass objectionable proactive product bans with no proof of harm.[104] It also appeared in the *Southern Bluefin Tuna Cases* at ITLOS, where the tribunal held that with regards to threats to fish stocks, scientific uncertainty did not constitute a reason to delay adopting precautionary measures.[105] A quarter of a century later, the precautionary principle continues to be controversial, blamed for being irrational, unscientific and bad for innovation,[106] but also celebrated by those who are hopeful that its reach will spread to even more areas of law.[107]

[100] JD Graham, 'Europe's Precautionary Principle: Promise and Pitfalls' (2002) 371 *Journal of Risk Research* 371, 373–74.

[101] M Recuerda, 'Dangerous Interpretations of the Precautionary Principle and the Foundational Values of the European Union Food Law: Risk versus Risk' (2008) 4(1) *Journal of Food Law & Policy* 1, 31.

[102] N Vig and M Faure, *Green Giants? Environmental Policies of the United States and the European Union* (Cambridge MA, MIT Press, 2004).

[103] N Morag-Levine, 'The History of Precaution' (2014) 62 *American Journal of Comparative Law* 1095, 1095–96.

[104] Dispute Settlement, *United States – Continued Suppression of Obligations in the EC – Hormones Dispute*, WT/DS320/12 (2 June 2008).

[105] *Southern Bluefin Tuna Cases*, Provisional Measures, ITLOS Case No 3, Order, 117 ILR 148, International Tribunal for the Law of the Sea (27 August 1999) paras 77–80.

[106] B Durodié, 'The True Cost of Precautionary Chemicals Regulation' (2004) 23 *Risk Analysis* 389.

[107] N Geiling, 'Can the Precautionary Principle Save the Endangered Species Act from an Uncertain Climate Future?' (2020) 47 *Ecology Law Quarterly* 305; J Wieding, J Stubenrauch and F Ekardt, 'Human Rights and Precautionary Principle: Limits to Geoengineering, SRM, and IPCC Scenarios' (2020) 12(21) *Sustainability* 8858.

IV. Discussion

This historical overview of the origins of three international environmental law principles allows for a rough theoretical model to understand how and when earth system law-inspired norms might ever become 'principles' in international law.

First, it demonstrates that international legal principles come into being when legal and policy actors convert norms into principles at moments when there is a demand for them. Second, that demand arises when those actors confront new problems that complicate the ordinary work of states and international organisations. Third, when such actors convert a pre-existing concept or norm into a formal legal principle, they do so to optimise or facilitate their decision-making to deal with the new complications they are facing. Fourth, once a new principle is demonstrably able to perform that optimising or facilitating function relatively well, other actors may adapt and transpose it to address other legal and policy dilemmas, which causes its meaning, content and legal utility to evolve and expand but also fragment over time. Finally, and perhaps least surprisingly, states in general will resist principles that threaten to encroach on their sovereignty, and one should expect (at least some of) them to expend efforts in international forums to limit this. International tribunals, on the other hand, are less restrained in recognising and expanding the sovereignty-limiting ambits of principles when they help them to resolve conflicts between states. This tussle between states and courts will also affect how a principle evolves in international law.

One could read the three principles studied here and be hopeful that the more that earth system science develops, the greater the likelihood that demand for earth system law principles might arise. After all, in all three cases it was the emergent science of pollution and climate change in the second half of the last century that created new problems that needed new legal solutions. However, before one makes easy analogies between that and earth system science, it is notable that none of the three principles was first proposed as a legal solution to the problems of climate change or pollution per se. Rather, they were created and adopted in order to help states do relatively ordinary things: to better allocate costs, respect the national sovereignty of one's neighbours, promote international trade, and make justifiable choices in the face of an uncertain future. Thus, one can wonder what might the (relatively mundane) concerns of states be in the future that would give rise to their demand for earth system law principles as solutions. One cannot simply assume that climate change itself will present those conditions: the climate is already known to be changing, yet the question remains open of how and in what ways laws should change to deal with it. Furthermore, the three principles reviewed here did not originate as parts of a proactive and coherent programme to reform law according to a new or even coherent reframed vision of the world, or even to fix the environment.

It follows, therefore, that the scope of opportunity for new legal principles in international law is relatively limited and highly contextualised. Recognising this can focus one's attention on certain kinds of analytical questions, such as: To what degree is there or will there ever be 'demand' for earth system-oriented legal principles in the international system today? How might the earth system as a concept help states with their relations with one another? How does the earth system facilitate or optimise state policy-making at the international and domestic levels? How fertile might the earth system concept be for translation and adaptation to resolve multiple legal conundrums? And how or under what conditions might states see the earth system as not being something that will threaten their sovereignty? The argument here is that without answers to these questions, it becomes difficult, if not impossible, to predict or anticipate how, when or even if the earth system might ever become part of the tapestry of international law in the form of one or more legal principles.

The principles reviewed here are examples of incremental legal change, even though they represent significant, and still controversial, transformations in international environmental law. They demonstrate that principles become part of international law when a specific demand arises for them among international actors in need of guidance in their decision-making. Furthermore, they also reveal that, regardless of how scholars and jurists may imagine them before the fact, once they emerge as principles, they are subject to change and evolution as they are applied to ever-increasing areas of law over time. In short, this implies that the causal relationship between principles and legal orders is better understood as one where contextual changes to the latter create demands for the former, rather than the other way around. If this is so, then one should expect earth system law principles to become principles of law only after legal actors working within international orders willingly orient themselves towards something resembling the concept of the 'earth system', thereby sparking a demand for earth system-inspired principles to guide their future decision-making and dispute resolution.

This approach can easily be critiqued for staying too faithfully within the bounds of traditional international law scholarship with its interest in state relations, trade, transboundary harms, etc. This is an important and relevant critique, given that some earth system law scholarship is explicit in its intention to move beyond the confines of international law.[108] Compared to more creative and visionary efforts to imagine earth system law, or even law in general, for the Anthropocene, the pragmatism of the approach offered here might seem restrained, conservative, even unimaginative. In its defence, the logic behind it rests on a recognition that great, revolutionary transformations of entire legal orders around new normative frameworks are historically rare, and most legal transformation in history has happened incrementally.[109]

[108] L du Toit and LJ Kotzé, 'Reimagining International Environmental Law for the Anthropocene: An Earth System Law Perspective' (2022) 11 *Earth System Governance* 100132.

[109] R Grace, 'Incrementalism in International Lawmaking: The Development of Normative Frameworks of Protection for Forcibly Displaced Persons' in K Polackova van der Ploeg, L Pasquet and L Castellanos-Jankiewicz (eds), *International Law and Time* (Heidelberg, Springer 2002); S Block-Lieb and TC Halliday, 'Incrementalisms in Global Lawmaking' (2007) 32 *Brooklyn Journal of International Law* 851.

V. Conclusion

The foregoing thought experiment poses a challenge to the notion of the earth system becoming a legal concept given how earth system law, and even earth system governance, as fields of inquiry intentionally aim to disrupt the self-interested logic of states and state behaviour. Indeed, the conceptual framework of the earth system in a way is radical enough in its singular collective focus that attempting to imagine its underlying legal principles often leads one to imagine an entirely different legal regime than the international one that currently prevails. This, of course, invites the question not only about what an earth system-oriented legal regime would look like (which earth system law scholars have started to ask), but also, and more pragmatically, what it would take to shift the international legal order from its current footing to that imagined alternative.

The argument offered here is that one should not expect earth system law principles to be the engines of that work. Instead, one should expect earth system law principles to emerge on the global stage as legal instruments only when demand for them arises once the international political and legal order has shifted itself to an earth system orientation. How or what will bring about that shift, though, is not a question that lawyers are trained to answer, and we would be well advised to rely on our earth system governance and other colleagues for help and guidance on that front.

5

Earth System Law and The Praxis of Being De-Principled*

EMILLE BOULOT, LAURA MAI AND SHAUN SELLERS

I. Introduction

Legal principles have long shaped environmental law doctrine and jurisprudence and played a central role in crystallising paradigms which characterise and demarcate environmental law as a distinct field of legal expertise. Legal principles have, as it were, become part of environmental law's DNA – normatively, procedurally and politically. Examples include 'polluter pays', 'prevention', 'precaution' and 'sustainable development' amongst others.[1] But international environmental law and its principles have failed to arrest dramatic socio-ecological decline and the ravages of what has been termed the 'Anthropocene'.[2] As a result, there has been significant scholarly consideration of alternative legal paradigms, including what has been termed earth system law.[3] In response to the questions raised by this book, our intervention critically asks: Does earth system law need to set out 'better' principles, in terms of re-designed, updated and revised normative substance, to respond

* The authors would like to thank Anja Hilkermeijer for her helpful commentary, sound-boarding, and critical eyes in our writing of this chapter. Whatever mistakes exist remain our fault alone.

[1] See also Kotzé and Du Toit, Chapter 3, and Leach, Chapter 4 in this book.

[2] The term 'Anthropocene' has been criticised for being a totalising and homogenising discourse of an undifferentiated humanity. The term puts forward a technocratic and de-political discourse which co-exists with ongoing capital accumulation, despite the roots of the crisis having been closely linked to modernity and capitalism. H Ernstson and E Swyngedouw (eds), *Urban Political Ecology in the Anthropo-Obscene: Interruptions and Possibilities* (Abingdon-on-Thames, Routledge, 2019); V De Lucia, 'Critical Environmental Law and the Double Register of the Anthropocene: A Biopolitical Reading' in LJ Kotzé (ed), *Environmental Law and Governance for the Anthropocene* (Oxford, Hart Publishing, 2019). Alternative terms such as 'Capitalocene', 'Plantationocene', and 'Cthulucene' have been put forward in an effort to acknowledge the conceptual limitations of the 'Anthropocene' and to describe more accurately the manner in which the narratives of industrial capitalism, colonialism, and civilisation shape this new geological epoch and to acknowledge that the distribution of harm and responsibility is deeply inequitable and uneven. See eg D Haraway, 'Anthropocene, Capitalocene, Plantationocene, Chthulucene: Making Kin' (2015) 6 *Environmental Humanities* 159.

[3] LJ Kotzé and RE Kim, 'Earth System Law: The Juridical Dimensions of Earth System Governance' (2019) *Earth System Governance* 1.

to the crisis (crises)? Or, would it be useful, and in fact necessary, to re-think the legal forms, strategies and techniques which we mobilise in scholarly efforts?[4]

Engaging with these questions, we show that there are real risks in relying on statements of principle in efforts to reimagine law without considering the social, political and economic contexts that prevent transformation.[5] Legal principles without consideration of existing shortcomings and complicities of international environmental law will fail to respond to 'environmental' crises. Our point is that in reimagining law, we cannot simply repeat the process of how modern international environmental law came into being at the beginning of the 1970s but should rather think more deeply about the interweaving of international environmental law with the global economy and about the processes of change required to shift away from harmful life-ways. Relying on legal principles as the primary legal technique for transformation has the potential to re-inscribe the very tendencies which alternative conceptions of law seek to overcome. These include prioritising economic over socio-ecological interests, including by upholding corporate exploitation, sustaining structural injustices of colonialism and neo-colonialism between the Global South and North, and maintaining claims to universalism and concomitant forms of epistemic exclusion.

Accordingly, we present an approach that we have termed 'being de-principled' as a strategic practice which allows us to resist the urge to follow the mainstream disciplinary dispositions to conceive law as a normative phenomenon with an internal order, a hierarchical structure and a pre-defined purpose – as something that can simply be reconfigured abstractly through scholarly discourse. Instead, we want to open up possibilities and give resonance to practices which allow for *thinking and doing law differently*. We argue that becoming de-principled means taking space to render law more open to plural ways of knowing, doing and relating and to become attuned to how law is both socially and materially imagined, produced, sustained and, at times, allowed to wither away. We address our intervention specifically to emerging earth system law scholarship and present it in the

[4] See also L Mai, 'The "Question of Possibilities" as a Leitmotif for Re-imagining Law for the "Anthropocene"' (2022) 13(53) *Global Policy* (Special Issue) 49.

[5] Mai describes transformations as processes of change that render real what seems impossible at present, but which could arguably be realised if different conditions were in place, identifying transformative temporality, change, and action as three central features of transformation processes. L Mai, 'Navigating Transformations: Climate Change and International Law' (2024) 37(3) *Leiden Journal of International Law* 535. The Intergovernmental Panel on Climate Change (IPCC) refers to transformation as a change in the 'fundamental attributes' of a system, and we might add that transformational change results in qualitatively distinct system outcomes from those previous. IPCC, 'Annex I: Glossary' in V Masson-Delmotte and others (eds), *Global Warming of 1.5°C: An IPCC Special Report on the Impacts of Global Warming of 1.5°C above Pre-industrial Levels and Related Global Greenhouse Gas Emission Pathways, in the Context of Strengthening the Global Response to the Threat of Climate Change, Sustainable Development, and Efforts to Eradicate Poverty* (IPCC, 2019; Cambridge, Cambridge University Press, 2022).

hope that it assists in the ongoing development of a theory of change within this scholarship.

This chapter begins by providing a brief overview of the scholarship of earth system law,[6] before considering the roles and functions of international environmental law principles. We set out the limitations of a principles-based approach for transformative change that earth system law seeks, before articulating what we have termed a 'de-principled' praxis. Crucially, being de-principled is not simply an absence of principles. It requires both normative prescription and methodological processes attendant to theories of change to international environmental law's legal and political contexts to imagine and develop post-Anthropocene futures through legal means. We elaborate the approach further through the method of thinking of principles as techniques and applying it to the global trade regime.

II. The Roles, Functions and Limitations of Legal Principles

A. Earth System Law as a Normative Endeavour

Earth system law, as put forward by Kotzé and Kim,[7] aims to consider the 'juridical elements of earth systems governance' by extending the Earth System Governance Project scientific agenda to introduce a systems approach to legal thinking and governance practices.[8] The 'earth system', from the perspective of earth system law is considered to be a planetary social-ecological system. This system is composed of different sub-systems that are interdependent and complex, resulting in human and ecological mutual vulnerability.[9] The driving rationale for the development of a 'new' international legal paradigm is the looming spectre of the Anthropocene, a geological era in which humans have categorically impacted the capability of the earth system to sustain a biodiverse community and all life. Earth system law seeks to make law 'more responsive to the Anthropocene's normative, ethical and regulatory challenges'.[10]

Earth system law is a particular epistemic endeavour in that it takes the modalities of knowledge-production of earth system science and relates these scientific insights to constructions of law, ie legal theory and legal doctrine. Earth system science has been described as a 'paradigm shift' within Western

[6] See also Kotzé, Angstadt and Kim, Chapter 2 in this book.
[7] Kotzé and Kim (n 2) 19.
[8] https://www.earthsystemgovernance.org/research-framework/.
[9] LJ Kotzé, 'Earth System Law for the Anthropocene' (2019) 11 *Sustainability* 6796; LJ Kotzé, 'Earth System Law for the Anthropocene: Rethinking Environmental Law alongside the Earth System Metaphor' (2020) 11 *Transnational Legal Theory* 75.
[10] Kotzé and Kim (n 2) 10.

knowledge traditions, 'a markedly new thinking about the Earth', with Hamilton writing:

> Ecological thinking, which emerged in the early 20th century and surged in the 1960s and 1970s, is the biological science of the relationship within communities of organisms and between them and their local environments, whereas Earth System thinking, which emerged in the 1990s, is the integrative meta-science of the whole planet as a unified, complex, evolving system beyond the sum of its parts.[11]

Earth system law takes this claim uncritically[12] and this makes the very basis for its normative dimension. The question that earth system law wants to answer then is: What does the notion of the earth system, and earth system sciences that this notion makes possible, mean for law? In what ways does it prompt us to reconsider law? While earth system law, in line with the broader Earth System Governance Project, recognises transdisciplinarity and epistemic plurality, its core epistemic commitment can be found within the earth system sciences.[13]

While revolutionary and holistic in many respects, earth system science has been criticised for its potential to exclude certain knowledges.[14] Certainly, this is something that the Earth System Governance Project recognises, acknowledging as it does that there is a lack of diversity with respect to the theorisation of knowledge, ontologies, epistemologies, and research methodologies within earth system governance.[15] Additionally, as has been identified by Leach,[16] there is an evident tension that arises in the relationship between complexity and normativity. Drawing on Luhmann's theory of law as an autopoietic system, Leach argues that a greater attendance to earth system law's normative endeavour is required along with careful consideration of the social function of law and legal systems and the ways in which they change.

We have previously argued there is a concern that without considering the political and social and other contexts of law, the norms and principles developed by earth system law scholars risk being siloed to the halls of academia.[17] Indeed, as we detail below, the focus on the development of principles and norms, without consideration of the political economy and situated and

[11] C Hamilton, 'The Anthropocene as Rupture' (2016) 3 *The Anthropocene Review* 93, 94.

[12] Kotzé and Kim (n 2).

[13] LJ Kotzé and others, 'Earth System Law: Exploring New Frontiers in Legal Science' (2022) 11 *Earth System Governance* 100126.

[14] M Heymann and AD Dalmedico, 'Epistemology and Politics in Earth System Modeling: Historical Perspectives' (2019) 11(5) *Journal of Advances in Modeling Earth Systems* 1139; E Boulot and J Sterlin, 'Steps Towards a Legal Ontological Turn: Proposals for Law's Place beyond the Human' (2021) 11 *Transnational Environmental Law* 13; DR Coen and FA Jonsson, 'Between History and Earth System Science' (2022) 113 *Isis* 407; C Soriano, 'Epistemological Limitations of Earth System Science to Confront the Anthropocene Crisis' (2022) 9 *The Anthropocene Review* 111.

[15] https://www.earthsystemgovernance.org/research-framework/.

[16] MC Leach, 'Seeking "Systems" in Earth System Law: Boundaries, Identity, and Purpose in an Emergent Field' (2023) 15 *Earth System Governance* 100162.

[17] L Mai and E Boulot, 'Harnessing the Transformative Potential of Earth System Law: From Theory to Practice' (2021) 7 *Earth System Governance* 100103.

diverse knowledges and perspectives, risks co-option and the reification of the status quo.

B. The Roles, Functions and Limitations of Legal Principles

Legal principles have long had a key role in the operation and development of international law. In comparison to a rule that is considered to be binding and mandatory, a principle is a consideration that must be taken into account in making decisions.[18] Rules specify certain actions, principles do not, but the line can be blurry. Principles have been derived from treaties, with the United Nations Charter, for example, setting out key principles of public international law such as the promotion of human rights and state sovereignty. In addition to principles derived from treaties, a key component of international law has been what are known as general principles of law which are derived from common legal practices of nations or customary law, such as the legal personality of corporations. Other principles have emerged from customary law such as the principle of non-intervention.

Legal principles have been especially prominent in the development of international environmental law.[19] The first principle usually articulated in any list is the principle of sovereignty over natural resources, with the corresponding responsibility not to cause transboundary environmental harm.[20] This has been articulated in the Stockholm Declaration (Principle 21)[21] and the Rio Declaration (Principle 2).[22] These principles are often followed by the principles of cooperation, preventative action, and sustainable development, the precautionary principle, the polluter pays principle, and the principle of common but differentiated responsibilities.

While the existence and global applicability of international environmental law principles was affirmed in the arbitration of the *Iron Rhine* case, there remains considerable debate about what is a rule or a principle.[23] Principles are often imprecisely defined to allow for broad applicability but often have questionable legal status or enforceability. It is likely that the principle of sovereignty over natural resources, the responsibility not to cause harm and the prevention and cooperation principles are each sufficient to be a cause of action under

[18] P Sands and J Peel, *Principles of International Environmental Law*, 4th edn (Cambridge, Cambridge University Press, 2018).

[19] See also Leach, Chapter 4 in this book.

[20] Sands and Peel (n 18); MV Soto, 'General Principles of International Environmental Law' (1996) 3 *ILSA Journal of International & Comparative Law* 193.

[21] 1972 Declaration of the United Nations Conference on the Human Environment, UN Doc A/RES/2994(XXVII) (Stockholm Declaration).

[22] 1992 Rio Declaration on Environment and Development, A/CONF.151/26, vol I (Rio Declaration).

[23] *Iron Rhine Railway Arbitration (Belgium v Netherlands)*, Award, 24th May 2005, ICGJ 373 (PCA, 2005), Permanent Court of Arbitration, at [58].

international customary law, but the justiciability of the remaining principles is questionable.[24]

There exist some significant critiques of the development, implementation and operation of international environmental law principles. Despite significant efforts on behalf of the Global South for legal recognition that the Global North is responsible for the majority of the world's consumption and waste, with the associated introduction of principles such as sustainable development and common but differentiated responsibilities, there has been little change to the rate of environmental degradation caused by the Global North. The Global North has consistently ignored, and indeed rejected, differential responsibilities and has instead sought to ensure that any legal environmental obligations are voluntary and aspirational, rather than mandatory.[25]

International environmental law principles have been criticised, amongst other things, for being co-opted or hijacked.[26] Gramsci called co-option 'hegemony through neutralisation' which means that transformative strategies, which aim to transform existing institutional hegemonies, are appropriated by the existing system, neutralising their transformative potential.[27] Examples from international environmental law include the principle of sustainable development, which despite its revolutionary beginnings, has been heavily criticised for maintaining exploitative forms of 'development'.[28] Article XX of the General Agreement on Tariffs and Trade (GATT), in principle, allows for the protection of the environment within the borders of a country, yet trade law and the specificities around the interpretation/ application of Article XX have instead produced much more leverage for those industries and interests that seek to prevent the protection of the environment (see further below).

What is evident on a closer reading of international environmental law principles is an ongoing commitment to state sovereignty and a description and framing of nature as a resource for economic development, with environmental degradation being considered an economic externality. Natarajan and Khoday[29] argue that this ontological framework embeds a deeply inequitable distribution of harms and benefits. They write:

> [I]nternational lawyers have helped normalize a world-view where nature is understood predominantly as a natural resource, where humanity is at the centre of the

[24] Sands and Peel (n 18).

[25] J Dehm, 'Carbon Colonialism or Climate Justice? Interrogating the International Climate Regime from a TWAIL Perspective' (2016) 33 *Windsor Yearbook of Access to Justice* 129.

[26] GL Porras, 'Integrating the Mexican Water Law into the Earth System Law Perspective' in T Cadman, M Hurlbert and AC Simonelli (eds), *Earth System Law: Standing on the Precipice of the Anthropocene* (Abingdon-on-Thames, Routledge, 2022); LJ Kotzé and S Adelman, 'Environmental Law and the Unsustainability of Sustainable Development: A Tale of Disenchantment and of Hope' (2023) 34 *Law and Critique* 227.

[27] Q Hoare and G Nowell Smith (eds and trans), *Selections from the Prison Notebooks of Antonio Gramsci* (New York, International Publishers, 1971).

[28] Kotzé and Adelman (n 26).

[29] U Natarajan and K Khoday, 'Locating Nature: Making and Unmaking International Law' (2014) 27 *Leiden Journal of International Law* 573.

> environment and privileged above all else, where progress is defined by our degree of control over nature, and where this capacity to control is believed to be limitless.[30]

State sovereignty is deeply tied to natural resources, with the legitimacy and sovereignty of the state maintained by the construction and reconstruction of socio-ecological processes and practices. As Parenti[31] argues, the state 'does not have a relationship with nature, it is a relationship with nature' with the 'control and management of nature … always central to the realization and consolidation of state power'.[32] Ioris[33] shows that the core task of the modern (Western) state is, therefore, to naturalise and maximise anti-commons institutions (such as institutions which codify and enforce privatisation and the commodification of ecological systems) and to undertake the administration of the socio-ecological impacts of resource production. This approach is no different within the arena of international law, as states seek to promote the exploitation of natural resources while also seeking to contain environmental conflicts. Examples of this approach can be found in the usual operation of international trade law, investment law, commercial contracts and the lending practices of international financial corporations. Through the architecture of international law, transnational corporations have been able to acquire labour, resources, land, water, food, minerals and energy from the Global South and leave pollution, waste and post-extractive landscapes at the expense of Indigenous, poor and marginalised communities, all under the auspices of sustainable development.[34]

Not all peoples are afforded the same control over their natural resources. Authors such as Sultana,[35] Pahuja,[36] Natarajan and Khoday,[37] have comprehensively argued that the resource management processes facilitated by international environmental law continue a deep coloniality. Much of international law is dedicated to maintaining markets with demands for particular governmental systems and particular relationships between the state and the economy evident across multinational trade regimes. International environmental law solutions, such as carbon markets and offsets, have been tied to land grabs, displacement and dispossession of local people.[38] Nation states do not have equal footing in the

[30] ibid 586.

[31] C Parenti, 'The 2013 *ANTIPODE* AAG Lecture. The Environment Making State: Territory, Nature, and Value' (2015) 47 *Antipode* 829, 830.

[32] M Whitehead, R Jones and M Jones, *The Nature of the State: Excavating the Political Ecologies of the Modern State*, Oxford Geographical and Environmental Studies (Oxford, Oxford University Press, 2007) 6.

[33] AAR Ioris, 'Theorizing State-Environment Relationships: Antinomies of Flexibility and Legitimacy' (2015) 39 *Progress in Human Geography* 167.

[34] U Natarajan and J Dehm, 'Introduction: Where Is the Environment? Locating Nature in International Law' in U Natarajan and J Dehm (eds), *Locating Nature: Making and Unmaking International Law* (Cambridge, Cambridge University Press, 2022).

[35] F Sultana, 'The Unbearable Heaviness of Climate Coloniality' (2022) 99 *Political Geography* 102638.

[36] S Pahuja, *Decolonising International Law: Development, Economic Growth and the Politics of Universality* (Cambridge, Cambridge University Press, 2011).

[37] Natarajan and Khoday (n 29).

[38] Sultana (n 35).

negotiation of Conferences of the Parties on climate change, or in trade treaties or development programmes,[39] with this inequality leading to extraction and dispossession in the Global South.

The bifurcation of economy and ecology in international law 'produces convenient regulatory schizophrenia that allows environmentalism itself to be captured by the unrestrainable pursuit of economic growth'.[40] This 'regulatory schizophrenia' can be seen in the overwhelming reaction to climate disruptions as an opportunity to increase trade liberalisation through growth in so-called 'environmental services and goods', which has been criticised as being a category with no fixed definition[41] and arguably co-opted as 'environmental' in principle if not in quality. The ongoing degradation of ecologies is therefore an inherent part of international law, with international environmental law and its principles unable to arrest an unsustainable economic system. International environmental law continues and maintains the structural injustices and inequalities of colonialism and associated capital accumulation.

The final critique that we level at international environmental law principles is that of an unwavering commitment to universalism. Western modernity has tended to make universal assumptions about the environment,[42] which international law has continued, putting forward universal values from a presumed position of external objectivity.[43] But, despite significant efforts on behalf of legal positivism and modernist hegemonies, we do not live in a single reality.[44] The universality of international law produces what Pahuja[45] calls the continuation of violence against collectives who practice other forms of law. As a result, there has been significant scholarly interest in designing transformative theories of change that are pluralistic, open ended and informed by democratic processes.[46] This has been led by Indigenous and Global South activism and scholarship.[47]

[39] D Robertson, 'EU-ACP Economic Partnership Agreements: Modern Colonialism Disguised in Violation of the WTO' (2021) 50 *Vanderbilt Law Review* 463; D Falzon, 'The Ideal Delegation: How Institutional Privilege Silences "Developing" Nations in the UN Climate Negotiations' (2021) 70 *Social Problems* 185.

[40] Natarajan and Dehm (n 34) 7.

[41] W Brown, *Undoing the Demos: Neoliberalism's Stealth Revolution* (Brooklyn NY, Zone Books, 2017).

[42] V Argyrou, *The Logic of Environmentalism: Anthropology, Ecology and Postcoloniality* (New York, Berghahn Books, 2005).

[43] A Anghie, *Imperialism, Sovereignty and the Making of International Law* (Cambridge, Cambridge University Press, 2005); MC Petersmann, 'Sympoietic Thinking and Earth System Law: The Earth, Its Subjects and the Law' (2021) 9 *Earth System Governance* 100114; E Jones, *Feminist Theory and International Law: Posthuman Perspectives* (London, Routledge, 2022).

[44] M Davies, EcoLaw: Legality, Life and the Normativity of Nature (London, Routledge, 2022) 105.

[45] Pahuja (n 36).

[46] G Munda, 'Social Multi-Criteria Evaluation: Methodological Foundations and Operational Consequences' (2004) 158 *European Journal of Operational Research* 662; R White, 'Multicriteria Mapping' in CL Spash (ed), *Routledge Handbook of Ecological Economics: Nature and Society* (London, Routledge, 2017).

[47] Z Todd, 'An Indigenous Feminist's Take on the Ontological Turn: "Ontology" Is Just Another Word for Colonialism' (2016) 29(1) *Journal of Historical Sociology* 4, 20; A Escobar, 'Thinking-Feeling with the Earth: Territorial Struggles and the Ontological Dimension of the Epistemologies of the South' (2016) 11(1) *AIBR, Revista de Antropología Iberoamericana* 11.

Principles have been a dominant feature of international environmental law development and practice, but we believe that an additional approach is needed to avoid co-option and the continuation of the deeply inequitable harms between the Global North and South. Other ways of knowing and being are required outside of the hegemonic narrative of resource extraction and development, and outside of the disciplinary silos that we find ourselves in.[48] We seek to contribute to the discussion a 'de-principled' approach that aims to articulate one theory of change for the task of earth system law. As Parker and Haines[49] observe in relation to regulation, 'A focus on how regulation *should* occur glosses over the political, social and economic challenges that will be faced in ensuring it *does* occur'.

III. A De-principled Praxis

A. What do We Mean by Being De-principled?

We propose the neologism of being 'de-principled' to describe a move beyond an exclusively positivist, abstract and universalising approach to reimagining law for the Anthropocene. In our view, this approach risks re-inscribing the modern state-centric legal paradigm with its tendencies to reify law as a monolithic abstract object and an aesthetic of coherence, systematicity and orderliness. As we have discussed, critical legal analysis and political economy scholarship have shown how these disciplinary presuppositions and commitments have created a culture within legal scholarship which tends to marginalise, and in fact, render invisible, forms of legality which do not conform to positivist assumptions. International environmental law and critical legal scholars have highlighted the disruptive effects of the Anthropocene and the way in which they force us to fundamentally question and rebuild the ontological foundations of legal systems.[50] It is to that call that we turn by focusing specifically on legal form and praxis. Accordingly, we propose being de-principled as a practice to help create spaces within legal scholarship, and in discussion with other fields of knowledge, that allows imaginative re-thinking and experimenting with law in ways that are attuned to plural ways of knowing, doing and relating. In this sense, the prefix 'de-' is intended to signify a practice of unsettling learned ways of engaging with, thinking about and doing law. Such unsettling involves critical self-reflection, un-learning and looking for blind spots.

[48] Kotzé and others (n 13).

[49] C Parker and F Haines, 'An Ecological Approach to Regulatory Studies?' (2018) 45 *Journal of Law and Society* 136, 150.

[50] A Philippopoulos-Mihalopoulos, 'Critical Autopoiesis and the Materiality of Law' (2014) 27 *International Journal for the Semiotics of Law – Revue Internationale de Sémiotique Juridique* 389; LJ Kotzé (ed), *Environmental Law and Governance for the Anthropocene* (Oxford, Hart Publishing, 2017); Boulot and Sterlin (n 14).

Being de-principled is to reimagine law for the Anthropocene in ways that are unfamiliar to the legal discipline and established legal categories and disciplinary truths that a critical mass of legal scholarship continues to take for granted.

In our previous writing on the transformative potential of earth system law we suggested that to stretch the legal mind, a three-step exercise could be helpful: first, taking stock and becoming aware of collectively held mental models; second having uncovered problematic assumptions, looking for alternatives; and third, working to ensure that these alternatives find resonance in scholarly discourse and practice.[51] The practice of being de-principled is a practical iteration of this three-step exercise. It is intended to challenge tacitly held assumptions about legal principles, specifically, assumptions about what they can and cannot do; it is intended to help alternative conceptions of legal change to emerge and gain traction; and it is mindful of the need to spread emerging ideas beyond disciplinary pockets into mainstream discourse and practice. To be clear, being de-principled emerges as practice – something that is continuously worked into engagements with law. Accordingly, being de-principled is not a principle by another name. It is not another abstract normative maxim, but rather exemplifies reflexive and critical engagement with and in legal thinking and practice. To put this another way, instead of an 'add-on' that modifies existing ways of thinking about law, 'being de-principled' is always and already included in legal thinking and praxis. Accordingly, rather than ex-post adjustments to the status quo that leave existing disciplinary presuppositions about law unchallenged, being de-principled requires a readiness to think critically of ideas, ideals and imaginaries which continue to shape legal knowledge production, craft and praxis.

As legal theorist Margaret Davies[52] explains, it is useful to heuristically distinguish between three forms of legal change: changes in the normative substance of law; changes in the conceptual understanding of law; and changes in the background knowledge which makes legal thinking and doing possible in the first place. Being de-principled, then, we suggest, emerges as a praxis – a theoretically informed practice with 'reflection and action upon the world to transform it'[53] – which pursues the latter two instantiations of change – modifications to the ways in which we conceptualise law, and deep-running processes of un-learning and un-doing that allow us to re-make the presuppositions which are foundational for legal thinking and doing.

B. Applying a De-principled Praxis

Being de-principled is challenging. The unsettling of legal paradigms risks leaving a space capable of being co-opted by interests that further imbed the status quo or

[51] Mai and Boulot (n 17) 8.

[52] M Davies, *Law Unlimited: Materialism, Pluralism, and Legal Theory* (Abingdon-on-Thames, Routledge, 2017).

[53] P Freire, *Pedagogy of the Oppressed* (London, Continuum, 1970) 51.

facilitate undemocratic approaches. As has long been recognised by political ecology, critical institutional theory, and science and technology studies, institutions are shaped by power relations, conflicting interests and values.[54] In order to explicitly consider some of these issues, we suggest one approach for actually practising it and apply that approach to the example of international trade law.

We suggest that in practising a de-principled approach it can be helpful to think of principles as a form of what legal ethnographer Annelise Riles refers to as 'legal technicalities' – those elements of law, understood as a field of study and practice, that define and hold the field together. Legal technicalities include: technical ways of sorting, including and excluding, reasoning, interpreting and argumentation; drafting techniques and other highly specific ways of composing documents; as well as etiquette and mannerisms that define the culture of the legal profession and the spaces in which it unfolds.[55] Re-framing legal principles as a specific form of legal technique allows us to move beyond the normative substance of principles – the ideas and ideals which legal principles aspire to. A focus on normative content is a way of thinking about law in terms of a means–ends relationship – law emerges as a tool for use in governance and regulatory processes to achieve desirable societal ends, a regulatory intervention that has impacts, outcomes and effects. A focus on legal technicalities, by contrast, allows us to centre law itself as the object of investigation, to ask questions about what it means to be law, to focus on law as a socially and materially constructed phenomenon that is worthy of analysis and critique in its own right.[56] As Riles explains, it is important to focus on law itself because: 'our tools … shape how we think, what we aspire to achieve, where we choose to go'.[57] To make this point, Riles draws a comparison with tools for writing. What and how we write is fundamentally influenced in different ways depending on whether there is pen and paper involved, a typewriter, a smartphone or a computer keyboard. Applying this perspective to the project of reimagining law for the Anthropocene, it becomes evident how navigating changing planetary realities is not only mediated through normative prescriptions and aspirations (some of which are enshrined in legal principles), but also through the technical means (such as, for instance, drafting techniques, document formats, interpretative conventions, etiquette, assumptions, and mannerisms, and the disciplinary sense of purpose) that carry these prescriptions and aspirations.

[54] S Jasanoff (ed), *States of Knowledge: The Co-Production of Science and Social Order. Transferred to Digital Print. International Library of Sociology* (London, Routledge, 2010); M Fabinyi, L Evans and SJ Foale, 'Social-Ecological Systems, Social Diversity, and Power: Insights from Anthropology and Political Ecology' (2014) 19 *Ecology and Society* 28; F Cleaver and L Whaley, 'Understanding Process, Power, and Meaning in Adaptive Governance: A Critical Institutional Reading' (2018) 23 *Ecology and Society* 49.

[55] A Riles, 'A New Agenda for the Cultural Study of Law: Taking on the Technicalities' (2005) 53 *Buffalo Law Review* 973, 976.

[56] A Riles and R Michaels, 'Law as Technique' in MC Foblets, M Goodale, M Sapignoli and O Zenker (eds), *The Oxford Handbook of Law and Anthropology* (Oxford, Oxford University Press, 2022).

[57] A Riles, *Collateral Knowledge: Legal Reasoning in the Global Financial Markets* (Chicago IL, University of Chicago Press, 2011) 72.

A focus on legal technique, then, allows us to reflect not only on which alternative normative aspirations may be necessary to meaningfully respond to Anthropocene realities, but also which alternative forms of legal knowledge, craft and culture may be required to effect such realities. As Feichtner[58] has argued, it is not only the content of law but also 'the legal form itself [which] limits the possibilities for remaking the global political economy'. Keeping in mind that legal techniques and legal forms will always have effects beyond their intended instrumental aims,[59] we want to ask the earth system law community: What could alternative forms of legal knowledge, expertise, craft and culture look like?

C. A Case Study of Trade Law

Trade law is a striking example of not just principles in action, but also the complexities involved with how to de-principle and to what end. There are three core principles around which the General Agreement on Tariffs and Trade (GATT), the World Trade Organization (WTO), and subsidiary trade agreements are organised, and which create, monitor, and enforce the rules of market access. Membership of the WTO, and access to global markets are based on principles of: 'like goods' in which goods are grouped according to end use, 'national treatment' in which products from other countries must be treated like domestic goods,[60] and 'most-favoured-nation' in which each member country must be accorded the same benefits as other member countries.[61] The principle of 'like goods' largely does not allow for nation states to discriminate between commodities on the basis of anything that occurs in production or transport or precedes their end use, such as embodied energy, labour practices, or material intensity, although there is some flexibility regarding process and production methods.

The fundamental principles of trade law have had significant effects upon environmental protection policies, with environmental protection regularly coming into conflict with trade liberalisation measures.[62] Disputes under the GATT and WTO such as *US – Tuna I*,[63] *Shrimp/Turtle*,[64] *US – Gasoline*,[65] and

[58] I Feichtner, 'Critical Scholarship and Responsible Practice of International Law. How Can the Two Be Reconciled' (2016) 29 *Leiden Journal of International Law* 979, 993.

[59] ibid.

[60] See General Agreement on Tariffs and Trade (GATT), Art 3; General Agreement on Trade in Services (GATS) Art 17; Agreement on Trade-Related Aspects of Intellectual Property Rights (TRIPS) Art 3.

[61] GATT Art 1; GATS Art 2; TRIPS Art 4.

[62] M Wu and J Salzman, The Next Generation of Trade and Environment Conflicts: The Rise of Green Industrial Policy (2014) 108 *Northwestern University Law Review* 401.

[63] Panel Report, *United States – Restriction on Imports of Tuna*, DS2I/R (3 September 1991), GATT.

[64] Panel Report, *United States – Import Prohibition of Certain Shrimp and Shrimp Products*, 2.4–2.14, WT/DS58/R (15 May 1998).

[65] Panel Report, *United States – Standards for Reformulated and Conventional Gasoline*, IT, 2.5–2.7, WT/DS2/R (29 January 1996); Appellate Body Report, *United States – Standards for Reformulated and Conventional Gasoline*, IB, WT/DS2/AB/R (29 April 1996).

EC – Seal Products,[66] are examples that highlight how trade principles can come into conflict with environmental concerns.

In the *US – Tuna I* case, the United States developed an environmental policy abolishing the use of purse-seine nets for the national tuna fisheries in order to protect dolphins under the US Marine Mammal Protection Act (1972). To prevent the policy from putting US national fisheries at a competitive disadvantage, the US required all imports to meet the same standard. Mexico complained in 1991 under the GATT dispute settlement procedure that this requirement was discriminatory, arguing that the 'like goods' were being treated differently and that this was inconsistent with Articles XI, XIII and III of GATT as well as not meeting the exceptions of Article XX. Article XX sets out general exceptions to the WTO rules where such rules are 'necessary to protect public morals'; 'necessary to protect human, animal or plant life or health'; or relevant for measures 'relating to the conservation of exhaustible natural resources', as long as those measures are not applied in a way that results in discrimination between countries.

The GATT panel convened to decide the issue reported that the US could not embargo imports of tuna products due to the way in which tuna was *produced*. But the US could apply its regulations to the *quality or* content of the tuna imported. This is known as a 'product versus process' issue, which means that the process is irrelevant if the product is the same, under the requirement of 'like goods'. This GATT panel finding was ultimately not accepted and Mexico and the US held bilateral consultations outside of GATT. This complex dispute did not conclude until 2019 when the WTO Dispute Settlement Body in *US – Tuna II* found that the 'dolphin-safe' labelling requirements were compatible with the multilateral trade system and WTO compliant.[67]

Shrimp/Turtle involved similar facts but was again quite complex. In this dispute, India, Malaysia, Pakistan and Thailand brought a joint complaint against a US embargo on the importation of certain shrimp and shrimp products which was imposed for the purpose of protecting sea turtles. The embargo applied unless the country in which the shrimp were being caught legally required fisherman to use a 'turtle excluder device' (TED). The Appellate Body of the WTO found that 'we have not decided that the sovereign nations that are Members of the WTO cannot adopt effective measures to protect endangered species, such as sea turtles';[68] clearly, they can and should. With the embargo measures being legitimate under GATT Article XX, the US ultimately lost the case due to the way in which the US measures discriminated between WTO members. Countries largely in the Caribbean were provided with technical and financial assistance, whereas

[66] *European Communities – Measures Prohibiting the Importation and Marketing of Seal Products* WT/DS400/13; WT/DS401/14 (19 June 2014).

[67] *United States – Measures Concerning the Importation, Marketing and Sale of Tuna and Tuna Products* – Appellate Body Report and Panel Reports pursuant to Article 21.5 of the DSU – Action by the Dispute Settlement Body – Revision WT/DS381/49/Rev.1 (17 January 2019).

[68] *United States – Import Prohibition of Certain Shrimp and Shrimp Products*, Appellate Body Report WT/DS58/AB/R (12 October 1998), [185].

the complainant countries were not. The US ban was therefore inconsistent with GATT Article XI and not justified under GATT Article XX.

In *EC – Seal Products*, Canada made a complaint about the regulations of the European Union which prohibited the importation of seal products except in certain circumstances which included seal from hunts conducted by Inuit or Indigenous communities and for marine resource management purposes. Canada claimed that the implementation of these regulations was inconsistent with the Technical Barriers to Trade (TBT) Agreement, the GATT, and the WTO Agreement on Agriculture. The Panel found that the 'Indigenous communities' exception in the EC regulations violated Article I:1 of the GATT because an advantage granted by the European Union to seal products originating in Greenland (whose Inuit population produces practically all of its exported seal products) is not accorded immediately and unconditionally to the like products originating in Canada, where only a small percentage of seal products were Inuit produced. With respect to the 'marine resources management' exception, the panel found that it violated Article III:4 of the GATT as it was discriminatory by treating imported seal products less favourably than like domestic seal products and therefore did not meet the exception under Article XX of the GATT. On appeal, the Appellate Body largely agreed.

In all these cases, the relevant trade dispute bodies conducted a two-part analysis which is known as the balancing test. First, does the (environmental) policy serve the substantive purpose being claimed? Then, if so, the question is asked whether the measure is acting as 'a disguised restriction on international trade' or is being implemented in a discriminatory manner. In such cases the legitimacy of environmental regulation is weighed against the potential negative impact on trade.

This balancing test codifies a commodity episteme in which ecological degradation in the name of productivity and cost shifting for so-called efficiency along global value chains are neither visible nor readily included in international trade law (although there have been recent voluntary attempts at the national level).[69] Principles of 'national treatment' and 'most favoured nation' have emerged by envisioning global value chains as pathways of commodity movement, and regulation as a space for ensuring that commodities can freely move across borders. Any negotiated multi- or bilateral trade agreements must conform with these principles. The principles of international trade governance maintain and enforce commodity markets, allowing for the leveraging of state power for the purposes of market regulation and reinforcement. While trade governance does not always trump environmental policy (as the complexity of the cases above demonstrates),[70] it does assure commodity rights. As noted

[69] F Baetens, BM Hoekman and PC Mavroidis, 'Production Requirements and WTO Rules: The Case of Environmental and Labor Standards', Report prepared for the Ministry of Foreign Affairs, Netherlands (2022).

[70] Wu and Salzman (n 62).

by economic historian Slobodian,[71] neoliberal theorists have worked hard to protect commodity flows, arguing that the world must be 'flattened' for the purposes of commodity rights. This is also evidenced, for example, by pressures upon Member States to develop and adhere to international standards for goods and plant and animal products such as the Codex Alimentarius. The principles of trade law ensure that commodities can move unhindered by context, history, or knowledge of anything other than a commodity's end use. This commodity episteme can exist within current legal structures precisely because it reinforces Western ontological claims about the world as a series of discrete, separate objects, unhindered by histories, relationality, or power structures. The complex relations and entangledness of ecological knowledges are erased by the principle of 'like goods' and prevented, through principles of 'national treatment' and 'most favoured nation', from being visibilised.

It is here, within trade law and the intersections with international environmental law, that we can see the potential of cultivating a praxis of being de-principled. By engaging in contexts outside of the disciplinary silo of international environmental law and avoiding the compartmentalisation of the legal discipline, we can identify problematic assumptions that can undermine the development of earth system law. Measures designed to protect a state's natural environment or even the global commons could be challenged as being protectionist and discriminatory. To develop alternative and appropriate values and systems that directly challenge commodification economies and promote earth system law values, we can use principles as techniques to shift normative prescriptions by paying attention to the existing legal frameworks and barriers to alternative and life-sustaining legalities. We are not arguing here for an absence of principles, as to do so would risk creating space for increased forms of non-environmental protectionism that often have serious environmental outcomes, but rather to set forward an approach that makes explicit the *praxis required for systemic change*.

A de-principled approach that seeks to rupture the legal fallacies that maintain the Anthropocene, however, requires international environmental law scholars to take seriously the global political economy and to avoid the compartmentalisation that occurs within the legal discipline. Through thinking not only about principles, ideals and interests, but also about institutions, practices, legal forms and techniques, earth system law scholars can experiment with new institutional arrangements and imaginaries for global governance. It is to this imaginative exercise that we now turn and put forward some potential examples of further experimentation.

Our first example of an avenue of social change in line with earth system law within the trade space is located within what has been termed a 'new generation' of sustainability-orientated trade policies. These policies, such as forms of carbon taxation or regulating deforestation-related commodity trade, have been based

[71] Q Slobodian, *Globalists: The End of Empire and the Birth of Neoliberalism* (Cambridge MA, Harvard University Press, 2018).

on non-product related 'process and production methods' (PPMs). PPMs refer to the methods used to produce goods and services that may impact the environment, and human and animal health and safety, but are not directly related to the quality or physical characteristics of the final product.[72] For example, sustainably produced sugar, when measured by physical characteristics alone, is identical to sugar produced relying on labour in breach of human rights, or produced on deforested land. However, if the production methods are taken into account, the products can be perceived as substantially different. These 'non-product-related' PPMs are now well accepted as not being a priori illegal under WTO law.[73]

An additional avenue for experimentation could be through supporting a WTO climate waiver for national climate policies[74] under the waiver power of the WTO.[75] The waiver power allows the Ministerial Conference and the General Council to suspend WTO law and obligations on the request of a WTO member, which could allow a member to take measures (such as environmental ones) that would otherwise violate WTO law.[76] But as Bacchus[77] notes, this will be a significant political challenge, with the WTO decision-makers needing to be convinced that a WTO climate waiver is necessary, and will require trade and climate change disciplinary silos to work together.

Key to all the measures proposed above is the requirement of setting out new normative understandings that prioritise social and ecological well-being over capitalist constructions of well-being, while being attendant to the political realities that inhibit transformation and the political persuasion required for change. In the development of such cultural and political transformation, it is important to allow for understandings that challenge neo-colonialism and allow for non-universalising principles.

The examples given above demonstrate the potential for reframing WTO objectives by making use of existing legal forms and techniques. The examples explicitly challenge tacitly held assumptions about legal principles and could allow for alternative ideas of legal change to emerge and gain traction, as well as being mindful of the need to spread ideas beyond the disciplinary silo of international environmental law. De-principling trade governance must be part of re-contextualising trade law within broader social movements, lifeways, and ecologies that are subjects of and subject to that governance.

In paying attention to broader social movements, we can look to already existing examples that have sought to re-contextualise trade law beyond

[72] A Oeschger and EB Bonanomi, 'PPMs Are Back: The Rise of New Sustainability-Oriented Trade Policies Based on Process and Production Methods' (2023) 3(2) *IISD Trade and Sustainability Review*.

[73] ibid.

[74] J Bacchus, *The Case for a WTO Climate Waiver* (Centre for International Governance Innovation, 2017).

[75] Marrakesh Agreement Establishing the World Trade Organization (WTO Agreement) 15 April 1994, Art IX:3.

[76] Feichtner (n 58).

[77] Bacchus (n 74).

WTO rules. We put forward fair trade as an example of an attempt to transform trade beyond existing dominant regimes. Fair trade and alternative practices of trade subsidiarity, in which subjects of trade governance participate in formulating and iteratively negotiating that governance, do not place the state (or increasingly the corporation) as the subject of trade law, but rather allow for multiple voices, plural ontologies, and reflexive praxis, in which prices and norms are negotiated by producers and brokers directly. This makes the context, relationship, process and product visible as well as embedded in trade governance practices. Analysing fair trade through a lens of being de-principled demonstrates practices of subsidiarity, negotiation, and intentionally making space for plurality, often resulting in worker cooperatives with measurably different social and ecological outcomes for participants.[78] It also illuminates how the tools of participation, relationship, consent, and negotiation can result in collaborative markets instead of competitive market relations, a market network that includes commodities but is not mediated by them, and does not uphold a commodity episteme through hegemonic principles.

IV. Conclusion

The Anthropocene requires us to challenge dominant positivist approaches to law and identify new foundations for legal realities along with new techniques and approaches. We cannot, and never have, approached international environmental law from a mono-disciplinary framing, with international environmental law often being informed by environmental sciences. The challenge now in effecting transformation is to engage with the complexities within and between disciplines, theory and practice, as well as within and between politics, and law. The challenge in setting forward a de-principled praxis is to directly address the positivist framing of law that has been exported around the world through the processes of colonisation, development and globalisation and that 'signals a self-serving set of rules that imperialize the desires of the powerful',[79] and to identify necessarily incomplete exemplars that prioritise social and ecological well-being and directly challenge a neoliberal international system.

The Gramscian concept of the integral state has been invoked by scholars and activists in transformative movements, such as degrowth, agroecology and

[78] A Le Mare, 'The Impact of Fair Trade on Social and Economic Development: A Review of the Literature' (2008) 2(6) *Geography Compass* 1922; AC Dammert and S Mohan, 'A Survey of the Economics of Fair Trade' (2015) 29 *Journal of Economic Surveys* 855.

[79] A Escobar, 'Transiciones: A Space for Research and Design for Transitions to the Pluriverse' (2015) 13(1) *Design Philosophy Papers* 13, 19. See also J Law, 'What's Wrong with a One-World World?' (2015) 16 *Distinktion: Journal of Social Theory* 126; J Borrows, 'Heroes, Tricksters, Monsters, and Caretakers: Indigenous Law and Legal Education' (2016) 61 *McGill Law Journal* 795; A Mills, 'The Lifeworlds of Law: On Revitalizing Indigenous Legal Orders Today' (2016) 61 *McGill Law Journal* 847.

emancipatory education, to highlight the ways in which resituating the state as a relationship between civil and political society and the institutions that maintain these varied communities is itself part of a transformative process. To de-principle law is to consider law in a corollary manner, as something that is integral to and constitutive of the social and political practices and structures of its moment. It also requires paying close attention to prioritising the democratic common good and social and ecological well-being in our legal structures, with the direct participation of local communities (in line with their specific social, ecological and cultural understandings) to determine what the common good looks like from place to place and over time. The outcome of such collective creation and praxis cannot be known. The challenge will be to support multiple strategies and approaches and to promote and protect pluralist democracies. A praxis of being de-principled may help to do some of this work.

PART III

Alternative Worldviews and New Ethics Shaping Earth System Law

6

The Imperative Need for a New Relational Ethic to Underpin Earth System Law for the Anthropocene

KAREN MORROW

I. Introduction – Law, the Earth System and the Ambiguous Anthropocene

While growing understanding of the earth system and its interlocked natural and human dimensions requires a change in our ways of doing the business of law and governance, and above all a shift from what we now know to be an outmoded, state-centric international law model to a new framework of earth system law that is fit to engage with planetary-scale challenges,[1] in most circles the urgency of this need is not recognised. This chapter argues that a paradigm shift is required and that it must be informed by an expanded conception of human relationality, viewing humanity as in relationship with the Earth on which we depend and in relation with one another as a species.

The complexity and urgency of such a transition invoke a dense and increasingly pressing mix of practical and ethical considerations which cannot be addressed by existing law and governance arrangements that pit state against state in ways that run counter to planetary- and species-level flourishing. Instead, law and governance that work for the earth system are urgently required as we begin to come to terms with living in the Anthropocene and humanity's unique role as a planet-shaping species. Indeed, the rapidly developing earth system law episteme and its evolving framework, focused on addressing planetary governance challenges, is instructive to further explore viable futures for humanity.

The Anthropocene itself is, even from first principles, ambiguous: do we live in it or not? The answer to this question is also ambiguous – it depends on who you ask. After a decade and a half of research and discussion, in March 2024 the body

[1] LJ Kotzé and RE Kim, 'Towards Planetary Nexus Governance in the Anthropocene: An Earth System Law Perspective' (2022) 13 *Global Policy* 86.

charged with determining whether or not the Anthropocene qualifies as a geological epoch, the Subcommission on Quaternary Stratigraphy of the International Commission on Stratigraphy, voted that it does not. However, the vote itself was mired in controversy, and it seems doubtful that the matter is settled. In any case, other geologists, including the chair and vice-chair of the Subcommission (unhappy with proceedings and having abstained from the vote) pithily stated: 'It's real, it's already made geology, and it won't go away. Best to acknowledge it, to help us cope with its consequences'.[2]

This view coincides with broader views of the Anthropocene,[3] which – geology aside – understand it to be a new age, simultaneously quotidian and epochal in nature, characterised by anthropogenic threats to human flourishing operating on a global scale. Refashioning law to better fit what we now understand about what it is to be human in the new world that we are making, represents a crucially important element in this process,[4] but in order to do so, we must interrogate the ethics and principles that inform current practice to grasp what this requires.

The discussion that follows focuses on some additional ambiguities of the Anthropocene. It begins in section II by setting out earth system science as an Anthropocene-appropriate framing for understanding the human–Earth relationship, briefly considering the human-facing dimensions of the Anthropocene, and the urgent need to address practices infringing planetary boundaries as impinging on the safe operating space for humanity that has characterised the Holocene.[5] In section III, the chapter discusses the unique position of human responsibility in the Anthropocene, looking first at humanity as threat-maker, responsible for generating negative planetary impacts and the attitudes, ethics and conduct that created and continue them. It goes on to consider humanity's unique potential to function as a threat-breaker and how this requires an urgent and drastic recalibration of how we view the human–Earth relationship.[6] In section IV, the chapter considers a care-based ethic as an alternative basis for the human–Earth relationship, identifying and discussing three core elements of such an approach: responsibility, relationality and responsiveness. In section V it examines the most basic application required of a normative ethical imperative – harm prevention – and compares the 'first do no harm' principle of the Hippocratic oath in medicine with the 'no-harm' principle in international

[2] S Turner, C Waters, J Salasiewicz and MJ Head, 'What the Anthropocene's Critics Overlook – and Why It Really Should Be a New Geological Epoch', *The Conversation*, 12 March 2024: https://theconversation.com/what-the-anthropocenes-critics-overlook-and-why-it-really-should-be-a-new-geological-epoch-225493.

[3] K Morrow, 'Tackling Climate Change and Gender Justice – Integral; Not Optional' (2021) 11(1) *Oñati Socio-Legal Series* 207.

[4] LJ Kotzé, 'Earth System Law for the Anthropocene: Rethinking Environmental Law Alongside the Earth System Metaphor' (2020) 11 *Transnational Legal Theory* 75.

[5] W Steffen, 'Planetary Boundaries: Guiding Human Development on a Changing Planet' (2020) 347 *Science* 1259855.

[6] S Hartman and P Degeorges, '"DON'T PANIC": Fear and Acceptance in the Anthropocene' (2019) 26 *Interdisciplinary Studies in Literature and Environment* 256.

environmental law in this regard. It concludes that the key difference between these principles lies not in their approach, but rather in the ethical underpinnings that orient their application. In consequence it posits extending a new (or, more accurately, *renewed*) care-based, relational ethic as the necessary foundation for a re-set of the human–Earth relationship. It considers how responsibility, relationality and responsiveness could play out, responding to an eco-realistic view of humanity's place in the earth system and the consequent need to be circumspect in our dealings with it. In section VI, the chapter considers how a care-based relational ethic could be applied in the context of considering significant Earth system-level interventions, using geoengineering to ameliorate polar ice-melt as an example, to place harm prevention to the fore.

As would be expected, increasing support for planetary-scale geoengineering is emerging in some quarters (considered below) and this is only likely to gain weight and prominence as the impacts of the Anthropocene become ever more apparent. The same can be said for opposition to such projects, prompting calls for them to be banned outright for fear of disaster spawned by a perpetuation of the hubris and blind technological optimism that has led humanity to its present pass.[7] Past experience suggests that those on the side of banning planetary-scale geoengineering recommend the safest course. However, history also suggests that the voices of caution are unlikely to prevail and that some nation states and/ or commercial actors will seek to pursue geoengineering projects. Such schemes are not adequately addressed by international law,[8] their impacts extending across the earth system and potentially affecting numerous states – for good or ill. With that in mind it is imperative that our approach to law and governance is prepared for decision-making on these activities as a matter of planetary concern. Law and governance fit to ensure the functioning and flourishing of the earth system and humanity as a species are urgently needed. This chapter considers what ethical underpinnings would need to be put in place to enable earth system law to rise to the challenge.

II. Earth System Science – A Necessary Framing for Viewing the Anthropocene

Grasping the implications of earth system science, adopting an integrative view of the human-Earth relationship that encapsulates its intertwined non-human and human components, is central to understanding both the roots of the

[7] J Gupta and others, 'Earth System Boundaries and Earth System Justice: Sharing the Ecospace' (2024) 33(7) *Environmental Politics* 1286.

[8] H Du, *An International Legal Framework for Geoengineering: Managing the Risks of an Emerging Technology* (Abingdon-on-Thames, Routledge, 2018); A Gupta and others, 'Towards a Non-Use Regime on Solar Geoengineering: Lessons from International Law and Governance' (2024) 13(2) *Transnational Environmental Law* 368.

Anthropocene and how we need to adapt our ways of being in the world to negotiate it.[9] Likewise, Harari's[10] observation that: 'In the Anthropocene, the planet became for the first time a single ecological unit', is germane and the discussion that follows must ultimately take a planetary bent. Also foundational to the task in hand is the recognition that the Anthropocene is at root bifurcated, simultaneously positioning humanity as a world-breaking and 'world-making' species.[11] It is the deepest of ironies that humanity is in many ways in the vanguard of those most threatened by the world that we are making. The Anthropocene planetary re-set, in ending the relative perceived Holocene stability which has supported our species for its entire history, and the emerging earth system instabilities characterising the Anthropocene, are already threatening humanity by constraining human flourishing. Even before we consider the more extreme manifestations of the Anthropocene – tipping points and tipping cascades[12] – it seems set to hugely diminish both human quality of life and numbers. The range of vulnerabilities along this continuum is shared with many (though not all) other living beings. Life will go on, though it may – not for the first time in planetary history – be radically reconfigured; and we cannot assume that humanity will be among the species that will survive, let alone flourish in this age to which we have given our name.

Human vulnerability in the Anthropocene is simultaneously unique in adding a social and relational dimension to species survival;[13] the former is exclusively inter-human, the latter is additionally shared with other species with whom we are inextricably enmeshed. There are a number of possible responses to this entanglement, with post-modern new materialist thought, for example, ascribing agency to other species and even to the non-living world in a decisive rejection of human exceptionalism.[14] However, adopting this type of ontologically flat approach is arguably counterproductive, as it facilitates the denial of the particular nature and scope of human agency and allows for the evasion of human responsibility for both originating the Anthropocene and responding to it. To do so misses the core essence of the Anthropocene, for, as Hamilton,[15] puts it with characteristic bluntness: 'We look across the unbridgeable gulf that separates us from other beings: it is the gulf of responsibility. We have it; they don't'.

[9] F Biermann, 'The Future of 'Environmental' Policy in the Anthropocene: Time for a Paradigm Shift' (2021) 30 *Environmental Politics* 61; YN Harari, *Homo Deus: A Brief History of Tomorrow* (New York, Vintage, 2016) 86.

[10] YN Harari, *Homo Deus: A Brief History of Tomorrow* (London, Vintage, 2016) 86.

[11] C Hamilton, *Defiant Earth: The Fate of Humans in the Anthropocene* (Cambridge, Polity Press, 2017) 52.

[12] DI Armstrong McKay, 'Exceeding 1.5°C. Global Warming Could Trigger Multiple Climate Tipping Points' (2022) 377 *Science* eabn7950.

[13] LJ Kotzé, 'The Anthropocene, Earth System Vulnerability and Socio-Ecological Injustice in an Age of Human Rights' (2019) 10 *Journal of Human Rights and the Environment* 62.

[14] MH Benson, 'New Materialism: An Ontology for the Anthropocene' (2019) 59 *Natural Resources Journal* 251.

[15] Hamilton (n 11) 12.

III. Human Agency in the Anthropocene

A. Humanity: World-Maker and World-Breaker

Although presented by some as a 'great rupture',[16] the Anthropocene is more logically regarded as combining the consequences of doing the business of humanity as we have long done, exploiting the world around us to our own ends, with the increasingly apparent inability of crucial elements of the altering earth system to continue to tolerate this. The dual human cause and consequences of the Anthropocene raise interesting and evolving considerations pertaining to human agency and responsibility. Some indicators of the Anthropocene, such as evidence of nuclear testing appearing in the fossil record,[17] are not readily attributable or even apparent to ordinary people; nor, for the most part, are their impacts obvious in everyday life. The emergent, maturing threats posed by the Anthropocene today, however, differ from their precursors in important ways: they are often mundane in their origins, implicate the bulk of humanity, albeit to highly varying degrees,[18] and are increasingly dramatic in their effects, which are readily observable and increasingly impinging on many aspects of human life. Furthermore, the Anthropocene compounds long-known anthropogenic interferences – for example, biodiversity depletion – with new/ emerging ones such as interference with the phosphorus and nitrogen cycles, all interacting and interconnecting at the earth system level.[19]

B. Mastery: An Ethic of Hierarchy and Exploitation

The Anthropocene is attributable not just to human behaviours, but also to the attitudes that underpin them that express how humanity views the earth system and its place in relation to it. The ongoing, multiple, interconnected, and above all *cumulative*, threats to the Holocene setting of the earth system, rooted in anthropogenic resource depletion and pollution, are now rendering the future unpredictable. This amply demonstrates that we have long deluded ourselves as to what constitutes a viable relationship between humanity and planet Earth. Foundationally, this has, since the Enlightenment, been characterised by a notional split between humanity and the rest of the biosphere, accompanied by the assumed superiority of the former over the latter. This has resulted in a hierarchical, exploitative basis for interactions between humanity and the Earth, succinctly characterised in what Val

[16] ibid.

[17] SL Lewis and MA Maslin, 'A Transparent Framework for Defining the Anthropocene Epoch' (2015) 2 *The Anthropocene Review* 128.

[18] S Dalby, 'Framing the Anthropocene: The Good, the Bad and the Ugly' (2016) 3 *The Anthropocene Review* 33.

[19] Steffen (n 5).

Plumwood[20] terms the 'paradigm of mastery'. This instrumental treatment of the Earth reached its zenith in modernity.

Human mastery over the environment has, however, always been illusory, as evidenced not only by natural disasters, but also by the frequent unforeseen consequences of human actions. The Anthropocene makes it clear that no semblance of human control over the environment can be upheld while human actions threaten the subsistence of earth system conditions and functions that are favourable to our own species and many other living beings. The advent of the Anthropocene gives the lie to the foundational hierarchical dualism that has come to dominate the human–Earth relationship. Humanity's position may be unique in the biosphere – no other species can interfere with the earth system on a geological scale – but our uniqueness neither removes us from nature nor insulates us from the consequences of our actions and inaction towards it.[21]

For humanity, the Anthropocene as it is developing, is a self-inflicted threat, necessitating change on our part as this is the only agency that we have to bring to bear on the acts and omissions that have brought us to this point. For the earth system, the Anthropocene is a matter of cause and effect – not an expression of anger,[22] or even revenge.[23] While ascribing such attributes dramatises what is at stake in relational terms, which is helpful in cultivating approaches that no longer see the earth system as the inert backdrop to the human drama, they also unhelpfully anthropomorphise its responses to anthropogenic impacts, drawing focus from the unique role of humanity in this context.

C. The Anthropocene and the End of Mastery

Hamilton[24] argues that the Anthropocene came about 'more or less consciously'; but this oversimplifies the case. Until quite recently it would have been possible to argue that the adverse impacts of the Anthropocene were by-products of human enterprise and inadvertent, or at worst negligent: this fiction is no longer tenable. While many of the adverse impacts of the Anthropocene remain unintended, humanity is not thereby absolved of responsibility for them, as our state of knowledge now renders our behaviour reckless, involving unreasonable or unjustified risk-taking. In conceptualising the Anthropocene in an educative light it behoves us to reflect on how we reached this point, and in consequence to reorient our values and behaviours to take responsibility for anthropogenic impacts, repairing where we can and adapting where we cannot, to offer the best option for a viable future.

[20] V Plumwood, *Feminism and the Mastery of Nature* (London, Routledge, 1993).
[21] Hamilton (n 11) 131.
[22] ibid 99.
[23] J Lovelock, *Gaia: A New Look at Life on Earth* (Oxford, Oxford University Press, 2000).
[24] Hamilton (n 11) 103.

We must therefore engage with profound questions, starting with interrogating anthropocentrism, as it is arguable that even our most ambitious attempts at ecocentrism betray human biases. We tend, for example, to cast appropriate treatment for non-human others after our own image, deploying the language of agency or rights,[25] which originate and sit most easily in the context of human endeavours.[26] Acknowledging that anthropocentrism is a default position that is difficult (and perhaps impossible) to escape, it is perhaps more useful to ask if it may be adapted to better fit our understanding of humanity's place within the earth system in the Anthropocene. Anthropocentrism need not be viewed as synonymous with human chauvinism and (contrary to some views),[27] it can play a positive role in invoking responsibility for human actions. What may be understood as a contextualised anthropocentrism could serve as an important stage in progressing a shift away from a disastrous, myopic, narrowly instrumental treatment of the earth system, to a more ecologically realistic and sustainable stance. Hamilton's conception of a 'new anthropocentrism' has much to offer in this regard, distinguishing between what he terms 'monstrous anthropocentrism' that 'elevates the human to an exalted place of power-without-responsibility', and a 'humble anthropocentrism'.[28] Hamilton's new anthropocentrism is built on the acknowledgement that while human agency now operates at a planetary level, it is: 'always constrained by its embeddedness in the processes of nature'.[29] This type of anthropocentrism also explicitly recognises that the 'special place humans occupy as the world-making creature, rather than conferring entitlement to the Earth … imposes unique responsibility for it'.[30] In short, humble anthropocentrism urges us to eschew dualism and mastery, replacing them with embeddedness and responsibility.

There is curative potential in reconstituting the human–Earth relationship based on taking responsibility for human actions and their impacts, as expressed through a care-based relational ethic, to fashion a more sustainable incarnation of the human-Earth relationship. While such a change would be radical in some ways, by remaining broadly anthropocentric in its orientation and drawing on established inter-human ethics of care approaches, it is less so in others. As such, it would present a useful step towards developing an integrated ethical framework to address the enmeshed concerns of humanity and other constituents of the Earth system. In so doing, it does not suggest a destination so much as a practicable direction of travel to meet an urgent need.

[25] Benson (n 14) 258–59.

[26] Hartman and Degeorges (n 6) 468–69.

[27] H Kopnina, 'Anthropocentrism: More than Just a Misunderstood Problem' (2018) 31 *Journal of Agricultural Environmental Ethics* 109.

[28] Hamilton (n 11) 44.

[29] ibid 51.

[30] ibid 54.

IV. Relational Care-based Ethics

A. Sustainable Development – A Failed Attempt at a New Ethic

Recognition that the human–Earth relationship requires radical reframing to fit practice to ecological reality is not new and predates current debate around the Anthropocene. On its face, sustainable development – the exhaustively researched creation of the World Commission on Environment and Development's (WCED) report, *Our Common Future* – recognised the need for and sought precisely the sort of ethical re-set required. It defined sustainable development as meeting

> the needs of the present without compromising the ability of future generations to meet their own needs. The concept of sustainable development does imply limits – not absolute limits but limitations imposed by the present state of technology and social organization on environmental resources and by the ability of the biosphere to absorb the effects of human activities.[31]

Defined thus, the Brundtland conception of sustainability contains the core elements that would be required for the necessary ethical re-set to counter the paradigm of mastery, inferring relationality (both inter-human and human–Earth), and responsibility as crucial in recognising and responding to environmental limits and their implications for people and planet. However, while the first part of this statement is now a well-worn aphorism; the second, the necessary acknowledgement of the multiple dimensions of limits which could have made a stark difference to our understanding of the human–Earth relationship, is known only to those who have read the report closely. The reasons for this are compellingly expressed by Jim MacNeil, the Secretary General to the WCED, who observes: 'Neither governments nor industries wanted to hear their activities described as *un*sustainable … And unfortunately, absent any notion of limits, our intergenerational "definition" lent itself to … manipulation'.[32]

As popularly understood, sustainable development actually represents an abnegation of human responsibility for environmental degradation and as such, it inevitably failed to reset the human–Earth relationship. Sustainable development instead became used to effectively normalise the 'business as usual' approach it ostensibly sought to replace.[33] It is also arguable that, even

[31] World Commission on Environment and Development (WCED), *Report of the World Commission on Environment and Development: Our Common Future* (1987) 16.

[32] J MacNeill, 'Foreword' in I Borowy, *Defining Sustainable Development for Our Common Future: A History of the World Commission on Environment and Development* (Abingdon-on-Thames, Routledge, 2014) ix.

[33] NK Dawe and KL Ryan, 'The Faulty Three-Legged-Stool Model of Sustainable Development' (2003) 17 *Conservation Biology* 1458.

if sustainable development had been fully pursued, the famous 'three pillars' approach that it popularised, in placing the environment as coequal with social and economic issues, rather than foundational to them, was never ecologically realistic.[34] Sustainable development, far from acting as a reset for the human–Earth relationship, has instead been used to continue the exploitative paradigm of mastery.[35]

Accepting responsibility for the impact of an exploitative ethic on the plight of the planet and non-privileged humans in principle, and addressing its ramifications for change in practice, requiring preventative, informed self-control, and responses to damage already done, remain extremely far apart. However, if the half-hearted pursuit of sustainable development saw the adoption of an ecologically realistic reformulation of the human–Earth relationship deferred, the Anthropocene makes the need for such a shift imperative. It is argued here that a new, ecologically realistic approach towards human responsibility, founded on a relational, care-based ethic, can furnish the necessary ethical basis to inform and orient earth system law by explicitly articulating the reality of the human–Earth relationship as foundational to it.

B. Care-based Ethics

If a new ethic that eschews dualism and exploitation and heeds the relational foundation of what it means to be human in the environment is required to provide an explicit rationale for human actions in the Anthropocene, what might this look like? Shifting to a care-based approach could offer much in informing the answer to this question. While, as discussed briefly below, originating in new feminist ethics of interpersonal relationships, ethics of care approaches as an ethical grounding for decision-making and conduct, in rejecting hitherto dominant notions of power and entitlement, are capable of much broader application.[36] Thus relational, care-based ethics could offer a viable framing for the human–earth system relationship. This would not require a shift as radical as, for example, adopting ecocentrism, instead charting a much more prosaic course in pursuing an expanded idea of human self-interest as being rooted in care for the environment, which would be sufficient to inform the required ethical re-set in the first instance.

The ethics of care emerged in Carol Gilligan's pioneering work in psychology, wherein it articulated an alternative to hegemonic rights and justice-based moral philosophy as the basis for decision-making,[37] which is particularly interesting

[34] ibid 1459.

[35] LJ Kotzé and S Adelman, 'Environmental Law and the Unsustainability of Sustainable Development: A Tale of Disenchantment and of Hope' (2023) 34 *Law & Critique* 227.

[36] V Held, *The Ethics of Care: Personal, Political, and Global* (Oxford, Oxford University Press, 2006) 150.

[37] C Gilligan, *In a Different Voice: Psychological Theory and Women's Development* (Cambridge MA, Harvard University Press 1982).

for present purposes. Subsequent authors have viewed the two ethical systems as complementary rather than alternatives, rejecting a single grand narrative.[38] Nevertheless, Gilligan's core idea remains highly salient in addressing lacunae in approaching ethical challenges. The ethics of care she crafted was in essence: situated/ contextual, relational, dialogic, deductive, and responsive.[39] Gilligan's work located ethics of care approaches in interpersonal relations, but its core conceptual foundations, relationship and responsibility, are capable of adaptation and can extend to groups, up to and including the global level.[40] Likewise, the relational and responsibility axes, as the basis of moral obligation, can extend beyond humans to encapsulate other types of vulnerable subject[41] and systemic concerns.[42]

Thus, the environment, in being vulnerable to the overweening effects of human agency, can be viewed as an appropriate object of care at all levels from the local to the planetary. Ultimately, recognising that the Anthropocene is the product of human agency places responsibility for it with humanity. This is not to say that all of humanity is either equally implicated in the acts and omissions that are forging the Anthropocene, or, in the short term at least, congruently exposed to its impacts.[43] However, ultimately, humanity (individually and collectively) and the earth system are interdependent; we are in relation. Furthermore, human dependence on the environment for all that we have and all that we are means that Earth-care is inextricably bound up with the familiar obligations of inter-human care for both present and future generations.[44]

C. The Core Elements of an Ethics of Care-based Approach

While the current chapter will not accommodate a fully developed account of an ethics of care-based approach to the human–Earth relationship, it will allow consideration of its three co-requisite foundational elements: responsibility, relationality, and responsiveness. These issues are crucial to an earth system law approach. Responsibility points to the basis for law that considers, controls and remediates (or where this is not possible – ameliorates) the adverse impacts of human agency on the Earth system. Relationality frames a basis for addressing the reciprocal ramifications of anthropogenic impacts for both human–Earth and

[38] Held (n 36) 15.
[39] Gilligan (n 37).
[40] Held (n 36) 153.
[41] HO Stensota, 'Public Ethics of Care – A General Public Ethics' (2015) 9 *Ethics and Social Welfare* 183.
[42] Held (n 36).
[43] Dalby (n 18).
[44] K Morrow, 'The Fragility of Climate, Human Responsibility and Finding the Impetus to Act Decisively – Investigating the Potential of the Ethics of Care' in J Jaria-Manzano and S Borràs (eds), *Research Handbook on Global Climate Constitutionalism* (Cheltenham, Edward Elgar Publishing, 2019).

inter-human interactions. Responsiveness speaks to the imperative to act with speed (further temporising is both immoral and compounds the magnitude of the challenges we face) but also with justice to other components of the earth system and humanity as a species.

(i) Responsibility

The recognition of responsibility is foundational to a care-based ethic. If, as considered above, the role of human agency and the unsustainable footing of a human–Earth relationship based on exploitation was already clear by the early 1990s, it has only become more apparent in the interim. Responsibility is grounded in concrete scientific attribution of key aspects of the Anthropocene to human actions and this is growing apace.[45] However, it is clear that, even now, factual attribution has not cut through sufficiently to ascribe moral, political, and legal responsibility for key Anthropocene threats, prompting necessary change in dominant human attitudes and conduct towards the environment. The signal failure of international law to deliver the necessary progress in key areas makes it is abundantly clear that scientific attribution is not yet equated with taking responsibility for human actions.[46]

Where the notion of responsibility appears explicitly in international treaty law, it tends to do so in a very particular guise, using the politically and legally expedient language of the principle of 'common but differentiated responsibilities' (CBDR).[47] CBDR, although pre-dating its current usage,[48] is ubiquitous in multilateral environmental agreements. In principle the concept of CBDR stands to serve the cause of inter-human equity and justice, placing greater obligations to act on developed nations that have historically been responsible for the environmental exploitation that has prompted the Anthropocene. In practice, though, the conception of responsibility involved in CBDR is very limited, generally involving the unilateral undertaking by developed countries of (inadequate) financial commitments to developing countries and even this is consistently underdelivered.[49] In turn, the dearth of finance has inevitably seen developing nations continue to pursue unsustainable development. Essentially, the shared

[45] Intergovernmental Panel on Climate Change (IPCC), *Climate Change 2021: The Physical Science Basis*, https://www.ipcc.ch/report/ar6/wg1/; Intergovernmental Science-Policy Platform on Biodiversity and Ecosystem Services (IPBES), *Global Assessment Report on Biodiversity and Ecosystem Services*, https://doi.org/10.5281/zenodo.3831673.

[46] United Nations Environment Programme (UNEP), *Global Environment Outlook 6: Healthy Planet, Healthy People*, chapters 5–6, https://www.unep.org/resources/global-environment-outlook-6.

[47] V Barral, 'Common but Differentiated Responsibilities and Justice: Broadening the Notion of Responsibility in International Law' in H Hansen-Magnusson and A Vetterlein (eds), *The Rise of Responsibility in World Politics* (Cambridge, Cambridge University Press, 2020).

[48] M Williams and MF Montes, 'Common but Differentiated Responsibilities: Which Way Forward?' (2017) 59 *Development* 114.

[49] M Kolmaš, 'The Failure of CBDR in Global Environmental Politics' (2023) 23 *Global Environmental Politics* 11.

fiction that human responsibility for planetary degradation lies elsewhere means that action to address the Anthropocene is stymied. CBDR, as currently understood, is not sufficient to meet the challenges of the Anthropocene; nor can it play the sort of role that would be required of it by earth system law. To function as required, CBDR would need to be radically changed from a comparatively nebulous principle into a legally enforceable obligation aligning with imposing moral, political, and legal responsibility for human actions (historic and ongoing) for causing harm to the Earth system.[50] Experience shows that such a move would be contested on all sides.[51]

In rare cases, there are potentially promising signs of practical progress on questions of responsibility for the societal impacts of environmental harms. We can see an example in the establishment of the new loss and damage fund under the United Nations Framework Convention on Climate Change (UNFCCC). Significantly though, the politically and legally unpalatable (to developed nations at least)[52] notion of responsibility is not actually articulated as the basis for action at any stage. As is typically the case, funds are voluntarily committed, and the record on delivery of previously promised resources does not inspire confidence that they will actually be delivered.[53] The contortions involved in eschewing even the language of responsibility in this limited guise are considerable, and while they have not ultimately prevented action, they have certainly limited it. Likewise, while voluntaristic loss and damage initiatives can help,[54] they do not suffice to deal with the scale of the challenges we already face, and they will certainly not be adequate to address future needs. We need to move swiftly beyond this sort of equivocation to accept the invocation of responsibility as a basis to act regarding the harms in question. If we can achieve this vis-à-vis societal harms, this may ultimately pave the way for the broader invocation of responsibility for environmental harms.

Even on the very rare occasions where responsibility is ostensibly centre stage in international law, for example, in the soft law 1997 United Nations Educational, Scientific and Cultural Organization Declaration on the Responsibilities of the Present Generations Towards Future Generations,[55] it has been understood in

[50] See also Kotzé, Angstadt and Kim, Chapter 2 in this book.

[51] Kolmaš (n 49).

[52] P Bhandari, N Warszawski, D Cogan and R Gerholdt, 'What Is "Loss and Damage" from Climate Change? 8 Key Questions, Answered' (2022) *World Resources Institute Insights*, updated 5 May 2025, https://www.wri.org/insights/loss-damage-climate-change.

[53] Christian Aid, *The Loss and Damage Fund: Where Does the Money Come From?* https://www.christianaid.org.uk/sites/default/files/2023-04/the-loss-and-damage-fund_final.pdf.

[54] K Cheng, 'From Scotland to Malawi: Climate Survivors Are Rebuilding with World First Loss and Damage Fund', *The Guardian*, 31 July 2024, https://www.theguardian.com/global-development/article/2024/jul/31/loss-and-damage-how-the-first-climate-survivors-to-receive-funds-are-rebuilding-their-lives-in-malawi.

[55] UNESCO, *Declaration on the Responsibilities of the Present Generations Towards Future Generations*, https://www.unesco.org/en/legal-affairs/declaration-responsibilities-present-generations-towards-future-generations.

limited terms, as primarily an inter-human rather than a human–Earth obligation. Of the 12 articles of the Declaration, 11 are directly focused on human interests. Only Article 5 – Protection of the Environment – is ostensibly concerned with the environment, but it takes an entirely instrumental view of it, framing coverage around human priorities: 'In order to ensure that future generations benefit from the richness of the Earth's ecosystems, the present generations should strive for sustainable development and preserve living conditions, particularly the quality and integrity of the environment'.[56] The content of the provision is in fact more closely allied to an ethic of exploitation than care. In any case, responsibility has remained, at best, a peripheral issue in this sphere of international law.[57] The rapidly advancing threats of the Anthropocene make continuing such evasion at best unwise, and it is imperative to revisit and legally mainstream human responsibility for it. Acting as a new legal paradigm to envision law for the Anthropocene, earth system law could provide the necessary vehicle to achieve this.

(ii) *Relationality*

An environmentally applied ethics of care is, as with any care-oriented approach,[58] characterised as inherently relational; in this case it encapsulates inter-human and human–Earth relationships, expressed in terms of connection and vulnerability. In the context of inter-human views of relationality, vulnerability tends to be (relatively speaking) conceived of as a one-sided concept. Broadly speaking, one party to the relationship needs care because of vulnerability and the other offers care in response.[59] In an Anthropocene environmental context, however, vulnerability is more complex than this, encapsulating but extending beyond inter-human issues into the complex constellations of human–Earth relationships.[60] As the anthropogenic threats of the Anthropocene materialise, relationality is born of ecological realism and requires that humanity recognises and acts in acknowledgment of being situated in the earth system that is vulnerable to change and re-shaping itself in response to human agency, which in turn renders our species vulnerable by ending the Holocene conditions under which we have flourished.[61] Ultimately the Anthropocene represents the apogee of human power and its nadir, as an anthropocentric threat: 'The planet will survive, in changed form no doubt, but it will survive. The question is whether we will be here to witness it'.[62]

[56] ibid 5.1.

[57] K Morrow, 'Of Human Responsibility: Considering the Human/Environment Relationship and Ecosystems in the Anthropocene' in LJ Kotzé (ed), *Environmental Law and Governance for the Anthropocene* (Oxford, Hart Publishing, 2017).

[58] Held (n 36) 57.

[59] Gilligan (n 37).

[60] Morrow, 'The Fragility of Climate' (n 44).

[61] Steffen (n 5) 737.

[62] C Figueres and T Rivett-Carnac, *The Future We Choose: Surviving the Climate Crisis* (Stockholm, Manilla Press, 2020) 10.

That humanity is altering the earth system in the Anthropocene is a given; so too is the fact that, as currently manifesting, Anthropocene conditions threaten humanity. At the same time, this understanding presents an opportunity, for 'our maturing ecological awareness [and] … opens up new possibilities for reconnecting with the world.[63] In addition to responsibility (considered above) relationality, itself understood in terms of interdependence and mutual but distinct vulnerability, must be addressed to place the human–earth system relationship on a viable footing. Hartman and Degeorges also view what I have termed relationality and responsibility as inextricably bound: 'Caring means not neglecting our relationships of dependence and interdependence as we rely on what is also reliant on us'.[64]

(iii) Responsiveness

Finally, to complete the core of an ethics of care-based approach, it is necessary to address what we have hitherto neglected in basing the human–Earth relationship on exploitation and the myth of mastery. Responsiveness provides the practical link between responsibility, relationality and reality. In an environmentally applied ethics of care a recognition of responsibility, and even an understanding of its real-world inter-human and environmental relationality, is insufficient. Responsibility and relationality must prompt responsiveness.

As a starting point, tackling the threats of the Anthropocene at base requires ecological realism. This requires significantly more thorough and ambitious engagement with planetary boundaries than that offered by international law. The concerns in question being planetary – understood as extending to the earth system – they cannot be either understood or addressed in the purely human transnational and/ or international terms of international law as currently practised.[65] The challenges involved in shifting to a planetary framing are undoubtedly immense, necessitating unprecedented global agreement on how to deal with environmental limits, and meaningful action to do so – but they are also a matter of necessity, not choice. The advent of the Anthropocene, its damaging encroachments on the Earth system, and the need for self-restraint on the part of humanity, are matters of survival that require truly global action to succeed and 'buy-in' to this must be secured.

What responsiveness requires will vary for different actors, though discussion here will focus only on states. Insofar as the global application of an ethics of care is concerned, while Article 2 of the United Nations Charter invokes the sovereign equality of states,[66] the fault lines of inequality and injustice permeate international law generally and environmental law in particular, and while

[63] Hartman and Degeorges (n 6) 465.
[64] ibid 467.
[65] D French and LJ Kotzé (eds), *Research Handbook on Law, Governance and Planetary Boundaries* (Cheltenham, Edward Elgar Publishing, 2021).
[66] United Nations Charter 1945.

arguments about them are well-worn, they are nowhere close to being resolved.[67] The Anthropocene only amplifies this long-established debate. Thus, the content and extent of care-based obligations pertaining to states must be responsibility and capabilities based, and multi-scalar in reach. A state's environmental care-based obligations to its people and its environment apply internally, as short-term abuse of sovereign entitlements by states can undermine the safe operating space available for their population.[68] In addition, collective societal interests in the safe operating space overlap with individual human rights concerns but are not easily or adequately addressed by human rights law, which focuses primarily on the rights of individuals. This makes care-based obligations an attractive alternative route to secure a state's responsibility for optimal environmental conditions within its borders.[69]

Discussion here, however, will focus on the fact acknowledged in Principle 2 of the Rio Declaration on Environment and Development[70] (see further below), that states' behaviour has impacts on other states and the broader environment. As we now know, these impacts are no longer only cross-border, as they were always perceived to be, but extend to the earth system at a planetary level; even to outer space.[71] This knowledge requires a revised approach to Principle 2; responsiveness to responsibility and relationality would acknowledge limits on state sovereignty on the basis that no state is entitled to undermine planetary systems to the detriment of their ability to support human flourishing and/ or to compromise the ability of any state to secure a safe operating space for its citizens. Although space precludes discussion here, on a like basis, the application of an ethics of care-based approach would also necessarily invoke an expansive temporal dimension for states' care obligations, reaching forward to embrace future generations to secure a safe operating space for those who will succeed us.[72]

V. Harm Prevention

The most basic tenet of humanity taking responsibility for its acts and omissions and the consequences is that harm prevention is placed centre stage. Thus, a central issue to be addressed by a care-based approach to the planet lies in

[67] CD Stone, 'Common but Differentiated Responsibilities in International Law' (2004) 98 *American Journal of International Law* 276; See also Leach, Chapter 4 in this book.

[68] K Morrow, 'Human Rights and the Environment: Substantive Rights' in M Fitzmaurice, M Brus and P Merkouris (eds), *Research Handbook on International Environmental Law* (Cheltenham, Edward Elgar Publishing, 2021).

[69] ibid.

[70] United Nations Conference on Environment and Development (UNCED), *Report of the United Nations Conference on Environment and Development* (1992) vol I, Annex I.

[71] Y Xiao-Shan and RE Kim, 'Towards earth-space governance in a multi-planetary era' (2023) 16 *Earth System Governance* 100173.

[72] Morrow, 'Human Rights and the Environment: Substantive Rights' (n 68).

minimising adverse impacts of unqualified anthropocentrism on the biosphere. Harm prevention therefore needs to be prioritised so as to limit, where possible, harms to earth system functions, in full acknowledgement that once damage is done it is often difficult, and in some cases impossible, to repair. This type of thinking is well established in many aspects of ethical normative practice ordering relational human activity. The discussion which follows considers and reflects on two examples of it, with quite different impacts, which can provide the raw material we need to build anew. The first is the *primum non nocere* – first, do no harm – ethical principle, a core part of the modern incarnation of the ancient Hippocratic Oath in medicine.[73] The second is the no-harm principle in international environmental law.

A. First, Do No Harm

Relational, care-based ethics, while popularised in this guise by feminist scholarship since the early 1980s, are far from novel in substance in the context of individually-focused inter-human relations. An extraordinarily long-lived and ubiquitous example of a relational care-based ethic can be found in the Hippocratic Oath (hereafter, the oath).[74] As an ethic for the practice of medicine, the specific physician–patient care orientation of the oath is so obvious that it has long been little discussed in these terms. Its longevity has been extraordinary, and failure to observe its professional moral code is the exception rather than the rule.

For present purposes it is significant that the injunction against harm is one of the enduring core elements of the oath, cutting across what it is now deemed to require: 'respect for autonomy, non maleficence, beneficence and justice'.[75] The centrality of the injunction against harm was both confirmed and endorsed in law at the Nuremburg trials in regard to the barbaric experimentation on humans by doctors during the Holocaust.[76] Furthermore, in prioritising the prohibition of harm, the oath is neither unique nor confined to Western thought, indicating the broad importance attached to this ethical principle in patient care.[77]

Contrary to its face value, 'first do no harm' is not interpreted as imposing a total prohibition on harm, which would be a practical impossibility in conducting many forms of treatment.[78] Sokol argues that 'A more accurate formulation is "first

[73] DK Sokol, '"First no no harm" Revisited' (2013) 347 *British Medical Journal* f6426.
[74] W Stigall, 'The Hippocratic Oath' (2022) 89 *The Linacre Quarterly* 277.
[75] H Askitopoulou and AN Vgontzas, 'The Relevance of the Hippocratic Oath to the Ethical and Moral Values of Contemporary Medicine. Part I: The Hippocratic Oath from Antiquity to Modern Times' (2018) 27(7) *European Spine Journal* 1481, 1486.
[76] ibid 1487.
[77] GA Ogunbanjo and KD Bogaert, 'The Hippocratic Oath: Revisited' (2009) 51 *South African Family Practice* 30.
[78] Stigall (n 74) 276.

do no net harm'".[79] The prohibition of harm as practised, then, is at base principled but also pragmatic. It is partly deontological in its duty/ obligation component and in the injunction to ensure that any harm done is outweighed by the benefit it brings to the patient. At the same time, the prohibition is care-based in its interpersonal, relational setting, acknowledging the vulnerability of the patient and the responsibility of the doctor in treatment scenarios and in its consequentialist dimensions.

The conception of care in the application of the oath has, while always being patient-centred, shifted in a variety of ways over time to accommodate huge changes in medicine itself and application across a wide range of social mores, for example, in modernity evolving from paternalism to respect for patient autonomy.[80] Nevertheless, the centrality of the patient as the object of care and the obligations placed on the medical professional in consequence have been pivotal in the oath. More importantly, observing the ethical priorities of the oath is regarded as the norm and departures from it aberrant.

Normalising the pursuit of the core goal of acting for the net benefit of the object of care, founded on a responsibility-based care relationship, arguably maps well onto what would be required to fashion a sustainable human–Earth relationship. At the very least, it provides evidence of the type of approach that is required and sees it successfully sustained across time and multiple cultures, which can inspire the sort of durable ethical project that we now need to undertake.

B. The No-Harm Principle in International Environmental Law

A significant aspect of the planetary nature of the Anthropocene lies in the fact that, while humanity is both vulnerable to and (albeit variably) responsible for it as a species, we do not (as yet and may perhaps never) function coherently as one in our dealings with the Earth system. Our macro-level legal and political systems are international – not global. In international law we do find potential kin to a notionally care-based human–Earth ethic through the imposition of obligations on states as both putative agents of harm in their own right and in regulating their subjects. It is, however, necessary to engage with the foundational concept of state sovereignty in international law in order to consider how recognition of planetary boundaries must further constrain it, curtailing states' ability to act independently in altering the earth system to the detriment of humanity as a whole.[81]

[79] Sokol (n 73) 23.
[80] Askitopoulou and Vgontzas (n 75) 1486–87.
[81] See also, J Rockström and others, 'The Planetary Commons: A New Paradigm for Safeguarding Earth-Regulating Systems in the Anthropocene' (2024) 121 *Proceedings of the National Academy of Sciences* e2301531121.

State sovereignty as currently understood is integrally connected with the paradigm of mastery, not least through its expression in extractivism.[82] Sovereignty has, throughout its history, served as a tool to facilitate the exploitation of the environment and is therefore one of the engines for cumulative planetary-level impacts that transgress planetary boundaries and eat into the safe operating space for humanity. In consequence, some argue for the root-and-branch reform of sovereignty into a collective endeavour to 'save the planet'.[83] A more pragmatic way forward lies in explicitly linking already recognised limits on state sovereignty with the need to respect planetary boundaries. State sovereignty is already qualified (albeit to varying effect) in many ways,[84] not least in regard to some of its adverse environmental impacts. One of the earliest principles of customary international environmental law, recognised in the foundational *Trail Smelter* arbitration on state responsibility, affirms that:

> No state has the right to use or permit the use of its territory in such a manner as to cause injury in or to the territory of another or the properties of persons therein, when the case is of serious consequence and the injury is established by clear and convincing evidence.[85]

This statement articulates what has come to be known as the 'no-harm' principle, and, debate surrounding its lack of precision notwithstanding, it has been upheld in copious subsequent case law and deployed in a plethora of environmental treaties. Significantly, the no-harm principle has also been codified in the overarching foundational soft law texts of international environmental law, first as Principle 21 of the Stockholm Declaration,[86] and then Principle 2 of the Rio Declaration,[87] which asserts that:

> States have, in accordance with the Charter of the United Nations and the principles of international law, the sovereign right to exploit their own resources pursuant to their own environmental and developmental policies, and *the responsibility to ensure that activities within their jurisdiction or control do not cause damage to the environment of other States or of areas beyond the limits of national jurisdiction* (emphasis added).[88]

The no-harm principle, then, does speak very clearly to state responsibility for environmental harm, although it invokes a limited concept of relationality. The

[82] L Cotula, '(Dis)Integration in Global Resource Governance: Extractivism, Human Rights, and Investment Treaties' (2020) 23 *Journal of International Economic Law* 233.

[83] G Mann and J Wainwright, *Climate Leviathan: A Political Theory of Our Planetary Future* (London, Verso Books, 2018).

[84] OA Hathaway, 'International Delegation and State Sovereignty' (2008) 71 *Law and Contemporary Problems* 115.

[85] Reports of International Arbitral Awards (*Trail Smelter Case, United States v Canada*), April 1938 and March 1941, vol III, RIAA pp 1905–1982.

[86] United Nations Conference on the Human Environment, 'Stockholm Declaration on the Human Environment', *Report of the United Nations Conference on the Human Environment*, UN Doc A/CONF.48/14, at 2 and Corr.1 (1972), https://lpr.adb.org/resource/declaration-united-nations-conference-human-environment-report-united-nations-conference.

[87] UNCED (n 70).

[88] ibid.

conception of harm to be avoided focuses on a narrow definition of human interests: primarily those of other states within their own sovereign territory or, in the alternative – and more to the point regarding planetary boundaries – shared human interests in those areas of the planet that do not fall under the remit of any individual state – the global commons. However, the notion of harm countenanced in Principle 2 casts the environment in an instrumental light, appealing primarily to the need to protect the interests of other states in their own territories and regarding areas where no state exercises jurisdiction. While the wording of the final clause of Principle 2 could potentially be open to a more planetary interpretation, this seems unlikely given the rest of the provision. Indeed, in a seemingly small but telling move, in adding the term 'developmental' to the 'environmental policies' that had been referred to in Principle 21 of the Stockholm Declaration, Principle 2, far from setting the human–Earth relationship on a new ethical footing, actually represents a retrograde shift, augmenting exploitative approaches towards the environment.

In this, Principle 2 arguably represents the apex of the myth of sustainable development, in its preoccupation with human concerns and its effective subjugation of the environment to them. Far from re-fashioning the human–Earth relationship, it reinforces a mastery narrative. In terms of responsiveness, it is glaringly apparent that, as currently conceived, the no-harm principle is failing to safeguard even the narrow interests of states, let alone the environment, from damage. However, our state of knowledge and the state of the earth system itself have shifted seismically since 1992, and it is now imperative that state sovereignty be explicitly qualified, in light of the necessary restraint to operate within planetary boundaries and secure a safe operating space for humanity.[89]

C. Re-framing Harm Prevention

It is now evident that a legal conception of 'no harm' rooted not in care, but in exploitation, and appealing to self-restraint exercised on a purely inter-human basis, is woefully inadequate. The Anthropocene sees the functional constraints of planetary systems imposing restraints on human exploitation of the biosphere as a whole rather than on a narrow, inter-state basis. In consequence, Principle 2 urgently requires an 'earth systems-literate' rethink for the Anthropocene, expanding the notions of responsibility and relationality beyond narrow human interests to account for the ecological realities of the altered world that we are making. Such a rethink occupies a central role in the project of earth system law.

States and sovereignty endure, albeit increasingly constrained by the self-inflicted encroachments of the Anthropocene in their ability to secure the welfare of their citizens. Adopting a human–Earth ethic for the Anthropocene

[89] P Heikkurinen, 'Managing the Anthropocene: Relational Agency and Power to Respect Planetary Boundaries' (2019) 34 *Organization and Environment* 18.

that ascribes a foundational significance to our ecological context and responsibility for the planetary care that is required for human (and many other species') flourishing, and ultimately *survival*, is an urgent necessity. This endeavour requires a fundamentally relational view of what it is to be human in the world.[90] The planetary nature of the earth system and the global impacts of Anthropocene conditions require us to accept and act on the knowledge that our activities are constrained by planetary boundaries. The alternative is to continue to pretend that we can bend the planet to humanity's wants, all the while compromising its ability to meet our needs.

While the changes suggested to fashion a new approach to the human–Earth relationship may seem enormous, the prospect is less daunting than it appears. Adopting an expanded, relational conception of states and their sovereignty on ethical and practical grounds is hardly unprecedented. For example, international cooperation has sometimes seen sovereignty pooled and even delegated.[91] Globalisation, too, has wrought practical changes on how sovereignty operates while allowing it to remain the foundational fiction of international affairs. Commentary on globalisation in particular tends to speak to the increasing interconnectedness of the world, albeit largely in human terms. In practical terms though, globalisation is necessarily embodied in the earth system and itself acts as a potent driver of the Anthropocene;[92] and the ecological realities involved are surely a more potent incentive to seek global, relational ways forward than any previous challenge that has prompted attenuations in state sovereignty. However, there is no guarantee that the threats of the Anthropocene will prompt a rational, relational response, as amply evidenced by the rise of populism in the face of new global uncertainties. Populism denies both human interdependence and the global context of the human–Earth relationship in the Anthropocene. It sees the nation state resurgent, as the fears and loss of control that characterise the Anthropocene predicament cause some to seek to retreat to old state-centric certainties, unfit as they are for present, never mind future, purposes.[93]

VI. A Case in Point – Ethics, Harm Prevention and Planetary Geoengineering

In replacing the erroneous paradigm of mastery, the control that we need to achieve most urgently is not over the Earth system, but rather our own environmentally

[90] ibid.

[91] CE Pavel, *Divided Sovereignty: International Institutions and the Limits of State Authority* (Oxford, Oxford University Press, 2015).

[92] CS Reddy, 'Globalisation and the Sovereignty of the Nation-State' (2012) 16 *World Affairs: The Journal of International Issues* 66, 70–71.

[93] A Kallis, 'Populism, Sovereigntism, and the Unlikely Re-Emergence of the Territorial Nation-State' (2018) 11 *Fudan Journal of the Humanities and Social Sciences* 285.

damaging behaviours and so, the question of harm prevention must come to the fore. In this, the idea of doing no net harm, drawn from the Hippocratic Oath, offers a helpful framing. Treating the ills that we have already inflicted on the earth system will inevitably involve further human interventions with key parts of it and, like administering treatment to an ailing patient, such interventions may well involve inflicting therapeutic harms, which makes the need for those promoting such actions to show a clear net benefit centrally important. This species of framing requires a profound recalibration, founded on relational terms, of how we regard our role and place in the Earth community. We are not masters, but members of the earth system – though members with particular power and privilege and the responsibilities that come with it. The response required is one of humility rather than hubris in our interactions with the Earth system. Applying a care-based ethic, founded on responsibility, relationality and responsiveness to human–Earth interactions would provide a sound foundation for the difficult decisions we are likely to face.

One area where human self-restraint will be crucial is in the fledgling field of geoengineering. This is an area where the siren song of technological optimism and the appeal of the technical fix, above more radical attitude and behaviour change, is already beginning to beguile.[94] Controversial as it undoubtedly is on scientific, political and moral grounds,[95] geoengineering, in multiple guises, is already being mooted as a potential response to 'baked in' climate change impacts. However, given that the Anthropocene itself is a consequence in large part of misplaced faith in the benign consequences of human ingenuity, where such planetary engineering is contemplated, the question of harm prevention will need to be central.[96] The issues are complex, in inter-human terms alone; the distribution of costs and harms involved raise significant geopolitical issues that only an incredibly optimistic interpretation can deem capable of being adequately addressed by international law in its current form.[97] The possible unforeseen environmental consequences of planetary-scale interventions could also see putative 'solutions' being counterproductive,[98] or worse. With this in mind, prevention of harm, where possible, and its substantial amelioration where not, must be considered, as must the need to ensure that further human interventions do not impose greater net harm than that which they seek to address. To address this, a relational ethic that regards its object as protecting the earth system as humanity's life support system and in its own right, has much to offer over a business-as-usual approach. The latter would place states (or even private actors) and their interests centre-stage which stands to replicate

[94] R Heinberg, 'Restoring Nature Is Our Only Climate Solution', *Resilience*, 1 July 2024.

[95] S Huttunen, E Skytén and M Hildén, 'Emerging Policy Perspectives on Geoengineering: An International Comparison' (2015) 2(1) *The Anthropocene Review* 14; Gupta and others (n 7).

[96] F Biermann and others, 'Solar Geoengineering: The Case for an International Non-Use Agreement' (2022) 13(3) *WIREs Climate Change* e754.

[97] Dalby (n 18); Du (n 8) 170–78.

[98] Heinberg (n 94); Du (n 8) 186–91.

and compound the errors of supposed mastery that have brought humanity to its current pass.

The topic of geoengineering is a broad one, so this discussion will focus on glacial climate engineering as an example which demonstrates the key concerns that need to be addressed. Among the plethora of climate change impact records currently being broken, sea-ice loss and glacier retreat have reached new record levels,[99] and the consequent speed and rate of sea-level rise is now a major concern. A recent consultation process and White Paper, articulating a research vision for glacial engineering, sponsored by the University of Chicago and focusing on the Antarctic and Greenland ice-sheets,[100] provides an interesting snapshot of the types of issues of principle involved. As a starting point, it is important to note that geoengineering would not halt the irreversible process of ice-sheet melt; at best it would slow the process. In a particular instance of the mechanics of Anthropocene threats, in addition to the environmental harm done by loss of ice eg (exacerbating climate change and shifts/loss of biodiversity) the sea-level rise that it generates and the emerging ocean conditions it contributes to pose major threats to humanity. Although claiming to offer a 'new ethos' in its approach, the White Paper focuses on the impact of sea-level rise and of any geoengineering solution on 'the well-being of global societies', and places humanity squarely to the fore, invoking the

> robust participation of sociologists, humanists, ecologists, community leaders, scientific and engineering governing bodies, international treaty organizations, and other relevant stakeholders in guiding the research so that it provides the answers needed for informed decisions about interventions.[101]

The 'well-being of human societies' ethos clearly locates the ethical setting of the discussion within the mastery paradigm: while those who advocate for the non-human world appear in the list of stakeholders whose contributions to the debate are deemed desirable (non-governmental organisations are also mentioned later in the paper),[102] the tenor of the document is anthropocentric.

With that in mind, let us consider how a care-based ethic might look in a proposal of this nature. There would be some common ground: namely, acknowledging that human responsibility for the problem is now unavoidable and accounted for here to a degree in seeking to intervene in a key element of the earth system that has been destabilised by human agency. From the perspective of relationality, the White Paper promotes inclusive governance to draw perspectives from the developing as well as the developed world into the discussion – which is valuable given the current dominance of the developed world in

[99] World Meteorological Organization, *State of the Global Climate 2023*, https://wmo.int/publication-series/state-of-global-climate-2023.

[100] D Macayeal and others, 'Glacial Climate Intervention: A Research Vision', https://www.usap-dc.org/view/dataset/601797.

[101] ibid 6.

[102] ibid 20.

this area.[103] However, the conception of relationality used is primarily inter-human, the factors to be considered in evaluating potential research being described as: 'local and global costs and benefits, for human and environmental systems'. This adopts an instrumental framing of the environment, even while acknowledging the 'high probability' of 'unforeseen' human and environmental consequences of geoengineering,[104] which should suggest a human–Earth relational framing. While some attention is paid to the environment in general terms, the technological optimist approach that dominates the document means that this acts as a veneer applied to an essentially business-as-usual setting. This in turn colours the responsiveness of what is proposed. In centring concern on the human impacts of ice-sheet melt and on ameliorating their consequences as the dominant framing for a discussion about research in this field of geoengineering, short-term human interests will inevitably prevail.

This is precisely the type of thinking that has seen realistic engagement with the Anthropocene deferred to the point that it is now an existential threat to humanity. Responsibility is already clear if a care-based approach of the type suggested in this chapter were to be applied to researching geoengineering for ice-sheet melt. Relationality would include not only the full range of human interests affected (including those of future generations), but also the dependence of humanity on the environment at local, regional and planetary levels. In short, an ecologically realistic view of relationality requires the well-being of the Earth and the functioning of its systems to be placed front and centre in any decision-making process. It is no longer tenable (if it ever was) to assume that what is good for humanity is beneficial to the world, but we can surely acknowledge that shifting the earth system out of the Holocene stability is bad for humanity. The threshold for undertaking geoengineering set by a no-net-harm approach would be a very high one – and it should be – the risks are so enormous that it should be a last resort. The stakes are simply too high for unadulterated technological optimism to drive action; earth system (ecological) realism must be applied instead. This requires a humble approach to relationality that sets guard-rails on responsiveness, which must prioritise avoiding net harm. Taking first the re-stabilisation and then, where possible, the repair of the earth system as the object of care is the best route to securing humanity's survival, and hopefully sustainable flourishing in the Anthropocene.

VII. Conclusion

The Anthropocene at once represents the apotheosis of human power within the earth system and also its ultimately illusory nature and limits. We can no longer

[103] ibid 9.
[104] ibid 19.

delude ourselves that the Anthropocene can be ignored out of existence, argued into submission or 'fixed' by technology. How we choose to act on this knowledge is crucial. The Anthropocene exposes the true nature of human–earth system interdependence and its impact on planetary conditions favourable to the flourishing of all species. The constraints that this imposes on the human enterprise, even viewed through an anthropocentric lens, furnish the context within which we operate, providing a hybrid practical and moral prompt to re-set the human–earth system relationship. Our old ways of being in the world are no longer viable. Averting the potentially existential threats humanity faces therefore requires a deep-seated shift in our ethics away from exploitation towards a care-based orientation that attends to the planetary realities within which we must either function and thrive, or transgress and fail. This is one of the key tasks that the evolving project of earth system law will have to assume: earth system law must, and likely would, be instrumental in propagating a new ethics of care that is both ensconced in and responsive to the earth system and all its living beings.

The changes that are required in the dominant ethical underpinning of the human–Earth relationship are undoubtedly profound and demanding, but they are not beyond humanity, at least in principle. Significant legal transformations that have fundamentally changed society have happened in the past; they can – and must – happen again. The motivation for transformations is clear: 'if we stay long enough with our feelings of rage, of helplessness, of sorrow, of wanting to shut off what we didn't want to know about, we can find a way too towards a new ethics of responsibility'.[105]

Make no mistake, this is absolutely necessary in practice. The world we are making is already changing at terrifying speed from the one we have always known. The new, unfamiliar, and unpredictable reality requires a new way of thinking about what it is to be human in the world, one that we can act on. A care-based ethical orientation that is expressed earth system-oriented imaginaries of law, can help in the necessary transition, harnessing a relatable, familiar, concrete concept, albeit newly applied. This offers a degree of legibility in efforts to re-shape the human–earth system paradigm, which promises a much-needed boon in uncertain times. Humanity is undoubtedly responsible for the Anthropocene and, ironically, among the species most threatened by it. The new world we are creating forces us to reflect relationally on what it is to be a planet-breaking species and what this means for our social systems, such as law, and the ways we engage with and further develop our legal systems. Finding new modes of responsiveness to the Anthropocene that are embedded in earth system law, in recognition of our species' power and peril, to re-make a world we can flourish in, is a matter of choice – for now. It will not be so for long.

[105] S Orbach, 'We Don't Have to Be Overwhelmed by Climate Anxiety. Feel the Pain, Then Act' (2023) *The Guardian*.

7

Earth Made Up of Territories of Life: An Inspiration for Earth System Law

GEOFFREY GARVER AND IVÁN D VARGAS RONCANCIO*

I. Introduction

Six hundred years after the early modern era of transoceanic European exploration and conquest began, the modern world's dominant legal systems still reflect the capitalist and colonialist orientations of this quest for new places to expand and exploit. Just as early modern voyages of conquest and dispossession had legal and moral sanction and wealthy backers expecting a financial return,[1] modern states grant transnational corporations and foreign investors legal authority to assert remote ownership or control over faraway places, to reap profits, maintain global capitalist growth and support consumerist lifestyles for enough people in enough places to retain social licence.[2] As Western people and their ideas gradually progressed on a centuries-long path to global economic domination, capitalism and colonialism co-evolved and eventually hardened into a firmly entrenched legal and socio-economic order in which the exploitation of people and places perpetually yields ever-expanding opportunities for new capital investment and profit-making.[3]

The key elements of this legal and economic order are a human relationship with territory that is grounded in the social construct of property; an international system of nation states whose legal systems are largely built around private property relationships with territory; and an international commitment to endlessly perpetuating capitalist economic growth.[4] The United Nations (UN), World Bank,

* The co-authors contributed equally to this chapter.

[1] R Patel and JW Moore, *A History of the World in Seven Cheap Things* (Oakland CA, University of California Press, 2018).

[2] G Garver, 'Confronting Remote Ownership Problems with Ecological Law' (2019) 43 *Vermont Law Review* 425.

[3] Patel and Moore (n 1).

[4] F Capra and U Mattei, *The Ecology of Law: Toward a Legal System in Tune with Nature and Community* (Oakland CA, Berrett Koehler, 2015).

International Monetary Fund, World Trade Organization and other international institutions maintain this economic and legal order, which is reflected in their charters, in the de facto hierarchies of economic and legal power they constitute and maintain, and in overarching policy frameworks like the UN Sustainable Development Goals.[5]

Within this global system, earnest efforts to address international environmental concerns are left to relatively isolated environmental agreements that allow economic, political and technological considerations to limit environmental regulation, and to relatively toothless elements of sustainable development and international trade policies and agreements that collectively entrench the *status quo ante*. This imbues national governments with an overarching desire to be economically competitive and with incentives either to offshore environmentally harmful production to other countries, or to adopt weak environmental governance regimes to attract economic activity.[6] Serious efforts to address looming ecological crises, most critically those of climate change and biodiversity loss,[7] are perpetually pushed off into the future.

A core problem that earth system law attempts to confront is the failure of the dominant modern economic and legal order to constrain human activities sufficiently to prevent increasingly dangerous levels of anthropogenic ecological dystopia.[8] The ongoing ecological deterioration that the growth-insistent global economy continues to wreak varies from place to place, but as both planetary boundaries research and the Intergovernmental Panel on Climate Change have made clear, it is now on a global scale and getting worse.[9] Indeed, it has given rise to the Anthropocene, whose name underscores the integral and dominant role of humans in the earth system that they are negatively impacting at an alarming rate. The hubristic assumption of ecomodernists and other adherents of a growth-insistent paradigm that the same global economic and legal order that has enabled this unprecedented level of ecological peril will also yield a lasting solution through the generation of yet more wealth and more commodification and financialisation of life systems, must urgently give way to new ecologically-oriented social constructs.[10] This includes law.

[5] G Garver, *Ecological Law and the Planetary Crisis: A Legal Guide for Harmony on Earth* (Abingdon-on-Thames, Routledge, 2021) 48, 185–88; LJ Kotzé and D French, 'The Anthropocentric Ontology of International Environmental Law and the Sustainable Development Goals: Towards an Ecocentric Rule of Law in the Anthropocene' (2018) 7 *Global Journal of Comparative Law* 5.

[6] WE Rees, 'Globalization and Sustainability: Conflict or Convergence?' (2002) 22 *Bulletin of Science, Technology & Society* 249.

[7] W Steffen and others, 'Planetary Boundaries: Guiding Human Development on a Changing Planet' (2015) 347 *Science* 1259885.

[8] G Garver, 'The Rule of Ecological Law: The Legal Complement to Degrowth Economics' (2013) 5 *Sustainability* 316; LJ Kotzé, 'Earth System Law for the Anthropocene: Rethinking Environmental Law alongside the Earth System Metaphor' (2020) 11 *Transnational Legal Theory* 75.

[9] Steffen and others (n 7); Intergovernmental Panel on Climate Change (IPCC), *Climate Change 2023: AR6 Synthesis Report* (March 2023), https://www.ipcc.ch/report/ar6/syr/.

[10] LJ Kotzé and S Adelman, 'Environmental Law and the Unsustainability of Sustainable Development: A Tale of Disenchantment and Hope' (2023) 34 *Law and Critique* 227.

Earth system law, the focus of this book, and related approaches such as ecological law, are emerging as legal constructs that pave an alternative, pluralistic, life-enhancing path to the future.[11] With roots in Bosselmann's notion of *ökologischen Recht*,[12] these 'alternative' visions for law in the Anthropocene weave together concepts of care, relationality and responsibility associated with Earth jurisprudence,[13] oriented around a mutually enhancing human–Earth relationship; human-inclusive ecocentrism; the systems-based framework of the planetary boundaries; intragenerational, intergenerational and interspecies justice; and a strong critique of growth-insistent economics, along with several other features.

These features are largely reflected in earth system law.[14] Earth system law grew out of an interest in developing a juridical focus within the broad multidisciplinary framework of the Earth System Governance Project, the aim of which is to work across disciplines using systems-based approaches to study and develop responses to earth system governance challenges in the Anthropocene.

The formulation of earth system law is in the process of being developed and made more coherent. What is clear is that earth system law consistently refers to the need for a local-to-global systems approach to law, attuned to Anthropocene challenges, with reference to planetary boundaries and other ecological limits, as well as to juridical themes of rights and justice, and a new ethic.[15] Notably, scholars of earth system law have highlighted the need for legal systems to move past environmental law, and proposals exist to align earth system law with degrowth concepts.[16] Moreover, ecocentrism, recognition of more-than-human legalities and the inclusion of humans and more-than-humans as subjects of law are key themes in earth system law.[17]

This chapter focuses on the way in which the modern capitalist-colonialist complex treats territory and the life systems attached to it as private property that can be exploited, harmed or destroyed, and sacrificed in the name of the common good or the public interest, defined around a fundamental commitment to perpetual capitalistic wealth accumulation and growth. It also shows how law

[11] LJ Kotzé and RE Kim, 'Earth System Law: The Juridical Dimensions of Earth System Governance' (2019) *Earth System Governance* 100003; Garver (n 5).

[12] K Bosselmann, 'Eigene Rechte für die Natur? Ansätze einer ökologischen Rechtsauffassung' (1986) 19 *Kritische Justiz* 1.

[13] T Berry, *The Great Work: Our Way into the Future* (New York, Three Rivers Press, 1999).

[14] See, Kotzé, Angstadt and Kim, Chapter 2 in this book.

[15] LJ Kotzé and others, 'Earth System Law: Exploring New Frontiers in Legal Science' (2022) 11 *Earth System Governance* 100126; K Anker and others (eds), *From Environmental to Ecological Law* (Abingdon-on-Thames, Routledge, 2021).

[16] Garver (n 5).

[17] ID Vargas Roncancio and others (eds), *Posthuman Legalities: New Materialism and Law Beyond the Human* (Cheltenham, Edward Elgar Publishing, 2021); ID Vargas Roncancio, *Law, Humans, and Plants in the Andes-Amazon: The Lawness of Life* (Abingdon-on-Thames, Routledge, 2024); MC Petersmann, 'Sympoietic Thinking and Earth System Law: The Earth, Its Subjects and the Law' (2021) 9 *Earth System Governance* 100114; L Mai and E Boulot, 'Harnessing the Transformative Potential of Earth System Law: From Theory to Practice' (2021) 7 *Earth System Governance* 100103.

is complicit in this practice. Our central thesis is that earth system law should include a long-term vision of Earth as entirely made up of a diversity of territories of life with a non-hierarchical plurality of life-enhancing legal regimes. Transitional measures toward earth system law must strive to be consistent with that vision: a vision that is informed by conceptions of territories as both areas 'governed, managed and conserved by custodian indigenous peoples and local communities'[18] and as living and sentient meshworks of human and non-human lifeways with legal agency.[19] Thus, the response to the continued reliance on life-depleting 'sacrifice zones'[20] to further the colonialist-capitalist global agenda is to treat territories and the life systems attached to them as territories of life,[21] where place-based, life-enhancing law and governance regimes allow for fulfilling lives without destroying the ecological foundations that make them possible. This is how we understand territories of life, in short: a place where living beings co-habit within the territory's ecological means.

We first explain the need and reasons for a territories-of-life framing in law. We then describe the territories-of-life concept in more detail by focusing on an instance of a territory of life in the Colombian Amazon whose Indigenous custodians perceive the territory and its meshwork of life as kin with socio-legal agency. In the final section, we explain how a vision of Earth made up entirely of territories of life illuminates a transitional pathway for earth system law. This transitional pathway is intended to shape the evolution of earth system law and hopefully might lead to a global plurality of place-based law that should ultimately be re-grounded in a commitment to sustaining thriving communities of all life forms.

II. The Need for Territories-of-Life Framing in Law

The need for a long-term vision in law of Earth made up of territories of life arises from the current dire socio-ecological circumstances to which historical pathways have led humanity.

[18] G Borrini-Feyerabend with T Jaeger, *Territories of Life. Exploring Vitality of Goverance for Conserved and Protected Areas* (ICCA-GSI with ICCA Consortium, IUCN and UNDP GEF SGP, 2024); ICCA Consortium, 'ICCAs-Territories of Life': https://toolbox.iccaconsortium.org/meanings-and-more/iccas-territories-of-life/. We recognise the inappropriateness of conflating Indigenous peoples and local communities in some circumstances, especially in the context of the rights of Indigenous peoples and their status as belonging to sovereign Nations.

[19] T Ingold, *Being Alive: Essays on Movement, Knowledge, and Description* (Abingdon-on-Thames, Routledge, 2011).

[20] M Souza, 'Sacrifice Zone: The Environment-Territory-Place of Disposable Lives' (2021) 56 *Community Development Journal* 220.

[21] ICCA Consortium (n 18).

A. Co-emergence of Conquest, Colonialism and Capitalism

The most consequential arc of history began in the early modern era when European powers ramped up efforts to extend their empires outside of their borders. Already at the dawn of the fifteenth century, provisioning Europe's growing populations from within was running up against environmental constraints, as well as structural problems of feudalism, exacerbated by the Little Ice Age that began in the fourteenth century following a period of agricultural expansion and deforestation.[22] Metal mining and refining within Europe was on the rise but required wood fuel that was becoming increasingly scarce.[23]

If a territory of life is a place where people live within the territory's ecological means, Europe had fewer and fewer of them. Hence, although ventures such as the Crusades had occurred and trade routes within and beyond Europe were established, ocean voyages to seek new sources of provisioning began in earnest at that time, setting the stage for the long co-evolution of colonialism and the quest for returns on investment that became capitalism. Although the details of the legal regimes that opened the pathway for this co-evolution are important and discussed elsewhere,[24] we simply note here that the law that paved the way emerged as the power elites created it, as an enabler of their competitive quests for wealth and power.

The economic and legal orders in Europe at the beginning of the early modern era enabled profit-seekers, backed by private lenders, to externalise the provisioning, wealth accumulation and empire building of European monarchies through conquest and colonisation of new lands. The unpopulated *Isla de Madeira* ('Island of Wood') was an early example of the co-emergence of capitalism and conquest. After Portuguese sailors discovered the heavily forested island in 1419, it became a source of timber and then, as cleared land became available for cultivation, wheat farming.[25] In the second half of the fifteenth century, with the appetite for sugar rising in Europe, sugar production took over,[26] the production of which had particular requirements. Harvested sugar needed to be processed quickly; thus, workers other than the cane cutters were needed to process it. On Madeira, those labourers included some of the first African slaves working in European enterprises, and the assembly-line nature of the production process made sugar mills early prototypes of modern factories. Sugar mills were fuelled with wood and '[l]ike palm and soy monocultures today, [sugar] cleared forests, exhausted soils,

[22] C Ponting, *A New Green History of the World: The Environment and the Collapse of Great Civilizations* (London, Penguin Books, 2007).
[23] RP Sieferle, *The Subterranean Forest: Energy Systems and the Industrial Revolution* (Winwick, The White Horse Press, 2001) 65.
[24] Capra and Mattei (n 4).
[25] Patel and Moore (n 1) 14–15.
[26] SM Greenfield, 'Plantations, Sugar Cane and Slavery' (1979) 6 *Historical Reflections* 85.

and encouraged pests at breakneck speed'.[27] By the 1530s, the 'island of wood' was essentially deforested, and Portuguese sugar production, along with its African slave labour, moved on to Brazil and the Caribbean. Yet, '[c]apitalism didn't leave Madeira – it reinvented itself'[28] as an outpost for the African slave trade and a centre of production of the fortified wine named after the island, with barrels ironically produced with wood from the Americas.

While Madeira was being deforested, the impetus for European trans-oceanic voyages of conquest grew, and the pattern of privateers acting under royal charters with private financing undertaking voyages to Africa, Asia and the Americas in search of precious metals, spices and places to colonise took hold.[29] Spain, the Netherlands, France and England had the advantage of major Atlantic ports and were the principal realms jockeying for advantage and domination through control of trade, conquered lands and new colonies.[30] Among the legal provisions at play at the time were the fifteenth-century papal bulls that gave legal and moral authority, through the doctrine of discovery, to European monarchs to claim sovereignty over new lands and overtake, kill, dispossess or enslave the non-Christian people who lived there.[31]

The rise of mercantilism in the sixteenth century, grounded mostly in stores of gold and silver that nations sought to maximise through trade surpluses, was part of the frenzy of conquest and plunder of the early modern era. The competitive search for new sources of precious metals catalysed the financialisation of trans-oceanic trade. As Patel and Moore put it, '[m]oney facilitates and compels action at a distance', and because of the ecological change that financing can unleash, 'money *is* an ecological relation'.[32] The pattern that took hold in places like Madeira long ago – of investors seeking returns to reinvest in all kinds of new ways in ever expanding frontiers – persists, now powered by fossil fuels, modern trade regimes, and an intractable commitment to endless economic growth.[33]

B. Privatisation, State Sovereignty, Remote Ownership, and the Rise in Monocultures

Although the forms of private ownership and state sovereignty that prevail in the modern global capitalist economic and legal regime emerged from Europe,

[27] Patel and Moore (n 1) 16.

[28] ibid 17–18.

[29] DW Bromley, 'The Commons, Common Property, and Environmental Policy' (1992) 2 *Environmental and Resource Economics* 1; D Korten, *The Great Turning: From Empire to Earth Community* (Oakland CA, Berrett-Koehler, 2006).

[30] Greenfield (n 26).

[31] *Romanus Pontifex*, 1455, *Inter Caetera*, 1493.

[32] Patel and Moore (n 1) 67.

[33] F Pearce, *The Land Grabbers: The New Fight Over Who Owns the Earth* (Boston MA, Beacon Press, 2013).

sovereign states and private actors – most notably large transnational corporations – now mutually support and maintain each other. They do so in accordance with the mechanistic paradigm of early Enlightenment thinkers that is now out of step with newer and still-evolving scientific understandings of the functioning of Earth's interdependent social and ecological systems.[34]

The Westphalian state model that took hold in Europe in the seventeenth century has spread globally, and a political entity's membership in the international community of equal sovereign states now requires it to be identified as, and meet the criteria for, a state in that model. According to this model, Indigenous peoples and local communities acting as custodians of lands have no agency equivalent to statehood in the international sphere, and what agency they do have is inferior and subservient to states.[35] Thus, although dealings between countries like Canada and the United States and the nations of their original Indigenous peoples are sometimes referred to as sovereign-to-sovereign relations, they are not relations between equals in terms of the controlling hierarchies of power. The Supreme Courts in both countries have recognised a duty to consult with Indigenous peoples in certain circumstances, but have made clear that consent of Indigenous peoples or Nations is not required for decisions that affect their interests (even though both countries formally endorsed the United Nations Declaration on the Rights of Indigenous Peoples).[36] In short, 'the monoculture that has been constructed around state sovereignty is a monolith that tends to destroy life and impede the possibility of alternative relationships for the maintenance or recovery of places contaminated and threatened by this cultural form'.[37]

The colonial-capitalist model of economics, law and governance depends on complicity between states and the private actors they depend on for employment, tax revenue and competitivity in global markets.[38] Indeed, the market societies in nations linked via globalisation are 'run largely by private market rules and interests'.[39] Rather than being natural and immutable, the legal regime grounded in mechanistic paradigms of private property and state sovereignty is merely a cultural and political choice, from among many alternatives, to facilitate that 'nature's essence could be transformed into a commodity, a physical object that humans could exploit or "improve"'.[40] Consequently, the symbiosis among private property, corporations and nation states (all human inventions), has allowed much

[34] Capra and Mattei (n 4).

[35] J Borrows, *Canada's Indigenous Constitution* (Toronto, University of Toronto Press, 2010) 12–22.

[36] RJ Miller, 'Consultation or Consent: The United States' Duty to Confer with American Indian Governments' (2015) 91 *North Dakota Law Review* 37.

[37] G Garver and C Derani, 'Moving from monocultures to resilience' in K Gwiazdon, L Bosselmann, and V Zambrano (eds), *Ecological Integrity and International Law: Peace, Public Health, and Global Security* (Abingdon-on-Thames, Routledge, 2025).

[38] Capra and Mattei (n 4).

[39] J Erickson, *The Progress Illusion: Reclaiming Our Future from the Fairytale of Economics* (Washington DC, Island Press, 2022) 56.

[40] Capra and Mattei (n 4) 7.

of the world's commons to be appropriated as private property in various forms of capital.[41]

Accounts of resource and land grabbing around the world, including 'green' land grabs (land grabs for conservation purposes) that often involve removing custodian Indigenous peoples or local communities from territories to which they are intimately attached (typically with exclusionary control), reveal the extent to which co-evolved ideologies grounded in expansionist colonialism and capitalism remain affixed in the modern world.[42] Inherent in the global phenomenon of land and resource grabbing is remote ownership and control of land, territory and ecosystems. Private property owners or other decision-makers act at a considerable distance, far removed from the ecosystems and local communities that their decisions negatively affect, and without the knowledge or care needed to govern those faraway places and people in an ecologically sustainable or just manner.

Around the world, remote owners and decision-makers, including investors, drive conversion of ecosystems or land tenures from generally small-scale, traditional, locally controlled uses, or relatively pristine undeveloped ecosystems, to large tracts of industrial agriculture serving global markets.[43] The same dynamic drives extraction of fossil fuels, mining of metals and minerals, and industrial fisheries. Modern trade and investment treaties have arisen as global or regional catalysts for ongoing remote ownership and control that causes harmful social and ecological disruption. In the most abstract forms of remote ownership, investors in private corporate land grabs typically have little knowledge of or interest in the cultural history, ecological functioning, or local-level human–Earth interactions of the land underlying their investment.[44] Acquiring the greatest financial return possible is the primary objective, regardless of ecological or social costs.

One alarming consequence of the co-evolution of colonialism and capitalism has been the concurrent concentration of both material and conceptual processes in harmful monocultures. Material monocultures include vast landscapes of single-crop cultivation. Corn, wheat, soy and even-aged managed forests of palm or timber wood are examples. All material monocultures are systems designed to efficiently produce uniform results in terms of the quantity, quality and nature of the product. The cost exacted for this uniformity is the axiomatic loss of diversity in monocultures, along with a reduction in ecologically valuable redundancy.[45] Monocultures increase efficiency but inevitably reduce ecological resilience,

[41] ibid 6.

[42] B Yang and J He, 'Global Land Grabbing: A Critical Review of Case Studies across the World' (2021) 10 *Land* 324.

[43] Garver (n 2) 437.

[44] ibid 449–50.

[45] Ecologically valuable redundancy is a core feature of ecosystem resilience whereby a similar function is served by multiple species, providing a 'biological insurance policy' against the decline or loss of some species.

while interfering with the inclusivity, interconnectedness and complexity that are essential to an earth system functioning in a life-enhancing way.[46]

Monocultures can also arise within conceptual domains: '[C]onceptual monocultures reflect a universal worldview or other conceptual framing that is put forth as absolute and unquestionable, or superior to, dominant over or exclusive of all others'.[47] Examples include money as an expression of value; state-centred Western legal systems as a form of law; Western science as a form of knowledge; universities with siloed disciplines as a form of pedagogy; and consumerism as a form of well-being and happiness. Modern material and conceptual monocultures are mutually constitutive and reinforcing and can come together in sweeping societal narratives, such as the dominant global narrative of progress grounded in the colonial-capitalist complex. This overarching narrative, and the monocultures that characterise and maintain it, undermine the socio-ecological integrity and resilience necessary for long-term security and stability of social and ecological systems.

III. Territories of Life[48]

Is it possible to rethink the type of growth-insistent regimes discussed above in ways that render them altogether more regenerative, caring, inclusive, relational, and ultimately, ecologically sustainable? We argue that the territories-of-life framing offers a potentially instructive way to do so. In this section, we explore the territories-of-life concept in more detail, and focus specifically on Colombia as a case study. We ask: How can humans learn to co-create knowledge with living territories to live-well together? How can Indigenous experiences with territory re-shape or even displace conventional decision-making protocols that rely on rational deliberation among humans alone? Ultimately, how can reflections upon such questions influence conceptions of law and help design an earth system law from the vantage point of living territories? Our hypothesis is that an Earth-oriented form of law and governance necessitates both a definition of territories as more than the backdrop of human action – to include the more-than-human dimensions of a living place – and a new definition of law beyond the human that emerges from a living territory itself. Earth system law should embrace such an expansive, all-embracing, definition of law.

[46] CS Holling and GK Meffe, 'Command and Control and the Pathology of Natural Resource Management' (1996) 10 *Conservation Biology* 328.

[47] Garver and Derani (n 37) Introduction, para 2.

[48] This section also draws on interviews that Ivan Vargas Roncancio conducted with several Inga practitioners from the regions of Putumayo and Caquetá in the Colombian Amazon in February 2021. See www.deveniruniversidad.org. Thanks to the Inga people of Colombia, particularly Hernando Chindoy Chindoy, Waira Jacanamijoy Mutumbajoy, Flora Macas, and members of the intercultural team that supports the Indigenous Biocultural University.

'Territory' is typically understood as a backdrop for human action; a collection of natural resources in a defined space to be extracted in pursuit of the modernist notion of a good life. Territories continue to be represented and acted upon as sources of biogenetic material, plants, trees, animals and minerals to fulfil national and international development demands. The story is well known and widely discussed in the ethnographic record.[49] Plants and animals are rendered as objects of study across a wide spectrum of disciplinary silos, from biology, ecology, botany and resource economics to animal husbandry and environmental law. In contrast to Indigenous ways of learning, knowing and acting, this compartmentalisation reveals a profound rift between biophysical processes, knowledge, and the wisdom to care for the living community of which humans are only a small part.

Connected to this fundamental separation between the human and the more-than-human is the notion that territories exist *out-there*, separated from socio-ecological systems, and can be reduced to 'data' about the functioning of those systems. For example, ecosystem functions such as regulating clean air and filtering water are considered services for humans.[50] This instrumentalisation of nature further reveals how conventional knowledge systems based on an ontology of separation predominantly foreclose alternative ways of understanding the territory and the living relations that constitute it:[51] the sentience and cognitive dispositions of other beings are relegated to the status of myth and/ or cultural belief that militate against Western 'logic' and rationality.[52]

In contrast, the notion of territories of life offers a lens for conceiving territoriality and socio-ecological governance in ways aligned with an Earth-centred orientation of law and governance. Territories of life, as a concept and practice of life, offers an alternative territoriality based on Indigenous cosmologies, and non-monocultural, place-based understandings of relationships. From this point of view, a territory cannot be mechanically reduced to its biophysical components, as it also includes emergent properties and non-visible dimensions.[53] From the perspective of earth system law, this placed-based lens reveals how Earth as a whole consists of a diverse array of local territories and knowledge practices that exist in continuity with them. Each place is a unique expression of the inexorable forces that create life's diversity across the planet.

Territories of life vary across cultural contexts and may also be referred to, for example, as commons and 'greens', ancestral domains, 'country', community

[49] A Escobar, *Territories of Difference: Place, Movements, Life, Redes. New Ecologies for the Twenty-First Century* (Durham NC, Duke University Press, 2008).

[50] Millennium Ecosystem Assessment, 'Guide to the Millennium Assessment Reports', https://www.millenniumassessment.org/en/index.html.

[51] A Escobar, *Designs for the Pluriverse: Radical Interdependence, Autonomy and the Making of Worlds* (Durham NC, Duke University Press, 2018).

[52] M Cadena, 'Indigenous Cosmopolitics in the Andes: Conceptual Reflections Beyond Politics' (2010) 25 *Cultural Anthropology* 334.

[53] Vargas Roncancio, *Law, Humans, and Plants* (n 17) 114.

conserved areas, territories for living well, and sacred natural sites. Although these concepts refer to site-specific territories-of-life experiences, they all share an intimate material and spiritual interconnection between communities and the territories they are part of. This interconnection goes far beyond any linguistic representation to encompass a meshwork of lively relations in constant co-emergence and renewal.[54]

Alongside these visible and non-visible dimensions are the dignity and self-determination of local communities that care for and are cared for by territories of life. In this sense, the reciprocal nature of territories of life is instructive to inform an earth system orientation of law in three ways. First, there is a close and deep connection between a territory or area and its custodian Indigenous people or local community. This relationship is usually embedded in history, social and cultural identity, spirituality and/ or people's reliance on the territory for their material and non-material well-being. Second, the custodian people or community makes and enforces decisions and rules about the territory or area through a governing institution. Third, governance efforts of the community contribute directly to the conservation of nature as well as to community livelihoods and well-being. In 'defined' territories of life, the territories fulfil these three characteristics, while 'disrupted' territories of life are known to have fulfilled them in the past but are unable to do so today because of historical processes and disturbances that can still be reversed or counteracted. A 'desired' territory of life has 'the potential of developing the three characteristics, and their custodian communities are ready to work for this'.[55]

Living in the Andean-Amazonian territories of southern Colombia, Quichua-speaking Inga communities offer a sophisticated vision of territory that can be considered an instance of a 'desired' territory of life. While the rich soils of the Andean slopes have favoured an economy based on coffee, beans and other cash crops, Amazonian ecosystems are characterised by their fragility as most of them are located on poor soils that are vulnerable to rain and direct sun exposure.[56] Once the forest is cut down, the fertility of these acidic and thin soils quickly depletes. The biological variability and resilience of the Amazon region is due to the way in which its ecosystems function in a feeding cycle of aerial and subterranean interaction of Andean Amazonian geographies; the prevailing environmental conditions of high humidity and heat; and the intimate ecological knowledge and efficaciousness of Indigenous territorial governance systems.[57] The territory has a spiritual and cultural dimension that both encompasses and transcends this biophysical dimension.

[54] Ingold (n 19).

[55] ICCA Consortium 2024, para 6.

[56] FJ Luizão, 'Soil Acidity and Nutrient Deficiency in Central Amazonian Heath Forest Soils' (2007) 192 *Plant Ecology* 209.

[57] Vargas Roncancio, *Law, Humans, and Plants* (n 17); KL Thompson, T Lantz and NC Ban, 'A Review of Indigenous Knowledge and Participation in Environmental Monitoring' (2020) 25 *Ecology and Society* 10.

For Inga political leader and intellectual Hernando Chindoy, the territory is Mother, our mother, and the Sun is Father, our father. The condor, the tapir and other beings are members of the *human* family, and the territory is their home:

> [W]hen I plant corn, when I cultivate the *chagra* (small food garden), I can't sow only for my family, for me, for my wife and children to have food. When there is a harvest, the squirrel, the deer, the tapir, the turkey, the parrots will come to harvest this corn and those beans too.[58]

The territory, then, is a network of human and non-human people: a multitude of persons organised as a socio-ecological kinship.[59] These typical local articulations of territory as people vary across the Andean Amazonian ethnographic record. The territory is also a meeting place:

> [O]ne Inga family in the Sibundoy Valley told us that to put up a fence means to divide: From this point here to this fence over there, you command, you are the owner; and from that fence over there to where I stand here, I am the owner: I am in charge, and no one is allowed to enter without my permission. However, those limits that we were taught to think of as barriers for our cultures and communities are, in fact, not lines that divide but meeting places: points of encounter between different beings.[60]

The territory is also a socio-ecological family. It is a place where lifeways meet and cross each other, forming a living tapestry. Anthropologist Tim Ingold defines a way of life as the trajectory of movement and growth of all beings. Every being is instantiated in the world 'as a path of movement along a way of life',[61] and these paths or lines form a tapestry of co-emergent lifeways that he calls a 'meshwork'.[62] He contrasts the meshwork with the idea of a network, which represents the interconnection between pre-existent entities in space. He notes that what is commonly known as the web of life – that is, the material relationships between organisms in an ecological community – is not a network of connected points but a meshwork of interwoven lines making up a place.[63] For example, winding rivers, growing plants, roaming animals and humans, and languages, are all ways of life or trajectories of growth and movement relentlessly co-emerging.

For Hernando, this meshwork of lifeways expresses both a sense of movement and direction, as well as a state of rest and a meeting point to learn something new about a place:

> [T]he black jaguar that inhabits these sacred points between the Andes and the Amazon is the spirit of protection who day by day safeguards this region; the jaguar, our most powerful *wasikama*, or guardian, is the protector of the ancestral knowledge of the Inga people.

[58] Interview with Hernando Chinoy, 2021.
[59] See also Warner, Chapter 9 in this book.
[60] Interview with Hernando Chindoy, 2021.
[61] Ingold (n 19) 4.
[62] ibid 63.
[63] Ingold (n 19).

> This territory has the form of a jaguar in a state of *samai*, at rest, and that is why the black jaguar is a very important symbol of knowledge, protection, and harmony: having the color of the soil – *el color de la tierra* – that sustains our lives, this territory is embraced with the spirituality of the black jaguar who is the *wasikama* of these sacred, strategic, and emblematic territories.[64]

As a people and meeting place, the territory moves and rests. The territory is in motion in two ways: insofar as humans are 'territories that breathe and walk on two legs',[65] the territory moves when the human roams through the forest to hunt and collect wild seeds to sow in the *chagra* (a defined portion of terrain designated for ecological cultivation strategies); and when the same *chagra* co-shapes the forest as it successionally moves to another plot to allow the previous one to rest, regenerate, and make the forest anew. When the territory rests, humans can also see other facets of reality beyond the physicality of their own immediate experience. These facets or dimensions are not always visible and often require the mediation of powerful beings such as plants. For Hernando, the territory encompasses visible and invisible realms woven together as a tapestry (*tejido*). Hernando poetically describes the territory as the dress of the Earth (*el vestido de la tierra*). This dress is composed of

> all the plants, the leaves, and trees. And between them and the soil, there are many connections. We, humans, destroy this dress; in times of deep separation and socio-ecological crisis it is important to reconnect with the forgotten principle that teaches that all forms of life are sentient and family, and they deserve to live … when the *abuelos* [elders] teach us how to intake the medicine [*yage*][66] they also teach us that the vine gives that connection across time and space; when you look down from the sky [during a *yagé* vision], this very stream is also like a hair. If there is a snowy mountain, if there is a lagoon above, those are like the eyes of the territory that are watching over us; they communicate with the rest of the family: the jaguar, the tapir, the plants … Everything talks, everything connects. Nothing is separate.[67]

This territory as people or kinship, and as meeting place, is simultaneously singular and multiple: the territory is an assortment of persons in relentless continuity of communication and metabolic exchange. A person can learn about this multitude of people *peopling* the territory as they make *territory* by participating in the modes of emergence of this complex self through labour, ritual, and care:

> The territory is like one's body, says Hernando, if something smashes one's toe, one feels even the hairs in one's head [like an electric shock] … If something happens in your head, even your toenails will feel that pain, wouldn't they? What happens in one place

[64] Interview with Hernando Chindoy, 2021.

[65] M Zaiduni, 'The Rights of the Living Pristine Rainforest' (ICCS Global, 2021), https://www.youtube.com/watch?v=dGMK-R9u95M.

[66] The yage concoction combines two different plants: *Banisteriopsis caapi*, which is a vine, and the chacruna (*Psychotria viridis*) a perennial shrub. Chacruna comes from the Quechua verb '*chaqruy*' meaning 'to mix'. *Yajé o ambihuasca* means 'vine of the soul'.

[67] Interview with Hernando Chindoy, 2021.

> can be felt in others, and this sense of inter-connectedness spreads across different life forms, while making the territorial body simultaneously multiple in her lifeways [ie, peoples and places] and singular in her modes of emergence or coming into being [ie, radical interdependence of beings].[68]

Territories like the Inga territory that Hernando's community relates to as kin, teacher and multi-dimensional meeting place are seen differently by those seeking to exploit them for profit. The antitheses of territories of life are so-called 'sacrifice zones', which are places where the quality of human and non-human life is 'compromised in the name of "economic development" or "progress" – but ultimately for the sake of capitalist interests'.[69] Dominant legal regimes worldwide, including environmental law, incorporate sacrifice zones as legally valid necessities on the path to economic growth and capitalist wealth accumulation. Environmental impact assessments, environmental quality criteria, emissions limits, toxic chemicals tolerances, protected lands, and species laws are not designed to require respect for ecologically-based limits. Instead, they legalise diverse kinds of exploitative sacrifice zones.

Sacrifice zones are most readily conceptualised as discrete geographic areas, such as the countless poor or minority communities worldwide living near toxic industries, hazardous waste sites or mining sites.[70] These are often landscapes rendered virtually beyond ecological rehabilitation following mining,[71] or areas poisoned with pesticides to grow soy and other crops.[72] These zones also extend to the atmosphere, other vast expanses, or even the bodies of humans and other beings, where discrete increments of harmful impacts, often seemingly de minimis, accumulate over time with devastating consequences. Thus, while the sacrifice zones often evoke images of highly visible industrial zones, in the case of areas impacted by far-away pollution sources, as well as living beings, every action causing an incremental contribution to such contamination inherently relies on a sacrifice zone.

Sacrifice zones also include 'green' sacrifice zones, which can take several forms. One type is created when a mining or other development project is undertaken in the name of the green energy transition, as in the case of lithium mining.[73] The other resembles 'green land grabbing' that occurs when Indigenous or local communities are driven from their homelands or territories to create human-free wildernesses or protected areas in the name of biodiversity.[74]

[68] ibid.

[69] Souza (n 20) 220.

[70] K Valenzuela-Fuentes, E Alarcón-Barrueta and R Torres-Salinas, 'From Resistance to Creation: Socio-Environmental Activism in Chile's "Sacrifice Zones"' (2021) 13 *Sustainability* 3481.

[71] R Juskus, 'Sacrifice Zones: A Genealogy and Analysis of an Environmental Justice Concept' (2023) 15 *Environmental Humanities* 3.

[72] D Egger and others, 'Ecocide in the Cerrados (Brazilian Savanna): Agribusiness, Water Spoliation and Pesticide Contamination' (2021) 57 *Desenvolvimento e Meio Ambiente* 16.

[73] J Canelas and J Carvalho, 'The Dark Side of the Energy Transition: Extractivist Violence, Energy (in) Justice and Lithium Mining in Portugal' (2023) 100 *Energy Research & Social Science* 103096.

[74] LM Pereira and others, 'Equity and Justice Should Underpin the Discourse on Tipping Points' (2023) 15 *Earth System Dynamics* 341.

Territories of life, too, can involve sacrifices when the lives of plants or animals are taken to provide for the human custodians of the territories. The difference, however, is in what is held sacred, as well as the scale of the 'sacrifice'. With the sacrifice zones of exploitative capitalism, private property and a capitalist growth-insistent economy are held 'sacred', and life systems that include humans are cheapened and sacrificed to promote wealth accumulation, profit and perpetual growth.[75] In a territory of life, sacrifices are made to perpetuate mutually-enhancing relationships between human communities and the living worlds in which they are embedded, and principles of respect, kinship, reciprocity and sufficiency guide the kinds of sacrifices that are made.[76] The scale of sacrifice in a territory of life does not compromise the integrity and renewal of the territory: it is instead *regenerative*.

Table 1 below highlights the values that tend to guide the sacrifices that are made in the growth-insistent regime of modernity in contrast to an ideal set of values aligned with the regenerative regimes of territories of life. We argue that the values associated with regenerative regimes are those that earth system law should embrace.

Table 1 Guiding principles for regenerative regimes

Growth-Insistent Regime	Regenerative Regime
Anthropocentrism	Human-inclusive ecocentrism
Colonialism	Localism and attachment to place
Relationships of property	Relationships of kinship and meshwork
Efficiency to produce more	Sufficiency to produce enough
Production based on utilitarian desires	Production based on true needs
Commodification and profit	Respect and reciprocity
Individuals and private interests	Communities and common good
Material and conceptual monocultures	Diversity and socio-ecological integrity
Selfishness	Sharing and solidarity
Hubris and techno-optimism	Humility and precaution

IV. Territories of Life as a Frame for Earth System Law

This section explores the potential of territories of life to have a broader application and impact, as a visionary frame, that could help shape legal systems to better

[75] Patel and Moore (n 1).

[76] RW Kimmerer, *Braiding Sweetgrass: Indigenous Wisdom, Scientific Knowledge and the Teachings of Plants* (Minneapolis MN, Milkweed Editions, 2015).

respond to the planetary crisis. We posit that earth system law could usefully be framed around a vision of Earth made up of territories of life, which implies an embrace of legal plurality and law beyond the human, a focus on bottom-up commonalities as a source of law across territories and globally, acceptance of rights of nature as a transitional feature of law, and a strong emphasis on ecological and eco-cultural restoration.

A. Legal Plurality and Law Beyond the Human

A vision of territories of life across the Earth includes a broad acceptance of legal plurality and notions of law that go beyond giving legal agency only to humans. In the Andes-Amazon, territories are often considered sources of knowledge and authority, as we have shown above; they play key normative roles and are sometimes cast as primary sources of law and justice. Living and cognitive territories can serve as a prototype of legal analysis and practice modelled after socio-ecological relationalities in what can be conceptualised as 'law beyond the human'.[77] This is a crucial step towards a broader paradigm shift in the law that reckons with the limits of environmental law.[78] This shift requires a new legal ontology that goes beyond symbolic representation.[79] In this view, law surpasses linguistic reductionism and embraces socio-ecological relations, lived experience; possibly even dreams.[80] This 'law unlimited'[81] rests on a bold onto-epistemic and methodological assumption: humans are not the only thinking beings in the world,[82] which means that non-human life is not only sentient, but also meaning-making itself.

Extending the notion of representation to other beings has important implications for legal thought and practice globally. An expansive definition of law is untenable unless humans become more open to a mode of socio-legal reasoning and agency that *exceeds* the human; that is, a mode of acting *with* the world (rather than *in* the world as the backdrop of human action), whereby human perspectives are considered only one among many in a larger cosmological meshwork of lifeways.[83]

[77] A Grear and others (eds), *Posthuman Legalities: New Materialism and Law Beyond the Human* (Cheltenham, Edward Elgar Publishing, 2021).

[78] N Sachs, 'A Wrong Turn with the Rights of Nature Movement' (2023) 36 *Georgetown Environmental Law Review* 39.

[79] A Grear, 'Towards a New Horizon: In Search of a Renewing Socio-Juridical Imaginary' (2013) 3(5) *Oñanti Socio-Legal Series* 966; S Vermeylen, 'Materiality and the Ontological Turn in the Anthropocene: Establishing a Dialogue between Law, Anthropology, and Eco-Philosphy' in LJ Kotzé (ed), *Environmental Law and Governance for the Anthropocene* (Oxford, Hart Publishing, 2017).

[80] A Pelizzon and M Gagliano, 'The Sentience of Plants: Toward a New Regime of Plant Rights, or the Intersection of Animal Rights and Rights of Nature?' (2015) 11 *Australian Animal Protection Law Journal* 5.

[81] M Davies, *Law Unlimited: Materialism, Pluralism, and Legal Theory* (London, Routledge, 2017).

[82] E Kohn, *How Forests Think. Toward and Anthropology beyond the Human* (Oakland CA, University of California Press, 2013).

[83] Vargas Roncancio, *Law, Humans, and Plants* (n 17) 231–32.

B. Bottom-up Commonalities Instead of Top-down Imposition of Uniformity

A territories-of-life approach to law and governance is a way to shift from life-diminishing material and conceptual monocultures to life-enhancing diversity in the conduct of human activities, including through law. This entails a fresh perspective on the quest for universality and uniformity regarding some aspects of law. The critical distinction is between the top-down imposition of uniformity that is dominant in the existing international legal order and a bottom-up recognition of commonalities emerging from different territories of life; a theme that already has been brought indirectly into earth system law discourse.[84] For those who live in them, sacrifice zones are not typically accepted voluntarily. With a territories-of-life framing, universality at societal levels above the local would arise primarily through recognition of commonalities that transcend the place-based particularities of individual territories of life.

In the contemporary world, the commonalities reflected in the Universal Declaration of Human Rights may represent this kind of bottom-up commonality. Likewise, the earth system dilemma that the Anthropocene signifies presents to Earth's people a common problem with spatially and temporally heterogeneous drivers and impacts. Earth system law built on a territories-of-life vision to deal with this dilemma would need to derive from some commonly held notions of justice and fairness that respect local communities and ecosystems. Sbert[85] proposes a notion of ecological justice, encompassing intragenerational, intergenerational and interspecies dimensions, and a shared core principle of avoiding consumption that has harmful impacts beyond essential, minimum needs that enable fulfilling, meaningful lives. Ecological justice of this kind might also lead to social discourse and inclusive decisions involving potentially affected communities that include the consent of those impacted.

C. Rights of Nature as a Bridge

Rights of nature are emerging as a powerful narrative that could helpfully inform a vision for earth system law that embraces the idea of Earth made up of territories of life.[86] Two basic models are emerging. The top-down model involves

[84] L du Toit and LJ Kotzé, 'Reimagining International Environmental Law for the Anthropocene: An Earth System Law Perspective' (2022) 11 *Earth System Governance* 100132.

[85] C Sbert, *The Lens of Ecological Law: A Look at Mining* (Cheltenham, Edward Elgar Publishing, 2020) 92.

[86] G Garver, 'Are Rights of Nature Radical Enough for Ecological Law?' in G Garver and others (eds), *From Environmental to Ecological Law* (London, Routledge 2021) 90–104; Joshua C Gellers, 'Earth System Law and the Legal Status of Non-Humans in the Anthropocene' (2021) 7 *Earth System Governance* 100083.

the recognition of rights of nature in national constitutions or legislation. For example, Ecuador amended its Constitution in 2008 to establish that 'Nature, or Pacha Mama, where life is reproduced and occurs, has the right to integral respect for its existence and for the maintenance and regeneration of its life cycles, structure, functions and evolutionary processes'.[87] Likewise, Bolivia's Law 071, the Ley de Derechos de la Madre Tierra, adopted in 2010, and Law 300, the Ley Marco de la Madre Tierra y Desarrollo Integral para Vivir Bien, adopted in 2012, set out rights of nature and a framework for implementing them.[88] The bottom-up model involves the declaration or formal recognition of rights of nature in specific contexts and places, often with the involvement of Indigenous peoples or local communities attached to those places. A prominent example is the settlement and subsequent legislation that resolved over a century of Māori treaty claims regarding the Whanganui River in Aotearoa New Zealand.

Both models are tenuous, on the one hand raising hopes for transformative change, and on the other hand stirring fears of being subsumed by the dominant colonialist-capitalist economic and legal systems in which they are embedded.[89] Ecuador's Constitutional Court rejected government and industry arguments in delivering several interpretations of constitutional rights of nature that had the effect of halting ecologically-destructive projects, such as metal mining in a protected forest and a coastal aquaculture project in a mangrove forest.[90] In Bolivia, key Indigenous groups opposed rights of nature legislation which they argued watered down versions of the law they supported. Moreover, the rights of nature legislation conflicts with provisions of the Bolivian Constitution that dictate that government must place the highest value on human beings, while promoting industrialisation, among other development activities.[91]

In the case of the Whanganui River, the legislation granting legal personhood to the river requires any decisions by key stakeholders to afford 'particular regard' to principles from the Māori worldview:[92] for example, 'I am the river and the river is me'.[93] However, this 'particular regard' does not include a clear and binding substantive mandate on how to resolve conflicts, and the legislation defers to previous legislation that promotes mining and other extractive uses of the river, as well as to existing private property rights, rights of public access and

[87] Constitution of the Republic of Ecuador (2008) Art 71.

[88] L Muñoz, 'Bolivia's Mother Earth Laws: Is the Ecocentric Legislation Misleading?', *ReVista*, 6 February 2023, https://revista.drclas.harvard.edu/bolivias-mother-earth-laws-is-the-ecocentric-legislation-misleading/.

[89] ID Vargas Roncancio, 'Conjuring Sentient Beings and Relations in the Law: Rights of Nature and a Comparative Praxis of Legal Cosmologies' in K Anker and others (eds), *From Environmental to Ecological Law* (London, Routledge, 2021).

[90] G Prieto, 'The Los Cedros Forest Has Rights: The Ecuadorian Constitutional Court Affirms the Rights of Nature', *Verfassungsblog*, 10 December 2021, https://verfassungsblog.de/the-los-cedros-forest-has-rights/.

[91] Muñoz (n 88) 2.

[92] Te Awa Tupua Act, Arts 15, 30.

[93] Te Awa Tupua Act, Art 13(c).

use, and rights of state-owned and other enterprises.[94] In short, whether rights of nature will resist being subsumed and rendered ineffectual by the neoliberal forces of globalisation and 'development' remains to be seen, but they do offer a meaningfully transformative – and above all, hopeful – alternative to the *status quo ante*; an alternative that also responds to and aligns with the essence of territories of life.

D. Restoration as a Core Transitional Process

Given the extent of disrupted territories of life around the world, the transition toward the vision of Earth made up entirely of territories of life, and a form of law that derives from such a tapestried vision, must arguably also include a strong focus on eco-cultural restoration. Restoration is not only needed for damaged ecosystems, but also for lost connections between people and the places they inhabit, and it often requires giving the common good greater emphasis than private property rights and transactional relationships tied to the globalised economy. A restorative approach in line with a territories-of-life framing is reciprocal restoration.[95] Kimmerer explains that '[r]estoration of reciprocal relationships with land is central to the indigenous vision of restoration'.[96] This approach to restoration could involve restoration of subsistence uses of ecosystems and their gifts, a focus on cultural keystone species, a return to traditional diets, revitalisation of language and cultural practices, use of traditional ecological knowledge, and restoration that benefits non-human life.[97]

To be clear, reciprocal restoration is not a quest to return to an unrecoverable past, but rather a future-oriented and goal-driven course that instils place-attuned 'diverse lifeways and livelihoods as a matter of daily habit, resisting cultural homogenization and supporting diverse ways of living, restorative activities, and habitats and co-inhabitants'.[98] A key challenge is to respond to the 'shifting baseline' syndrome, by which generational decreases in opportunities to connect with nature, a lack of knowledge of the range of historical ecocultural conditions, and societal conditioning to degraded and deteriorated ecosystems can result in inadequate baselines and goals for restoration.[99] The Mannahatta Project – in which a future vision of the highly disrupted pre-colonial ecosystems of Manhattan in the

[94] T Collins and S Esterling, 'Fluid Personality: Indigenous Rights and the Te Awa Tupua (Whanganui River Claims Settlement) Act 2017 in Aotearoa New Zealand' (2019) 20 *Melbourne Journal of International Law* 197.

[95] R Kimmerer, 'Restoration and Reciprocity: The Contributions of Traditional Ecological Knowledge, Chapter 18' in D Egan, EE Hjerpe and J Abrams (eds), *Human Dimensions of Ecological Restoration: Integrating Science, Nature, and Culture* (Washington DC, Island Press, 2011).

[96] ibid 259.

[97] ibid.

[98] H Bliska, RL Vidra and MJ Burke, 'Embracing eco-cultural restoration' (2023) 32 *Restoration Ecology* 14069.

[99] M Soga and KJ Gaston, 'Shifting Baseline Syndrome: Causes, Consequences, and Implications' (2018) 16 *Frontiers in Ecology and the Environment* 222.

United States is aligned with a detailed recreation of its natural history going back to the day before Hudson arrived there in 1609 – provides one inspiring model for envisioning reciprocally restored territories.[100]

E. Overcoming Troubling Counter-narratives

To achieve a long-term vision of Earth made up entirely of a diverse and pluralistic array of territories of life, powerful counter-narratives must consciously and continuously be confronted and overcome. Three of the most formidable of these interrelated counter-narratives are: the narrative of denial that an ecological crisis exists,[101] the narrative (famously per Margaret Thatcher) that 'there is no alternative' (TINA) to never-ending capitalistic economic growth,[102] and the narrative of ecomodernism. All these growth-insistent counter-narratives culminate in the fantasies of ecomodernism, which, along with denialism, is grounded in

> a desire to continue the modern project of walling societies off from their environments, either through positing an infinite series of technological fixes that could keep the illusion alive, or by denying that there is anything to worry about in the first place.[103]

The ongoing project of solar-geoengineering is a worrying example in this respect.[104] Ecomodernists envision in their 2015 Ecomodernist Manifesto a 'good Anthropocene' in which 'humans use their growing social, economic, and technological powers to make life better for people, stabilize the climate, and protect the natural world'.[105] The key to the ecomodernist narrative is decoupling economic growth and human consumption from ecological impacts and relying on fantastical technologies, such as solar-geoengineering. Ecomodernists believe that 'active, conscious and accelerated decoupling'[106] will enable a perpetually growing economy to provide the means to address ecological challenges and 'spare nature'. These means are almost always entirely technological: ever-increasing agricultural intensification, advanced nuclear and solar power, automation, de-salination of ocean water, capture and storage of atmospheric carbon, and climate engineering.[107]

[100] EW Sanderson, *Mannahatta: A Natural History of New York City* (New York, Abrams, 2009).

[101] A Phillips, 'How Republicans Are Echoing Climate Change Conspiracy Theories', *Newsweek*, 11 February 2023, https://www.newsweek.com/republicans-echo-climate-change-conspiracy-theories-1779865.

[102] BW Bateman, 'There Are Many Alternatives: Margaret Thatcher in the History of Economic Thought' (2002) 24 *Journal of the History of Economic Thought* 307.

[103] M Tănăsescu, *Ecocene Politics* (Cambridge, Open Book Publishers, 2019).

[104] See also Morrow, Chapter 6 in this book.

[105] J Asafu-Adjaye and others, *An Ecomodernist Manifesto* (April 2015), http://www.ecomodernism.org/manifesto-english.

[106] ibid 25.

[107] Asafu-Adjaye (n 105).

Contrary to the proposals in this chapter to frame earth system law around a vision of Earth made up of territories of life, ecomodernists reject the notion 'that human societies must harmonize with nature to avoid economic and ecological collapse'.[108] Ecomodernism is singled out because it is the most likely result of maintaining dominant growth-insistent approaches to law across the globe. Money and power are being heavily invested in that future vision. As a stark example, the ecomodernist fantasy of complete mastery and control of nature unites with the global capitalist-colonial project in the disturbingly detailed imaginings, plans and investments for the colonisation of Mars. Not surprisingly, themes of 'frontier conquest, colonization, and exploitation … are dominant in American space exploration rhetoric and in public discourse about the human future in space'.[109] NASA has already funded unmanned missions to Mars, and in 2020 its Artemis Plan was to establish a human-occupied base camp on the Moon by 2024 with a view to later using it for human missions to Mars.[110] Colonisation of Mars is envisioned as early as this century,[111] and a remarkable amount of detailed thinking and planning is already underway in regard to the kinds of energy and other infrastructure, human health care, continual funding, and employment opportunities, that would be needed on Mars.[112]

Our proposition is that it would be better to keep law firmly grounded on the one and only Earth that humanity can safely rely on for material, cultural and spiritual sustenance. Earth system law should firmly reject the ecomodernist path to the future and the legal regimes that enable it. The proposals in this chapter for placed-based law, grounded in territories of life, are anchors for the counter-narrative and legal alternative to ecomodernism.

V. Conclusion

The virulence of the dominant models of economics, law and governance that earth system law and related legal approaches should aim to radically transform and replace is abundantly clear. The beacon on the horizon that guides the current dominant socially-constructed normative regimes of law and economics is progress grounded in endless economic growth and wealth creation. A more hopeful beacon is one grounded in a vision of the entire Earth made up of a plurality of diverse territories of life, held together through a shared commitment to mutually-enhancing human–Earth relationships and to the flourishing

[108] ibid 6.
[109] L Billings, 'Colonizing Other Planets Is a Bad Idea' (2019) 110 *Futures* 44.
[110] NASA, 'Artemis Plan: NASA's Lunar Exploration Program Overview' (September 2020) https://www.nasa.gov/wp-content/uploads/2020/12/artemis_plan-20200921.pdf.
[111] RJ Gustafson and others, 'A View of Future Human Colonies on Mars' (2003) 654 *AIP Conference Proceedings* 1250.
[112] AR Johnson, 'Biodiversity Requirements for Self-Sustaining Space Colonies' (2019) 110 *Futures* 24.

of all life. This beacon would transcend the current quest for 30 per cent of the Earth to be treated as 'protected areas' by 2030,[113] (which leaves unresolved what is ordained for the 70 per cent left 'unprotected'), with a commitment to treat 100 per cent of the Earth as life-enhancing territories of life as soon as possible.

Difficult challenges, such as applying territories-of-life framing to the urban centres in which over half of the world's people now live, or dealing with complex spatial and temporal interdependencies among different territories, must be acknowledged. Addressing these and other challenges would benefit from additional research on how territories-of-life framing can reach from the local to the global. Notably, action-oriented research to achieve this refinement of territories-of-life-based approaches must be encouraged.

To be clear, it is not just environmental law that needs reforming, as has been the focus of some calls for earth system law. Instead, entire monocultural legal systems that serve to uphold the global colonial-capitalist narrative that is driving ever-more dire social-ecological disintegration need radical reform. The Earth and all its territories and life systems can be lead sources in a form of earth system law that, with the right kind of listening and interpretation, can guide humanity toward a flourishing, life-enhancing future. The vision of territories of life everywhere on Earth opens the door to such a much-needed radical transformation in a hopeful, albeit admittedly challenging, way.

[113] Convention on Biological Diversity, 'Kunming-Montreal Global Biodiversity Framework' (19 December 2022).

8

Stain-Guarding Earth System Law in the Enshittocene: Back to the Future for Sustainable Development

MICHELLE LIM

I. Introduction

'Enshittification' is the American Dialect Society's 2023 'Word of the Year'.[1] The word, coined by Cory Doctorow, explains the process by which digital platforms (eg Facebook, TikTok, X/ Twitter etc) become bad for both users and advertisers, and ultimately result in the demise of the platform. In the words of Ben Zimmer, Chair of the American Dialect Society, 'Enshittification is a sadly apt term for how our online lives have become gradually degraded'.[2]

Doctorow highlights the emergence of digital platforms as the 'dominant life forms' of the internet.[3] The core of his analysis is not that platforms have emerged. Rather, as the middlemen of the internet, these spaces, initially good to their users, self-implode in the pursuit of self-interest and profit.[4] The title of Doctorow's February 2024 *Financial Times* article heralds that '"Enshittification" is coming for absolutely everything'. Doctorow therefore refers to current times as the 'Enshittocene'.[5]

Meanwhile, earth system law has emerged with the aim to craft a legal response to planetary scale change in a more famous '-cene': the Anthropocene. The term Anthropocene emerged at the turn of the millennium.[6] It has come to refer to

[1] American Dialect Society, '2023 Word of the Year Is "Enshittification"', 5 January 2024, https://americandialect.org/2023-word-of-the-year-is-enshittification/; C Doctorow, '"Enshittification" Is Coming for Absolutely Everything', *Financial Times*, 8 February 2024, https://www.ft.com/content/5efa975d-9994-42e3-a718-5924e71e0938.

[2] ibid.

[3] 'Enshittification: A Monopoly Story with Cory Doctorow' (December 2023), https://www.youtube.com/watch?v=5tJ2vgNPXxs.

[4] Doctorow (n 1).

[5] ibid.

[6] PJ Crutzen and EF Stoermer, 'The Anthropocene' (2000) 41 *Global Change Newsletter* 17; PJ Crutzen, 'Geology of Mankind' (2002) 415 *Nature* 23.

the recent and unparalleled geological, ecological, sociological and anthropological planetary-scale shifts caused by human activity.[7] Doctorow's Enshittocene is inarguably a reference to the Anthropocene. The parallels are clear. The Enshittocene characterises the degradation of online life; the Anthropocene, the degradation of life on Earth and of the life of the planet itself.

The aim of earth system law is to develop law in acknowledgement of earth system change in the Anthropocene.[8] This is reflected in the title of this edited book: *Earth System Law: Governing Planetary Transformations in the Anthropocene*. Meanwhile, discussion of the need for earth system law often occurs alongside acknowledgement that existing law, and in particular environmental law, is ill-suited to address the global-scale social-ecological disruption of the Anthropocene.[9]

While other contributions to this book explore principles, pathways and plural worldviews at the frontiers of earth system law, my objective is more modest. My chapter seeks to examine how earth system law, and the novel principles, concepts, values and imaginaries that it inspires, can be protected from the corrupting factors of neoliberalism.[10] My starting point is that enshittification of the online space stems from the same neoliberal ideology that has wrought social-ecological destruction across the planet. Keeping with a discussion of principles, I explore the possibilities of 'stain-guarding' earth system law through the case-study of the principle of sustainable development.[11]

My contention is that sustainable development has been abducted by, and assimilated into, the powers of free-market capitalism. I argue that recalling what sustainable development was meant to be, and contrasting this with what it has become, allows an exploration of processes of enshittification far beyond

[7] ES Brondizio et al, 'Re-Conceptualizing the Anthropocene: A Call for Collaboration' (2016) 39 *Global Environmental Change* 318; CN Waters and others, 'The Anthropocene is Functionally and Stratigraphically Distinct from the Holocene' (2016) 351 *Science* 2622.

[8] LJ Kotzé and RE Kim, 'Earth System Law: The Juridical Dimensions of Earth System Governance' (2019) 1 *Earth System Governance* 100003.

[9] Kotzé and Kim (n 8); L Mai and E Boulot, 'Harnessing the Transformative Potential of Earth System Law: From Theory to Practice' (2021) 7 *Earth System Governance* 100103; L du Toit and LJ Kotzé, 'Reimagining International Environmental Law for the Anthropocene: An Earth System Law Perspective' (2022) 11 *Earth System Governance* 100132.

[10] See, for a related inquiry, Garver and Vargas Roncancio, Chapter 7 in this book.

[11] I am cognisant of the rivers of ink that have been spilt discussing the legal status of sustainable development. Is it a principle, customary law norm, or objective? Drawing on French and Scotford, I have argued elsewhere (M Lim, 'Sustainable Development Principles and the Global South in the Context of Planetary Change' in S Khair, S Alam and ME Haque (eds), *Implementation of Sustainable Development in the Global South: Strategies, Innovations and Challenges* (Oxford, Hart Publishing, 2024)) that sustainable development is best understood as a principle (D French, 'Sustainable Development' in M Fitzmaurice, D Ong and P Merkouris (eds), *Research Handbook on International Environmental Law* (Cheltenham, Edward Elgar Publishing, 2010); E Scotford, *Environmental Principles and the Evolution of Environmental Law* (Oxford, Hart Publishing, 2017)). Ultimately, I agree, however, with Schacherer (S Schacherer, 'Sustainable Development in the International Legal Order' in S Schacherer (ed), *Sustainable Development in EU Foreign Investment Law* (Leiden, Brill Nijhoff, 2021)) that discussions as to the specific legal status of sustainable development have become tedious, as the term clearly has normative effect.

the digital sphere. I argue that an exploration of the enshittification of sustainable development facilitates stain-guarding of similar aspirations of equity alongside multigenerational and multispecies flourishing set out in earth system justice and earth system law.

It is personally meaningful to have the discussion of this chapter in a book brought together by Louis Kotzé. Kotzé, of course, not only introduced the concept of earth system law alongside Rakhyun Kim[12] but also, with Sam Adelman and Felix Dube, has characterised sustainable development as an irredeemably flawed principle for the Anthropocene.[13]

My conversation with the work of Kotzé and colleagues begins from a point of 'furious agreement'. First, we are similarly appalled by what sustainable development *has become*. Second, we concur that capture by the neoliberal machine is the cause of sustainable development's grotesque mutation. We even agree on the corresponding need for transformations towards relational value systems. Where we differ, however, is on the question of what to do with sustainable development. While Kotzé and colleagues deem the concept unsalvageable; I am not yet prepared to give up on it – at least not on a particular version of sustainable development. Further, given the resonance of the aims of earth system law and justice with sustainable development in its pre-enshittified form, it is important that we understand *how* sustainable development was and continues to be co-opted. It is my hope that this understanding could go some way to ensuring that developments at the frontiers of earth system law (such as those set out in this book) are not similarly enshittified – and that enshittified concepts, such as sustainable development, may be redeemed.

This chapter therefore proceeds as follows: I first situate discussion within the foundational and evolving scholarship of earth system law. I also highlight here, like others in this book, earth system law's ambition towards transformations beyond the neoliberalised status quo.[14] Next, I discuss how enshittification in the digital space is but a manifestation of neoliberalism. Then I set out neoliberalism's enshittification of sustainable development. From there, I argue that sustainable development is salvageable if we go back to the future – to a time prior to the enshittification of the term and when neoliberalism had yet to gain a stranglehold on everything. It is from there, that I then discuss the stain-guarding of earth system law from neoliberalism through the transformative framework developed by Mai and Boulot in 2021.[15] From this, I aim to initiate a conversation around the pitfalls and opportunities for earth system law as it strives to innovate legal principles, concepts, processes and

[12] Kotzé and Kim (n 8).

[13] LJ Kotzé, S Adelman and F Dube, 'The Problem with Sustainable Development in the Anthropocene Epoch' in PD Burdon and J Martel (eds), *The Routledge Handbook of Law and the Anthropocene* (Abingdon-on-Thames, Routledge, 2023); LJ Kotzé and S Adelman, 'Environmental Law and the Unsustainability of Sustainable Development: A Tale of Disenchantment and of Hope' (2023) 34 *Law and Critique* 227.

[14] Eg, Morrow, Chapter 6 and Burdon, Chapter 10 in this book.

[15] Mai and Boulot (n 9).

actors, for the Anthropocene – lest these innovations are also debased by the stains of neoliberalism.

II. Evolving Understandings of Earth System Law

Earth system law is directed towards addressing, through law, Galaz's[16] 'Anthropocene gap'.[17] The legal gap Kotzé and Kim identify is the inability of dominant legal frameworks, epistemologies and ontologies to respond to earth system change. Earth system law therefore seeks to develop a research agenda, and ultimately 'a new overarching legal phenomenon' that adequately responds to planetary-scale disruption in the Anthropocene.[18] Earth system law opens up opportunities to take into account some of the most pressing current and future global-scale social-ecological considerations. These include uncertainty across scales (including the planetary scale) in relation to social and biophysical tipping points, as well as intergenerational and more-than-human interdependencies.[19]

In this section, I attempt to briefly describe what earth system law is. In doing so, I highlight links to earth system science and earth system justice. I conclude the section by highlighting where earth system law scholarship has recognised the need for ambition that transcends the neoliberal paradigm of the status quo.

A. Law in a Rapidly Changing Earth System

Earth system law has emerged in recognition of the limits of environmental law in the context of accelerated disruption of the earth system.[20] Earth system law thus aims to take an approach which considers law in light of earth system science. The approach therefore adopts a systems perspective – one which recognises the instability of the Anthropocene and the need for responses that differ from the earlier epoch of the Holocene.[21]

A key concept of earth system science is that of the planetary boundaries approach.[22] This science-based framework describes planetary processes that

[16] V Galaz, *Global Environmental Governance, Technology and Politics: The Anthropocene Gap* (Cheltenham, Edward Elgar Publishing, 2014).

[17] Kotzé and Kim (n 8).

[18] See also, Kotzé, Angstadt and Kim, Chapter 2 in this book.

[19] ibid.

[20] LJ Kotzé, 'Earth System Law for the Anthropocene: Rethinking Environmental Law Alongside the Earth System Metaphor' (2020) 11 *Transnational Legal Theory* 75.

[21] ibid.

[22] J Rockström and others, 'A Safe Operating Space for Humanity' (2009) 461 *Nature* 472; W Steffen and others, 'Planetary Boundaries: Guiding Human Development on a Changing Planet' (2015) 347 *Science* 1259885.

maintain the functioning of the earth system. The planetary boundaries framework explores global-scale limits that human activity needs to respect to in order to stay as close to safe Holocene conditions as possible.[23] The approach recognises, on the one hand, that the more planetary boundaries are transgressed, the greater the likelihood that the earth system will shift to an irreversible, undesirable state. On the other hand, efforts to stay within these boundaries can buy time to respond to abrupt changes to earth system functions.[24] While planetary boundaries were originally conceptualised at the biophysical level, there are increasing efforts to link understandings of biophysical systems with human systems.

In subsequent iterations of planetary boundaries, Rockström et al propose earth system boundaries which combine efforts to retain the integrity of the Earth's biophysical systems while taking justice considerations into account in order to limit harm to humans from earth system change.[25] At the core of these justice considerations sits the 'three "I"s' approach of earth system justice. The three 'I's emphasises inter- and intra- generational justice alongside interspecies justice and earth system stability,[26] thus echoing the foundational elements of sustainable development. Boundaries in the latest iteration also take into account limits on sub-global scales – in addition to those at the planetary level.[27]

In their foundational paper on earth system law, Kotzé and Kim contemplate the 'normative regulatory role' of law in contributing to earth system governance's aims to address the 'human-social aspects of earth system change'.[28] Due to the significant role that law plays in structuring society, the growing integration of social-ecological planetary concerns in earth system understandings described above[29] underscores the potential for earth system law to play an important role in adverting catastrophic earth system disruption.

B. The Normative Ambition of Earth System Law Beyond Neoliberalism

One of the characteristics that distinguishes earth system law from environmental law is the earth system law's aims of normative ambition.[30] Earth system law, centred on an earth system-oriented understanding of abrupt planetary-scale change and socio-ecological tipping points, appreciates the urgency with which legal frameworks need to challenge the status quo and compel anticipatory and

[23] ibid.
[24] Steffen and others (n 22).
[25] Rockström and others (n 22).
[26] J Gupta and others, 'Earth System Justice Needed to Identify and Live within Earth System Boundaries' (2023) 6 *Nature Sustainability* 630.
[27] J Rockström and others, 'Safe and Just Earth System Boundaries' (2023) 619 *Nature* 102.
[28] Kotzé and Kim (n 8).
[29] Rockström and others (n 22).
[30] Du Toit and Kotzé (n 9).

immediate action. At the same time, there is growing recognition within earth system law scholarship of neoliberalism as a structural barrier to ambition.[31] Meanwhile, unsustainable resource extraction and consumption have been identified by earth system scientists as the key drivers of transgression of earth system limits.[32]

In earth system law scholarship, du Toit and Kotzé[33] highlight the severe lack of ambition in instruments such as the United Nations (UN) Framework Convention on Climate Change, the Paris Agreement and the proposed Global Pact for the Environment. They point specifically to the inability of the Pact to 'radically transform the predatory neoliberal world order'. Similarly, Mai and Boulot[34] refer to Bartel and Graham,[35] who highlight how existing legal paradigms entrench an implicit hierarchy of corporate and property rights which take precedence over social-ecological concerns.

In the section that follows, I explore the characteristics of neoliberalism and its embeddedness as the status quo. I then highlight how neoliberalism has enabled enshittification of the digital space. This facilitates the discussion that then follows on the cautionary tale, for earth system law, of how sustainable development has been enshittified.

III. Enshittification = Neoliberalisation

A. What is Neoliberalism?

Neoliberalism has been variously described as today's 'dominant social paradigm';[36] the structure of the current status quo;[37] the 'predominant ideology of the past 40 years';[38] and a 'revolutionary turning point in the world's social and economic history'.[39] Key characteristics of neoliberalism can be synthesised

[31] Mai and Boulot (n 9).
[32] Rockström and others (n 22).
[33] Du Toit and Kotzé (n 9).
[34] Mai and Boulot (n 9).
[35] R Bartel and N Graham, 'Ecological Reconciliation on Private Agricultural Land: Moving beyond the Human–Nature Binary in Property-Environment Contests' in A Akhtar-Khavari and BJ Richardson (eds), *Ecological Restoration Law: Concepts and Case Studies* (Abingdon-on-Thames, Routledge, 2019).
[36] JM Bogert and others, 'Reviewing the Relationship between Neoliberal Societies and Nature: Implications of the Industrialized Dominant Social Paradigm for a Sustainable Future' (2022) 27 *Ecology and Society* (article 7) 1.
[37] A Datta and I Chakraborty, 'Are You Neoliberal Fit? The Politics of Consumption under Neoliberalism' in O Kravets and others (eds), *The SAGE Handbook of Consumer Culture* (London, Sage, 2018).
[38] JE Stiglitz, 'Neoliberalism, Keynesian Economics, and Responding to Today's Inflation' (2024) 12 *Review of Keynesian Economics* 1.
[39] D Harvey, *A Brief History of Neoliberalism* (Oxford, Oxford University Press, 2005) 2, cited in R Venugopal, 'Neoliberalism as Concept' (2015) 44 *Economy and Society* 165.

from the literature. First, neoliberalism is a form of capitalism. The ideology therefore emphasises profit, private ownership and competition. Neoliberalism further entrenches deregulation and associated minimal intervention from the state as well as individualisation and consumerism.[40] Neoliberalism, often understood as market fundamentalism,[41] therefore centres market relations in politics, economics and society such that the functions that were previously the domain of the state are now redirected to 'individual responsibility'.[42] A key problem of neoliberalism is that competitive markets become entrenched in all areas of life as not only an economic ideology but ultimately also as moral and 'practical' imperatives as well.

With an ideology centred on markets and profit-making, it is unsurprising that neoliberalism is further defined by marketing and media actively directed towards consumerism. This, in turn, has the tendency to crowd out other behaviour,[43] resulting in the structuring of society as an endless marketing campaign. Mythmaking, is, of course, central to any successful marketing campaign. Datta and Chakraborty illustrate how such mythmaking is central to maintaining the neoliberal economy (and by extension the neoliberal society). This fake world full of 'friendliness and not friendships' enables the emergence of 'new prophets of capital'. These prophets take the form of a 'new generation of wealthy mythmakers, masquerading as progressive thinkers' who champion the free market as the solution to societal challenges.[44] Datta and Chakraborty go on to highlight how masses of neoliberal subjects are thus inculcated to turn away from critical socio-economic and structural analyses of current times. Instead, they are taught to see themselves as commodities and to view failures to live up to neoliberal fantasies as personal failures. At the same time, Bogert et al[45] highlight how corporate ownership of mass media, and mass media's reliance on corporate advertising, result in the promotion of the neoliberal doctrine in service of corporate and political elites. This is done through claims to individualism and free choice and the message that neoliberal subjects are in charge of their own happiness so long as they 'work hard enough and make the correct purchasing decisions'.[46] Thus, the overarching indoctrination is that consumption is the source of happiness, and that overconsumption and personal gain are morally acceptable ways of structuring society.[47]

[40] Bogert and others (n 36); Stiglitz (n 38).

[41] Stiglitz (n 38).

[42] S Springer, K Birch and J MacLeavy, 'An Introduction to Neoliberalism' in S Springer, K Birch and J MacLeavy (eds), *Handbook of Neoliberalism* (Abingdon-on-Thames, Routledge, 2016).

[43] Bogert and others (n 36).

[44] Datta and Chakraborty (n 37).

[45] Bogert and others (n 36).

[46] S Kantartzis and M Molineux, 'The Influence of Western Society's Construction of a Healthy Daily Life on the Conceptualisation of Occupation' (2011) 18(1) *Journal of Occupational Science* 62; and P Leonard, *Postmodern Welfare: Reconstructing an Emancipatory Project* (London, Sage, 1997).

[47] ibid.

I argue below that Doctorow's observations of enshittification of the digital space represent an example of the logical end point of neoliberalism in a particular sector. In subsequent sections, I then build on observations of enshittification in the digital space to facilitate further understanding and anticipation of neoliberalism's enshittification of everything.

B. Neoliberalism as Enshittification

The term 'enshittification' was first published in 2022. Nevertheless, only in Doctorow's 2024 *Financial Times* piece does the term 'neoliberal' appear, and even then, only once. Further, Doctorow[48] anticipates, but does not address, potential suggestions that enshittification is an illustration of capitalism in practice. Yet, when articulating the driving forces of enshittification, Doctorow underscores causal patterns which can be directly linked to the core tenets of neoliberalism. Doctorow defines the four constraints on enshittification as: competition, regulation, self-help and labour unionisation. Of these, regulation and unionisation are clearly antidotes to neoliberalism's deregulation, privatisation and individualisation. Similarly, the availability of 'self-help' mechanisms in the tech space can readily be equated to the role of the state or other collective endeavours to impose limits on neoliberalism's (or indeed enshittification's) excesses.

'Aha!' you might say. 'What about competition? – Doctorow's first identified limit on enshittificatory impulses. Is competition not at the core of neoliberalism itself?' While competition is an identified part of neoliberal capitalism, to my mind, the lack of competition identified by Doctorow is in fact an observation of the monopoly and oligarchy that emerges at neoliberalism's logical conclusion. Stiglitz,[49] for example, identifies neoliberalism's fallacies as emerging from false assumptions based on 'simplistic models that ignored problems of imperfections of competition and information, externalities and public goods, and incompleteness of markets'.

At the same time, Myers[50] draws attention to the oligarchical 'rule by rich' in one of the most neoliberalised of all countries – the United States (US). She highlights how, in the US, the extremely affluent have a stranglehold over politics. Consequently, the excessively wealthy use law and policy, through their political power to enrich themselves to the detriment of everyone else.[51] Doctorow even presents examples of this. He highlights that the US Digital Millennium Copyright Act 1998 and Article 6 of the European Union's Copyright Directive 2019 prevent interoperability that would facilitate an alternative to Facebook or allow

[48] Doctorow (n 1).
[49] Stiglitz (n 38).
[50] E Myers, 'The Non-scandal of American Oligarchy' (2017) 20 *Theory & Event* 296.
[51] P Krugman, 'Oligarchy, American Style', *New York Times*, 4 November 2011.

Android phones to play iPhone apps. This is despite the fact that Apple machines were deliberately reconfigured to operate popular Microsoft Office software such as Word, Excel and PowerPoint. Similarly, Facebook was able to push MySpace into oblivion through the use of a bot that allowed users to migrate their data and networks to Facebook.[52] The limits to competition that Doctorow observes, therefore, can readily be attributed to the oligarchical 'neoliberal social settlement' of the past 40-plus years, where market values have been naturalised into virtually all parts of society and how law is weaponised to protect the interests of the wealthy.[53]

It is curious that while Doctorow seeks to establish street-cred through provocative phraseology, he nevertheless draws the line at provoking the status quo. By failing to attribute the woes of online platforms and indeed the 'enshittification of everything' to neoliberal capitalism, Doctorow steers well clear of engaging with enshittification's root cause.

There could be a simple explanation for this: the satisfaction of being the first to define a novel concept. As discussed above, however, it is clear that Doctorow's observations of enshittification are, in fact, observations of the manifestation of neoliberalism. Therefore, Doctorow's failure to recognise that enshittification is merely neoliberal capitalism playing out in the contemporary digital space highlights how entrenched neoliberalism has become as a dominant social paradigm. It also provides a further illustration of how neoliberalism has entered the realm of the 'taken for granted'.[54]

Nevertheless, I find Doctorow's enshittification to be a helpful articulation of present-day neoliberalism in action. In the remainder of this chapter, I continue to use enshittification with a firm sense of the term representing neoliberalism's powers to corrupt and co-opt.

IV. Neoliberalism's Enshittification of Sustainable Development

Sustainable development is

> development that meets the needs of the present without compromising the ability of future generations to meet their own needs.[55]

Ask anyone working on sustainable development what sustainable development is, and they will likely recite the above definition from the Brundtland Report. Kotzé and Adelman note that the 1987 Brundtland Report from the World Commission on Environment and Development (WCED) emerged alongside neoliberalism's

[52] Doctorow (n 1).
[53] Myers (n 50).
[54] Myers (n 50).
[55] World Commission on Environment and Development, *Report of the World Commission on Environment and Development: Our Common Future* (New York, United Nations, 1987).

ascendancy. They draw attention to the Report's emphasis on 'a new era of economic growth'.[56] Being a characteristically neoliberal brainchild, the Report aims to *have it all*. The Report speaks, in the same breath, of a 'forceful' growth which is 'at the same time socially and environmentally sustainable'.[57]

I argue that sustainable development should be interpreted in a way that reflects traditional human–nature relationships that go much further back into the past, long before 1987. This is precisely the argument of Vice-President Christopher Weeramantry in his Separate Opinion in the *Gabčíkovo-Nagymaros* case before the International Court of Justice (ICJ). This was the first instance where the ICJ was asked to consider the legal status of sustainable development.

In his Separate Opinion, Justice Weeramantry describes sustainable development as the need to reconcile environmental and development considerations. When recognising that 'the right to development and the right to environmental protection – are important principles of current international law',[58] it is Weeramantry's characterisation of 'development' that is instructive. Drawing on the UN's Declaration on the Right to Development, 1986, he states:

> 'Development' means, of course, development not merely for the sake of development and the economic gain it produces, but for its value in increasing the *sum total of human happiness and welfare*. That could perhaps be called the first principle of the law relating to development (emphasis added).[59]

Weeramantry then emphasises that environmental protection is a principle of international law and 'a *sine qua non* for numerous human rights'. For Weeramantry, sustainable development not only underscores understandings of 'development' as human development (as opposed to economic development and endless economic growth); he also recognises that the right to development is not absolute and must occur only within the boundaries of what can be tolerated by the environment. A core part of Weeramantry's Separate Opinion is a comprehensive survey, across civilisations and generations, of the understanding of the need for limits to development defined by the capacity of the environment to withstand such activities:

> Sustainable development is thus not merely a principle of modern international law. It is one of the most ancient ideas in the human heritage. Fortified by the rich insights that can be gained from millennia of human experience, it has an important part to play in the service of international law.[60]

Weeramantry articulates how sustainable development reflects millennia of insights. Meanwhile, Kotzé and Adelman highlight how sustainable development

[56] Kotzé and Adelman (n 13).
[57] WCED (n 55) xii.
[58] *Gabčíkovo-Nagymaros Project (Hungary v Slovakia)* [1997] ICJ 7, 25 September 1997, https://www.icj-cij.org/sites/default/files/case-related/92/092-19970925-JUD-01-03-EN.pdf, Separate Opinion of Vice-President Weeramantry, p 88, at 89.
[59] ibid 91 (footnote omitted).
[60] ibid 110–11.

can be traced, in the contemporary context, to the 1970s. They explain that the term originated as a 'noble idea' that individuals would choose a type of development that also enhanced human well-being, social justice and environmental protection. Despite this, Kotzé and Adelman advocate for abandoning the concept. Their central reason for doing so is the contemporary understanding of (neoliberal) 'development' in sustainable development. 'Development', they argue, becomes problematic in a world where 'all mainstream models of development' have become synonymous with economic growth, and where neoliberalism lies at the core of the sustained hegemony of dominating definitions of development.[61]

This, of course, raises the question of how sustainable development became enshittified in the first place. In some ways this is self-evident. Recalling neoliberalism's central premise that society should be structured through markets, eventually the dominant social paradigm came to claim that market forces *should* be used for the environment's own good.[62] Similar to Doctorow's enshittification, we have the situation where the concept of sustainable development is first good to 'users' – human and more-than-human subjects. However, in attempts to extract the value of multi-species worlds to attract corporate interests, sustainable development has been used to entice subjects and corporate interests into a sub-optimal situationship.

Further, Mohanty[63] draws attention to the current era of deferred liberalism that has emerged in the new wave of capitalism. Here, neoliberalism subjugates equality to liberty. This has been entrenched further with the hegemony of the United States, alongside the massive expansion of Western capital and technology. Western powers therefore claim Western values, culture and religion as superior while derogating from affirmations of equality, the dignity of nations, cultures and religions and rights to self-determination – principles expounded in the triumph of post-World War II global anti-colonial and independence movements. Thus, even in the Global South, one observes how the ascendancy of neoliberalism in, for example, India has come at the expense of equality.[64] Meanwhile, in China, 'harmony and order' have been prioritised over equality.[65] This explains how 'development' in sustainable development – a framing which should have equity between and within generations at its core, has similarly come to champion economic growth over the well-being of all humans.

[61] Kotzé and Adelman (n 13).

[62] C Bonneuil, 'Tell Me Where You Come from, I Will Tell You Who You Are: A Genealogy of Biodiversity Offsetting Mechanisms in Historical Context' (2015) 192 *Biological Conservation* 485; Bogert and others (n 36).

[63] M Mohanty, 'Inequality from the Perspective of the Global South' in M Juergensmeyer, S Sassen, MB Steger and V Faessel (eds), *The Oxford Handbook of Global Studies* (Oxford, Oxford University Press, 2018) 210–27.

[64] Dubey and Thorat (2012), cited in M Mohanty, 'Inequality from the Perspective of the Global South' in M Juergensmeyer, S Sassen, MB Steger and V Faessel (eds), *The Oxford Handbook of Global Studies* (Oxford, Oxford University Press, 2018) 210–27.

[65] R Gao, 'The unarticulated conception of equality in early Confucianism, and its relation to modern conceptions' in Y Xinzhong (ed), *Reconceptualising Confucian Philosophy in the 21st Century* (Heidelberg, Springer 2017) 241–56.

Specifically in the co-optation of sustainable development, Purvis, Mao and Robinson[66] trace the emergence of the term to the Club of Rome's calls for a sustainable world system in *The Limits to Growth*.[67] The discourse of the 1970s argued that the Western world's capitalist economic growth was incompatible with ecological and social flourishing.[68] However, by the 1980s, in the Brundtland Report, economic growth, once identified as the problem for environmental and social integrity, had now been repackaged as the solution.[69] This, Purvis, Mao and Robinson point out, was the end result of the co-optation of the earlier concepts which championed environmental and social considerations.[70]

In sum, Justice Weeramantry's Separate Opinion in *Gabčíkovo-Nagymaros* recognises inextricable and continued human–nature relationships across millennia. In this vein, sustainable development needs to be understood as multi-species flourishing within and between generations. Sustainable development has, however, become enshittified. This reflects the emergence of the concept in the decades of neoliberalism's ascendancy. The section that follows rallies against the enshittification powers of the dominant social paradigm. The section argues that sustainable development was, and can be, the antidote to the continued enshittification of the earth system and the lives of the majority of multi-species on our planet.

V. Back to the Future for Sustainable Development

Sustainable development and development need to be reclaimed from neoliberalism and returned to their original meaning and practice such as that set out in Justice Weeramantry's Separate Opinion in the *Gabčíkovo-Nagymaros* case. Kotzé and Adelman[71] point to suggestions that sustainable development may have crystallised as a principle of customary international law, thus bestowing on the concept a 'constitutional'-like status in international law. This is a further reason why sustainable development should not be abandoned: its embeddedness across international and domestic instruments and court decisions. Nevertheless, like all legal principles, sustainable development must be reclaimed and interpreted in the context of the times – a context which necessitates the abandonment of neoliberalism and the normalisation of human–nature relationships. In the sub-sections that follow, I highlight how a range of scholarship increasingly emphasises twin global

[66] B Purvis, Y Mao and D Robinson, 'Three Pillars of Sustainability: In Search of Conceptual Origins' (2019) 14 *Sustainability Science* 681.

[67] DH Meadows and others, *The Limits to Growth: A Report for the Club of Rome's Project on the Predicament of Mankind* (New York, Universe Books, 1972). The Club of Rome is an international think-tank established in 1968.

[68] Purvis, Mao and Robinson (n 66).

[69] ibid.

[70] ibid.

[71] Kotzé and Adelman (n 13).

priorities of people and planet without needing to 'balance' that with an insidious further pillar of profit. I then highlight how plural understandings of relationality bring further depth to this discourse.

A. From Three Pillars to Two Non-Negotiables

Purvis, Mao and Robinson[72] attempt to trace the genesis of the well-known 'three pillar' or Venn diagram framing of sustainable development. These visualisations of sustainable development are respectively three social, economic and environmental pillars holding up the 'roof' of sustainability; or three intersecting circles where the interaction of society, economy and environment constitute sustainable development. They note the difficulty of pin-pointing the origins of these conceptualisations while drawing attention to the varied disciplines that have contributed to sustainable development discourse. They identify Barbier[73] as the likely origin of the three circles diagram. Barbier and Altieri[74] both adopt the three-circle approach of trade-offs. Both reject economic *growth* as the definition of the 'economy' side of the diagram. The literature from the International Union for Conservation of Nature (IUCN) is similarly cautious of the economic system and instead focuses on relationships between environmental and social goals. This, Purvis, Mao and Robinson[75] point out, represents a stark contrast to the central narrative advanced by the UN where economic growth is an imperative.

The earlier framings of sustainable development in the literature are also more in line with the 'twin demands' of the environment and development championed by Justice Weeramantry.[76] The need to return to the two non-negotiables of people and planet is reflected in Griggs et al's[77] redefinition of sustainable development when adopting an earth system approach to sustainable development during the conceptualisation of the Sustainable Development Goals (SDGs). Here they define sustainable development as 'development that meets the needs of the present while safeguarding Earth's life support system, on which the welfare of current and future generations depends.' Similarly, Leach et al[78]

[72] Purvis, Mao and Robinson (n 66).

[73] E Barbier, 'The Concept of Sustainable Economic Development' (1987) 14(2) *Environmental Conservation* 101–10.

[74] MA Altieri, *Agroecology: The Scientific Basis of Alternative Agriculture* (Boulder CO, Westview, 1987).

[75] ibid.

[76] *Gabčíkovo-Nagymaros Project (Hungary v Slovakia)* (n 58) 95. I am also grateful to Karen Morrow, who highlighted in a workshop for this book, how the three circles or pillars constitute a 'double counting' of human concerns. The impact on environment and society of this double counting is exacerbated when 'economy' has been captured by neoliberalism (and as reflected in sustainable development's manifestation in the United Nations system) and championed as unabated economic growth. See Morrow, Chapter 6 in this book.

[77] D Griggs and others, 'Sustainable Development Goals for People and Planet' (2013) 495 *Nature* 305.

[78] M Leach and others, 'Equity and Sustainability in the Anthropocene: A Social–Ecological Systems Perspective on Their Intertwined Futures' (2018) 1 *Global Sustainability* e13.

develop the term 'equitable-sustainability', recognising the inextricable and dynamic connections between human and natural systems. This finds echoes too in the conceptual framework of the Intergovernmental Science-Policy Platform on Biodiversity and Ecosystem Services (IPBES).[79] The IPBES Conceptual Framework prioritises nature and good quality of life for humans without the inclusion of an economic pillar. Interactions between humans and nature are represented further as nature's contributions to people.[80] Meanwhile, Hickel and Sullivan[81] demonstrate that it is possible to provide decent living standards for current and future populations by prioritising the production of specific goods and services, and importantly, access to them. Contrary to the neoliberal capitalist view, they argue that what is needed is not generic production but rather a focus on the content and purpose of production.

Having centred two non-negotiables of people and planet while rejecting profit as a guiding principle, the next section expands exploration of equitable and sustainable multi-species relationships.

B. From Integration to Relationality

The IPBES Values Assessment underscores that the unprecedented global loss of nature stems from the prioritisation of instrumental values which can be traded in markets.[82] At the same time, West et al[83] draw attention to the interacting drivers of modernism, colonialism and industrial capitalism being at the core of severe social-ecological impacts on the planet and sustainability transformations that will require relational approaches as 'alternatives to the paradigms, practices, and policies that have generated social-ecological destruction and the Anthropocene'.

Meanwhile, large areas of the global South are pursuing 'development' based on unsustainable Northern models which prioritise instrumental values. Yet, out of the necessity presented by intersecting global crises, there is growing attention on traditional more-than-human relationships in the global South for visions of what a thriving planet could look like.[84] Many of these relationships champion relational values in contrast to the instrumental values of dominant neoliberal framings and even distinct from intrinsic values. Instrumental values largely focus on monetary

[79] S Díaz and others, 'The IPBES Conceptual Framework – Connecting Nature and People' (2015) 14 *Current Opinion in Environmental Sustainability* 1.

[80] ibid.

[81] J Hickel and D Sullivan, 'How Much Growth Is Required to Achieve Good Lives for All? Insights from Needs-Based Analysis' (2024) 35 *World Development Perspectives* 100612.

[82] IPBES, *Methodological Assessment Report on the Diverse Values and Valuation of Nature* (P Balvanera and others (eds), IPBES Secretariat, 2022).

[83] S West and others, 'Relational Approaches to Sustainability Transformations: Walking Together in a World of Many Worlds' (2024) 20 *Ecosystems and People* 2370539, 1.

[84] Lim (n 11).

quantification of the benefits that nature provides to humans. On the other end of the spectrum, the intrinsic valuation of nature treats the environment as having value in its own right, separate from humans (ie, the value of the environment is – or should be – independent from the human act of placing a value on her). With its focus on how people connect to each other in their relations with nature, relational values, on the other hand, bridge the gap between instrumental and intrinsic values.[85]

I am in firm agreement with Kotzé, Adelman and Dube[86] who argue for the foregrounding of relational ontologies and epistemologies; of worldviews, such as *Ubuntu*, which prioritise care, humility and mutual obligations across multi-species communities. This finds support too, in Justice Weeramantry's Separate Opinion in *Gabčíkovo-Nagymaros*, where he calls for the development of modern environmental law to draw on traditional principles 'at a time when such harmony between humanity and its planetary inheritance is a prerequisite for human survival'.[87]

Relationality is practised and theorised across a range of cultures, power relations and purposes. Relational approaches also occur within different knowledge and governance systems, scholarly traditions and disciplines. West et al[88] therefore emphasise the necessity of engaging diverse approaches to relationality. At the same time, they identify three areas of common to relationality's plurality. First, relational approaches rally against the cartesian separation of society and nature; second, relationality stems from understandings of multi-species interconnectedness, reciprocity and mutuality; and third, relational approaches are underpinned by ethical obligations of responsibility and care. The IPBES Values Assessment highlights that instrumental values take precedence in dominant societal norms and formal rules.[89] At the same time, in a recent publication, we use biodiversity offsetting as an example of how capitalist and human interests are prioritised in planning law, thus reinforcing the capitalist world view of hyperseparation where 'nature is commodified and fungible'.[90]

In sum, legal relationality therefore requires a fundamental shift in how law comes into being and how it is practised. It also requires addressing the corrupting power of neoliberalism's oligarchy head-on.

VI. Stain-Guarding Earth System Law

Despite sustainable development being mentioned in this chapter's title, and despite the space dedicated above to discussing sustainable development, this

[85] KM Chan and others, 'Why Protect Nature? Rethinking Values and the Environment' (2016) 113 *Proceedings of the National Academy of Sciences* 1462.

[86] Kotzé, Adelman and Dube (n 13).

[87] *Gabčíkovo-Nagymaros Project (Hungary v Slovakia)* (n 58) 110.

[88] West and others (n 83).

[89] IPBES (n 82).

[90] P Govind and others, 'Offsetting' (2024) 16 *Environmental Humanities* 426.

piece is less about the principle itself and more about the cautionary tale of sustainable development's enshittification. Some of the core tenets of sustainable development echo strongly in the aims of earth system law, earth system governance and earth system justice. For example, earth system justice's three 'I's (inter- and intra- generational justice alongside interspecies justice) and earth system stability,[91] reflect foundational concerns of sustainable development. In this final substantive section, I examine possible means of stain-guarding earth system law against neoliberalism's corruption. I do so through Mai and Boulot's[92] analytical framework that identifies structural, normative, ontological, epistemological-conceptual and methodological challenges to realising earth system law's transformative potential. Examining neoliberalism alongside these considerations, I suggest possible in-roads into the dominant social paradigm responsible for social-ecological destruction.

A. Structural Dimensions

Mai and Boulot[93] highlight the contradiction of aiming to bring about transformative change for the Anthropocene through the very institutions responsible for earth system decline. They point out that existing legal and organisational structures that are meant to address planetary change largely remain fixed in an 'environmental paradigm' that demonstrates insufficient appreciation that interconnected social, technical and natural factors shape planetary processes. This, the authors indicate, leads to specialisation as well as horizontal and vertical fragmentation.

In this chapter, I have brought a further issue of structure to the fore. That is, how power shapes social orders and institutions and in turn the use and allocation of resources. Stain-guarding earth system law requires scrutinisation of the structures that are institutionalised by neoliberalism. In the discussion above, I drew attention to the way in which sustainable development came into its current form once it had gone through the wash of the UN system: a system that prioritises economic growth.[94] Meanwhile, Alexander[95] points to the growth fetishism that characterises domestic law-making. Therefore, particularly as earth system law gains even greater prominence, vigilance is needed so that powerful actors and structures that fortify the status quo, while prioritising the economic interests of the wealthy, do not similarly enshittify earth system law and its principles.

[91] Gupta and others (n 26).
[92] Mai and Boulot (n 9).
[93] ibid.
[94] Purvis, Mao and Robinson (n 66).
[95] S Alexander, 'Wild Law from Below: Examining the Anarchist Challenge to Earth, Jurisprudence' in M Maloney and P Burdon (eds), *Wild Law – In Practice* (Abingdon-on-Thames, Routledge, 2014).

B. Normative Dimensions

Mai and Boulot[96] emphasise the need to engage with the values, ethics and politics of earth system law. When identifying the normative dimensions of earth system law, the authors underscore the difficult discussions that will need to be taken around trade-offs.[97] Meanwhile, to operationalise earth system justice, Gupta et al[98] call for orientation towards two ends: (i) stabilising the earth system to reduce harm; and (ii) access to material needs by all. At the same time, they underscore the importance of 'just means' to achieve the 'just ends' of earth system stability and access for all. Neoliberalism has actively sabotaged the capacity of sustainable development to achieve environmental protection and human well-being. Normative decisions are needed, including within and by means of earth system law, that prioritise twin-goals of people and nature. The 'have it all' approach of neoliberalism is a misnomer. Awareness of neoliberalism's tricks as it aims to 'balance' economic interests, as seen in sustainable development, will help to prevent similar corruption of the aims of earth system justice, and by extension, earth system law.

C. Ontological Dimensions

Mai and Boulot's call to go beyond nature–culture dichotomies of dominant worldviews reinforces my (and indeed Justice Weeramantry's) calls, above, to shift from sustainable development's focus on integration in favour of relationality. I will not repeat these here beyond pointing out that relationality is in stark contrast to neoliberalism's instrumentalism. Meanwhile, discussions of relationality create an important segue to the discussion of epistemological-conceptual dimensions below; that is, in order to give effect to relationality's diversity,[99] it is critical to embrace plural ways of knowing and knowledge systems.

D. Epistemological-Conceptual Dimensions

The *Gabčíkovo-Nagymaros* judgment is but one example (the *Advisory Opinion on the Legality of the Threat or Use of Nuclear Weapons* being another) of where Justice Weeramantry draws on knowledge systems from around the world. Justice Weeramantry does more than pay lip-service to the importance of plural ways of knowing. He also demonstrates how broad knowledge systems can be

[96] Mai and Boulot (n 9).
[97] ibid.
[98] Gupta and others (n 26).
[99] West and others (n 83).

incorporated into legal development. Gupta et al[100] reiterate that contributions from multiple knowledge systems are key to achieving just means, while in the specific context of earth system law, Mai and Boulot[101] see the accommodation of a wide range of knowledges to be central to earth system law achieving its transformative potential.

Grove[102] refers to the Anthropocene as the 'Great Homogenisation'. Neoliberalism's pervasiveness in the hyperconnected Anthropocene perpetuates homogenisation of thought alongside dubious fashion choices repeated globally ad nauseum. Across disparate parts of the planet, we are being sold the same products and (destructive) lifestyles. This, all when creativity and imagination are needed more than ever before.[103] Knowledges and knowledge systems are inherently important. In the face of unparalleled earth system change and corresponding homogenisation, epistemological and conceptual diversity takes on new significance.

E. Methodological Dimensions

How can legal scholarship be more-than-doctrinal? This is the fundamental question of the final dimension of Mai and Boulot's framework. My analysis of neoliberalism's enshittification of sustainable development has but scratched the surface of the type of inter- and trans-disciplinary scholarship that Mai and Boulot recommend. While I have engaged with the literature from earth system science, justice and governance as well as some scholarship in politics, economics and geography, there remains much scope to apply the methodologies of other disciplines to further understand the phenomenon of sustainable development's enshittification as described in this chapter.

VII. Conclusion

In this chapter, I have argued against rejecting the term sustainable development. As a principle/objective/concept enshrined across international and domestic instruments and case-law, the reclamation of sustainable development provides a Trojan horse into the heart of neoliberal global governance by which claims to the normalisation of human–nature relationships can be made. Conceptualisation of these relationships include those articulated in Justice Weeramantry's Separate

[100] Gupta and others (n 26).
[101] Mai and Boulot (n 9).
[102] JV Grove, *Savage Ecology: War and Geopolitics at the End of the World* (Durham NC, Duke University Press, 2019).
[103] M Lim, 'Fiction as Legal Method – Imagining with the More-than-Human to Awaken Our Plural Selves' (2021) 33 *Journal of Environmental Law* 501.

Opinion in *Gabčíkovo-Nagymaros* and leave room to be expanded and diversified through plural relational ontologies.

This chapter has therefore explored neoliberalism's enshittification of everything and how extractive human–nature relationships have become the status quo. Indeed, a large part of neoliberalism's omnipotence stems from its capacity to effectively market its exploitation as something that is good for us. Neoliberalism's dominance is sustained by continuing to benefit the most powerful at the expense of current and future human and more-than-human generations. Its further insidiousness arises from the banality of neoliberalism's normalisation. Current frameworks that allow the abuse and even annihilation of other humans are not normal. Human–nature interactions that elevate profit over all else are not normal. And yet, such practices occur with such regularity that they have become 'normal', *and even mundane.*

Earth system law presents a paradigm which enables cutting-edge understanding from earth system sciences to be factored into the analysis and design of legal frameworks. As a result, avant garde scholarship is possible by introducing to law a systems approach which takes interactions across sectors and feedbacks across geographical and temporal scales (including the planetary scale) into account. Nevertheless, as important as earth system science is to realising, through law, possibilities for thriving multi-species futures in the Anthropocene, biophysical knowledge of the earth system is, on its own, insufficient. A critical contribution of earth system law is in its bridging of earth system-focused social sciences (eg earth system governance and earth system justice). Earth system law therefore provides an important juridical space to interrogate dominant value systems that are the underlying drivers of earth system instability and inequality.

In this chapter, I have examined how the principle of sustainable development, which aimed to address interconnected social-ecological concerns, has been enshittified due to its capture by the dominant neoliberal ideology. I hope that this chapter may contribute, in some small way, to stain-guarding earth system law's most honourable aspirations. However, to realise these aspirations there is a need to embrace approaches to more-than-human relationships which discard neoliberalism in favour of ways of being that enabled stable earth system functioning across the ~11,700 years of the Holocene.

9

Kinship as a Metaphor for Earth System Law

ROSALIND WARNER

I. Introduction

This chapter uses a discourse analysis to evaluate how metaphors are used in prevailing systems of international environmental law.[1] It then deploys this evaluation to explore the transformative potential of kinship metaphors in earth system law. International environmental law, like other social systems, is the product of a social imaginary. A social imaginary is neither a theory nor an ideology, but an implicit 'background' that visualises and maps space and normalises a particular sense of time. Social imaginaries are formed from the everyday 'prototypes, framings and metaphors' that enable us to make sense of the world and our place in it, thus 'providing the bedrock on which social discourses and practices rest, creating a widely shared sense of their legitimacy'.[2]

Metaphors construct ways of understanding these relationships that illuminate the socio-ethical dimensions of the earth system. Recognising and using metaphors in different ways enables earth system law to more easily bridge disciplines. To the extent that earth system law intersects with science, economics, and social issues, metaphors can help create a common language between these disciplines, facilitating interdisciplinary collaboration. Metaphors can facilitate discussions across disciplinary siloes and help to surface underlying assumptions across disciplines that may interfere with the 'comprehensive and networked systems-oriented understanding of a problem and possible ways to address it'.[3]

[1] WE Connolly, *The Terms of Political Discourse* (Princeton NJ, Princeton Paperbacks, 1993); JS Dryzek, *The Politics of The Earth: Environmental Discourses*, 3rd edn (Oxford, Oxford University Press, 2013); G Lakoff and M Johnson, *Metaphors We Live By* (Chicago IL, University of Chicago Press, 1980); R Warner, *Discourses of Global Environmental Governance: From Colonialism to the 21st Century*, PhD Dissertation, Graduate Program in Political Science (Toronto, York University, 2005).

[2] H Patomäki and MB Steger, 'Social Imaginaries and Big History: Towards a New Planetary Consciousness?' (2010) 42 *Futures* 1056, 1057.

[3] LJ Kotzé and others, 'Earth System Law: Exploring New Frontiers in Legal Science' (2022) 11 *Earth System Governance* 100126, 4.

Ethical dimensions can also be highlighted by using metaphors, since these 'foster better understanding of the many ways in which humans relate to, care for, and value ecosystems'.[4] More centrally, from the transformational perspective of earth system law, the explicit and conscious exploration of metaphors can challenge existing paradigms and inspire innovative approaches to lawyering in the Anthropocene.[5] By reframing issues in novel ways, metaphors can encourage creative problem-solving and the development of new legal frameworks,[6] and even imaginaries of what the law could or should be in relation to a planet in crisis, as exemplified by the earth system law framework. For example, framing civil climate action as a 'war' activates a different set of ethical considerations than thinking of climate action as an act of consultation or dialogue. Metaphors are always partial and emphasise some features over others; they necessarily simplify what are otherwise complex sets of interactions and factors. Metaphors also co-exist, interact and even compete in different ways. Nevertheless, metaphors are the psychological way in which we make sense of the world and our place in it, and so they inevitably play a role in policy, law and governance and in the general process of social ordering.

Different metaphors can co-exist within the same system of law, although they can also be ethically incompatible and lead the law to contradictions that may become untenable over time. Thinking in terms of legal metaphors can help to identify gaps and issues in the legal system, especially the ethical basis for relative value. With respect to the latter, metaphors may create subjects and objects, define the scope for action, or hide domains of inaction. Accordingly, metaphors of property, which imply an instrumental relationship of ownership that underpins prevailing systems of international environmental law, can tend to reduce nature in value and limit the scope of ethical relationships that exist between humans and the environment.[7] Similarly, applying and embedding different metaphors can surround law in an alternative ethics more appropriate for the emerging complex of problems characteristic of the Anthropocene.

This chapter explores existing metaphors deployed in law, including those of property, sovereignty and the public trust.[8] The argument is that these metaphors constrain international environmental law and governance by constructing it as a residual domain, separate from and subordinate to the realm of private property. By using the term 'residual', it is recognised that a given system of international environmental law may contain different metaphorical images or principles, but

[4] CM Raymond and others, 'Ecosystem Services and Beyond: Using Multiple Metaphors to Understand Human–Environment Relationships' (2013) 63 *BioScience* 536.

[5] LJ Kotzé and RE Kim, 'Earth System Law: The Juridical Dimensions of Earth System Governance' (2019) *Earth System Governance* 100003.

[6] K Höne, 'Metaphors and Images: Illustrating Climate Change' (July 2012, updated April 2024) *Diplo*, https://www.diplomacy.edu/blog/metaphors-and-images-illustrating-climate-change/.

[7] See also Morrow, Chapter 6, and Garver and Vargas Roncancio, Chapter 7 in this book.

[8] K Sanders, '"Beyond Human Ownership"? Property, Power and Legal Personality for Nature in Aotearoa New Zealand' (2018) 30 *Journal of Environmental Law* 207.

that these may be incompatible, either when compared against each other, or against the prevailing systems in which they operate. So, in this imaginary, public policy and law begin from a world with constricting limitations on their scope that do not similarly limit the realms of private property and the agency of sovereign action in nature. The chapter argues that, as principles of law, property and sovereignty work to define subjectivity and agency in a permissive and expansive way, with property rights holders enjoying maximal freedom and little to no burden of proving their value or responsibilities. In the realm of environmental law and governance which has *protection* as its goal, the opposite is in fact the case: the value of 'the environment' (or nature) is reliant on explicit explanations and justifications for its *exemption* from the claims of private, individually-based rights. Such private claims and rights, including sovereign rights, are thus the legal default of international environmental law principles, with public or collective claims requiring explicit justification.

The chapter situates kinship metaphors in a pluralist approach to law as subaltern discourses in international environmental relations and law and then analyses the implications of a shift away from prevailing legal metaphors towards ones that are regenerative rather than destructive. The chapter explores the comparative meaning and application of property, sovereignty, and public trust doctrines with kinship-based metaphors, many of which are already found in law, and which are paralleled partially (but not exclusively) in Indigenous worldviews. The analysis concludes with reflections on the historical and cultural implications of adopting kinship as a metaphor in environmental governance, with the attendant implications for action, law and policy, used to protect, restore, and care for the planet in the Anthropocene.

II. Legal Pluralism and Metaphors

Legal pluralism as an approach to law recognises the sources of meaning in law as discursive. A discourse is defined by Hajer as 'an ensemble of ideas, concepts, and categorizations that is produced, reproduced, and transformed in a particular set of practices and through which meaning is given to physical and social realities'.[9] Discursive analysis of law recognises law as a function of a diversity of constructs rather than a single framework. Law is made through discourse, and it is understood through discursive frames.

A discursive approach to earth system law can reveal how the law interprets and defines its subjects, objects, guiding principles, and foundational values.[10]

[9] MA Hajer, 'Discourse Coalitions and the Institutionalization of Practice: The Case of Acid Rain in Britain' in F Fischer and J Forrester (eds), *The Argumentative Turn in Policy Analysis and Planning* (Durham NC, Duke University Press, 2002) 45.

[10] H Dancer, 'Harmony with Nature: Towards a New Deep Legal Pluralism' (2020) 53 *Environmental Policy and Law* 21.

With respect to earth system law, using metaphors can help to identify gaps and silences in the prevailing dominant system of international environmental law, while opening up more space for a pluralistic understanding that can leverage change.

Understanding how discourses work with metaphors to construct new framings is one way of transforming issues or things in novel ways. Understanding metaphors can encourage creative problem-solving, inspire innovative approaches, and help to develop new legal frameworks.[11] In particular, examining metaphors is one means of understanding how discourses work to ascribe meaning to the natural and social world in ways that permit some actions while proscribing others.[12] Thus, discourses, and metaphors which compose parts of those narratives of meaning, have important policy and action implications: notably also in the context of earth system law.

The inadequacy of existing legal principles for organising a complex and even damaging system of human–nature relationships is increasingly being pointed out. To contribute to the transformative potential of earth system law, new ways of thinking about systemic relationships is needed.[13] These new ways of thinking should articulate a normative and ethical image of social, economic, institutional and technological relationships that renews and sustains, rather than undermines, Earth's systems. Earth system law is an emerging approach that seeks to incorporate and articulate new ways of thinking about human–nature relationships. To do this, earth system law should address rich epistemological and ontological approaches that can more clearly illustrate the need for, and direction of, transformative change of the underlying basis of law.[14]

III. Dominant Metaphors of Human–Nature Relations

Existing legal systems mostly rely on metaphors of property and the related conception of sovereignty for their discursive power. These Western legal concepts are not immutable, but rather have evolved over time through case law, statutory changes, and deeper constitutional changes, among other legal development processes. Many of the most promising legal innovations have come through the interplay of politics with law, through case law and/ or new constitutionalist movements. Accordingly, even established legal principles should be understood as potentially subject to re-interpretation and revision.[15]

[11] Höne (n 6).

[12] S Bernstein and M Hoffmann, 'Climate Politics, Metaphors and the Fractal Carbon Trap' (2019) 9 *Nature Climate Change* 919; M Del Mar, 'Metaphor in International Law: Language, Imagination and Normative Inquiry' (2017) 86 *Nordic Journal of International Law* 170.

[13] Kotzé and Kim (n 5); LJ Kotzé and RE Kim, 'Exploring the Analytical, Normative and Transformative Dimensions of Earth System Law' (2020) 50 *Environmental Policy and Law* 457.

[14] L Mai and E Boulot, 'Harnessing the Transformative Potential of Earth System Law: From Theory to Practice' (2021) 7 *Earth System Governance* 100103.

[15] See also Kotzé and Du Toit, Chapter 3 and Leach, Chapter 4 in this book.

In Western jurisprudence, the notion of property is a key principle that governs who has subjectivity and standing, since standing is earned by the ability to demonstrate financial loss or damage, something that requires reference to ownership or interest.[16] Burdon correctly notes that the underlying assumption of human dominion over nature is 'the unquestioned presupposition upon which all other theories of property have since been based'.[17] As a metaphor for human–nature relations, the notion of property carries a bundle of cultural meanings whose significance is reproduced through international treaties, regulations, and laws around environmental issues. Greenhouse gas emissions trading agreements, debt-for-nature swaps, and arrangements for payments and financing through Reducing Emissions from Deforestation and Forest Degradation in Developing Countries (REDD+)[18] are all predicated on claims of exclusive ownership and the right to accumulate, trade, and dispose of nature. Property is also at the heart of international law, having been recognised by the United Nations General Assembly in 1962 in a resolution to establish state's permanent rights to natural resources, cementing states' rights as 'owners' of their environment (or 'nature').[19]

While the concept of property has a long pedigree in Western philosophical thinking, and is not by any means simple or straightforward, the interrelated concepts of property and sovereignty have nevertheless become ingrained in the context of globalised industrial capitalism, and therefore have direct implications for the non-human living world.[20] The existence of property implies the need for laws to protect ownership, and in general the bias of such laws has been to protected individual rather than collective versions of property ownership. In fact, 'liberal societies, which are predicated on the notion of individual self-interest, are faced with tremendous problems when trying to deal with issues requiring communal solutions'.[21]

Property essentially means 'the rights to exclude, to possess, to use and to transfer'.[22] As a colonial construction, the claim to property rights remains exceptionally powerful as a means of limiting the terms of new law and governance arrangements concerning environmental protection, and the domains

[16] K Bosselmann, 'Environmental and Human Rights in Ethical Context' in LJ Kotzé and A Grear (eds), *Research Handbook on Human Rights and the Environment* (Cheltenham, Edward Elgar Publishing, 2015).

[17] P Burdon, *Earth Jurisprudence: Private Property and the Environment* (Abingdon-on-Thames, Routledge, 2015) 22.

[18] M Lederer, 'REDD+ governance' (2012) 3 *WIREs Climate Change* 107.

[19] M Ojanen and others, 'What Are the Environmental Impacts of Property Rights Regimes in Forests, Fisheries and Rangelands?' (2017) 6 *Environmental Evidence* 12.

[20] M Ece, 'Creating Property out of Insecurity: Territorialization and Legitimation of REDD+ in Lindi, Tanzania' (2021) 53 *The Journal of Legal Pluralism and Unofficial Law* 78.

[21] MA Cahn and R O'Brien, *Thinking about the Environment: Readings on Politics, Property, and the Physical World* (Armonk NY, ME Sharpe, 1996) 63.

[22] M Strack, 'Land and Rivers Can Own Themselves' (2017) 9 *International Journal of Law in the Built Environment* 4.

within which they can be made. The exclusivity of property rights lends material support to legal claims that treat the non-human living world as a highly divisible and reductive object for the single purpose of human use. As a metaphor for human–nature relationships, property governs the relationships between humans and leaves little room for the idea of mutual obligation or social or collective rights. In other words, property as a legal metaphor has implications for human–nature relationships, since 'property rights represent social relations established between an entity (owner) and other entities (non-owners) regarding an object'.[23] Property as a metaphor also crowds out considerations of nature protection and excludes ecocentric notions of nature as a 'something-in-itself', since its socio-cultural Western context is premised on the assumption of human dominion over nature.[24] Because the domain of private property (including by extension the realm of sovereignty rights that governments hold over their territories), is expansive under the law, private property rights are highly permissive. Property is primarily a 'negative' right in the sense that it constrains and limits public claims or actions by governments without providing a positive basis for the exercise of protective laws.

Intimately related to the notions of sovereignty and property, is the idea of the public trust. The public trust doctrine provides that 'certain natural resources within national territories are common, shared property among citizens and should therefore be stewarded in perpetuity by the states'.[25] This ancient Roman doctrine has been used to protect and restore goods for public benefit such as ancient monuments, public education, wilderness areas, and animal and plant species. The track record for protection of these various 'goods' is uneven, with claims often being forgotten during times of austerity, or political instability. While international initiatives have been able to boost efforts to preserve and restore iconic structures like the Notre Dame Cathedral in France, the will and resources to fully apply the public trust doctrine to non-human nature has been more limited. For example, the expansion of a public trust doctrine to wildlife conservation in the United States (US) would effectively create such a wide easement on private property that it would enable a 'massive taking of private property'.[26]

While offering some promise, the doctrine of a public trust is sometimes interpreted as a 'modification' to property laws that allow public access to natural resources for economic or recreational use.[27] This is quite different from an

[23] O Beriozovas and others, 'Research Advancement in Forest Property Rights: A Thematic Review over Half a Decade Using Natural Language Processing' (2024) 16(19) *Sustainability* 8280.

[24] J Murray, 'Earth Jurisprudence, Wild Law, Emergent Law: The Emerging Field of Ecology and Law – Part 2' (2015) 36 *Liverpool Law Review* 105.

[25] J Orangias, 'Towards Global Public Trust Doctrines: An Analysis of the Transnationalisation of State Stewardship Duties' (2021) 12(4) *Transnational Legal Theory* 550.

[26] J Huffman, 'The Limits of the Public Trust Doctrine', *PERC*, 19 June 2019, https://www.perc.org/2019/06/19/the-limits-of-the-public-trust-doctrine/.

[27] H Ahmad, 'Boom or Bust: The Public Trust Doctrine in Canadian Climate Change Litigation' (2024) 49(2) *Queens Law Journal* 1.

understanding of a public trust that might infuse public authorities with an obligation to protect and value the non-human world in light of a higher moral calling. Accordingly, while the public trust can be used to limit specific special interests and private property claims, the same rationale of a public trust can also override protections, since states can argue that development is in the interest of *their* public. This is problematic in that it clashes with another value often associated with the notion of a public trust, which is to preserve nature for the benefit of future generations. Since unborn generations cannot under the current law fully exercise an ownership claim (also because they do not have standing to sue for loss and damage), their claims are discounted when they clash with the needs of present generations. Thus, the public trust is only a limited measure in protecting the non-human world from incursions from present-day property rightsholders, whether private or governmental. While some jurisdictions around the world have been able to apply a more expansive doctrine of the public trust to environmental protection, others have struggled to advance wider protections due to governmental resistance. For protection of the non-human world, a more innovative approach is needed to do justice to the planetary implications of environmental degradation in the Anthropocene.

In sum, property, sovereignty and the public trust, as metaphors, limit the capability of law to care for the entire living order. A more fulsome alternative approach that extends beyond, and even challenges, property rights, sovereignty and narrow visions of the public trust as described above, is needed to more clearly identify how public claims should be exercised and how obligations to the public, including future generations, should be observed and defined. Rather than doubling down on these foundational metaphors, it is preferable to explore what steps can push law towards an increasing recognition that nature is 'beyond' property; that it is endowed with intrinsic value and cannot be reduced to a tradable commodity. The metaphor of property, as it has been expressed through the public trust doctrine and other related doctrines such as national sovereignty over resources, has worked to construct nature as an object, inert and wasted until human effort awakens it to usefulness and productivity.

How might different metaphors shift the terrain of (environmental) law to allow for a wider range of legal categories and realms of legal practice? Alternative metaphors may be more likely to expand the space for common and/ or enlightened community-based legal principles and practices that span human–nature relationships on a planetary scale. The next section argues that alternative legal approaches, such as those based on the metaphor of kinship, could guide the much-needed transformation of law and legal systems away from their current predatory orientation to one that is altogether more embracive of a vulnerable living order.[28]

[28] LJ Kotzé, 'The Anthropocene, Earth System Vulnerability and Socio-Ecological Injustice in an Age of Human Rights' (2019) 10(1) *Journal of Human Rights and the Environment* 62.

IV. Exploring the Kinship Metaphor

The study of kinship as a social phenomenon has been associated most closely with anthropology, although it is also central to sociology and politics. Kinship is a structured system of relationships extending outward from those defined by family, lineal descent and marriage to a set of ramified relationships characterised by complex interlocking ties that are socially determined. The idea of kinship extends beyond face-to-face or simple blood relationships, to include what Herzfeld calls 'metaphorical' (or at least metonymic) elaborations of local moral communities or 'moral worlds'.[29] Kinship determines how groups are formed, what their relative structures and identities are, and provides a basis for social binding and organising social relations.

As a metaphor underlying law, kinship implies a relationship based on mutual obligation, intergenerational connection, and interdependence. A kinship metaphor potentially represents a preferable way of describing human–nature relations compared to those discussed above, which are mechanical, reductionist and hierarchical.[30]

Kinship metaphors are found within Western international relations theory, although they are less often applied to human–nature relationships.[31] In international relations, kinship metaphors have been used to frame relationships between states, justify political actions, structure international organisations, and conceptualise governance systems in international relations and law. In 1957 Karl Deutsch identified a sense of shared identity and commonality amongst the North Atlantic countries – what he termed 'we-feeling' as a basis for a security community.[32] As evidenced by the extensive use of kinship language throughout international relations history, practice and discourse, kinship is more than a *category* of social relations. It is rather an *organising principle* for social relations, most often based on friendship and trust: 'new communities – nations – are often thought of as extended families. They are motherlands, so they are mothers, and they are fatherlands, so they are fathers'.[33]

In the foregoing context, kinship also serves to define how social groupings are formed. So, we could imagine ways in which the 'planetary family' is organised according to affinity and kin-like relationships. The ecosystem of a forest, including its humans, would contain varieties of familial relationships characterised by a

[29] M Herzfeld, 'Global Kinship: Anthropology and the Politics of Knowing' (2007) 80 *Anthropological Quarterly* 313, 314.

[30] S Dalby, 'Ecological Metaphors of Security: World Politics in the Biosphere' (1998) 23(3) *Alternatives: Global, Local, Political* 291, 293.

[31] LC Pecharroman, 'Rights of Nature: Rivers That Can Stand in Court' (2018) 7 *Resources* 13.

[32] K Deutsch, *Political Community and the North Atlantic Area* (Princeton NJ, Princeton University Press, 1957).

[33] IB Neumann, K Haugevick and JHS Lie, 'Kinship in International Relations: Introduction and Framework' in K Haugevick and IB Neumann (eds), *Kinship in International Relations* (Abingdon-on-Thames, Routledge, 2019) 4.

mutual interest in co-existence, active relationship maintenance, adaptability, and a sense of affinity or pro-social respect for each other's existence and contribution to the whole. Because metaphors work to enable and constrain certain forms of social relations, kinship is more often used as an 'enabling metaphor' (as a means of construction) than as a means of constraint. A kinship metaphor, in contrast to those legal metaphors discussed above, is an ethical metaphorical relationship based on affinity, familiarity, and respect – if not always for the individuals, then at least for the overall social structure. It is suggestive of a relationship of mutual rights and responsibilities in the context of a common origin and fate, and a collective and stable identity which can be defined in different ways with a common root.

Metaphors of kinship are often articulated within legal arguments from Indigenous peoples as part of a framing of nature and territorial belonging.[34] For example, it is common in Indigenous origin stories across North America to find the natural world making a conscious effort to produce the first humans, and there is rarely a strict instrumental division in these tales between humans and nature.[35] Callicott and others have focused on the potential universality of Indigenous beliefs that regard nature as part of the human family, and point to kinship metaphors of nature that are common in Hindu and Buddhist thought.[36] As noted by Peterson, 'this emphasis on relationship and common origins accords with evolutionary science and thus with the exigencies of an adequate environmental ethic'.[37]

Viewing human–nature relationships in kinship terms elevates the 'community' basis of law over the privileges and rights of private property owners in a way that notions like a 'public trust' fail to do. In particular, the embeddedness of kinship relations within a community could act as a counterweight to the individualistic instrumentalism and utilitarianism of Western law and other forms of social organisation.[38]

The key shift that a kinship metaphor brings is its power to envision a non-instrumental relationship with the planet that recognises a common shared origin while preventing the reduction of nature to a single fixed imaginary. In contrast to existing dominant metaphors that reproduce nature as fixed and objective, a metaphor of 'kinship' precludes the instrumental use and reduction of nature by reframing the ethical relationships in terms of family and relations. Since the

[34] V Watts, 'Indigenous Place-Thought and Agency Amongst Humans and Non-Humans (First Woman and Sky Woman Go On a European World Tour!)' (2013) 2(1) *Decolonization: Indigeneity, Education & Society* 20.

[35] JD Belshaw, S Nickel and C Horton, *Histories of Indigenous Peoples and Canada* (Montreal, Pressbooks, 2020); MC Petersmann, 'Sympoietic Thinking and Earth System Law: The Earth, Its Subjects and the Law' (2021) 9 *Earth System Governance* 100114.

[36] JB Callicott, *Thinking Like a Planet: The Land Ethic and the Earth Ethic* (Oxford, Oxford University Press, 2013).

[37] AL Peterson, *Being Human* (Oakland CA, University of California Press, 2001) 14.

[38] G Chapron, Y Epstein and JV López-Bao, 'A Rights Revolution for Nature' (2019) 363(6434) *Science* 1392.

emergence of ecological studies in the late nineteenth century, and the growth of earth system science in the 1980s, it has become well established that the discursive reduction of nature to a mere object is one of the key means by which exploitation and extraction – and indeed, devaluing – of nature has been facilitated. To the degree that human activities now threaten and undermine modern civilisation and exceed planetary boundaries, the necessity of overcoming the human–nature paradox is clear.[39]

What might a shift to a discursive metaphor for law do to achieve a more resilient, sustainable and regenerative human–nature relationship? How can this transform or re-constitute law in ways that might shift thinking towards alternatives such as earth system law? As described above, metaphors can create or limit imagination and can be permissive, proscriptive or regulatory when adopted into law. One complicating factor is the cultural fluidity of kinship metaphors and meanings. Is kinship universal, or particular to specific contexts and systems of social organisation?[40] Kin may be friendly or not, depending on the social context,[41] but there is an implied community, shared origin, and interdependence among kin in every society that is, at least potentially, comprehensible. The word 'ecology' derives from the Greek *Oikos*, meaning 'house' or 'place to live in'.[42] It is not impossible, then, to consider nature as 'those that we live with'; nature is kin. Practically speaking, if nature is kin, has subjectivity, and has intrinsic value, then the degrees of harm arising from human activities should ideally be considered by courts as a first principle and measure of justice.

V. Conclusion

Understanding law as a social imaginary that is constructed through metaphors enables an account of legal pluralism that shifts the ground for reimagining human–nature relationships in law. This chapter has sought to explore the gaps in prevailing metaphors of (environmental) law rooted in mechanistic, instrumentalist human–nature relationships. It is argued that dominant metaphors in the historical development of law have contributed to the degradation of nature by design or neglect. Imagining the relationship as one of property or sovereign ownership limits the scope for community imaginaries and collective agency.

A kinship metaphor, however, precludes instrumentalism as the core modus operandi between humans and nature, while understanding that generations are part of a single continuous community with mutual rights and obligations to each other. The dominant imaginaries of property and sovereignty are profoundly

[39] Petersmann (n 35).
[40] Neumann, Haugevick and Lie (n 33).
[41] Peterson (n 37) 15–16.
[42] Burdon (n 17).

dysfunctional and contradictory. Kinship potentially offers a far more expansive and maximal basis for building a new human–nature ethical community. In short, kinship is a very different contrasting metaphoric basis for law that allows for legal subjectivity, moral agency, intergenerational ethics, and intrinsic value for nature. As such, re-casting the relationship between humans and nature as one of kinship may prompt an ethical shift towards the more transformative agenda that earth system law seeks to pursue.

10

Between Idealism and Reality: Reflecting on the Viability of Earth System Law Through the Lens of Ecological Integrity

PETER D BURDON*

I. Introduction

In this chapter, I engage in a critique of the concept of ecological integrity and its suitability for thinking about law in the Anthropocene, with a specific focus on its potential role within the earth system law paradigm. Earth system law is an emerging legal paradigm that aims to align legal systems with the complexities of the Earth as an interconnected system.[1] As the other chapters in this book argue, it seeks to move beyond traditional environmental law approaches in order to address the challenges of the Anthropocene epoch.

My analysis explores whether ecological integrity, or its more recent iteration as biosphere integrity, could serve as a foundational principle for earth system law. This inquiry is crucial because earth system law, in its quest to govern complex planetary systems, requires principles that can operate on a global scale while remaining responsive to local realities. Ecological integrity, with its focus on ecosystem health, presents an intriguing candidate for such a principle.

My method of critique is grounded in Ron Engel's notion of critical loyalty, which requires that interlocutors are read generously, and engagements are offered in 'the spirit of self-reflective criticism' toward the 'vocation we share'.[2] I situate critique alongside Karl Marx's method, namely, as a systematic analysis that tries to bring to light premises and presuppositions that might not be readily

* This chapter draws on P Burdon, *The Anthropocene: New Trajectories in Law* (Abingdon-on-Thames, Routledge, 2023).

[1] LJ Kotzé and RE Kim, 'Earth System Law: The Juridical Dimensions of Earth System Governance' (2019) 1 *Earth System Governance* 100003.

[2] JR Engel, 'Summons to a New Axial Age: The Promise, Limits, and Future of the Earth Charter' in L Westra and M Vilela (eds), *Ecological Integrity, and Social Movements* (London, Earthscan, 2014) xv.

available on the surface.[3] Even if those foundations are misplaced, I contend that we can still learn something about what their wrongness systematises or represents. Marx's method of critique is not about rejection; it is a tool to help us unpack the presumptions and presuppositions of an idea that is not readily available, so that we can see a problem more clearly and formulate an appropriate political response.

Throughout this chapter I draw on Marx's method of critique and his engagement with the limits of philosophical idealism, as articulated in his essay 'On the Jewish Question'.[4] In this essay, Marx argues that the state, by representing its subjects as free and equal, creates an abstract representation of reality that feigns indifference to concrete forms of social power. This idealism is reflected in modes of legal analysis that focus on law reform and create abstractions from the material conditions of daily life. In the context of ecological integrity, I argue that the concept creates an abstract representation of the environment that is disconnected from the material causes of the Anthropocene rupture. The Anthropocene demands a mode of analysis that is grounded in the material world and the real conditions of human existence.

This critique is particularly relevant to earth system law, which aims to move beyond the abstractions of traditional environmental law.[5] By examining the concept of ecological integrity through this lens, we can better understand the challenges and opportunities it presents for earth system law's ambition to create a more holistic, materially grounded legal framework.

The chapter begins by tracing the emergence of ecological integrity in philosophy, theology, and science. This exposition not only clarifies the original meaning of ecological integrity but is also important for my argument that the definitional possibilities of concepts are not boundless but marked by their history. Toward the end of this analysis, I argue that, in its standard form, the concept of ecological integrity is not suitable for thinking about law in the Anthropocene or as a principle for earth system law. This is for two reasons. First is the issue of scale: while ecological integrity measures health at the local level, the Anthropocene and earth system law compel us to think about the Earth as a planetary system. Second, the orthodox concept of ecological integrity remains connected to notions of purity and wilderness which are no longer tenable in the Anthropocene.

In response to this critique, scholars have begun thinking about the idea of biosphere integrity. After unpacking this theory, I turn once again to critique in order to understand the presumptions that underpin biosphere integrity and its potential as a principle for earth system law. Here I argue that the turn to biosphere integrity reproduces some of the existing concerns with the idea of ecological integrity. Specifically, I am concerned with the retention of the term

[3] K Marx, 'On the Jewish Question' in RC Tucker (ed), *The Marx-Engels Reader* (New York, Norton & Co, 1978 [1843]).

[4] ibid.

[5] Kotzé and Kim (n 1).

'integrity', which I do not think can be fully removed from its history. More fundamentally, I argue that biosphere integrity is an idealist discourse that creates an abstraction from reality and is silent on the material causes of the Anthropocene rupture.

By engaging in critique, I aim to open new ways of thinking about ecological integrity that respond to earth system science and move away from the idealism that pervades environmental legal scholarship. This critique extends to earth system law itself, questioning whether it, too, might fall into idealist traps in its pursuit of a more holistic legal framework. The analysis presented here is less about advocating for a specific legal principle and more about developing a methodology for critically examining potential principles for earth system law.[6]

Ultimately, this chapter argues that the Anthropocene and the project of earth system law demand a mode of analysis that is grounded in the material world and the real conditions of human existence. By critically examining ecological and biosphere integrity through this lens, we can better understand the challenges of developing principles for earth system law that truly respond to the complexities of our planetary reality.

II. Intellectual Origins

Many concepts in environmental and ecological law derive from an intellectual engagement with the science of ecology. The concept of integrity entered environmental thought earlier in the context of nascent wilderness ethics. The first reference can be noted in the writing of James Hall who lived in Illinois in the 1820s. Hall's writing evinces a troubling strand in some approaches to wilderness ethics – namely, the affirmation of civilisational progress as Indigenous people were displaced from the frontier. In 1828 Hall wrote: 'From this land, so lately a wilderness the savage has been expelled; towns and colleges have arisen; farms have been made; the mechanic arts cherished; the necessaries of life abound, and many of its luxuries are enjoyed'.[7] While authors like Nash[8] have sought to distinguish these sentiments from Hall's writing on wilderness, I contend that the two are connected. For Hall, wilderness has integrity not simply because people are absent – Hall was there after all; wilderness gains integrity once it is cleansed through civilisational progress. This reading is consistent with Hall's subsequent reflections on the industry of the pioneers which he framed in terms of the 'beautiful consummation of that promise, "thou shalt have dominion over all the earth"'.[9]

[6] An approach similar to Boulot, Mai and Sellers, Chapter 5 in this book.
[7] J Hall, *Letters from the West* (Whitefish MT, Literary Licensing, 2014 [1828]) 165.
[8] R Nash, *Wilderness and the American Mind* (New Haven CT, Yale University Press, 2014) 59.
[9] J Hall, 'Chase's Statutes of Ohio' (1836) 5 *Western Monthly Magazine* 631, 631–32; Nash (n 8) 59.

It is in this context that Hall first wrote about the idea of integrity. Reflecting on how settlers had transformed the Ohio Valley 'from a desert to a paradise' he noted: 'I know of nothing more splendid than a forest of the west, standing *in its original integrity*, adorned with the exuberant beauties of a powerful vegetation, and crowned with the honors of a venerable age' (emphasis added). This romantic sensibility celebrated an imagined wilderness which was vast and abundant: 'the forest is seen in its majesty; the pomp and pride of the wilderness is here. Here is nature unspoiled, and silence undisturbed'.[10]

Prior to Hall the idea of integrity was confined to moral and ethical thinking. In this context, the term was used to describe a state of being whole and undivided in oneself. A person had integrity if they demonstrated internal consistency and could withstand hypocrisy. At its most idealistic, the idea of integrity can be linked to purity. I say idealistic because no ancient philosopher held out purity as something that could be fully realised. Part of the human condition meant that we are limited or flawed (something Christian philosophers developed with the idea of original sin). However, no such limitations needed to be placed on the environment – here was a canvass upon which environmental thinkers could project ideas of perfection. This is particularly true in the context of wilderness which was defined through the absence of human beings and the impurities of culture.

The best example is Aldo Leopold's *Land Ethic*. Here Leopold held that an action is 'right when it tends to preserve the integrity, stability, and beauty of the biotic community. It is wrong when it tends otherwise'.[11] This is a deontological statement which Leopold used to make further prescriptions about ethics and land management. Two points stand out. First, the land is conceived with respect to wilderness and wild animals; it does not apply to exotic plants, domesticated animals or animals undergoing vivisection.[12] Those components of the 'biotic community' were part of human culture and Leopold did not challenge legal concepts of property and ownership. Second, Leopold did not use the land ethic to argue for the intrinsic value or rights of all wild animals. Leopold himself was a game catcher, and his writings are filled with arguments in favour of culling a species once it had exceeded the carrying capacity of the land and risked its 'beauty' or the 'healthy functioning' of the 'biotic mechanism'.[13] For this reason, Leopold's land ethic should not be read as an extension of natural rights from human beings to the environment. His idea is concerned with the good of the whole. If individual biotic value is recognised it is only to the extent that it helps preserve the entire ecosystem.[14]

From this sketch we can make three observations about Leopold's *Land Ethic*: (i) wilderness has its own integrity; (ii) that integrity is knowable by ecologists

[10] Nash (n 8) 54.
[11] A Leopold, *A Sand County Almanac* (Oxford, Oxford University Press, 1949) 224–25.
[12] R Nash, *The Rights of Nature* (Madison WI, University of Wisconsin Press, 1989) 71.
[13] Leopold (n 11) 214.
[14] JN Moline, 'Aldo Leopold and the Moral Community' (1986) 8 *Environmental Ethics* 99.

or those close to the land; and (iii) its integrity can be preserved through careful management. Integrity in this schema means more than a healthy and functioning ecosystem. It is closer to the idea that here is a balance in nature like homeostasis in the human body. The role of land management is to find this balance through positive actions (ie culling) or through withdrawal and preservation. We can extend this final point to say that the land ethic is concerned with the good of the whole and not the individual or component parts of an ecosystem.

After Leopold, the idea of ecological integrity was developed in two directions – theology and secular ethics. In theology, ecological integrity was interpreted with reference to natural law concepts like human dignity. While scathing of the contribution of Christianity to the ecological crisis, Lyn White Jnr followed Leopold in arguing for the 'integrity' of ecosystems. For White, this integrity was knowable through the science of ecology which he felt could provide 'new religious understandings of our own being, of other beings, and of being'.[15] White's appeal to integrity was grounded in natural law, which he argued derived its authority from God. This was a common perspective which was promoted by the Faith-Man-Nature Groups which sprung up in the United States in the middle of the twentieth century.[16] Daniel Williams, for example, stated simply: 'Things have a value and integrity in themselves' because they are part of the 'ongoing reality'.[17] In agreement, Allan Brockway[18] constructed a 'theology for the natural world' which declared that

> the non-human world has just as much right to its internal integrity as does the human world, that human beings transgress their divine authority when they destroy or fundamentally alter the rocks, the trees, the air, the water, the soil, the animals – just as they do when they murder other human beings.

Secular environmental philosophy was influenced by these theological currents. This was most evident in the shift from utilitarian conservation toward the view that environmental protection should be promoted 'independent of the usefulness of the nonhuman world for human purposes'.[19] One proponent of this view was John Rodman,[20] who argued that animals and the environment should be respected 'for having their own existence, their own character and potentialities, their own forms of excellence, their own integrity, their own grandeur'. However, because secular ethics were unbounded from natural law (at least in theory) many scholars also returned to the ethical priority that Leopold placed on the whole ecosystem. The most prominent writer in this tradition was John Callicott. Callicott is best read

[15] L White Jr, 'Continuing the Conversation' in I Barbour (ed), *Western Man and Environmental Ethics* (Boston MA, Addison-Wesley Publishing Company, 1973) 62.

[16] Nash (n 12) 103.

[17] Cited in Nash (n 12) 104.

[18] AR Brockway, 'A Theology of the Natural World' (1973) 23 *Engage! Social Action* 37.

[19] B Devall and G Sessions, *Deep Ecology: Living as if Nature Mattered* (Layton UT, Gibbs Smith, 1985) 4.

[20] J Rodman, 'The Liberation of Nature?' (1977) 20 *Inquiry: An Interdisciplinary Journal of Philosophy* 83, 94.

as writing against the grain of the animal rights movement, which he critiqued for being 'atomistic' in its focus on individual organisms.[21] Against this approach, Callicott argued that the whole had more ethical value than any component part: 'Oceans and lakes, mountains, forests, and wetlands are assigned a greater value than individual animals', including human beings.[22]

This is a fundamentally anti-natural law perspective because it holds that individual organisms have no absolute dignity that must be respected. While I suspect Callicott would have baulked at the comparison, I read Callicott's views as sharing important similarities with utilitarian ethics. All one needs to do is replace the utility principle with holism – an action is judged right or wrong in terms of whether it contributes to the integrity of the comprehensive ecological community. Callicott was consistent in his application of this theory and pushed Leopold's concern with integrity in a new direction. Specifically, Callicott argued that in protection of ecosystem integrity, it may be necessary to prioritise the life of a single endangered or keystone species. He also argued that bacteria and ocean plankton had more ethical importance than human beings.[23] Roderick Nash has observed that Callicott softened some of these claims toward the end of his career and accepted ideals concerning the value of the individual. This is a tight-rope to walk but Callicott does so by affirming that the 'health and integrity of the social whole is literally essential to a socially constituted individual's well-being'.[24]

As the concept of ecological integrity was being constructed in the humanities it was simultaneously being developed by ecologists and adapted by policy-makers. Far from developing in isolation, it is best to think of it in terms of cross-pollination with each discipline learning and adapting in response to the other. The earliest example can be noted in the Marine Mammal Protection Act, HR 6558 1972 (United States) (MMPA) which was developed in response to the impact that overfishing and bottom-trawling were having on marine biodiversity.[25] The original intention of the Act was radical – an absolute ban on hunting or killing marine animals.[26] However, due to the impact this would have had on capital accumulation, the Act was watered down to prioritise the integrity of the marine ecosystem. To achieve this, the Act provided that marine animals would not be 'permitted to diminish beyond the point at which they cease to be a significant functioning element in the ecosystem of which they are a part'. Here the term integrity has been stripped of notions of purity which dominated early philosophical interpretations. But one

[21] J Callicott, 'Animal Liberation: A Triangular Affair' (1980) 4 *Environmental Ethics* 324.
[22] ibid 326.
[23] ibid 337.
[24] J Callicott and FM Lappe, 'Marx Meets Muir: Toward a Synthesis of the Progressive Political and Ecological Visions' (1987) 2 *Tikkun* 337.
[25] For an overview of how the term has been used in multinational agreements and international documents, see P Bridgewater, RE Kim and K Bosselmann, 'Ecological Integrity: A Relevant Concept for International Environmental Law in the Anthropocene?' (2015) 25(1) *Yearbook of International Environmental Law* 72.
[26] Nash (n 12) 174.

can see the influence of Leopold and his contention that the ecosystem has more ethical weight than individual parts. Moreover, one might also view the turn to 'integrity' to pacify the more radical demand that marine life be given individual moral value.

Following the passing of the MMPA, over 80 nations signed the Convention on International Trade in Endangered Species of Wild Fauna and Flora (CITES). The intention of CITES was to create a mechanism for measuring the health and integrity of ecosystems. Rather than measuring each aspect of an ecosystem, the convention used extinction as proxy and established processes for identifying at-risk species. Once an animal species was classified as at-risk, signatory countries were obligated to restrict trade in that animal and/ or associated products. A lot more could be said, but for my argument it is important to understand why extinction was used as a proxy for deeper notions of integrity. No doubt pragmatism played a role, but there was also deeper philosophical reflection. For example, in 1972, Senator Alan Cranston of California cited Lyn White Jnr to articulate a sophisticated understanding of the way individual organisms contribute to ecological integrity. When a species dies Cranston noted: 'nature has lost one of its components, which played a role in the interrelationship of life on earth'. Extinction gives rise to a 'void' that can never be recovered.[27] This reasoning formed the dominant logic upon which subsequent legislation was based. For example, the Endangered Species Act of 1973 not only protected vulnerable species in the United States but also the 'critical habitat' on which they depend.[28] For the first time the legislation went beyond federally-owned land and applied to private property. For Senator James Buckley, this represented a 'quantum jump in man's acknowledgment of his moral responsibility for the integrity of the natural world'.[29]

While I do not have the space here to highlight every legislative instrument ever to recognise ecological integrity,[30] another common example cited by proponents is the Clean Water Act (1972). The legislation empowers the US Environmental Protection Agency to 'preserve and restore the physical, chemical, and biological integrity of the Nation's waters'.[31] It is tempting to regard the term biological integrity as distinct from ecological integrity. Does not the former shift our attention away from an ecosystem and toward organisms? However, this is not how the term is defined by scientists. For example, James Karr and Daniel Dudley[32]

[27] US Congress, 'Subcommittee on Fisheries and Wildlife Conservation: Hearings, Predatory Mammals and Endangered Species' (92nd Congress, 2nd session, 1972) A Cranston, 479 at 484.

[28] Endangered Species Act (1973) 87 Stat. 884.

[29] Nash (n 12) 177.

[30] The literature is vast. Stephen Woodley has noted that ecological integrity is the 'most entrenched [term] in the scientific literature, in national and provincial legislation, and in the language of international agreements and treaties': S Woodley, 'Ecological Integrity and Canada's National Parks' (2010) 27(2) *George Wright Forum* 151.

[31] Clean Water Act (1972) 86 Stat. 916.

[32] J Karr and D Dudley, 'Ecological Perspective on Water Quality Goals' (1981) 5 *Environmental Management* 56.

defined biological integrity as referring to the capacity of an ecosystem to 'support and maintain a balanced, integrated, adaptive community of organisms having a species composition, diversity, and functional organization comparable to that of the natural habitat of the region'.

This is similar to the idea of ecological integrity discussed above. However, note that the last part of Karr and Dudley's definition references a comparison to 'natural habitat'. This is not isolated and has been repeated by many proponents of ecological integrity. Laura Westra,[33] for example, defines integrity as 'a valuable whole, the state of being whole or undiminished, unimpaired, or in perfect condition'. Due to human impact on natural systems, Westra argues that 'wild nature provides the paradigmatic example of ecological integrity'.[34] For a time Karr worked with Westra in the Global Ecological Integrity Group and he developed the Index of Biological Integrity (IBI) as a tool to enable 'scientists to provide an approximate description of the extent to which systems deviate from verifiable integrity levels calibrated from a baseline condition of wild nature'.[35] In the Clean Water Act (1972) integrity is analysed predominately with reference to the 'physico-chemical properties of water'.[36] However, in other contexts, the IBI attempts to assess integrity by 'evaluating the degree to which waters provide for beneficial uses … water supply, recreational and other uses'.[37]

What would a generous reading of these statements look like? Unlike Westra, I do not think that Karr should be read as conflating integrity with purity. Borrowing from Holmes Rolston III,[38] I interpret the IBI as attempting to understand the extent to which an ecosystem is dynamic, stable and has a capacity for self-repair with minimal outside intervention. However, critics have pointed out that the IBI relies on questionable assumptions, particularly in how it selects and measures its data, and whether these metrics can truly be objectively assessed. To this I would add that the choice to place wild nature as the baseline index for measuring integrity is meaningless in the Anthropocene. This is for two reasons: the Anthropocene is grounded in earth system science, which

[33] L Westra, *Ecological Integrity and Global Governance: Science, Ethics and the Law* (Abingdon-on-Thames, Routledge Press, 2016) 5.

[34] This recent statement is surprising because Westra had previously warned against upholding pure notions of integrity. See for example J Lemons and L Westra, 'Introduction' in J Lemons and L Westra (eds), *Perspectives on Ecological Integrity* (Heidelberg, Springer, 1995) 3–4. This is consistent with a trend in Westra's writing which has gradually shifted to more pure statements on integrity.

[35] J Karr, 'Health, Integrity and Biological Assessment: The Importance of Wild Things' in D Pimentel, L Westra and R Noss (eds), *Ecological Integrity: Integrating Environment, Conservation and Health* (Washington DC, Island Press, 2000) 96.

[36] V Capmourteres, N Rooney and M Anand, 'Assessing the Causal Relationships of Ecological Integrity: A Re-Evaluation of Karr's Iconic Index of Biotic Integrity' (2018) *Ecosphere: An ESA Open Access Journal* 1.

[37] JR Karr, 'Assessment of Biotic Integrity Using Fish Communities' (1981) 6 *Fisheries* 22.

[38] H Rolston III, *A New Environmental Ethics: The Next Millennium for Life on Earth* (Abingdon-on-Thames, Routledge, 2011) 165.

encompasses but also surpasses the ecological sciences.[39] Rather than looking back to concepts derived from ecology, environmental legal thinking requires a systematic way of thinking about the new object of the Earth system. And this is precisely the entire project of earth system law. Earth system law seeks to develop a legal framework that can comprehend and respond to the complexities of the Earth as an interconnected system, moving beyond the limitations of traditional environmental law approaches. By critiquing concepts like ecological integrity through this lens, we can better understand the challenges and opportunities in developing legal principles truly suited to the Anthropocene reality.

Second, and more fundamentally, if the idea of integrity is to have meaning today it must consider human impact on living systems from the local to the global scale, in other words, the entire planetary scale. In making this argument I am trying to articulate something more than the common argument that nature includes human beings; I am saying that ecological systems like water are not immune to the rupture of the earth system which the Anthropocene describes. As Geoffrey Garver[40] has noted: 'The Anthropocene underscores the near certainty that ecosystems completely free of anthropogenic impacts no longer exist – and that widespread human impacts on "wild nature" have occurred since Paleolithic times'.

These are facts that proponents of ecological integrity need to come to terms with or the word itself should be replaced by something that is more suited to the Anthropocene. This recognition of pervasive human impact and the need for concepts that reflect our current reality is at the heart of earth system law. Earth system law seeks to develop legal frameworks and principles that can address the complexities of human–nature interactions on a planetary scale. It challenges us to move beyond traditional notions of ecological integrity towards more holistic concepts that can capture the interconnected nature of Earth's systems in the Anthropocene. As such, the critique of ecological integrity presented here aligns with earth system law's goal of reimagining legal concepts to better reflect and respond to our current planetary condition. I turn now to discuss the most promising attempt to think in terms of the Earth system, and point out limits to this approach, considering how these attempts align with or challenge the developing framework of earth system law.

III. Biosphere Integrity

In the previous section, I argued that the Anthropocene has made redundant conceptions of ecological integrity which are linked to notions of purity or

[39] C Hamilton, *Defiant Earth: The Fate of Humans in the Anthropocene* (Cambridge, Polity Press, 2017) 12.

[40] G Garver, 'Ecological Integrity in the Anthropocene: Lessons for Law from Ecological Restoration and Beyond' in L Westra, J Gray and F Gottwald (eds), *The Role of Integrity in the Governance of the Commons* (Heidelberg, Springer, 2017).

wilderness. The rupture of the earth system has fused human and Earth history and there is no place to hide from his reality. Moreover, while ecological integrity has focused at the local and regional levels, earth system law requires a mode of investigation that brings the earth system into focus. It is not a matter of adapting ecological integrity to the larger system – we either need a new way of thinking about law or else the term ecological integrity should be abandoned.[41]

This has led some writers to redefine ecological integrity at a global level and reimagine its parameters for the Anthropocene. The most developed example is Peter Bridgewater, Rakhyun E Kim, and Klaus Bosselmann[42] who reconceptualise ecological integrity as a 'combination of the biodiversity and ecosystem processes (functions) that characterize the area at a given point in time'. Integrity, on this understanding is composed of the 'goods and services' that are required for an ecosystem to maintain itself. This has similarities to the idea of biodiversity health and incorporates animals (including humans) and non-living systems. Moreover, rather than holding on to fixed ideas of purity or wilderness, the authors argue integrity should be measured 'at a point of time' to 'allow for elasticity in terms of potential change'.[43]

So far, we have an updated version of the concept of ecological integrity articulated above. To respond to the first challenge of scale we need some way to expand the notion of ecological integrity from the local to the planetary scale. The authors attempt this by noting that the earth system is made up of component parts that can be brought together to form a whole: 'ecological integrity then means the combination of the biodiversity and ecosystem processes that characterize the biosphere as a whole during the Holocene epoch'.[44] Viewed on this scale, the term 'ecological integrity' is no longer appropriate – we have transcended the ecological community. The authors propose 'biosphere integrity' as the appropriate term for Anthropocene scholarship.[45] Just as ecological integrity is measured at a point in time, the authors argue that 'biosphere integrity' is measured with reference to the Holocene. The authors do not engage in the debate about when the Anthropocene started and so we do not have firm dates for this measurement. Instead, the Holocene is chosen because it is 'the only state of the Earth System that we know for sure can support contemporary society'.[46]

[41] Kotzé and Kim (n 1); RE Kim, 'Taming Gaia 2.0: Earth System Law in the Ruptured Anthropocene' (2022) 9(3) *The Anthropocene Review* 411; LJ Kotzé and others, 'Earth System Law: Exploring New Frontiers in Legal Science' (2022) 11 *Earth System Governance* 100126.

[42] Bridgewater, Kim and Bosselmann (n 25).

[43] ibid 73.

[44] ibid.

[45] ibid.

[46] ibid.

While the earth system may be made up of component parts, the authors are aware that the biosphere is also a unique entity and vastly more complicated than measurements made in a local ecosystem. To overcome this issue, the authors attempt to measure biosphere integrity with reference to planetary boundaries.[47] The concept of planetary boundaries emerged from an attempt to 'identify which of Earth's processes are most important to maintaining the stability of the planet as we know it', and to establish what needs to be done 'to maintain Holocene-like conditions on Earth, now that we, in the Anthropocene, have become a global force of change'.[48] Johan Rockström and his colleagues identified nine boundaries which, if transgressed, could result in linear, abrupt environmental change within continental-to-planetary-scale systems. These boundaries are: climate change, changes in biosphere integrity, biogeochemical flows, stratospheric ozone depletion, ocean acidification, freshwater use, land-system change, atmospheric aerosol loading, and the introduction of novel entities. While itemised as separate points of measurement, it is important to understand that each boundary is tightly linked such that if 'one boundary is transgressed, then other boundaries are also under serious risk'.[49] Recent research has further emphasised these interconnections, showing that transgressing one planetary boundary can change risk gradients for other boundaries.[50] For example, there is increasing evidence to suggest that transgressing either the 'climate change' or 'biosphere integrity' planetary boundary can potentially lead to more steeply increasing risk to the other.[51] The most recent assessment of these boundaries finds that seven of the nine are now transgressed, suggesting that Earth is well outside of the safe operating space for humanity.[52]

Planetary boundaries are a useful tool for thinking about Earth as an interconnected system. We can see, for example, how 'significant land use-changes in the Amazon could influence water resources as far as away as Tibet'.[53] And yet it is important to note that the boundaries are best conceived as guardrails, not tipping points.[54] Steffen et al[55] note:

> A zone of uncertainty, sometimes large, is associated with each of the boundaries … This zone encapsulates both gaps and weaknesses in the scientific knowledge base and intrinsic uncertainties in the functioning of the Earth system. At the 'safe' end of the

[47] J Rockström and others, 'A Safe Operating Space for Humanity' (2009) 461 *Nature* 472.

[48] J Rockström and M Klum, *Big World, Small Planet: Abundance within Planetary Boundaries* (New Haven CT, Yale University Press, 2015) 59.

[49] Rockström and others (n 47) 474.

[50] K Richardson, 'Earth beyond Six of Nine Planetary Boundaries' (2023) 9 *Science Advances* 1.

[51] ibid.

[52] Planetary Boundaries Science (PBScience), *Planetary Health Check 2025* (Potsdam Institute for Climate Impact Research, 2025).

[53] Rockström and others (n 47) 474.

[54] Although the planetary boundaries are sometimes referenced in the context of and connected with tipping points. See, eg V Lam and Y Rousselot, 'Anthropocene, Planetary Boundaries and Tipping Points: Interdisciplinarity and Values in Earth System Science' (2024) 14 *European Journal for Philosophy of Science* 18.

[55] W Steffen and others, 'Planetary Boundaries: Guiding Human Development on a Changing Planet' (2015) 347 *Science* 1259855.

> zone of uncertainty, current scientific knowledge suggests that there is a very low probability of crossing a critical threshold or significantly eroding the resilience of the Earth system. Beyond the 'danger' end of the zone of uncertainty, current knowledge suggests a much higher probability of a change to the functioning of the Earth system that could potentially be devastating for human societies.

Given the severity of these transgressions and the interconnected nature of Earth's biophysical systems, there is an urgent need to reconsider how we conceptualise and measure ecological integrity in the Anthropocene. It is within this context that the proposal from Bridgewater, Kim and Bosselmann offers a compelling restatement of ecological integrity for the Anthropocene. Their approach seeks to align the concept with the planetary-scale challenges we now face, while also leveraging its established presence in international sustainable development instruments. Moreover, the proposal addresses the problem of scale, and while I maintain that the definitional possibilities for the term 'integrity' are not boundless but marked by its history, the authors have distanced themselves from notions of purity. Moreover, by measuring integrity with reference to planetary boundaries, the authors have attached their theory to an internationally recognised method for measuring aspects of the Earth system. I also find laudable the motivation for their restatement – reconceptualising ecological integrity allows us to 'leverage' a concept that is 'already included in major international instruments in the field of sustainable development'.[56]

This is a pragmatic position, motivated (in part) by the magnitude of the crisis and the timeframes for responding. And yet I also uphold Marx's[57] dictum in 'For a Ruthless Criticism of Everything Existing' that 'the work of our time [is to] clarify to itself (critical philosophy) the meaning of its own struggle and its own desires'. We must make time for the work of critique, or we risk moving ahead in the wrong direction to reconsider how we conceptualise and measure ecological integrity in the Anthropocene.

The first strand of my critique is conceptual. Bridgewater, Kim and Bosselmann are fully cognisant that ecological integrity is an elastic idea with varying interpretations. They note, for example, that while ecological integrity is a common term, 'there is still no scientific or societal consensus on what it really means'.[58] To resolve this problem, the authors propose that basic elements of statutory interpretation be employed: 'using both the letter of international agreements and the apparent intentions of the parties as interpreted through decisions and recommendations'.[59] Of course, this will only get us so far because, as the authors note, the term has been used by a wide variety of parties, for different purposes and with

[56] Bridgewater, Kim and Bosselmann (n 25) 74.
[57] K Marx, 'For a Ruthless Criticism of Everything Existing' in RC Tucker (ed), *The Marx-Engels Reader* (New York, Norton & Co, 1978) 15.
[58] Bridgewater, Kim and Bosselmann (n 25) 64.
[59] ibid 68.

interpretations ranging from 'holistic health' to biodiversity. As many lawyers will attest, it can be hard to determine *intention* in a domestic legal system, never mind at the global level.

Arguably the connection to planetary boundaries provides some conceptual clarity in terms of measuring biosphere integrity. As noted above, biosphere integrity is one of the nine planetary boundaries being measured. I interpret Bridgewater, Kim and Bosselmann as being concerned with this specific boundary rather than treating biosphere integrity as the culmination of all nine boundaries. If that is the case, it's worth noting that in their 2009 article, Steffen[60] and colleagues didn't mention biosphere integrity. This changed in their 2015 article where biosphere integrity was introduced to replace biodiversity loss and include measurements on genetic diversity. Because Steffen and colleagues were not writing with reference to ecological integrity, their approach differs from that expressed in ecological law scholarship. Simply put, proponents of planetary boundaries are interested in the specific role the biosphere plays in the Earth system, rather than treating the biosphere as equivalent to the entire Earth system.

The measurements also differ. Within the planetary boundaries literature, biosphere integrity is measured in two ways: (i) genetic diversity, which 'provides the long-term capacity of the biosphere to persist under and adapt to abrupt and gradual abiotic change';[61] and (ii) the role of the biosphere and measures of biodiversity at the global and large biome levels.[62] To illustrate this with a concrete example, scientists might measure genetic diversity by tracking the variety of genes within a species of rainforest tree across different regions, while also assessing how that tree species contributes to the overall functioning of the rainforest ecosystem. Conceived in this narrower form, the concept of biosphere integrity may provide a useful tool for thinking about one aspect of the Earth system. However, if I have misinterpreted Bridgewater, Kim and Bosselmann, and they intend their concept of biosphere integrity to be measured with reference to *all nine* planetary boundaries, then we must ask what their concept adds that is not already covered by planetary boundaries scholarship.

Finally, we must consider how proposals for law reform, including those related to earth system law, might reflect an idealistic approach to philosophy and history. I've previously argued that there's a fundamental connection between liberal proposals for law reform and philosophical idealism.[63] This involves legislating for an ideal or abstract version of something (be it a person or the biosphere) which may not align with material reality. It is important to note that biosphere integrity does not have this idealistic quality when investigated

[60] W Steffen, 'The Trajectory of the Anthropocene: The Great Acceleration' (2015) 2 *The Anthropocene Review* 81.

[61] Steffen and others (n 55).

[62] ibid.

[63] P Burdon, *The Anthropocene: New Trajectories in Law* (Abingdon-on-Thames, Routledge, 2023).

by earth system scientists. For them, it's a tool for collecting data and providing decision-makers with practical reasons for action. This is precisely why earth system law proposes using earth system science to inform legal reform processes. However, when the concept moves from science into legal prescriptions (eg, a mandate to maintain integrity), it risks adopting a similar idealism to that found in rights-based approaches to law.

Focusing on ecological or biosphere integrity we might again note the limits of a politics that relies on ideal abstractions. This approach does not name the material causes of environmental harm or engage those forces that course through civil society and render the environment an object for exploitation. Assuming a position of neutrality in response to these forces may seem value free, but it risks reifying the status quo. To follow Marx,[64] legal abstractions liberate the state from having to engage with the material causes of environmental harm. But individuals still need to navigate those powers on their own and in a depoliticised way. To be more direct, a state may legislate for biosphere integrity rather than addressing extractive capitalism or its own reliance on revenue generated from fossil fuels. The biosphere is legally represented as having integrity but those forces that have caused a rupture in the earth system may not be addressed. Instead, the state has the freedom to promote integrity through notions of individual responsibility, purchasing carbon credits, denouncing foreign polluters or arguing that it has a moral responsibility to open new coal mines to support the developing world.

A politics that relies on ideal abstractions will always be at some distance from material reality. To repurpose an idea from Wendy Brown,[65] the biosphere is 'ideally emancipated' through its promulgation as an abstract entity and is 'practically resubordinated' through the idealist disavowal of the material reasons for its active subordination at the level of the economy. Until these material causes of the Anthropocene rupture are addressed, any notion of integrity must be a 'narrow', 'partial' or perhaps even a 'devious' form of emancipation.[66] In the context of earth system law, we must critically examine how these concepts of integrity and abstraction are operationalised.

Earth system law, as an emerging legal paradigm, has the potential to bridge the gap between abstract legal principles and material realities of the Earth system. However, for earth system law to be an effective vehicle for change, it must grapple with several key questions: How can earth system law incorporate materialist perspectives to address the root causes of environmental degradation? What alternative justice claims might emerge from an earth system law framework that prioritises the interconnectedness of the earth system over abstract notions of integrity? How can earth system law drive legal reforms that reflect the complex, dynamic nature of the earth system rather than relying on idealised abstractions?

[64] Marx (n 3) 32.

[65] W Brown, *Undoing the Demos: Neoliberalism's Stealth Revolution* (Brooklyn NY, Zone Books, 2015) 106.

[66] Marx (n 3) 32.

By engaging with these questions, earth system law could potentially offer a more nuanced and effective approach to earth system governance: one that acknowledges the material realities of the Anthropocene while still leveraging the power of legal frameworks to effect change. This approach would require a fundamental rethinking of how we conceptualise, implement and reform (environmental) law, moving beyond traditional notions of integrity towards a more holistic, systems-based understanding of Earth's processes and humanity's place within them.

IV. Conclusion

In this chapter, I have presented two main arguments within the context of earth system law. The first is that the concept of ecological integrity, while historically significant in environmental legal thought, is not suitable for thinking about law in the Anthropocene or as a principle for earth system law. This is due to issues of scale and its insistence on affirming notions of purity and imagined wilderness that are incompatible with the realities of the Anthropocene epoch. The concept of biosphere integrity, which emerged as a response to these limitations, has addressed some concerns by shifting our attention to the biosphere and measuring health at a point in time in the Holocene. However, my critique revealed that biosphere integrity, despite its attempts to align with earth system scholarship, still participates in an idealistic discourse that abstracts from physical reality.

This insight is crucial for the future development of earth system law, which aims to create a legal framework capable of addressing the complexities of the planetary system. By subjecting these key concepts to critique, I have demonstrated the need for earth system law to move beyond the idealistic tendencies that have characterised much of environmental legal thought. The inability of concepts like ecological and biosphere integrity to name the material causes of the Anthropocene rupture highlights a significant challenge for earth system law: *how to develop principles that are truly grounded in the material realities of our planet.* I argue that it is time for earth system law to consider what a materialist approach to the Anthropocene might look like. This is a challenging task because liberal approaches to law reform, which have influenced much of environmental law and potentially earth system law itself, tend to be idealistic in nature. They create abstract representations of reality that are disconnected from the material conditions of daily life. However, I contend that a materialist approach is necessary if earth system law is to respond effectively to the challenges of the Anthropocene in a way that is grounded in the real conditions of human and non-human existence.

Second, the Anthropocene demands that earth system law develops a mode of analysis that engages directly with the material world and the forces that have caused the rupture in the Earth system. This requires moving beyond idealistic discourses that create abstractions from reality and instead grappling with the complex interplay of social, economic, and political factors that have brought us to this point. It also requires a willingness to challenge the status quo and imagine new ways of organising society that are more sustainable and equitable. While I have focused on the limitations of ecological and biosphere integrity in this chapter, my critique is not meant to be a rejection of these concepts entirely. Rather, by unpacking the presumptions and presuppositions that underpin these ideas, I aim to open new ways of thinking about (environmental) law and policy that are better suited to meeting the challenges of the Anthropocene. This is a key purpose of this book and indeed of the broader project of earth system law: to critically examine existing legal concepts and principles, and to develop new ones that can effectively address the complexities of our planetary reality.

This chapter thus contributes to the larger project of earth system law by demonstrating the need for a critical, materialist approach to developing legal principles for the Anthropocene. It suggests that earth system law must be vigilant against reproducing the idealistic tendencies of traditional environmental law and instead strive for a framework that is deeply engaged with the material realities of our planet. This is a difficult and ongoing task, but one that is essential if earth system law is to fulfil its promise of being a new legal paradigm to think about law's contribution to building a more just and sustainable future for all inhabitants of our planet.

PART IV

Earth System Lawyering: In Search of New Actors, Architectures and Institutions

11

Architectural Principles for Earth System Law: Constitutive Regulation

CAMERON HOLLEY, CLIFFORD SHEARING AND SAMANTHA MOYO*

I. Introduction

As human activities have continued to impact the earth system in ways that have breached the biophysical and biochemical planetary boundaries that characterised the Holocene epoch, the issue of earth system governance[1] and how this might be reformed so as to provide for the maintenance of these boundaries, has moved increasingly to the centre of the socio-legal regulatory stage.[2] Legal debates in the earth system governance community focus on the domain of earth system law, and these debates question what regulatory (legal) approach to governing the earth system might, and should, be adopted.[3]

In exploring this question, we recognise and build upon a well-established critique of regulatory scholarship that dates back to the 1960s, that has drawn attention to the failure to attend to the constitutive features of regulatory tools. Law, in this critique, must, it is argued, be understood not simply as a set of directions (rules) for ordering relationships between objects within a field, but also as

* We are grateful for the research assistance of Cameron Greig. Parts of this chapter draw on work that previously appeared in C Holley and C Shearing, 'A Nodal Perspective of Governance: Advances in Nodal Governance Thinking' in P Drahos (ed), *Regulatory Theory: Foundations and Applications* (Canberra, ANU E-Press, 2017) 163–80; and C Holley, A Kennedy and C Shearing, 'Power, Conflict and Energy Law: Learning from Unconventional Natural Gas, Non-State Actors, Industry and Government' (2022) 18 *Texas Journal of Oil, Gas and Energy Law* 1.

[1] F Biermann, *Earth System Governance: World Politics in the Anthropocene* (Cambridge MA, MIT Press, 2014).

[2] LJ Kotzé and RE Kim, 'Earth System Law: The Juridical Dimensions of Earth System Governance' (2019) 1 *Earth System Governance* 100003.

[3] LJ Kotzé, 'Earth System Law for the Anthropocene' (2019) 11 *Sustainability* 6796.

constituting the objects and the field itself.[4] In this chapter, we seek to remedy this neglect in relation to the regulation of anthropogenic impacts on planetary boundaries, by considering the possibility of earth system law adopting a constitutive conception of regulation as a foundational principle. In doing so, we draw upon and extend Shearing's[5] 'constitutive conception of regulation' to develop a constitutive principle that could provide a sound conceptual foundation for earth system law scholarship as it tackles complex planetary challenges and contributes to realising the ambitious transformations they require.

Our analysis sketches out a constitutive conception of regulation which argues that 'reality' is not simply given but rather must be understood as socially constructed.[6] We draw upon developments within the legal, sociological, and criminological literature suggesting that law constitutes the realities it seeks to regulate, through processes of social construction that have consistently produced inequitable power relations. These constitutive features must be recognised and addressed in any regulatory initiative.

In what follows we begin by providing a short history of some of this critical scholarship before highlighting the limits of established legal regulatory instruments and examining how constitutive regulation might be established as a guiding principle of earth system law to help it identify, map and reform the multiple structures, sectors, actants, actors, politics and power that are present within a complex earth system.

II. Law and the Social Construction of Reality

The concept of reality has long been a subject of philosophical and sociological inquiry. Rather than a fixed and objective entity, scholars have argued that reality is socially constructed. This has been explored through numerous lenses, including the influences of social interactions, language, and power. Berger and Luckmann[7] argue that society is an ongoing human production, and reality is a social construct. The idea is that reality, as experienced, is not an objective, pre-existing entity but rather a social product. Human beings collectively create and maintain their understanding of reality through social interactions which occur within a social context and are influenced by cultural, historical, and institutional factors.

[4] C Scott, 'Regulation in the Age of Governance: The Rise of the Post-Regulatory State' in J Jordana and D Levi-Faur (eds), *The Politics of Regulation* (Cheltenham, Edward Elgar Publishing, 2004).

[5] C Shearing, 'A Constitutive Conception of Regulation' in P Grabosky and J Braithwaite (eds), *Business Regulation and Australia's Future* (Canberra, Australian Institute of Criminology, 1993).

[6] PL Berger and T Luckmann, *The Social Construction of Reality: A Treatise in the Sociology of Knowledge* (New York, Anchor Books, 1967).

[7] ibid.

As such, reality is socially constructed through interpersonal interaction as well as interaction with others, depending on the situation and the time. Freedman and Combs[8] reiterate that the main principle of social constructionism is that the beliefs, institutions, and divisions of labour that produce our social realities are created through daily interaction by the members of a society from generation to generation. Sociological literature appreciates the construction of reality through relations and attempts to understand how such reality influences the lives of society.[9] This idea contends that multiple unstable realities are facilitated through history, culture, and language.[10] People view the world differently and meanings change with time and context.[11]

A. Ethnomethodology

Garfinkel[12] delves into the foundations of ethnomethodology, a sociological approach that focuses on the study of everyday social interactions and the methods people use to make sense of the world. Ethnomethodology, as he describes it, is concerned with the 'everyday methods' people employ to navigate and understand their social world. Ethnomethodology is interested in the practical methods individuals use to produce and interpret social order. Garfinkel introduces the notion that meaning in social interactions is context-dependent and indexical. This means that the meaning of actions, statements, or gestures is not fixed but is contingent on the specific context in which they occur.

Ethnomethodologists are concerned with unravelling the indexical expressions that people use in their everyday interactions to construct and interpret the social world. Garfinkel emphasises the practical nature of social order, arguing that it is an accomplishment that individuals continually produce through their actions and interpretations. He challenges the idea that social order is predefined and dictated by formal structures, asserting that it is an ongoing, practical achievement that arises in the flow of everyday life. Ethnomethodology seeks to uncover the methods people employ to maintain the orderly processes of social life. Garfinkel's ideas served as an invitation to rethink traditional sociological approaches and engage with the everyday methods people employ to construct and interpret their social reality. This invitation challenges sociology to consider the practical accomplishments of everyday life.

[8] J Freedman and G Combs, *Narrative Therapy: The Social Construction of Preferred Realities* (New York, Norton & Company, 1996).

[9] Berger and Luckmann (n 6); K Gergen, 'Social Constructionism' in T Teo (ed), *Encyclopedia of Critical Psychology* (Heidelberg, Springer, 2014); V Burr and P Dick, 'Social Constructionism' in B Gough (ed), *The Palgrave Handbook of Critical Social Psychology* (London, Palgrave Macmillan/Springer, 2017).

[10] Gergen (n 9).

[11] A Galbin, 'An Introduction to Social Constructionism' (2014) 6 *Social Research Reports* 82–92.

[12] H Garfinkel, *Studies in Ethnomethodology* (Cambridge, Polity Press, 1984).

B. Language and Legal Texts

The world is conceptually and communicatively constituted. Paraphrasing Heidegger,[13] one might say that we do not have our language so much as it has us. Who and what we are, how we arrange and classify and think about our world, and how we act in it, is deeply delimited by the rhetorical resources of our language. Our shared reality transforms as the meanings of the fundamental concepts that shape it evolve. According to Kierkegaard,[14] concepts, like individuals, have their own histories and are equally vulnerable to the effects of time. Authors such as White[15] question how 'words lose their meaning', and worlds their coherence, and consider how meanings, once lost might be regained or created anew and the world made whole. By doing so, White delves into the ways in which language shapes our understanding of legal texts, character, and community, and how it can be reconstituted to adapt to changing social contexts. White[16] uses the term 'language' to recognise 'common understandings of the world, shared behaviours and values, shared resources and expectations, and methods for communication and thought' that shape and define communities.

White's perspective shares similarities with Dewey's,[17] as both suggest that society not only endures *through* communication but can be described as existing *within* communication. The connection between the words 'common', 'community', and 'communication' is instructive. People form communities based on the things they share, and communication is how they acquire shared elements. White is intrigued not just by the nature of ways of seeing and being,[18] but also by the potential for their complete and radical reconstitution. He invites us to contemplate a method of interpreting texts and comprehending their meaning. White's argument that certain classical texts in our tradition – whether labelled as literary, poetic, or political – are not solely narratives about communities grappling with events. Rather, they are inventive responses to the crises they portray. These texts are endeavours to establish communities by reconstituting language and forging new connections, whether between actual or fictional subjects or between the text and its readers. White challenges the traditional understanding of legal texts as fixed and unchanging entities. He argues that language is inherently dynamic and evolves over time, reflecting the evolving values and beliefs of society. Legal texts, including constitutions, are not immune to this linguistic evolution. White contends that the interpretation of legal texts should not be rigid

[13] M Heidegger, *The Piety of Thinking* (Bloomington IN, Indiana University Press, 1976) 28.

[14] S Kierkegaard, *The Concept of Irony, With Constant Reference to Socrates* (Glasgow, Collins, 1966) 47.

[15] JB White, *When Words Lose Their Meaning: Constitutions and Reconstitutions of Language, Character, and Community* (Chicago IL, University of Chicago Press, 1985).

[16] ibid 193.

[17] J Dewey, *Democracy and Education: An Introduction to the Philosophy of Education* (New York, MacMillan, 1916).

[18] B Morizot, *Ways of Being Alive* (Cambridge, Polity Press, 2022).

and literal but should embrace the fluidity of language. He advocates for a more nuanced approach that recognises the contextual and cultural factors influencing the interpretation of legal documents. In the realm of law, language shapes our perceptions of character and moral standing. He emphasises the importance of recognising the power of language to construct and deconstruct worlds in legal discourse.

As White delves into the concept of community and how language contributes to the formation of communal identity, he explores how shared language and narratives create a sense of belonging and community among individuals. He argues that legal texts play a crucial role in defining and redefining the boundaries of communities. He examines how legal language can promote either inclusivity or exclusion, depending on how it is constructed and interpreted. Therefore, legal texts should not be engaged with merely as technical documents but as rich sources of meaning and symbolism. In doing so, White encourages a more reflective and critical approach to legal interpretation and social discourse, by highlighting the malleability of language and its impact on our understanding of law, character, and community.

C. Legal Texts and Power

Carol Smart[19] delves into the complex relationship between law, power, and society. Her analysis revolves around the idea that law is not just a neutral set of rules and regulations but a dynamic force that reflects and reinforces power structures within society. Smart questions the traditional view of law as an objective and impartial system that exists to maintain social order, and argues that law is deeply entangled with power relations, shaping and reshaping social dynamics in profound ways. Smart emphasises that legal definitions are not fixed but are influenced by social, political, and economic factors. These definitions often serve the interests of dominant groups in society, reinforcing existing power imbalances. She considers how the criminal justice system, through its practices and policies, can disproportionately target marginalised communities, perpetuating social inequalities. Thus, law, according to Smart, is not just a tool for social control but a mechanism through which power is exercised and contested. Smart explores how societal attitudes and stereotypes regarding women's sexuality influence legal judgments. Women's sexual behaviour, clothing, and relationship status are often scrutinised in court, reinforcing notions of 'respectable victimhood'. She argues that such scrutiny serves to disqualify women as credible witnesses to their own victimisation, perpetuating the idea that some women are more deserving of protection and justice than others, thus highlighting courtroom dynamics.

[19] C Smart, 'The Power of Law' in J Muncie, E McLaughlin and M Langan (eds), *Criminological Perspectives: A Reader* (London, Sage, 1996).

Smart exposes law as a form of symbolic power. She argues that legal language and discourse are used strategically to legitimise certain actions and delegitimise others. Legal terminology can create narratives that justify social injustices or discriminatory practices. Thus, by controlling language and framing legal issues, those in power can shape public perceptions and attitudes, further consolidating their dominance. Through the exploration of how law intersects with gender, Smart discusses how legal definitions of crimes such as domestic violence and sexual assault have evolved and how feminist movements have challenged these definitions, leading to significant changes in legal discourse and policies.

Ecofeminists have drawn similar conclusions showing how the ideologies that authorise oppression, such as those based on gender, race, physical abilities, and species, are the same ideologies which sanction the oppression of nature.[20] Smart underscores the multifaceted power of law in shaping social reality. By examining law not just as a set of rules but as a dynamic instrument of power, she illuminates how legal systems can perpetuate or challenge social inequalities. Her analysis prompts critical reconsideration of understanding law and encourages a more nuanced perspective that recognises the intricate relationship between law, power, and society.

D. Power and Capture

Drawing on the above ideas and other antecedents,[21] interdisciplinary scholars increasingly study how different sections of society vie for their values and interests to be evident in the design and implementation of laws and regulation.[22] This is a rich area of inquiry that encompasses a variety of theoretical approaches.[23] All these approaches recognise, in different ways and with different emphases, that systems of laws and regulation encourage, and enable, different sets of interests to vie for political influence through processes that allow one or more sets of interests to influence and capture rule-making and implementation. As Stigler[24] pointed out in his classic paper 'The Theory of Economic Regulation', regulatory processes are a prize that different economic constituencies seek to harness for their own benefit. Capture, and contests over capture, are thus at the heart of the regulatory game. This is something that Stigler stated very clearly, and very bluntly, in

[20] G Gaard, 'Living Interconnections with Animals and Nature' in G Gaard (ed), *Ecofeminism* (Philadelphia PA, Temple University Press, 1993).

[21] M Foucault, *Discipline and Punish: The Birth of the Prison* (London, Allen Lane, 1977).

[22] C Carrigan and C Coglianese, 'The Politics of Regulation: From New Institutionalism to New Governance' (2011) 14 *Annual Review of Political Science* 107; F Haines, 'Compliance and Contestation' in B Rooij and DD Sokol (eds), *The Cambridge Handbook of Compliance* (Cambridge, Cambridge University Press, 2021); JL Short, 'The Politics of Regulatory Enforcement and Compliance: Theorizing and Operationalizing Political Influences' (2021) 15 *Regulation and Governance* 653.

[23] Short (n 22).

[24] G Stigler, 'The Theory of Economic Regulation' (1971) 2 *The Bell Journal of Economics and Management Science* 3.

the opening sentence of his 1971 paper: 'The state – the machinery and power of the state – is a potential resource or threat to every industry in the society'.[25] This challenges the widespread instrumental and idealistic view of law and regulation as standing above partisan politics to protect an untarnished public interest that, in Stigler's words, is 'deeply imbedded in professional economic thought', and, we would add, in the thought of many legal and regulatory scholars.[26]

However, the difficulty with Stigler's well-known framing is that it suggests that only major players in economies are involved, and that capture is a one-way process. Regulatory capture is undoubtedly of concern, but the flows of power and control are complicated and multidirectional, rendering simple or 'deterministic' explanations of control problematic.[27] For example, Gaventa's[28] study of coal miners in Central Appalachia's Clear Fork Valley some 40 years ago demonstrates that, even in the face of inequality and exploitation, a state of 'quiescence' or non-rebellion against the status quo might persist. In his research, a complex patchwork of historical practices, ownership structures, co-option of local government, and narratives which devalued the local culture and way of life, each contributed to a general acceptance by the miners of their exploitation.[29]

In a similar vein, recent studies expand their focus to other non-state actors and flows of power at micro and macro levels, with politics seen as constituting (as opposed to causing) regulatory arrangements, inputs, and outcomes.[30] Such approaches recognise the layers of contests that occur in law and regulation when balancing multiple economic, social, political, and environmental goals, such as responding to demands for a 'more conducive' regulatory environment for social and economic ends, while meeting other demands for greater environmental protection.[31] This broadening of the concept of capture – to include other interests and flows of power in contests and resistance over legal design, regulatory implementation and ends – highlights the need to unveil and decipher the 'power geometries' within legal and regulatory frameworks.[32] These geometries can be structural (based upon economic and political frameworks), material (based upon objects), and even discursive (based upon language), and they can be used to constrain policy development by prioritising certain scales of assessment (eg, international economic interests over local environmental concerns), promote particular ideologies (including historical perspectives), or exclude interests that

[25] ibid 3.

[26] ibid 17.

[27] Carrigan and Coglianese (n 22) 107; A Stirling, 'Transforming Power: Social Science and the Politics of Energy Choices' (2014) 1 *Energy Research & Social Science* 84.

[28] J Gaventa, *Power and Powerlessness: Quiescence and Rebellion in an Appalachian Valley* (Urbana IL, University of Illinois Press, 1980).

[29] ibid viii–x.

[30] Short (n 22) 658–59.

[31] Haines (n 22).

[32] D Massey, 'Power-Geometry and a Progressive Sense of Place' in J Bird and others (eds), *Mapping the Futures: Local Cultures, Global Change* (Abingdon-on-Thames, Routledge, 1993).

do not fit within the dominant paradigm.[33] On this view, it is not just laws that become a focus, but the 'constellation of laws, actors, institutions and dynamics' that should be scrutinised to determine how – and to what extent – power is mobilised in the service of particular interests.[34]

This perspective encourages a deeper understanding of how law and regulations interact with social, economic, and political contexts and how they can contribute to broader social goals and transformations. In the realm of law, this means that legal systems are not impartial frameworks but active participants in shaping social norms, behaviours, and power dynamics. Laws, regulations, and legal processes influence the way people perceive reality, defining what is acceptable, normal, and deviant behaviour. A 'constitutive conception of regulation'[35] highlights the idea that regulations are not merely rulebooks but active forces in shaping the dynamics of markets, society and industries. Such a view echoes various lines of thinking on law and markets, which highlight the social 'embeddedness' of markets and the influence of ex ante regulation in establishing the legal framework within which economic activity and market order and processes take place.[36]

Bringing a constitutive conception of regulation to the earth system law conversation can highlight the intricate ways in which law and regulations actively shape and are shaped by the realities they intend to regulate. Drawing upon developments within legal, sociological, and criminological literature, the law, far from being neutral, is seen as playing a pivotal role in, being constructed by and constructing social realities, often leading to inequitable power relations.

III. A Constitutive Principle for Earth System Law

Despite the long and varied precursors and threads, a constitutive understanding of law and regulation has often sat at the margins of legal scholarship. It is true that the 'law and …' movements, such as 'law and society' and 'law and economics' provided a broadening of constitutive understandings.[37] However, as Braithwaite points out, while they helped reshape legal disciplinary boundaries, over time, these scholars have found it professionally more secure to 'huddle together' in ways that reinforce

[33] G Walker, *Environmental Justice: Concepts, Evidence and Politics* (Abingdon-on-Thames, Routledge, 2012).

[34] BE Apple, 'Mapping Fracking: An Analysis of Law, Power, and Regional Distribution in the United States' (2014) 38 *Harvard Environmental Law Review* 243; TH Morrison and others, 'Mitigation and Adaptation in Polycentric Systems: Sources of Power in the Pursuit of Collective Goals' (2017) 8 *WIREs Climate Change* e479, 1.

[35] Shearing (n 5).

[36] K Polanyi, *The Great Transformation: The Political and Economic Origins of Our Time* (Boston MA, Beacon Press, 1944); B Lange, F Haines and D Thomas, *Regulatory Transformations: Rethinking Economy-Society Interactions* (Oxford, Hart Publishing, 2015); T Seddon, 'Markets, Regulation and Drug Law Reform: Towards a Constitutive Approach' (2020) 29 *Social & Legal Studies* 313.

[37] S Taekema and W Burg, 'Introduction: The Incorporation Problem in Interdisciplinary Research – Part 1: Theoretical Discussions' (2015) 8 *Erasmus Law Review* 39.

legal myopia.[38] As he puts it: 'The discipline of law would become a straitjacket smothering the promise of interdisciplinary social science in law schools'.[39]

There has been much deeper engagement with constitutive understandings in environmental governance literature, not least earth system governance through its focus on architecture and agency.[40] Rather than spotlight treaties or states, earth system governance's lens of 'architecture' foregrounds governance spaces and structures that are regulated by multiple organisations, regimes, and norms.[41] As Biermann and Kim[42] explain, under an architecture framing, the focus is placed on

> the structures that shape the overall interplay, dynamics, and effectiveness of global governance. We thus move, as it were, upwards from looking at single parts to assessing the larger whole. It is not about having better cake: it is about reinventing and restructuring the entire bakery … such an analytical move allows for a new vision on the fundamental restructuring of world politics and global governance.

Earth system governance defines governance architectures 'as the overarching system of public and private institutions, principles, norms, regulations, decision-making procedures and organizations that are valid or active in a given area of global governance'.[43] This macro-level view is not exclusively focused on the global level, nor is it static; rather, it recognises polycentric and multilevel regimes and embraces a fluid and dynamic architecture that is continuously changing in response to governance processes. Such an approach emphasises attention to state and non-state actors, transnational networks, intergovernmental institutions and regime complexes, and the influence and shaping that occurs between structures and agents.[44] This way of thinking has given rise to various analytical approaches to studying complexity of architectures, including a focus on treaties, institutional designs, bureaucracies or financial resources, discursive structures, as well as social networks.[45]

Despite similarities with the constitutive understanding of regulation that we elaborate below, earth system governance's architectural framing has yet to devote substantial time to law, and thus has found limited traction in legal and regulatory analysis or practice. As Kotzé and Kim[46] point out

[38] J Braithwaite, 'In Praise of Tents: Regulatory Studies and Transformative Social Science' (2014) 10 *Annual Review of Law and Social Science* 1, 5.

[39] ibid 18.

[40] OR Young, 'The Architecture of Global Environmental Governance: Bringing Science to Bear on Policy' (2008) 8 *Global Environmental Politics* 14; F Biermann, MM Betsill and J Gupta, *Earth System Governance: People, Places and the Planet. Science and Implementation Plan of the Earth System Governance Project* (Earth System Governance Project, 2009); F Biermann and RE Kim, 'The Boundaries of the Planetary Boundary Framework: A Critical Appraisal of Approaches to Define a 'Safe Operating Space' for Humanity' (2020) 45 *Annual Review of Environment and Resources* 497.

[41] Biermann and Kim (n 40).

[42] ibid 2.

[43] ibid 4.

[44] ibid 4–5.

[45] Biermann and Kim (n 40); RE Kim, 'Is Global Governance Fragmented, Polycentric, or Complex? The State of the Art of the Network Approach' (2020) 22 *International Studies Review* 903.

[46] Kotzé and Kim (n 2) 2.

> it remains unclear how law could respond from a regulatory perspective to some of the key problem characteristics of earth system governance … despite its relative maturity, environmental law remains a regulatory intervention at the periphery of the social regulatory system. It is essentially a collection of prohibitions with modest impacts on deeply intertwined socio-ecological relationships.

One solution to this issue, we argue, is for earth system law to adopt a *principle of constitutive regulation*, which offers a pathway to rethinking regulatory approaches of law and overcoming many of its existing limits.

To progress this analysis, we use as a heuristic Kotzé and Kim's[47] analysis of the limits of current environmental law, showing how constitutive regulation can enable earth system law to overcome these limits. There have been ongoing attempts to define earth system law's key features,[48] as this current book also demonstrates. Broadly speaking, it has been common to define earth system law by reference to what it must avoid and solve, namely a set of limits that plague traditional environmental law and its response to earth system problems.[49] Many nuanced challenges have been identified,[50] with some of the most common being state-centrism; anthropocentrism; assumptions of Holocene stability; reductionism; and the absence of ambition for deep structural reform. Below we briefly highlight these issues and explore what a principle of constitutive regulation may do to move earth system law past these challenges.

A. Understanding Regulatory Space

We commence with one of the more obvious limits of traditional environmental law, namely state-centrism. As Kotzé and Kim[51] put it: 'The multilateral environmental law and governance domain remains predominantly state-centric, largely depending on the state as the central source of its legitimacy and authority'. In response, they argue that earth system law needs to explore new ways in which law can elevate and meaningfully facilitate the participation and influence of non-state actors in governing the earth system.[52]

Thinking constitutively is well suited to helping earth system law deliver on these sentiments. For constitutive regulation scholars, an exclusive focus on

[47] Kotzé and Kim (n 2).

[48] Kotzé and Kim (n 2); LJ Kotzé and RE Kim, 'Exploring the Analytical, Normative and Transformative Dimensions of Earth System Law' (2020) 50 *Environmental Policy and Law* 457; L du Toit and LJ Kotzé, 'Reimagining International Environmental Law for the Anthropocene: An Earth System Law Perspective' (2022) 11 *Earth System Governance* 100132.

[49] Kotzé and Kim (n 2); Du Toit and Kotzé (n 48).

[50] RE Kim and LJ Kotzé, 'Planetary Boundaries at the Intersection of Earth System Law, Science and Governance: A State-of-the-Art Review' (2020) 30 *Review of European, Comparative and International Environmental Law* 3; Du Toit and Kotzé (n 48); LJ Kotzé and others, 'Earth System Law: Exploring New Frontiers in Legal Science' (2022) 11 *Earth System Governance* 100126.

[51] Kotzé and Kim (n 2) 4.

[52] ibid 5.

state regulation is a both 'peculiar and conservative' response to many regulatory problems.[53] It is true that states have at times conceptually dominated legal and regulatory responses, as is evident from the terms of the Peace of Westphalia of 1648, in which the parties to this treaty conceived of sovereign states as enjoying exclusive authority within their geographic regions.[54] However, as Kotzé and Kim[55] and others acknowledge, this idea has never constituted a satisfactory empirical account of the realities of law and regulation. Scott[56] drew attention to this in his historical study of the 2,000-year history of the hill-people of Zomia in South-East Asia, who have deliberately and consistently strategically organised themselves to keep the state at arm's length. This more polycentric view of the flow of events has been confirmed by a host of other studies within political science, criminology, and earth system governance.[57]

What many variants of law and regulation lack is a defined starting point that avoids privileging the state.[58] To halt this myopia, constitutive thinking starts with the metaphor of 'regulatory space'.[59] The core of this metaphor is that resources relevant to holding and exercising regulatory power and capacities are dispersed and often fragmented among state bodies, and between state and non-state bodies.[60] These resources are not simply state authority via treaties or legislation; they are also things such as information, wealth, knowledge, technologies, connections, and organisational capacities.[61] Such a constitutive conception of regulation assumes it will be rare to find a single, central, hierarchical locus of control. Rather, the means and ends of earth system law would be viewed as a matter of networks.[62]

This way of viewing the world has been called various terms, such as polycentric governance[63] and nodal governance.[64] Numerous studies have

[53] Shearing (n 5) 72; Seddon (n 36) 322.

[54] S Krasna, *Problematic Sovereignty: Contested Rules and Political Possibilities* (New York, Columbia University Press, 2001); C Shearing and L Johnston, 'Nodal Wars and Network Fallacies: A Genealogical Analysis of Global Insecurities' (2010) 14 *Theoretical Criminology* 495–514.

[55] Kotzé and Kim (n 2).

[56] JC Scott, *The Art of Not Being Governed* (New Haven CT, Yale University Press, 2009).

[57] RA Rhodes, 'Understanding Governance: Ten Years On' (2007) 28 *Organization Studies* 1243; JP Brodeur, *The Policing Web* (Oxford, Oxford University Press, 2010); MM Betsill, TM Benney and AK Gerlak (eds), *Agency in Earth System Governance* (Cambridge, Cambridge University Press, 2020).

[58] M Galanter, 'Justice in Many Rooms: Courts, Private Ordering and Indigenous Law' (1981) 13 *The Journal of Legal Pluralism and Unofficial Law* 1; S Merry, 'Legal Pluralism' (1988) 22 *Law and Society Review* 869.

[59] L Hancher and M Moran, 'Organizing Regulatory Space' in L Hancher and M Moran (eds), *Capitalism, Culture and Economic Regulation* (Oxford, Oxford University Press, 1998); C Scott, *Analysing Regulatory Space: Fragmented Resources and Institutional Design* (Oxford, Public Law, 2001) 283–305.

[60] C Scott (n 59) 284–87; Seddon (n 36) 322.

[61] C Scott (n 59) 2.

[62] J Braithwaite and P Drahos, *Global Business Regulation* (Cambridge, Cambridge University Press, 2000); C Scott (n 59) 285.

[63] E Ostrom, 'Beyond Markets and States: Polycentric Governance of Complex Economic Systems' (2010) 100 *American Economic Review* 641.

[64] C Holley and C Shearing, 'A Nodal Perspective of Governance: Advances in Nodal Governance Thinking' in P Drahos (ed), *Regulatory Theory: Foundations and Applications* (Canberra, ANU E-Press, 2017).

explored how networks and nodes are increasingly commonplace in regulatory activities. Even where states are recognised as significant governors, they are conceived of as existing in a broader context of other auspices and providers of regulation.[65] Within these governing assemblages,[66] states, through their legal frameworks, have long been recognised as playing a significant constitutive role in constructing reality.[67]

By commencing with a regulatory space metaphor, earth system law would accept that questions of who regulates, and how they regulate, are not issues that are determined a priori. For example, earth system law would not simply assume that tackling climate change required creating a new legal norm and treaties that prohibited carbon emissions and established a mechanism to enforce it. Instead, a constitutively informed earth system law would be aware that such questions can only be answered through careful empirical exploration of a regulatory space.

While there are multiple approaches to such inquiries, Johnston and Shearing[68] developed an eight-point framework to be used in guiding exploration. Kerr[69] and others have applied this framework and shown the importance of understanding how different auspices and providers of governance relate to one another and how, and when, they enrol the capacities and resources of others in realising regulatory objectives. These empirical 'post-Foucauldian'[70] inquiries into 'multilateral'[71] or 'multidimensional'[72] forms of regulation invite earth system law 'to consider more squarely the limits (and implicitly) the potential for law as one instrument of governance' and emphasise the need for a focus on the dispersion of regulatory authority negotiated between the actors within the regulatory space.[73] Echoes of this approach are already evident in the work of scholars who have recognised for some time now the role of international organisations in steering private and public–private governance,[74] as well as in earth system governance.[75]

[65] DH Bayley and CD Shearing, *The New Structure of Policing: Description, Conceptualization, and Research Agenda* (Washington DC, National Institute of Justice, 2001).

[66] R Abrahamsen and M Williams, *Security Beyond the State: Private Security in International Politics* (Cambridge, Cambridge University Press, 2009).

[67] C Smart, *Feminism and the Power of Law* (Abingdon-on-Thames, Routledge, 1989); Smart (n 19); C Scott (n 4).

[68] L Johnston and C Shearing, *Governing Security: Explorations in Policing and Justice* (Abingdon-on-Thames, Routledge, 2003) 22–30.

[69] J Kerr, *Securitization and Policing of Art Theft: The Case of London* (Farnham, Ashgate, 2015).

[70] K McKee, 'Post-Foucauldian Governmentality: What Does It Offer Critical Social Policy Analysis?' (2009) 29 *Critical Social Policy* 465.

[71] Bayley and Shearing (n 65).

[72] Rhodes (n 57).

[73] C Scott (n 59) 283, 284–92; T Seddon, *Rethinking Drug Laws: Theory, History, Politics* (Oxford, Oxford University Press, 2023).

[74] KW Abbott and D Snidal, 'International Regulation without International Government: Improving IO Performance through Orchestration' (2010) 5 *The Review of International Organizations* 1.

[75] Kim (n 45); A Burke, 'An Architecture for a Net Zero World: Global Climate Governance beyond the Epoch of Failure' (2022) 13 *Global Policy* 24.

An important but obvious insight that this regulatory space orientation brings to earth system law is that its regulatory design will be more effective if it pays attention to the full range of actors who potentially have a stake in the environmental regulatory enterprise.[76] Constitutive frameworks have in fact been used by a variety of scholars to map both existing and potential occupants of regulatory spaces in order to shape and guide subsequent normative regulatory strategies that emphasise how different actors might be enlisted, incentivised, and 'steered' to contribute to regulatory goals.[77] This approach can help earth system law to achieve the kind of innovation argued for by Bulkeley and Newell,[78] who highlight the limits of exclusively focusing on treaties to solve issues like climate change. Instead, they encourage other strategies for steering non-government actors and economic behaviours. As they explain,

> one approach would be to consider the global processes through which emissions of GHG [greenhouse gasses] are generated – flows of production, trade, and consumption, for example – which would signal a very different geography of responsibility suggesting that multinational corporations and consumers had a more significant role to play.[79]

B. Acknowledging Actors, Actants and Assemblages

Importantly, constitutive regulation's emphasis on considering 'the full range of actors'[80] in a regulatory space is particularly helpful in responding to the second critique of environmental law, namely its anthropocentrism. According to Kotzé and Kim,[81] environmental law has largely promoted 'a short-termist, utilitarian, and neoliberal human growth agenda by protecting environmental resources for the socio-economic (and therefore unsustainable) development of some privileged humans of the present generation'. They argue that an important part of earth system law's response to this state of affairs is to fully embrace all present and future earth system constituents, not least the non-human world.[82]

Constitutive regulation draws on Latour[83] and actor network theory to encourage the consideration of non-human 'actants' when exploring regulatory spaces. Adopting this Latourian view would see earth system law focus on the social as an assemblage of biophysical and physical entities, where various human and

[76] Seddon (n 36) 323.

[77] Holley and Shearing (n 64); Seddon (n 36) 323; Seddon (n 73).

[78] H Bulkeley and P Newell, *Governing Climate Change*, 3rd edn (Abingdon-on-Thames, Routledge 2023).

[79] ibid 3.

[80] Seddon (n 36) 323.

[81] Kotzé and Kim (n 2) 5.

[82] Kotzé (n 3); JC Gellers, 'Earth System Law and the Legal Status of Non-Humans in the Anthropocene' (2021) 7 *Earth System Governance* 100083.

[83] B Latour, *Politics of Nature: How to Bring the Sciences into Democracy* (Cambridge MA, Harvard University Press, 2004).

non-human actants take action and 'do things'.[84] This would enable a shift away from traditional law's anthropocentrism and instead foreground earth system law's entwinement with the power of the non-human (and the human).[85] Studies into the power of non-human actants in regulatory spaces has included a focus on wild law,[86] nature rights,[87] natural disasters (eg heat waves, sustained smoke pollution from bushfires),[88] as well as human made objects such as walls and dams.[89] From this viewpoint, earth system law can see actants in the same way as it would human stakeholders, with the biophysical properties of natural resources shaping the organisational and institutional systems within regulatory spaces.[90] A good illustration of such thinking is Jacob et al's[91] investigation of marine biodiversity offsets regulation in California, where they examine the relations between different human (eg Port of Los Angeles) and non-human (eg eel grass, wetlands) influences on marine offsetting approaches and outcomes.

C. Mapping the Dynamic Interactions of Nodes and Networks

Implicit in constitutive thinking's emphasis on understanding the interplay between multiple actors and actants within a regulatory space is a recognition that these relationships are dynamic, and that actors and actants (or nodes) may be connected across multiple networks and regulatory spaces. Recognising these connections and their dynamism is important for enabling earth system law to respond to Kotzé and Kim's[92] critique of traditional environmental law's reductionism and belief in Holocene stability. The former is argued to lead to silos and a lack of integrated and holistic thinking, while the latter makes traditional law unable to respond to 'a non-linear Earth system characterized by unpredictable, potentially catastrophic shifts at multiple scales ranging from the local to the global sphere'.[93]

[84] B Latour, *Reassembling the Social* (Oxford, Oxford University Press, 2005); C Holley, T Mutongwizo and C Shearing, 'Conceptualizing Policing and Security: New Harmscapes, the Anthropocene, and Technology' (2020) 3 *Annual Review of Criminology* 341, 348.

[85] Burke (n 75) 27.

[86] C Cullinan, *Wild Law: A Manifesto for Earth Justice* (Oxford, Green Books, 2003).

[87] Gellers (n 82).

[88] D Sanderson, *Urban Humanitarian Response* (London, Overseas Development Institute, 2019).

[89] M Marks, RM Matsha and C Caruso, 'Cities, Walls and the Anthropocene: When Consciousness and Purpose Fail to Coincide' in C Holley and C Shearing (eds), *Criminology and the Anthropocene* (Abingdon-on-Thames, Routledge, 2017); R Cury, M Kennelly and M Howes, 'Enacting Environmental Commitments and Initiatives in Australian Olympic Sport: An Actor-Network Theory Perspective' (2024) *Managing Sport and Leisure* 1.

[90] C Jacob, S Thorin and S Pioch, 'Marine Biodiversity Offsetting: An Analysis of the Emergence of an Environmental Governance System in California' (2018) 93 *Marine Policy* 128.

[91] ibid.

[92] Kotzé (n 3).

[93] Kotzé and Kim (n 2) 5.

A principle of constitutive regulation is premised on an acknowledgment of complexity, instability, and unpredictability within regulatory spaces, making it well suited to guiding earth system law toward a view of the Earth 'as a single dynamic system with multiple intersecting environmental subsystems'.[94] By focusing on regulatory spaces and all that inhabit them, earth system law will need to look to specific contexts and accept as given that there will be multiple legal schemes at work within such spaces, including energy law, financial law, property law, natural resources law and so on.[95] This recognition is important for avoiding the type of reductionism that has plagued existing environmental law approaches.

Central to understanding these multiple schemes is foregrounding the multi-nodal networks that influence and inform these schemes and the intra- and inter-network flows within and across networks and regulatory spaces.[96] The assumption, to be verified empirically, is that actors and actants are individually and collectively seeking to manage events.[97] In doing so, these actors and actants are constantly planning and reconstituting themselves, circulating power through evolving nodal structures and enabling regulatory orders to emerge.[98] Baumgartner and Pahl-Wostl's[99] study of UN–Water provides a useful illustration of how constitutive thinking can unpack complex social and ecological systems, enabling them to reveal UN–Water's constant adaptation to complex networks, but ultimate lack of influence over the effectiveness of global water governance.

In summary, by recognising that there is an ongoing interactive process of action, reaction and adaptation by the variety of actors and actants in a regulatory space, constitutive thinking can help guide earth system law away from assumptions of stability. This means earth system law will need to not only prioritise an empirical understanding of the regulatory space, but also ensure this understanding is regularly updated and fed by consistent information flows.[100]

D. Sensitivity to Economics, Power and Politics when Pursuing Structural Reform

Constitutive regulation's emphasis on the organised existence of a regulatory space, the human and non-human actors and actants that inhabit it, and the dynamism

[94] T Stephens, 'What Is the Point of International Environmental Law Scholarship in the Anthropocene?' in O Pedersen (ed), *Perspectives on Environmental Law Scholarship: Essays on Purpose, Shape and Direction* (Cambridge, Cambridge University Press, 2018) 124.

[95] Shearing (n 5); C Scott (n 59); Seddon (n 36).

[96] Seddon (n 36) 323.

[97] T Baumgartner and C Pahl-Wostl, 'UN-Water and Its Role in Global Water Governance' (2013) 18(3) *Ecology and Society* Art 3, 1.

[98] Baumgartner and Pahl-Wostl (n 97).

[99] ibid.

[100] Seddon (n 36) 320.

and flows of power between them can bring into focus the kind of holistic reforms envisioned by earth system law architects, who call for earth system law to embrace a normative ambition of deep structural reforms.[101] While traditional environmental law has achieved some success, such as limiting pollutions levels and protecting delimited ecosystems, planetary conditions have continued to decline across a range of markers.[102] Kotzé and Kim[103] argue this is because 'environmental law remains a regulatory intervention at the periphery of the social regulatory system. It is essentially a collection of prohibitions with modest impacts on deeply intertwined socio-ecological relationships'. On this view, prohibitions and regulatory systems that enforce them are essentially permitting individual and cumulative activities that are degrading the planet. For du Toit and Kotzé[104] this is because environmental law 'inevitably seems to chase the lowest common denominator that is shaped by political and economic interest'.

Adopting a principle of constitutive regulation can help earth system law to be more normatively ambitious and respond to this challenge. The constitutive viewpoint we have been sketching out implicitly recognises law and regulation as more than merely negative and constraining.[105] Instead, it is productive and constitutive.[106] That is to say, regulation is more than compliance with rules, it is the 'constitution of an order understood as a state of affairs'.[107] This is not an approach that says responses must come through the United Nations pursuing incremental change in the formal public sphere through more treaties and corresponding levels of enforcement intentionally and nationally.[108] Rather, it is one that may

> tackle not only the negative externalities of such pollution, but also the structural processes underlying the causes of that pollution including, for example, economic and consumption drivers that encourage development of coal power stations, spatial planning laws that allow such facilities to be built in sensitive areas, international relations and trade laws regulating the export of electricity to another country, investment laws that must ideally encourage the expansion of renewable energy plants, and labour and social security laws allowing cheap migrant labourers to temporarily work for minimum wages in the coal mines that feed the power plant.[109]

Constitutive thinking brings us to these structural considerations because its understanding of regulatory space acknowledges that 'economic and

[101] Seddon (n 36) 321–23; C Scott (n 59) 284–87.
[102] J Rockström and others, 'A Safe Operating Space for Humanity' (2009) 461 *Nature* 472; DI Armstrong McKay and others, 'Exceeding 1.5°C Global Warming Could Trigger Multiple Climate Tipping Points' (2022) 377(6671) *Science* 1; K Richardson and others, 'Earth beyond Six of Nine Planetary Boundaries' (2023) 9 *Science Advances* 1; Kotzé and Kim (n 2) 4.
[103] Kotzé and Kim (n 2) 4.
[104] Du Toit and Kotzé (n 48) 2.
[105] Seddon (n 36) 320.
[106] Foucault (n 21); Seddon (n 36) 320.
[107] Shearing (n 5) 77; Seddon (n 36) 323–24.
[108] Kotzé and Kim (n 2).
[109] LJ Kotzé, 'Earth System Law for the Anthropocene: Rethinking Environmental Law alongside the Earth System Metaphor' (2020) 11 *Transnational Legal Theory* 75, 96.

consumption drivers' are themselves a regulatory accomplishment created out of embedded social and legal and regulatory regimes and shaped by prior and ongoing allocations of resources.[110] This understanding seeks to do away with long-held neoliberal ideas of law and regulation as separate and external to the free market.[111] Instead, it takes as a given that all markets are organised via regulation (eg property allocation).[112]Guided by constitutive thinking, earth system law would empirically unpack this regulation, identifying the distributive consequences and outcomes arising out of economic and regulatory regimes.[113] Having done so, it would then look at ways to renegotiate the configuration of resources and relations within that space.[114] In Shearing's words,[115] the 'regulatory space as a whole should be made the subject of regulatory policy', including all economic and consumption drivers. Such an approach aligns with the critique of sustainability and global governance by Cardesa-Salzmann and Cocciolo,[116] who note that

> rather than a mere technical issue of more regulation and supervision, any reform aimed at resolving this systemic crisis goes right to the heart of the economic constitution … any reform of global governance requires anchoring legal discourse in the limits of the Earth system and meaningfully addressing global injustices in relation to the distribution of material wealth.

Instead of starting with more rules or enforcement, a constitutive earth system law approach would view its core normative task as imagining what a new preferred order should look like.[117] Importantly, in doing this imagining, earth system law would be required to transparently and seriously engage its regulatory imagination on difficult questions of politics. Waving away or submerging politics by viewing law as separate from these issues, or equally assuming law-makers can act free from the hand of politics is unwise, and perhaps part of the very reason why existing laws have failed.[118] Taking politics seriously can serve to open up regulatory solutions.[119] An example of this is the regulation of fracking and unconventional gas impacts on climate change and water. Traditional environmental laws in this space have received widespread criticism for perceived industry capture and collusion, noting strong economic returns, jobs and public tax benefits.[120] Taking a constitutive approach would acknowledge this organised state of affairs and look

[110] Shearing (n 5); Seddon (n 36) 321–25; C Scott (n 59) 284–85.
[111] FA Hayek, 'The Use of Knowledge in Society' (1945) 35(4) *The American Economic Review* 519.
[112] Shearing (n 5); Seddon (n 36) 321.
[113] Seddon (n 36) 321.
[114] ibid 322.
[115] Shearing (n 5) 72; Seddon (n 36) 322.
[116] A Cardesa-Salzmann and E Cocciolo, 'Global Governance, Sustainability and the Earth System: Critical Reflections on the Role of Global Law' (2019) 8 *Transnational Environmental Law* 437.
[117] Seddon (n 36) 324.
[118] C Scott (n 4); Seddon (n 36) 324.
[119] C Holley, A Kennedy and C Shearing, 'Power, Conflict and Energy Law: Learning from Unconventional Natural Gas, Nonstate Actors, Industry and Government' (2023) 18 *Texas Journal of Oil, Gas and Energy Law* 1.
[120] ibid.

not just to remedy collusion (weak or strong), but also acknowledge ways that law can create new and other forms of non-state ordering to effectively and fairly ensure planetary health and resilience.

Another central political and normative orientation of import for advancing earth system law is justice.[121] Rapid planetary-scale processes, and responses to them can and have reinforced injustices at international, national, and subnational levels.[122] The above constitutive methods can allow us to think through law's role in complex allocation challenges, such as addressing extreme concentrations of wealth in industrialised and middle-income countries and international redistributions of wealth and opportunities to help countries in the Global South to protect their populations against the catastrophic consequences of ecological collapse.[123]

IV. Conclusion

For earth system law to achieve its ambition and consider and address 'all at once'[124] the multiple structures, sectors, actants, actors, politics and power presents a complex, interdisciplinary and daunting task.[125] One of the reasons it is so daunting is because legal scholars have largely lacked a framework for starting with, mapping and then reforming such complexity. The constitutive conception of regulation we have mapped out offers a grounding principle for earth system law that can provide it with an orientation and method, albeit a complex one, for developing a new approach. As Teisman and Gerrits have argued: 'the complexity of an interconnected society and its governance require a complexity-informed approach'.[126] Constitutive thinking, as originally outlined by Shearing,[127] with its rich socio-legal foundation of social constructionism scholarship, offers an approach that could enable a more nuanced and evidence-based conceptualisation of complex planetary challenges to achieve more normatively ambitious transformations of our legal and regulatory systems.[128]

[121] F Biermann and A Kalfagianni, 'Planetary Justice: A Research Framework' (2020) 6 *Earth System Governance* 100049.
[122] Kotzé and Kim (n 2).
[123] P Kashwan and others, 'Planetary Justice: Prioritizing the Poor in Earth System Governance' (2020) 6 *Earth System Governance* 100075.
[124] Kotzé (n 3) 99.
[125] Kotzé and others (n 50).
[126] G Teisman and L Gerrits, 'The Emergence of Complexity in the Art and Science of Governance' (2014) 1 *Complexity, Governance & Networks* 17.
[127] Shearing (n 5).
[128] Burke (n 75).

12

The 'Near Frontier': Seeking Institutional Pathways to Earth System Law

J MICHAEL ANGSTADT

I. Introduction

Pressing planetary transformations pose unprecedented governance challenges to law and legal systems. Associated demands for justice and equity have yielded calls to transform legal institutions and procedures, and analysts advocate shifting legal frameworks away from mainstream environmental law towards new models and approaches. In particular, proponents of earth system law seek to 'reimagine law and legal scholarship in a more holistic way that cuts across silos, captures the bigger picture, and opens the closures of law to multiple stakeholders, including the marginalised, the unborn, and the non-human'.[1]

Yet, as many earth system law researchers acknowledge, this ideal model of law and governance differs significantly from many dominant environmental law practices. Therefore, advancing an earth system law agenda will require reimagining many contemporary understandings of how courts, legal actors, and juridical systems engage with environmental law and one another. It will also demand fundamental transformation of existing environmental law frameworks and judicial institutions in ways that advance identified earth system law objectives.

Frequently, these much-needed transformations are conceptualised theoretically, with researchers imagining how legal frameworks, provisions, and discourses can better address systems-oriented legal challenges. However, theoretical legal frameworks must be mapped onto real-world courts, tribunals, and other institutional architectures, implemented by their personnel, and contoured by their

[1] LJ Kotzé and others, 'Earth System Law: Exploring New Frontiers in Legal Science' (2022) 11 *Earth System Governance* 100126.

procedures and resources.[2] Thus, courts, other legal and quasi-judicial institutions, and the actors that shape these institutions, will tangibly determine how fully and effectively earth system law can be operationalised.

This chapter explores the adaptations that may be required to equip courts and related environmental law institutions to pursue earth system law objectives. As I note, much scholarship emphasises 'the here', or currently dominant environmental law approaches. Likewise, many earth system law accounts theorise 'the frontier', or ideal transformations. In this chapter, I highlight and emphasise the interstitial 'near frontier', where existing institutions and actors can undertake transformative work to pursue and operationalise earth system law objectives.

To pursue this inquiry, I first briefly highlight research evaluating (i) 'the here' – which considers contemporary law and its fitness to engage with systemic environmental governance issues; and (ii) 'the frontier' – which advocates necessary changes of institutions and structures towards an earth system law posture. By exploring both, I highlight opportunities for further exchange between the two. Accordingly, I next direct attention to how we might reimagine institutions in 'the near frontier', examining several potential structural determinants of systemic change. I evaluate the prospect of courts as sites of bottom-up, systemic transformation to earth system law. With this foundation laid, I next illustrate some of these pathways of institutional transformation by highlighting models of novel cognisance, jurisdiction, and disposition found within existing domestic courts. As I argue, many of these earth system law precepts are already viable, and I highlight established institutions that already incorporate elements that may be seen as advancing earth system law ideals. I highlight (i) widely studied courts in New Zealand, India, and elsewhere that have broadened their cognisance beyond purely anthropocentric considerations; (ii) water courts in Colorado, United States (US) and elsewhere that define geographic jurisdiction based on natural features, rather than purely political boundaries; and (iii) environmental courts and similar institutions that demonstrate the possibility of creating institutions with a purely environmental disposition. My institutional analysis affirms both their innovations and the real-world implementation challenges that they face. Nevertheless, I argue that these institutions indicate interest, spanning legal cultures and jurisdictions, in creating structures that can meaningfully address pressing earth system challenges. Finally, I explore the theoretical and applied value of analysing courts and their practitioners in the 'near frontier'. I suggest that examples of domestic and subnational innovation within the dominant governance framework highlight opportunities to further reimagine courts situated within and above the nation-state. Ultimately, I argue that a pathways approach to analysis can imbue the urgent theoretical precepts of earth system law with practice and stakeholder

[2] F Biermann and RE Kim, 'The Boundaries of the Planetary Boundary Framework: A Critical Appraisal of Approaches to Define a "Safe Operating Space" for Humanity' (2020) 45 *Annual Review of Environment and Resources* 497.

relevance, supporting ongoing efforts to communicate the transformative nature of earth system law.

II. Theorising the 'Here' and the 'Frontier'

Earth system law is a rapidly developing discourse, with researchers simultaneously exploring its promise, debating its implications, and interrogating its core content.[3] Many of earth system law's prescriptions and foci derive from critical engagement with mainstream international environmental law scholarship. Therefore, earth system law is simultaneously reactive and imaginative. Earth system law is reactive in that it contests core assumptions and orientations that have undergirded international environmental law. As noted elsewhere, these assumptions include its 'failure to respond to complex socio-legal challenges, its lack of deep engagement with state-centricity and implications of the Anthropocene in broader legal thought, and, troublingly, its inability to achieve structural reforms that can address systemic challenges'.[4]

Several earth system law researchers highlight the sectoral, geographical, and disciplinary constraints that mainstream environmental law faces when seeking to effectively address systemic environmental challenges. For instance, emergent research by Klimke and Zengerling[5] highlights the regulatory fragmentation of German agroforestry law as one localised illustration of how historical structures and frameworks can impede more systemic environmental responses. Elsewhere, Ahlström and others[6] show that the uncertain and transboundary character of hydrological resources, and their interconnection with other earth system processes all complicate efforts to develop more comprehensive legal governance of socio-hydrological cycles. Mai and Boulot[7] consider how the methodological and ontological fragmentation of legal research and practice can impede the transition to an earth system law orientation. Yet, in a more optimistic assessment, they note that available responses, including clinic-based education and the normalisation of interdisciplinary exchange, could combat these barriers.

[3] MC Leach, 'Seeking "Systems" in Earth System Law: Boundaries, Identity, and Purpose in an Emergent Field' (2023) 15 *Earth System Governance* 100162; and the chapters in this book.

[4] JM Angstadt and M Schink, 'Specialist Environmental Courts and Tribunals: A Systematic Literature Review and Case for Earth System Governance Analysis' (2023) 18 *Earth System Governance* 100192 (footnotes omitted).

[5] M Klimke and C Zengerling, 'A Pathway for Transforming Agroforestry Law from an Earth System Law Perspective', *Presentation, Radboud Conference on Earth System Governance* (24–26 October 2023, Nijmegen, Netherlands).

[6] H Ahlström and others, 'An Earth System Law Perspective on Governing Social-Hydrological Systems in the Anthropocene' (2021) 10 *Earth System Governance* 100120.

[7] L Mai and E Boulot, 'Harnessing the Transformative Potential of Earth System Law: From Theory to Practice' (2021) 7 *Earth System Governance* 100103.

In contrast to mainstream environmental law, many earth system law researchers, including those published within this book, emphasise that law can be reimagined in profound and transformative ways, and they underscore that law itself is dynamic, fluid, and capable of adapting to novel social and environmental pressures. When working to reconceptualise legal architectures in a more systemic fashion, researchers have highlighted earth system law's instrumental value, its capacity to engage more effectively with non-traditional legal subjects, and its ability to engage with non-traditional legal venues and sources. First, in examining earth system law's instrumental value, a recent editorial by Kim, Kotzé, and Blanchard[8] highlights how climate change and the associated intergenerational and rights-based considerations in emergent litigation complement earth system law's own emphasis of representational and longitudinal factors. Second, researchers have noted earth system law's capacity to engage with non-traditional legal subjects, including by maintaining a non-hierarchical openness to knowledge traditions and conceptions of human needs and values that can restructure law's engagement with environments at multiple spatial and temporal scales.[9] Third, researchers highlight the degree to which under-recognised venues, including eco-cinema, can catalyse shifts in public sentiment in ways that alter public consciousness, legal imaginary, and political capacity for more dramatic legal change and environmental engagement.[10]

III. Imagining Earth System Law's 'Near Frontier'

The previous section demonstrates that earth system law is malleable and porous. Its imaginative character enables scholars to constructively examine the dominant system while radically reimagining the legal landscape and its engagement with planetary challenges. Simultaneously, earth system law spotlights ontological and structural deficits of dominant environmental law frameworks and structures, inviting consideration of how and why the law has failed to satisfactorily address pressing socio-ecological challenges.

However, a middle ground exists between critique and holistic reimagination of new frontiers that a more systems-oriented Earth-embracing law could pursue. In this 'near frontier', exciting opportunities exist to leverage both critique and visionary thinking to meaningfully transform existing institutions. Exploring this 'near frontier' enables earth system law to actualise each of its three dimensions: analytical, normative, and transformative. First, whereas many existing institutions were shaped by dominant notions of environmental law, earth system law can

[8] RE Kim, C Blanchard and LJ Kotzé, 'Law, Systems, and Planet Earth: Editorial' (2022) 11 *Earth System Governance* 100127.

[9] See Garver and Vargas Roncancio, Chapter 7 in this book.

[10] Richardson, Chapter 14 in this book.

more expansively analyse how present institutions can reinterpret scale, process, and what might be considered 'law'.[11] Second, earth system law can support normative transformation of existing systems and structures of environmental regulation toward more inclusive and holistic responses by challenging them to more broadly consider what agreements and institutions 'should' be pursuing.[12] Third, in terms of its transformative potential, earth system law can underscore the need for urgent change and highlight the need to comprehensively reimagine the complex challenges and systems that regulate the planet.[13]

Each of these earth system law dimensions – the analytical, normative, and transformative – can support necessary reimagination of 'the here' and the promise and potential of 'the frontier'. However, they can also support multiple pathways of institutional transition. Three near-term pathways that merit attention are (i) the substantive, (ii) the procedural, and (iii) the institutional; and each may be explored through earth system law's normative, analytical, and transformative lenses. Each pathway (substantive, procedural, institutional) bears unique normative considerations and attributes. Examining the diverse configurations of potential responses carries analytical implications, as some proposals may have received more extensive attention to date.

However, examining potential pathways in the 'near frontier' also invites a certain degree of transformative risk. As earth system law theorists have cautioned, many celebrated innovations in environmental law suffer from a mechanistic, short-termist orientation that falls short of the ambitious objectives envisioned by earth system law. They have been described by some researchers as 'reductionist, one-dimensional, mono-disciplinary, linear … utilitarian, state-centred, top-down', and oriented towards concerns of the global North.[14] For example, dominant legal formulations reify the desirability of growth, emphasise the centrality of legal protections for individual rights and ownership, and regulate non-human entities in ways that benefit some humans.[15] Furthermore, many reforms advocated by scholars have been critiqued for their insufficiently ambitious character, 'creating a false feeling of change, legitimizing the continuity of the current development model and economic practices'.[16] Therefore, in exploring transformative pathways, a pressing question is: How can we imagine a 'near frontier' that meaningfully moves towards earth system law, rather than simply reimagining, remaking, and reproducing currently dominant biases and approaches?[17]

[11] LJ Kotzé and RE Kim, 'Exploring the Analytical, Normative and Transformative Dimensions of Earth System Law' (2020) 50 *Environmental Policy and Law* 457, 460.

[12] ibid 461–62.

[13] ibid 466.

[14] K Pope, M Bonatti and S Sieber, 'The What, Who and How of Socio-Ecological Justice: Tailoring a New Justice Model for Earth System Law' (2021) 10 *Earth System Governance* 100124.

[15] ibid.

[16] ibid.

[17] See also Boulot, Mai and Sellers, Chapter 5 in this book.

Simultaneously, and conversely, analysts of international environmental law have lauded the accomplishments that international approaches to environmental agreements have managed. Further, they reference leaders positioned within dominant institutions, including United Nations (UN) Secretary-General António Guterres and others, who themselves advocate ongoing 'reform' of international environmental law instruments and approaches and recognise that the problems addressed by the UN 'evolve over time and require new approaches and actions'.[18] Therefore, as earth system law seeks 'near frontier' solutions that do not simply reproduce existing patterns and problems, it must also consider whether, and how, near-term recommendations implied by an earth system law approach would be meaningfully distinct from the changes already accepted as necessary by international environmental law scholars and practitioners.

In imagining a meaningful 'near frontier' for earth system law, the foregoing pathways (substantive, procedural, institutional) have received differing levels of scholarly attention. Researchers have devoted considerable attention to the substance of earth system law and, to some degree, its process. However, far more emphasis could be directed to the institutional pathways that might support an earth system law transformation. To support this dialogue, this chapter briefly examines each pathway (substantive, procedural, and institutional) in the context of the 'near frontier', giving greatest attention to institutional dimensions.

A. Substantive Pathways in Earth System Law

Researchers examining earth system law have begun to evaluate substantive concepts that could support a transition from the dominant environmental law approaches to something more closely resembling the ideals of earth system law. Research in this area has proceeded in several directions relevant to the 'near frontier', including by (i) exploring the potential application of earth system law ideals in specific regimes, and (ii) examining precepts that earth system law might substantively include.

First, earth system law scholars have begun to examine earth system law's application to discrete issue areas and regimes. These include, for example, the governance of socio-hydrological systems.[19] However, earth system law's relevance has also been examined in the context of other regimes, notably climate change. There, earth system law scholars have noted the degree to which existing regulatory targets are insufficiently ambitious and have advocated for more comprehensive reimagination. While researchers applaud recent efforts to use the courts to initiate bold steps towards more ambitious climate actions, they suggest

[18] N Urho and others, *International Environmental Governance: Accomplishments and Way Forward* (Copenhagen, Nordic Council of Ministers, 2019).

[19] Ahlström and others (n 6).

that more systemic, substantive reimagination will be necessary.[20] However, researchers differ in their prescriptions of what, exactly, earth system law would require to satisfactorily address the climate crisis. For example, some suggest that reforms 'driven by states' will be necessary, even as they simultaneously critique the state-centric nature of international environmental law more broadly.[21] Leach[22] suggests that some of this contestation and imprecision derives, fundamentally, from earth system law's nascent conceptual status and ongoing scholarly elaboration. While acknowledging these debates and differing interpretations, earth system law clearly provides what many scholars perceive as an emancipatory platform from which to examine and reimagine key areas of law as they engage with systemic, planetary challenges.

Second, scholars have begun to consider how earth system law would amend dominant environmental law frameworks and what discrete precepts it could include. This area of research explores more focused changes that could be applied systemically. While these changes could occur in several ways, some have begun to consider new substantive principles and frameworks that could be introduced to environmental law. Some researchers examine the structural and architectural foundations of dominant and reimagined legal frameworks. For instance, Burdon[23] explores notions of 'ecological integrity' that can potentially contest many of environmental law's dominant challenges, while Holley and others[24] explore how a constitutive principle could support earth system law's overall development and integration. While these approaches are distinct in their prescriptions, they share a common effort to leverage theory towards principled application that contests and reshapes dominant legal frameworks.

B. Procedural Pathways in Earth System Law

Some scholars have begun to consider the role and promise of procedural provisions in advancing earth system law objectives. Procedural aspects of earth system law have thus far received comparatively less attention than substantive considerations. However, procedural provisions merit attention, since they would structure the application of substantive earth system law provisions. Most existing consideration in this space has been directed at mechanisms that could expand earth system law's application. For example, in acknowledgment of complementary

[20] L du Toit and LJ Kotzé, 'Reimagining International Environmental Law for the Anthropocene: An Earth System Law Perspective' (2022) 11 *Earth System Governance* 100132; LJ Kotzé, S Adelman and F Dube, 'The Problem with Sustainable Development in the Anthropocene Epoch' in PD Burdon and J Martel (eds), *The Routledge Handbook of Law and the Anthropocene* (Abingdon-on-Thames, Routledge, 2023).

[21] Kotzé, Adelman and Dube (n 20).

[22] Leach (n 3).

[23] Burdon, Chapter 10 in this book.

[24] Holley, Shearing and Moyo, Chapter 11 in this book.

discourses exploring 'rights of nature' movements and the justifications for expanding legal personhood, Gellers[25] explores how non-humans might beneficially be accommodated within the earth system law framework. Elsewhere, Pope and others[26] consider how distributive justice and related conceptions both challenge and provide toeholds from which to expand the ontological premise of earth system law. Their work emphasises the need to consider inter-temporal, -species, and -generational dimensions.[27] Finally, Petersmann[28] explores the novel, systems-oriented character of earth system law analysis, highlighting how contingent and evolving processes and communities will both contribute to – and be affected by – earth system law and related efforts to advance collective governance. There are certainly further opportunities to examine procedural considerations and pathways, and to more explicitly engage with considerations of procedural architecture and equity. However, these initial examinations clearly indicate the relevance of procedural pathways to the broader application of an earth system law framework.

C. Institutional Pathways in Earth System Law

Substantive and procedural legal provisions are ultimately mediated through institutional frameworks. In contemporary environmental law, these institutional architectures are diverse, encompassing formal legislative venues, legal institutions, and non-governmental regulatory frameworks. Earth system law could, in theory, be mapped onto each of these venues, as well as others not explicitly listed here. However, existing institutions can exhibit tremendous diversity in architecture, authority, and disposition. These attributes, in turn, hold considerable implications for the process and substance of environmental adjudication. While many institutions deserve further analysis as potential venues for engaging with earth system law, courts present especially useful objects of inquiry, given their status as sites for elaborating mainstream environmental law and contesting its development and application.[29]

In examining courts as sites for the implementation of earth system law, many institutional attributes merit deeper consideration, as each presents unique considerations. As an initial foundation for analysis, I examine three questions here, each bearing procedural and compositional considerations: (i) How can institutional models adapt to expand cognisance in ways that support earth system law recommendations? (ii) How can geographic attributes of courts better

[25] JC Gellers, 'Earth System Law and the Legal Status of Non-Humans in the Anthropocene' (2021) 7 *Earth System Governance* 100083.

[26] Pope, Bonatti and Sieber (n 14).

[27] ibid.

[28] MC Petersmann, 'Sympoietic Thinking and Earth System Law: The Earth, Its Subjects and the Law' (2021) 9 *Earth System Governance* 100114.

[29] Kotzé, Adelman and Dube (n 20).

accommodate the systemic character of earth system law? and (iii) How can courts' jurisdictional attributes better accommodate the breadth of earth system law considerations?

(i) Pathways to Reimagine and Expand Cognisance

Mainstream courts invite reimagination of cognisance, namely how an environmental dispute must be framed and presented so that a court may recognise and engage with it. Environmental law receives regular critique from earth system law scholars for being deeply anthropocentric.[30] In the context of courts, this often manifests in how disputes are framed; concrete harms must be demonstrated in the context of humans and their monetary losses, who can, in turn, be granted standing to seek redress for their (human) injuries. In addition to reinforcing the deeply anthropocentric character of environmental law, this dominant litigation approach tends to obscure the systemic character of many interlinked socio-ecological challenges, reducing them to granular disputes that affect individual humans, or that only explore very focused manifestations of much broader challenges.

Since many courts are reactive in posture and disposition, researchers and advocates could engage with these challenges by reimagining how lawsuits are framed and presented to courts, how underlying environmental statutes are framed, and how causes of action are authorised. However, from an institutional perspective, broader questions arise regarding how courts and litigation can accommodate many of the interests highlighted by emergent earth system law scholarship, particularly the interests of future generations and non-humans. Complementary discourses have long considered questions such as: how to give these future and non-human considerations meaningful voice in deeply presentist, anthropocentric venues; and how to develop trustee- or guardianship frameworks that could meaningfully present those concerns and considerations in the context of litigation.

Fascinatingly, however, courts are beginning to engage with these questions in an applied fashion. Several accounts document instances where the environmental interests of minors and future generations have been advocated in court, whether in the landmark 1993 timber licence case of *Oposa (Minors) v Factoran*[31] that enshrined intergenerational considerations in litigation, or in a 2023 US judgment that amplified youth interests in the context of climate trust litigation.[32]

Comparative legal studies would emphasise the need to acknowledge a clear correlation between successful litigation and a jurisdictions' statutory grounds that could support such claims. Nevertheless, intertemporal and environmental

[30] Eg Morrow, Chapter 6 in this book.

[31] *Oposa v Factoran*, GR No 101083, 224 SCRA 792 (Supreme Court of the Philippines), judgment of 30 July 1993, https://leap.unep.org/sites/default/files/court-case/Oposa%2520v%2520Factoran.pdf.

[32] *Held v State of Montana*, CDV-2020-307 (Montana 1st District Court – Lewis and Clark County), judgment of 14 August 2023.

personhood lawsuits pose fascinating institutional design questions regarding how to meaningfully incorporate and accommodate these interests in courts across legal cultures. As a result, it is valuable to explore how the (i) resources, and (ii) procedural provisions of courts and related institutions of environmental law can best support the expanded participation that earth system law envisions.

First, existing governance institutions, including courts, provide a foundation for exploring how resources and physical attributes can support expanded participation. Numerous barriers, including the technical nature of mainstream courts and related environmental law institutions, can impede meaningful participation and consideration of future generations and non-human interests. However, other examples demonstrate potential near-term institutional opportunities to support broader participation. In acknowledgment of the physical and resource barriers involved in attending proceedings, some courts have begun to facilitate completion of court business online: 'including filing, taking evidence, holding hearings, conducting site visits and publishing opinions'.[33]

Many of these innovations can arguably help promote access to justice by facilitating accessible, expedient, transparent, accountable, and cost-effective processes. For instance, India's National Green Tribunal regularly conducts video conferences that obviate the need for parties to travel to New Delhi.[34] Elsewhere, New Zealand's Environment Court conducts site visits that enable parties to illustrate the systemic character of environmental disputes and permit judges to more comprehensively understand what they are addressing. There are similar innovations in other jurisdictions, including Brazil, Nigeria, and the Philippines, each of which use mobile courthouses.[35] While many of these practices are long-standing, their rapid expansion in response to the pressures and governance challenges of the COVID-19 pandemic is also relevant to earth system law's 'near frontier', as it underscores the adaptive capacity of existing domestic courts, even as they are frequently presented as ossified institutional structures that impede the adoption of new governance frameworks.

Second, existing courts provide an opportunity to explore how procedural provisions can best promote participation. Whereas underlying enabling statutes can be amended to facilitate engagement, the procedural regulations that govern courts are often even more malleable, since they do not always require legislative approval. Accordingly, they provide courts with a mechanism to interpret their governance authority in ways that permissively support participation. Examples of such procedural mechanisms are numerous and widely documented, and they include efforts to relax requirements for *amicus* engagement by interested or

[33] United Nations Environment Programme, *Environmental Courts and Tribunals – 2021: A Guide for Policymakers* (UNEP, 2021) 8, https://www.unep.org/resources/publication/environmental-courts-and-tribunals-2021-guide-policy-makers.

[34] ibid 9.

[35] ibid 32.

potentially affected parties. The International Court of Justice's (ICJ) consideration of a request for an advisory opinion on the 'Obligations of States in respect of Climate Change' provides one compelling example, as few non-state parties have previously been authorised to participate in proceedings. The ICJ's overall approach is quite restrictive, with a default approach that constrains non-state party engagement and excludes non-governmental organisation statements and documents from being considered as part of a case's file.[36] Changing this approach would clearly counterbalance the primacy of state-based considerations, expanding courts' abilities to engage with the input and insight of advocates for youth, future generations, and non-human interests. Elsewhere, courts have relaxed the costs of filing or engaging in litigation as one mechanism to enhance participatory equity.[37] Finally, vibrant debates consider how to operationalise the trusteeship of natural objects that have been granted legal rights, including watercourses. For instance, New Zealand's Whanganui River Māori Trust Board, established in 1988, represents a formalised, institutional confluence of legal, ecosystem, and indigenous interests and perspectives. While the composition and constitution of such trusteeship arrangements have been contested, they nevertheless provide a compelling reminder of the ability to creatively imagine permissive pathways for engagement in contemporary legal systems.

(ii) Pathways to Reimagine Geographic Character

The preceding sub-section argues that institutional approaches to cognisance can be altered to provide clearer pathways toward earth system law. A related pathway of transition could reimagine how courts as institutions are defined by issues of geography, and, in turn, how they engage with considerations of geography in their rulings. Reimagining courts' engagement with geography and natural systems comports with the concept of systematicity which, in turn, undergirds much of the thinking around earth system law. Early earth system law publications engage with core precepts of earth system governance and science more broadly, emphasising the inherent feedbacks and interconnections of earth's systems, and rejecting a tendency towards reductionist or siloed legal approaches.[38] This systemic consideration further recognises that mainstream law's 'assumptions, orientations, operation and objectives, cannot be brought in line with the regulatory challenges of a complex earth system'.[39] For example, researchers have explored how law's

[36] JM Angstadt and MM Betsill, 'Non-State Actors' in L Rajamani and J Peel (eds), *Oxford Handbook of International Environmental Law* (Oxford, Oxford University Press, 2021). ICJ Advisory Opinion 'Obligations of States in Respect of Climate Change', 23 July 2025, https://www.icj-cij.org/sites/default/files/case-related/187/187-20250723-adv-01-00-en.pdf.

[37] United Nations Environment Programme, *Environmental Courts and Tribunals: A Guide for Policymakers* (n 33) iii.

[38] Kotzé and others (n 1). See also, LJ Kotzé, 'Earth System Law for the Anthropocene: Rethinking Environmental Law Alongside the Earth System Metaphor' (2020) 11(1–2) *Transnational Legal Theory* 75.

[39] ibid.

ability to meaningfully engage with the challenges posed by climate change will require more effective integration of a fragmented, multilevel, and transnational corpus of law.[40] However, these considerations also imply the need to consider the architecture and attributes of courts themselves.

Reimagining courts' geographic character provides an opportunity to explore transitional pathways that orient courts towards more holistic environmental considerations. Encouragingly, there are several ways that such a shift might be pursued.

First, courts can simply be granted comprehensive jurisdiction over a specified area of law, permitting more holistic engagement with earth system law-relevant considerations. International law offers numerous examples of how such an approach might look. For example, the request underlying the ICJ's 2025 climate change advisory opinion sought expansive clarification of obligations, in the global context, 'to ensure the protection of the climate system and other parts of the environment from anthropogenic emissions of greenhouse gases for States and for present and future generations'; and to identify legal obligations for states that have caused disproportionate harm to especially affected states, as well as 'Peoples and individuals of the present and future generations affected by the adverse effects of climate change'.[41] Scholars have also long considered (and, in some cases, advocated) establishing an international environmental tribunal that could be charged, explicitly, with considering environmental issues in their systemic context.[42] Such approaches are attractive from an earth system law perspective because they may permit more systemic consideration of environmental issues and their intertemporal character. However, they face many of the familiar limits of international law, including questions of enforceability, implementation, and its capacity to meaningfully engage with non-state actors. Therefore, exploring the promise of international courts and tribunals from an earth system law perspective would require weighing their capacity to highlight the systemic nature of environmental issues against their institutional constraints.

Second, and similarly, regional courts and tribunals could provide venues for more holistically considering earth system law-relevant issues. While more focused in geographic scope than international courts, regional courts can evaluate the contextual and transboundary issues that accompany natural resource disputes. This may be particularly true in regions such as Africa, where regional courts can support consideration of the human rights/ environment nexus by strengthening the rule of law and embracing innovations from other contexts.[43]

[40] H van Asselt and others, 'Global Climate Change and the Fragmentation of International Law' (2008) 30 *Law and Policy* 4.

[41] International Court Justice, 'Request for Advisory Opinion, Transmitted to the Court Pursuant to General Assembly Resolution 77/276' a, b, i-ii.

[42] A Rest, 'The Indispensability of an International Environmental Court' (1998) 7 *Review of European Comparative and International Environmental Law* 63.

[43] MM Mbengue, 'The Protection of the Environment Before African Regional Courts and Tribunals' in E Sobenes, S Mead and B Samson (eds), *The Environment Through the Lens of International Courts and Tribunals* (The Hague, TMC Asser Press, 2022).

At the same time, the many innovative, localised decisions concerning portions of the Amazon rainforest demonstrate the limitations of parcelised analysis. For example, the 2020 petition in *PSB et al v Brazil*[44] leveraged Brazil's national deforestation policy to challenge the government's perceived failure to address climate obligations, just as non-governmental organisation (NGO) petitioners filed suit in a French court to challenge BNP Paribas' financing of entities that contributed to Amazonian deforestation.[45] These and other innovative lawsuits certainly highlight tensions related to development and the Amazon rainforest's critical contributions to global biodiversity and carbon cycles, yet individual cases cannot comprehensively address the holistic challenges facing the biome. Therefore, earth system law could explore whether one transitional pathway might seek new regional courts and tribunals that could more holistically consider interlinked forestry, biodiversity, migratory species, and related challenges.

Third, earth system law emphasises legal responses to global and systemic issues, yet most courts exercise geographic jurisdiction of a national or subnational nature. This underlying tension need not imply a fundamental incompatibility, as earth system law scholars should reimagine how to better equip domestic courts to engage with environmental disputes in their broader context, either by reconceptualising what claims are admissible or by reimagining the competence of the courts that will resolve those claims. One illustration of such a potential response is provided by specialist water courts in the State of Colorado. Like some Western US jurisdictions, Colorado possesses a dedicated system of water courts. These courts resolve all disputes in the State concerning water matters, including the allocation, use, and administration of water rights.[46] However, Colorado's surface water hydrology is unique; as a headwater State, numerous major river systems originate in Colorado before flowing outward to other jurisdictions. Moreover, each river system possesses unique hydrological characteristics, water and land use considerations, and even regional climatic realities (snowpack can vary tremendously between basins, uniquely shaping spring runoff and, in turn, basin water availability). Acknowledging these natural features and processes, the geographic jurisdiction of Colorado water courts is allocated by river basin, rather than the political boundaries that structure jurisdiction for other State courts. For instance, Colorado Water Division 1 adjudicates only on disputes arising within the South Platte River Basin, Division 2 addresses Arkansas River disputes, and Division 3 engages those emerging in the Rio Grande basin.[47] Each division is staffed by a division engineer, a water judge, a water referee, and a water clerk, further facilitating the development of ecosystem-oriented resources and expertise.

[44] *Partido Socialista Brasileiro et al v Brazil* (Federal Supreme Court, Brazil).

[45] *Comissão Pastoral da Terra and Notre Affaire à Tous v BNP Paribas* (Judicial Court of Paris).

[46] GJ Hobbs, 'Colorado's 1969 Adjudication and Administration Act: Settling In' (1999) 3(1) *University of Denver Water Law Review* 1.

[47] ibid.

Across scales of operation, these examples demonstrate that courts' geographic jurisdiction and staffing can acknowledge and accommodate the systemic nature of environmental issues and natural resource features. Such institutions also show, as an earth system law framework advocates, how place-based institutions can engage with specialised areas of the law in ways that acknowledge their cross-cutting considerations, accommodate relevant scientific and technical expertise, and examine 'root causes' of systemic challenges, rather than simply the harms associated with them.

(iii) Pathways to Reimagine Subject-Matter Jurisdiction

Earth system law advocates can explore opportunities in the 'near frontier' by reimagining how courts and law engage with the core content and emphases of environmental law. As noted above, the lack of systematicity in dominant institutions highlights the need for institutional alternatives. Researchers examining how to effectively engage with these issues have identified several necessary considerations, including: (i) how to develop a 'coherent, collective and holistic way' to engage with environmental questions by considering 'all legal subdisciplines that are relevant';[48] and (ii) how to meaningfully incorporate insights and epistemologies from non-legal experts and professions in ways that can support holistic responses to environmental challenges. The fascinating emergence of specialist environmental courts highlights the potential for judicial structure to meaningfully engage with both.

At first examination, courts could seem inapt as institutions to address systemic environmental challenges, given the compartmentalised nature of most contemporary environmental litigation. However, the proliferating institutional model of environmental courts suggests that institutional design can afford courts greater latitude and competence to systematically engage with underlying questions. For instance, some environmental courts enjoy broad grants of authority, whether through expansive enabling legislation or authorisation to address numerous individual statutes with environmental relevance, or to address environmental questions in each geographic or political region. Here, examples are numerous and reflect several potential models. First, some courts are granted jurisdiction over expansive regulatory regimes. For instance, New Zealand's Environment Court can engage with appeals raised under the country's Resource Management Act 1991.[49] Second, enabling legislation for some environmental courts can affirm their jurisdictional breadth, with India's National Green Tribunal, for instance, enjoying jurisdiction over all civil cases that present a substantial environmental question.[50] Third, other jurisdictions explicitly reserve subject-matter jurisdiction

[48] Petersmann (n 28).

[49] JM Angstadt, 'Can Domestic Environmental Courts Implement International Environmental Law? A Framework for Institutional Analysis' (2023) 12 *Transnational Environmental Law* 318, 333.

[50] ibid.

for environmental courts in environmental issue areas not specified by statute, thereby permitting the understanding and interpretation of 'environmental' issues to evolve over time. For instance, Bolivia's Constitution reserves capacity for its Tribunal Agroambiental (Agro-environmental Tribunal) to engage with relevant environmental issues, even when the disputes arise from statutes falling outside those explicitly listed.[51]

Each foregoing approach illustrates how recommended practices for environmental courts can be operationalised, with a recent United Nations Environment Programme (UNEP) report advocating that such courts 'ought to have as wide a jurisdiction as possible'.[52] While prescriptions to operationalise this recommendation are broad, UNEP notes the benefit of granting a single court jurisdiction over 'all environment-related laws' to avoid, for example 'adjudicating a wetlands issue with authority over ecosystem laws but not water laws'.[53] Doing so appears highly relevant and complementary to recommendations presented by earth system law analysts.

Additionally, reimagining how courts can more meaningfully advance earth system law precepts also demands consideration of how traditional 'legal' and 'non-legal' insights and perspectives can be meaningfully integrated so as to engage with the holistic subject-matter of earth system challenges. Early consideration of earth system law has resulted in advocacy of deep inter- and trans-disciplinary engagement and recognition of the complex, bidirectional nature of this necessity and challenge.[54] For one reason, lawyers must understand scientific data and disciplines, modelling frameworks, and the methodologies of non-lawyers; simultaneously, non-lawyers must have avenues to translate scientific and technical complexity in ways that render them meaningful to lawyers, courts, and judges.[55]

While diverse in nature and imperfect in operationalisation, environmental courts, again, illustrate some potential pathways to creating institutions that more closely align with the needs identified by earth system law scholars. In one exemplar institutional response, environmental courts can explicitly require that judges hold environmental expertise – and even couple this requirement with continuing judicial education requirements to expand judges' fluency in environmental issues. For example, Kenya's Land and Environment Court requires that judges hold a minimum of 10 years' environmental experience and attend ongoing judicial education, while Sweden expects its judges to attend ongoing environmental legal education training.[56] In another example, panels for some environmental courts have been composed to include a mixture of legally-trained judges and scientific

[51] ibid 334.
[52] United Nations Environment Programme, *Environmental Courts and Tribunals – 2021: A Guide for Policymakers* (n 33) 32.
[53] ibid.
[54] Kotzé and others (n 1).
[55] Petersmann (n 28).
[56] Angstadt (n 49).

or technical experts. Environmental courts and tribunals in India, New Zealand, Sweden, and Trinidad and Tobago all employ variations of these models.[57]

Researchers have examined the implications of expert panellists' participation, both in India's National Green Tribunal and elsewhere. Their work highlights how expert presence has enhanced court capacity to engage in cumulative environmental impact assessment, to weigh the human impacts of rulings against environmental impacts, and to advance environmental justice through those rulings.[58] However, even with subject-matter specialisation and the inclusion of expert panellists, opportunities remain to better equip courts to address earth system challenges. Accordingly, debates continue within environmental courts scholarship regarding how to define 'environmental issues', just as questions remain regarding how to define, evaluate, and value expert scientists' credentials.[59] While recognising these continuing operational challenges, environmental courts – and environmental court practitioners – can nevertheless provide cause for optimism about the capacity to meaningfully reimagine and restructure courts and law in the 'near frontier'.

IV. The Value of Embracing Earth System Law's 'Near Frontier'

The near-term temporal space occupied by this chapter, as well as the analytical emphasis that it adopts (institutional attributes of courts and those who shape the courts, rather than the overall ontological orientation of earth system law), presents an opportunity to reimagine earth system law in proximately applicable context. It presents an optimistic assessment, drawing upon existing institutional innovations, to suggest that meaningful change is possible. At the same time, reimagining law in the 'near frontier' poses a risk: that the recommended interventions may be insufficiently impactful to support comprehensive structural change. As advocates of earth system law have noted, many contemporary legal responses have proven not only ineffective, but also insufficiently normatively ambitious 'when precisely such ambition is critically required in the Anthropocene'.[60]

How, then, can the earth system law imaginary be leveraged in ways that meaningfully advance systemic legal transformation, avoid pitfalls of complacency, and meaningfully drive courts on various scales to reimagine their purview in a more

[57] ibid.

[58] GN Gill, 'Environmental Justice in India: The National Green Tribunal and Expert Members' (2016) 5 *Transnational Environmental Law* 175.

[59] JM Angstadt, 'International Relations and the Analytical Foundations of Earth System Law' in T Cadman, M Hurlbert and A Simonelli (eds) *Earth System Law: Standing at the Precipice of the Anthropocene* (Abingdon-on-Thames, Routledge, 2023).

[60] LJ Kotzé and RE Kim, 'Earth System Law: The Juridical Dimensions of Earth System Governance' (2019) *Earth System Governance* 1, 100003.

systemic fashion? Such questions suggest the value inherent in exploring courts not just as institutions, but also as nexus points where policies, places, and practitioners intersect in ways that can be leveraged to better support earth system law. Therefore, as a complement to its institutional assessments of courts, this chapter concludes by broadening its analysis to identify, and briefly examine, three examples of initial steps that could better equip courts as environmental governance venues: (i) to reimagine the 'nearest frontier' of legal education and environmental law's pipeline; (ii) to adopt a 'theory-first' disposition to institutional design; and (iii) to decentre Western ontologies in Western legal frameworks.

First, there is a valuable opportunity to reimagine what arguably represents the nearest frontier pathway: the education and training of new 'environmental' lawyers. While scholarship frequently paints scholars and practitioners as two distinct constituencies, the reality is far more interlinked. From one direction, scholars regularly support the development and practice of environmental law, and earth system law scholars have highlighted opportunities to foster a 'theory-to-practice' agenda in this context.[61] However, there is a mirrored opportunity to integrate practice with earth system law theory, since legal practitioners begin their careers by training in the legal academy. Recognising this interconnection, especially early in lawyers' careers, provides an optimistic point of departure from which to reimagine how lawyers are socialised to conceptualise and engage with earth system challenges.

Briefly surveying the curricular requirements of the three top-ranked American environmental law programmes[62] illustrates the relative ease with which future 'environmental' lawyers could be attuned to more holistic, systemic consideration of issues that they will engage in practice. Each of the three law schools offers students the opportunity to focus their *juris doctor* training in ways that will yield a certificate of advanced specialisation in environmental law. At Pace University's Haub School of Law in New York, students must currently complete requirements including a specified number of credits and three courses: Administrative Law, Environmental Skills and Practice, and Environmental Survey.[63] Lewis & Clark Law School in Portland, Oregan, similarly requires students to complete a specified number of credits and two courses: Administrative Law, and Environmental Law.[64] Finally, the University of California Berkeley's Law School includes only two specific course requirements: Environmental Law and Policy, and Administrative Law.[65] However, each certificate programme also requires students to complete

[61] Mai and Boulot (n 7).

[62] Per US News & World Report, *Best Environmental Law Programs 2023–24*.

[63] Pace University, Elisabeth Haub School of Law, Advanced Certificate in Environmental Law, New York, https://www.pace.edu/law/academics/advanced-certificates/environmental-law.

[64] Lewis and Clark Law School, Certificate in Environmental and Natural Resources Law, https://law.lclark.edu/offices/registrar/certificate_programs/environmental_and_natural_resources_law/.

[65] Berkeley Law, Center for Law, Energy & the Environment, Certificate of Specialization in Environmental Law (JD), https://www.law.berkeley.edu/wp-content/uploads/2019/09/Environmental-Certificate-Requirements-JD-2019.pdf.

additional units of relevant courses, and each law school already offers courses that could introduce students to more systemic considerations: Science for Environmental Lawyers and Environmental Justice Seminar at Pace; Wildlife Law, Law of the Columbia Basin, and Native American Natural Resources Law at Lewis & Clark; and Climate Change and the Law, and multiple environmental justice offerings at Berkeley. Therefore, even the simplest practice of amending certificate programme requirements could fundamentally reorient a new generation of environmental lawyers. Undoubtedly, other opportunities exist to leverage more expansively existing resources to 'overcome ongoing barriers and develop clear pathways toward interdisciplinary solutions for the purpose of confronting earth system governance challenges'.[66]

Second, a reimagined 'near frontier' could more fruitfully engage with earth system law concepts by adopting a 'theory-first disposition'. Many current efforts begin by noting the attributes of present institutions, and by highlighting how they might, in turn, be adapted to more closely fit the ideals of earth system law. In one illustrative example, researchers highlight how courts' engagement with climate law suggests an opportunity for more explicit engagement with earth system law precepts.[67] The project highlights five specific domains where courts engage in work relevant to climate law: establishing accountability, redefining power relations, remedying vulnerabilities and injustices, increasing the reach and impact of international climate law, and applying climate science to adjudicate legal disputes.[68] In many ways, this approach aligns with the next steps advocated by this chapter, which examines how existing institutions exemplify potential manifestations of necessary or relevant transformations. Such a 'practice-first' disposition can also beneficially examine existing approaches to highlight unanticipated consequences that may result from 'locking in' existing governance pathways, supporting identification and exploration of necessary workarounds. For instance, alongside highlighting the contribution of courts to climate governance, researchers note and examine a rise in 'backlash litigation', where courts are increasingly sites for litigation brought by energy corporations and others opposing stricter climate regulation, not just for those seeking to compel urgent climate action.[69]

Simultaneously, however, earth system law advocates who seek practice-relevance could aim to support a 'theory-first disposition', where theorised needs can guide institutional design, and not vice versa. Doing so can help policy-makers and others to break free of existing, mainstream approaches and imagine new institutions that advance law's transformation, while supporting systemic engagement. However, it is important to remain mindful that a 'theory-first disposition'

[66] Kotzé and others (n 1).

[67] LJ Kotzé and others, 'Courts, Climate Litigation and the Evolution of Earth System Law' (2023) 15(1) *Global Policy* 5.

[68] ibid.

[69] ibid.

is quite different from a 'theory-only' disposition; indeed, many earth system law authors are quite adamant that their insights must be connected to practice-relevant discourse and institutional design. For instance, scholars have advocated moving beyond 'oftentimes elitist and exclusionary'[70] modes of information development and dissemination to embrace outreach and participation in ways that could maximise participation and efficacy, while legitimising the process and substance of earth system law.

Third, and finally, earth system law researchers can support the reimagination of earth system law's 'near frontier' by decentring Western ontologies that have, thus far, reinforced many problematic attributes of legal systems and institutions.[71] Courts, court employees, and litigants, more broadly, operationalise, interpret, and adjudicate in the context of dominantly Western legal systems and provisions. Therefore, courts and judges frequently reinforce these dynamics. In so doing, they have foregrounded human concerns, despite the far-reaching effects of planetary harm.[72] Likewise, they have inadequately acknowledged and responded to the unevenness of environmental harms and the unequal effects of these harms that courts are currently ill-fitted to address. As a result, earth system law analysts have highlighted the need to recognise the diverse human experiences within the earth system, and they have urged engagement with 'diverse knowledges, including those emerging from local communities as well as those coming from the arts and cultures'.[73] These potential approaches are diverse and could include other avenues advocated in this book, such as institutions that explore concepts of 'United Times' (to highlight dense, temporal interconnections), broader recognition of the role that cinema could play in expanding earth system law discourse, and consideration of how kinship could inform an earth system law sensitivity.[74]

While expanding ontological framing is broadly valuable in addressing earth system governance challenges, it seems particularly valuable in the context of courts and institutional design, where highly impactful institutions have historically been structured by parochial, fragmented, and unrepresentative discourses and communities of practice.[75] Earth system law researchers could support this necessary transformation by, among other ways, advocating and substantiating the need for more representative judicial oversight and administrative bodies, as these institutions frequently shape the functioning and disposition of domestic court systems.

Given the diversity of judicial systems, the forums and venues for this exchange could also vary tremendously by jurisdiction. However, this also suggests numerous

[70] Kim, Blanchard and Kotzé (n 8).
[71] See also Garver and Vargas Roncancio, Chapter 7 in this book.
[72] Kotzé and others (n 1).
[73] Mai and Boulot (n 7) footnote omitted.
[74] See, respectively, Hanusch, Chapter 15; Richardson, Chapter 14; and Warner, Chapter 9 in this book.
[75] See Morrow, Chapter 6 in this book.

distinct avenues to promote change that complements the 'theory-first' disposition advocated above. Local, subnational jurisdictions offer instructive cases to explore the multilevel mechanisms that could support such an objective, and the legal system in New York State represents one such example. I briefly examine it here to demonstrate the differing levels of engagement that could better integrate earth system law theory. First, earth system law researchers could begin to promote more expansive legal ontologies in bar journals and other practitioner outlets where judges and advocates can engage with expanded ideas. For example, the Environmental & Energy Law Section of the New York State Bar Association seeks to further the 'public interest in an effective and fair legal framework for protection of the human and natural environment'.[76] However, the group's practitioner-centric orientation means that the mission has not been pushed beyond its historically anthropocentric and subject-specific orientation. Secondly, and similarly, the court system of New York boasts a State judicial institute, whose purpose is to provide 'a venue for research and development regarding justice issues, as well as serving as a hub for judicial scholarship' and seeks to embrace 'innovation and progress'.[77] Therefore, while earth system law concepts seem rather foreign to the jurisdiction, they appear at least somewhat compatible with the mission of the institute. Thirdly, and finally, many jurisdictions operate institutes that function with the explicit objective of educating judges and other judicial practitioners. To provide one illustrative example, New York's 'Advisory Committee on Judicial Ethics' operates ongoing judicial education programmes.[78] Examining and pursuing opportunities to incorporate earth system law and complementary equity considerations within the existing training framework represents a third mechanism to better integrate earth system law's recognition of diverse ontologies and viewpoints into the form and fabric of New York State's judicial system.

V. Conclusion

This chapter has highlighted the energy and opportunity that exist at the 'near frontier' of earth system law. It has argued that the theoretical excitement and debate within the earth system law community can be productively leveraged, particularly within courts and judicial institutions, to meaningfully advance the application of earth system law precepts. It has examined three among many potential pathways to better align courts' structures with systemic environmental challenges: institutional transformation, geographic reorientation, and jurisdictional alteration. Simultaneously, it has highlighted three mechanisms to

[76] New York State Bar Association, Environmental & Energy Law Section, https://www.nysba.org/committees/environmental-energy-law-section/.
[77] New York State Judicial Institute, 'About Us', https://www.nycourts.gov/ip/judicialinstitute/.
[78] ibid.

ensure that these transformations are undertaken meaningfully, and in ways that do not reinforce existing dynamics: by reshaping the educational pipeline that socialises the practitioners who will staff the courts, by adopting a 'theory-first disposition' when undertaking institutional design, and by exploring multiple streams to decentre Western ontologies in legal systems. While these proposals are insufficient by themselves to foster necessary transformations, they provide a reminder of the prospect to reimagine legal institutions and effect meaningful change that could collectively promote more effective earth system governance.

13

The Earth System Law-Makers

BENOIT MAYER*

I. Introduction

A stream of academic literature has called for the development of new approaches to law aimed at addressing social impacts on multiple planetary systems.[1] This literature often builds on the idea that we have entered a new geological epoch – the Anthropocene – in which humankind has become the dominant driver of planetary change. Further, this literature shows that law and governance have yet to adapt to this new reality. In particular, it is argued that existing (environmental) law has been unable to regulate our widespread impact on the Earth system and, at times, may even have promoted harmful activities.[2] In this context, scholars have suggested that earth system law may be 'better suited to address the Anthropocene than traditional law'.[3] However, it is not entirely clear what precisely earth system law is – what it would consist of, how it would differ from 'traditional' law, whether it would really be better than 'traditional' law, or how this law would be created in the first place.[4]

While much of the literature on earth system law discusses what earth system law could entail, the present chapter aims to extend the debate and focus on the

* I am grateful to Louis Kotzé and Chris Hilson for comments on earlier drafts.

[1] LJ Kotzé, *Global Environmental Constitutionalism in the Anthropocene* (Oxford, Hart Publishing, 2016); LJ Kotzé (ed), *Environmental Law and Governance for the Anthropocene* (Oxford, Hart Publishing, 2017); LJ Kotzé, 'Earth System Law for the Anthropocene' (2019) 11 *Sustainability* 6796; LJ Kotzé and RE Kim, 'Earth System Law: The Juridical Dimensions of Earth System Governance' (2019) 1 *Earth System Governance* 100003; LJ Kotzé, 'Earth System Law for the Anthropocene: Rethinking Environmental Law Alongside the Earth System Metaphor' (2020) 11 *Transnational Legal Theory* 75; RE Kim, C Blanchard and LJ Kotzé, 'Law, Systems, and Planet Earth: Editorial' (2022) 11 *Earth System Governance* 100127; MC Petersmann, 'Sympoietic Thinking and Earth System Law: The Earth, Its Subjects and the Law' (2021) 9 *Earth System Governance* 100114; JE Viñuales, 'Two Layers of Self-Regulation' (2012) 23 *European Journal of International Law* 267.

[2] Kotzé (n 1) 75; Viñuales (n 1) 30.

[3] T Cadman, Hurlbert M and AC Simonelli, 'Dimensions and Definitions, Signposts and Silos in Earth System Law' in T Cadman, Hurlbert M and AC Simonelli (eds), *Earth System Law: Standing on the Precipice of the Anthropocene* (Abingdon-on-Thames, Routledge, 2022).

[4] Kim, Blanchard and Kotzé (n 1).

question of the identity of earth system law-makers. National, international, and scientific institutions could all conceivably play a role in the making of earth system law. Among these three types of institutions, the earth system law literature tends to promote the role of scientific institutions and international law-making while often discounting the importance of political processes unfolding in a national context. Yet, this chapter argues, each type of institution may have a legitimate role to play in earth system law-making and a balance needs to be struck between these three types of institutions. In particular, while scientific institutions must inform earth system law-making, they cannot legitimately make the value-based decisions required for the development of earth system law; and while international institutions are instrumental in addressing collective action issues, they might lack the legitimacy to decide how environmental protection is to be achieved. On these bases, this chapter suggests the need for earth system law to develop a principle akin to subsidiarity to determine the competence of each institution regarding the protection of the planet. According to this principle, each type of institution should only act if and insofar as it has a comparative advantage over other types of institution.

The next section reviews the literature on the making of earth system law and highlights the underlying questions regarding law-making competence. Sections III, IV and V discuss the roles of scientific, international, and national institutions in the making of earth system law. Section VI identifies potential principles for the sharing of law-making competence among these institutions.

II. The Making of Earth System Law

Scientists have long warned of society's impact on ecological processes, including on a planetary scale. For instance, the Intergovernmental Panel on Climate Change (IPCC) concluded its Sixth Assessment Report by noting that '[h]uman activities … have unequivocally caused global warming',[5] which 'has led to widespread adverse impacts and related losses and damages to nature and people'.[6] The United Nations Environment Programme (UNEP) has observed that '[b]iodiversity is declining at an unprecedented rate', that 'the pressures driving this decline are intensifying',[7] and that '[a]ll environmental impacts are on the rise', causing a 'planetary crisis'.[8] In a more controversial study, Steffen and colleagues argue that several 'planetary

[5] Intergovernmental Panel on Climate Change (IPCC), 'Climate Change 2023: Synthesis Report. Contribution of Working Groups I, II and III to the Sixth Assessment Report of the Intergovernmental Panel on Climate Change' (IPCC, 2023).

[6] ibid 5.

[7] United Nations Environment Programme, *Global Diversity Outlook* (2020) 5, 8.

[8] UN Environment Programme, *Bend the Trend: Pathways to a Liveable Planet as Resource Use Spikes* (Global Resources Outlook, UNEP, 2024) xiv.

boundaries' that define a 'safe operating space for humanity' have already been exceeded.

Such warnings are well known. National governments, in particular, have long recognised the need to address global environmental harms such as climate change and threats to biological diversity through international cooperation.[9] Yet, many observers have found that not enough is being done, and states themselves have noted, with increasingly emphatic concern, the insufficiency of their aggregate level of action, especially in relation to the mitigation of climate change. This shared dissatisfaction with the level of existing action has prompted scholars to propose new concepts and frameworks aimed at reconceptualising the way law and governance approach the protection and preservation of the environment. These concepts include earth system law,[10] and the overarching notion of earth system governance,[11] as well as planetary governance,[12] planetary justice,[13] and planetary stewardship,[14] among others. Rather than 'merely tinkering at the margins', these concepts are developed with the aim of fostering 'a new legal paradigm that is better fit for purpose' in the Anthropocene.[15]

Much of this literature considers what this new paradigm ought to be and, accordingly, which new types of law should be drafted, adopted, and implemented.[16] The present chapter does not engage with these substantive issues. Rather, this chapter notes that scholars have often approached these questions in the passive voice – discussing what needs to *be done*, without necessarily specifying *by whom* this ought to be done. *Who* acts – in particular, who makes earth system law – matters greatly because it will affect the legitimacy and acceptability of this new legal paradigm, influence the contents of earth system law, and determine how the costs and benefits (economic or otherwise) are distributed (assuming that earth system law-makers, like any other law-makers, would often put their own interests first).

The earth system law and governance literature can (also) be read as a critique of existing law-making arrangements. Thus, this literature has highlighted shortcomings in existing environmental laws that are directly related to well-known limitations in existing law-making processes. On the national plane, democratic

[9] United Nations Framework Convention on Climate Change (UNFCCC) (adopted 9 May 1992, entered into force 21 March 1994), 1771 UNTS 107 Preamble para 2, 10; Convention on Biological Diversity (adopted 5 June 1992, entered into force 29 December 1993), 1760 UNTS 79, Preamble para 15, Art 5.

[10] Kotzé and Kim (n 1).

[11] F Biermann, *Earth System Governance: World Politics in the Anthropocene* (Cambridge MA, MIT Press, 2014).

[12] OR Young, *Addressing the Grand Challenges of Planetary Governance: The Future of the Global Political Order* (Cambridge, Cambridge University Press, 2023); Kim, Blanchard and Kotzé (n 1).

[13] F Biermann and A Kalfagianni, 'Planetary Justice: A Research Framework' (2020) 6 *Earth System Governance* 100049.

[14] J Speth and P Haas, *Global Environmental Governance* (New York, Pearson Longman, 2006).

[15] Kotzé (n 1) 77.

[16] L Mai, '(Transnational) Law for the Anthropocene: Revisiting Jessup's Move from "What?" to "How?"' (2020) 11(1–2) *Transnational Legal Theory* 105.

institutions fail to ensure consideration for the interests of foreign populations, unborn generations, and non-human species.[17] On the international plane, meanwhile, negotiations are generally based on consensus, allowing any individual states to prioritise their own national interests over the pursuance of global goals, thus limiting the content of international agreements to the lowest common denominator acceptable to all.[18] Any major departure from existing law would likely start with a review of law-making processes with a view to overcoming these limitations.

In this regard, the earth system law literature seems to suggest that new law-making processes could differ from existing ones in two ways. First, new law-making processes could rely more heavily on expert institutions rather than on political ones. One way of justifying an extended role for expert institutions would be to approach earth system law as natural law whose content would need to be identified by technical experts, rather than positive law created by political institutions. The very concept of earth system law (or, even more explicitly, 'planetary boundaries law'),[19] is more directly rooted in scientific studies than in open-ended democratic or other political processes. Second, new law-making processes could also increasingly rely on international institutions, including global or transnational governance – or even government – rather than solely on intergovernmental negotiations. Earth system law's emphasis on 'Earth' suggests the need for Earthlings to act in concert, including through an extended role for global, rather than only national, institutions.

Notwithstanding whether the emphasis is on scientific or global institutions, the outcome of implementing these ideas would likely be a depoliticisation of law-making processes, as scientific or global institutions would expand across the domain traditionally reserved for (democratic) national institutions. Whether this move is desirable is a delicate moral and political question that ought to be contemplated carefully, given its far-reaching consequences, not just for the way we protect and preserve the planet, but also more broadly for (the rule of) law, governance, and ultimately, for society. The argument that important and urgent policy objectives justify setting democratic processes aside is a dangerous one, as it could set a precedent that could be used to justify many forms of illiberal government. If earth system law is to be developed, it should be through legitimate democratic processes, which are more likely to be found in national rather than

[17] S Caney, 'Global Climate Governance, Short-Termism, and the Vulnerability of Future Generations' (2022) 36 *Ethics & International Affairs* 137; A Burke and S Fishel, 'Across Species and Borders: Political Representation, Ecological Democracy and the Non-Human' in JC Pereira and A Saramago (eds), *Non-Human Nature in World Politics: Theory and Practice* (Heidelberg, Springer, 2020).

[18] J Brunnée, 'COPing with Consent: Law-Making Under Multilateral Environmental Agreements' (2002) 15(1) *Leiden Journal of International Law* 1; A Vihma, 'Climate of Consensus: Managing Decision Making in the UN Climate Change Negotiations' (2015) 58 *Comparative & International Environmental Law* 58.

[19] LJ Kotzé and D French, 'Staying Within the Planet's "Safe Operating Space"? Law and the Planetary Boundaries' in D French and LJ Kotzé (eds), *Research Handbook on Law, Governance and Planetary Boundaries* (Cheltenham, Edward Elgar Publishing, 2021).

global or scientific institutions. The role of scientific and global institutions, while essential, should be limited so as to ensure respect for such democratic processes and support them.

III. The Role of Scientific Institutions

The proponents of earth system law have often invoked science as a justification for new ways to approach law and governance. Frank Biermann, for instance, has pointed to 'a serious mismatch between the research and recommendations of Earth system analysists and the actions of political decisionmakers' as evidence of the need for earth system governance.[20] Further, according to Louis Kotzé, earth system law could 'serve as a coherent interdisciplinary epistemological bridge between law and other sciences'.[21] Non-governmental organisations (NGOs) have advocated for 'science-based targets' on the mitigation of climate change.[22] States too, have affirmed the need to act 'in accordance with best available science',[23] and have recognised 'the *scientific view* that the increase in global temperature should be below 2 degrees Celsius' (emphasis added).[24] And some courts have imposed on states and corporations an obligation to act consistently with temperature goals which they have identified as being 'derived from the IPCC reports'.[25]

There is no serious question that democratic law-making processes should be well informed, and that scientific findings are within the pool of relevant knowledge, in particular for environmental issues. What is more questionable, however, is the extent to which the content of the law should be *determined* by analysts, scientists, and other 'experts' – that is, the extent to which the law should not just *take into account*, but necessarily *follow* scientists' recommendations.

The scientific method helps to advance our knowledge of our world, based on observation.[26] In other words, this method helps us to understand what *is*. For instance, science shows with a high level of confidence that anthropogenic greenhouse gas emissions *are* causing profound changes to the Earth system.[27] Yet, an argument about what *ought to be* – for instance, about what society *ought to* do about climate change – is necessarily based on normative premises (eg moral

[20] Biermann (n 11) 8–9.
[21] Kotzé (n 1) 78.
[22] Eg, https://sciencebasedtargets.org/.
[23] Paris Agreement (adopted 12 December 2015, entered into force 4 November 2016), 3156 UNTS 79, Arts 2(1)(a), 4(1).
[24] Copenhagen Accord, 18 December 2009, para 1, in annex of Decision 2/CP.15, FCCC/CP/2009/11/Add.1, 4.
[25] *Milieudefensie and others v Royal Dutch Shell Plc* (26 May 2021) C/09/571932 / HA ZA 19-379, ECLI:NL:RBDHA:2021:5337, para 4.4.27.
[26] K Popper, *The Logic of Scientific Discovery*, 2nd edn (Abingdon-on-Thames, Routledge, 2002).
[27] IPCC (n 5).

values) as well as factual ones (eg science).[28] Scientists (or even, at times, some scientific institutions) can and do make policy recommendations that build not just on their scientific findings, but also, inevitably, on certain normative premises.[29] Such policy recommendations by scientists do not have the same authority as scientific findings.

This distinction between scientific findings and policy recommendations can be illustrated with the example of the goal of limiting global warming to two degrees Celsius above pre-industrial temperatures. Such targets are often 'perceived by the public' as having been 'identified by scientists as a safe limit that avoids dangerous climate change'; but scientists themselves have observed that '[t]his perception is incorrect: no scientific assessment has clearly justified or defended the 2 °C target as a safe level of warming, and indeed, this is not a problem that science alone can address'.[30] Certainly, earth system scientists can predict some of the consequences of global warming exceeding two degrees Celsius, and economists can even produce some rough estimates of the cost of limiting global warming to two degrees. However, values will necessarily play a critical role in an assessment that the benefits of achieving a two-degree target justifies the costs (economic or otherwise) of doing so. Different normative assumptions, for instance, about the way we value in our present decisions climate impacts that unfold in a distant future, have led well-established economists to widely different conclusions about the desirable level of global action on climate change mitigation – with Nobel Laureate in Economic Sciences William Nordhaus, at one end of the spectrum, actually suggesting that a three-degree target might actually be optimal.[31] The point here is not to advocate for one economic model over another, but merely to note that what policies 'scientists' may recommend are contingent on the values that inform their reasoning, with important implications even for issues as thoroughly studied as climate change. Determining the desirable level of global action on climate change mitigation is at least as much a political question as it is a scientific one: it depends at least as much on *how one values impacts* (as informed by our values) as it depends on these *actual impacts* (as predicted by science).[32]

Some scholars appear to believe that policy recommendations informing earth system law or governance are so strongly supported by science that they

[28] D Hume, *A Treatise of Human Nature* (Reprinted from the Original Edition in three volumes and edited, with an analytical index, by LA Selby-Bigge, Oxford, Clarendon Press, 1896 [1739]).

[29] D Gayle, 'More than 1,000 Climate Scientists Urge Public to Become Activists' (4 December 2023) *The Guardian*, https://www.theguardian.com/environment/2023/dec/04/more-than-1000-climate-scientists-urge-public-to-become-activists.

[30] R Knutti and others, 'A Scientific Critique of the Two-Degree Climate Change Target' (2016) 9 *Nature Geoscience* 13.

[31] WD Nordhaus, 'A Review of the *Stern Review on the Economics of Climate Change*' (2007) 45 *Journal of Economic Literature* 686; WD Nordhaus, 'Climate Change: The Ultimate Challenge for Economics' (2019) *American Economic Review* 1991.

[32] B Mayer, 'Temperature Targets and State Obligations on the Mitigation of Climate Change' (2021) 33 *Journal of Environmental Law* 585. A different issue is whether this question has been decided, for instance with the adoption of the temperature goals in the Paris Agreement.

do not need to rely on these wider values. Thus, a group of scientists who refer to themselves as 'the Earth Commission' have asserted that planetary boundaries are the object of a 'science-based political consensus' on the basis of which scientists can identify 'science-based targets' – omitting that such targets are necessarily grounded in some values. Frank Biermann himself, while critical of such scientific target-setting, once argued that the goal of respecting 'earth system boundaries' – that is, of ensuring that humankind does not self-destruct – is an objective that is 'in principle neutral toward human values and aspirations'.[33] What Biermann presumably meant was that the values underlying earth system boundaries are so obvious and so unlikely to be rejected by any reasonable mind that they can simply be taken for granted. The assumption that humanity should not self-destroy is a normative assumption, yet one that no one (hopefully) would argue against. Surely, one could write in support of Biermann's position, that humanity just cannot live in the twenty-first century in such a way that would necessarily preclude any form of life on Earth in the twenty-second century – not, at least, under any reasonable value-based system.

With this argument, Biermann seemed to suggest, at least in part, that new forms of law, politics, and governance, including earth system law, could emerge as a renewed form of natural law – that is to say, a set of rules that would be identified from empirical research (eg about the planetary boundaries) rather than primarily developed through pure political deliberation. Rather than clerics or philosophers as in previous iterations of the idea of a natural law,[34] it would be for scientists to determine what needs to be done for humanity to 'stay within the safe operating space as defined by earth system boundaries'.[35] Since scientists often disagree among themselves, in particular in social sciences like economics (assuming that social science would necessarily play a role), some procedures would need to be developed to determine which scientific views are sufficiently authoritative to be considered peremptory recommendations.[36]

The idea of earth system law as natural law, however, would face major practical hurdles in all but the most obvious cases. Most global environmental issues do not involve a clear-cut threshold beyond which life on Earth could reliably be predicted to become impossible; rather, they involve a gradual increase in complex, often ill-understood risks of widespread and irreversible degradation of the global environment. Even if tipping points are considered, the fact remains – considering the uncertainty associated with them and their multiplicity – that risks are increasing

[33] Biermann (n 11) 33. On Biermann's apparent change of mind, see below, text to note 39.

[34] J Finnis, 'Natural Law Theories' in EN Zalta and U Nodelman (eds), *The Stanford Encyclopedia of Philosophy* (Metaphysics Research Lab, Stanford University, updated March 2025) https://plato.stanford.edu/archives/sum2025/entries/natural-law-theories/.

[35] Biermann (n 11) 33–34.

[36] ibid 63. Biermann describes how 'state and nonstate actors establish mutually agreed procedures for determining an acceptable reading of knowledge and for assigning competence on delimiting accepted truth from other claims'. Yet Biermann does not expand on the legitimacy of these procedures, which certainly are not always fully agreeable to all actors concerned.

gradually with environmental impacts, and that even the best science cannot draw a clear line between what is and is not dangerous. Biermann recognises that 'the exact definition of earth system boundaries depends on normative assumptions about the risks that we, as humankind, are taking'.[37] In a sense, *any* alteration of global environmental conditions entails a risk for the survival of life on Earth. In another sense, some degree of global environmental degradation could be preferable to taking measures that would divert a finite pool of resources from more immediate priorities such as establishing peace and eradicating poverty.

Thus, observers may reasonably disagree as to the degree of risk society should be willing to take and the costs it should be willing to bear to ensure that humanity remains within a safe operating space. Since scientists are not representative of the global population, they would likely approach these questions differently. For instance, it might be the case that earth system scientists tend to attach greater value to the protection of ecological resources than others; or they would be less concerned about the economic cost of reducing greenhouse gas emissions than others are. In other words, the values informing scientists' policy recommendations may differ from the values supported by the rest of humanity, leading to some discrepancies between what scientists may recommend and what a democratic decision-making process would decide. In this regard, the Earth Commission's insistence on its independence does not address the more fundamental concern one may have with the potential for political biases in the selection of its members.[38] Allowing a group of self-selected scientists (clerics or philosophers) to impose on society what *they* believe to be the best balance between environmental and economic interests, informed by *their* values, would appear put to be fundamentally anti-democratic.

In conclusion, while science must play a role in the making of earth system law, it cannot do it alone. Indeed, in a subsequent publication co-authored with Rakhyun Kim, Biermann rejects the notion 'that science can conclusively resolve societal conflicts and set targets following the adage of "speaking truth to power"'.[39] Biermann and Kim further acknowledge that '[t]he global targets that our societies will need to adopt … must be defined in political processes'.[40]

IV. The Role of Global Institutions

Earth system law is, almost by definition, approached as a paradigm that is predominantly embedded in the international context. The challenges earth

[37] ibid 35.

[38] J Rockström and others, 'Safe and Just Earth System Boundaries' (2023) 619 *Nature* 102, 112.

[39] F Biermann and RE Kim, 'The Boundaries of the Planetary Boundary Framework: A Critical Appraisal of Approaches to Define a 'Safe Operating Space' for Humanity' (2020) 45 *Annual Review of Environment and Resources* 497.

[40] ibid 514.

system law seeks to address are global in nature, and the solutions, therefore, are often assumed to be global too. Among the various types of international institutions, the preference of the proponents of earth system law appears to be for multilevel 'global'[41] or 'transnational'[42] governance, rather than the more classic inter-governmental arrangement. Beyond national governments, transnational institutions could also seek to establish a form of global democracy and to account for the interests of future generations.[43]

Thus, a premise of the earth system law project is that national institutions are insufficient because they are ill equipped on their own to address issues unfolding 'at a planetary scale',[44] and that more international cooperation is needed, whether through formal intergovernmental agreements or through informal polycentric governance.[45] Louis Kotzé, for instance, agrees with François Venter's assertion that 'globalization produces a serious challenge to conventional premises' such as 'the axiomatic notion of the nation-state', and he insists that, '[i]n a globalised world, regulatory problems demand a global response and a body of regulatory arrangements'.[46] States themselves have repeatedly called for 'the widest possible cooperation by all countries' towards an international response to climate change – an ambiguous phrase which could either be redundant (if 'widest possible' *means* 'by all countries') or provide unlikely support for an ever-extending realm for international cooperation in all aspects of climate action (eg regarding the means of implementation).

While the limitations of national governance are self-evident, earth system law scholars are often well aware of the need to question the tacit assumption that international institutions could realistically do better. Biermann and Kim, for instance, have emphasised that not all planetary problems are best addressed at the planetary level – national governance may sometimes be more effective.[47] From a theoretical perspective, while there is some appeal in the idea of a centralised power deciding what is best for all, there is surely also some merit in preserving some diversity among cultures, civilisations, and political organisations.[48] From a more practical point of view, most peoples and governments may not be particularly keen to relinquish extended competence and autonomy to international institutions.

[41] A Cardesa-Salzmann and E Cocciolo, 'Global Governance, Sustainability and the Earth System: Critical Reflections on the Role of Global Law' (2019) 8 *Transnational Environmental Law* 437; Kotzé (n 1).

[42] E Webster and L Mai, 'Transnational Environmental Law in the Anthropocene' (2020) 11 *Transnational Legal Theory* 1.

[43] Caney (n 17).

[44] Biermann (n 11) 9.

[45] Cadman, Hurlbert and Simonelli (n 3) 20.

[46] Kotzé (n 1) 96.

[47] Biermann and Kim (n 39) 507.

[48] On the philosophical debate on the merits of cosmopolitanism, see P Kleingeld and E Brown, 'Cosmopolitanism' (Stanford Encyclopedia of Philosophy, revised edn, 2019) https://plato.stanford.edu/entries/cosmopolitanism/.

Further, international institutions, as they exist today, are not democratic in any meaningful sense, and the prospects for them to become so in the foreseeable future are unlikely.[49] Despite the principle of sovereign equality, international negotiations tend to be dominated by developed states due to their skilful diplomacy and their economic and political power to sway other states.[50] Non-state organisations might and sometimes do play a role, but these organisations appear even less representative of the global population than the assembly of states.[51]

On the one hand, the need for international institutions is at its strongest in relation to global collective action problems, where every nation is better off with cooperation, but better off still if it can free ride on measures implemented by others.[52] Thus, international negotiations have successfully defined a global pathway, agreed upon by most states, towards the phasing out of ozone-depleting substances.[53] By contrast, however, negotiations have struggled to define global objectives on climate change mitigation.[54] let alone national 'fair shares' towards the realisation of these objectives.[55] While the 1997 Kyoto Protocol contained agreed-upon national targets for developed countries,[56] the 2015 Paris Agreement reverted to a more explicitly 'bottom-up' system of 'nationally determined contributions'.[57]

On the other hand, however, Elinor Ostrom has famously shown the possibility of addressing collective action problems, including global ones such as climate change, through polycentric governance.[58] While Ostrom's work does not exclude the need for some sort of informal institutions, it questions the necessity of a centralized global decision-making authority, suggesting that something akin to the Paris Agreement might actually work best under existing geopolitical constraints. Relying on Ostrom's research, Rockström and colleagues have recently argued that a global law might be an unnecessary distraction from efforts aimed at preserving Earth's

[49] Kotzé (n 1) 237.

[50] D Bodansky, J Brunnée and L Rajamani, *International Climate Change Law* (Oxford, Oxford University Press, 2017) 73–82.

[51] A third of the NGOs admitted as observers under the UNFCCC are based in either the United States or the United Kingdom, while less than a quarter of admitted NGOs are based in a developing country. See data available at UNFCCC, 'List of Admitted NGOs', https://unfccc.int/process/parties-non-party-stakeholders/non-party-stakeholders/admitted-ngos/list-of-admitted-ngos.

[52] EA Posner and D Weisbach, *Climate Change Justice* (Princeton NJ, Princeton University Press, 2010).

[53] D Bodansky and H van Asselt, *The Art and Craft of International Environmental Law* 2nd ed (Oxford, Oxford University Press, 2024) 364–65.

[54] Mayer (n 32).

[55] L Rajamani and others, 'National 'Fair Shares' in Reducing Greenhouse Gas Emissions within the Principled Framework of International Environmental Law' (2021) 21 *Climate Policy* 983.

[56] Kyoto Protocol to the UNFCCC (adopted 11 December 1997, entered into force 16 February 2005) 2303 UNTS 162; J Depledge, 'The "Top-down" Kyoto Protocol? Exploring Caricature and Misrepresentation in Literature on Global Climate Change Governance' (2022) 22 *International Environmental Agreements: Politics, Law and Economics* 673.

[57] Paris Agreement (n 23) 4(2).

[58] E Ostrom, 'Polycentric Systems for Coping with Collective Action and Global Environmental Change' (2010) 20 *Global Environmental Change* 550.

'planetary commons', that could be more realistically and effectively achieved through more 'bottom-up' intergovernmental negotiations at scaled-down levels.[59]

While some types of international institutions surely need to play a role in addressing global collective action problems, international governance is less obviously needed with regard to the means of implementation, for instance to determine the particular national measures and policies aimed at limiting and reducing greenhouse gas emissions, as opposed to the national objective of limiting or reducing these emissions. In this regard, the 1992 United Nations Framework Convention on Climate Change (UNFCCC) recognised 'the principle of sovereignty of States in international cooperation to address climate change'.[60] This principle, however, has not been reaffirmed in any subsequent treaty or decision. On the contrary, negotiations have at times singled out some policies and measures,[61] or excluded others,[62] while developed states exerted pressure on developing ones for the adoption of some policies.[63]

It is generally well understood that an issue as complex as climate change can certainly not be addressed through policy-neutral global coordination. Assessing national 'fair shares' in global efforts on climate change mitigation requires far-reaching assumptions about the rate of emissions reduction, for instance, in the meat-production sector (a large source of emissions, eg, in New Zealand) as opposed to the coal sector (a large source of emissions, eg, in Australia).[64] Various national measures and policies on climate change mitigation – or even policies in other sectors – may affect emissions in other countries in multiple complex ways, including carbon leakage (eg, when polluting activities are relocated to another country), technological spillovers (when technological innovation facilitates emission reductions in another country), and regulatory influence (when technical standards imposed in one country influence global production processes).

V. The Role of National Institutions

Law usually develops in political communities, particularly in states. It is within such political communities that democracy is more likely to flourish, building on shared languages, cultures, and values. Even on the regional scale, such as the

[59] J Rockström and others, 'The Planetary Commons: A New Paradigm for Safeguarding Earth-Regulating Systems in the Anthropocene' (2024) 121 *Proceedings of the National Academy of Sciences* 1.

[60] UNFCCC (n 9) para 10.

[61] UNFCCC (1992) Decision 1/CMA.5, *Outcome of the First Global Stocktake* para 28.

[62] UNFCCC (n 9) para 7.

[63] K Hallding, G Han and M Jürisoo, *China's Carbon Emission Trading: An Overview of Current Development* (Stockholm Environment Institute and FORES, 2012).

[64] *Urgenda v the Netherlands* (2019) ECLI:NL:HR:2019:2007, para 7.2.3. Asserting that, 'in principle', an emission-reduction target applicable to all developed countries as a group 'also applies to the individual states'.

European Union, it is difficult to develop any meaningful democracy even among countries that share a common history.[65] International institutions have flourished in the last few decades but, by and large, they remain mostly dependent on national ones: it is states, after all, that negotiate, accept, and apply international law, while the budget of international organisations generally depends on funding paid (or left unpaid) by national governments. Thus, the proponents of earth system law and governance generally recognise that 'the state remains important'[66] even though it 'is … put under tremendous new challenges to adapt to the changed context of the Anthropocene'.[67] It is difficult to imagine a realistic and desirable scenario in which law and governance would do away with the central role of national institutions.

In this context, Kim and colleagues raise an important question underpinning the earth system law project: 'What if law has become unfit for purpose, and therefore incapable of effectively addressing the challenges at hand?'.[68] One could wish for the law to be reformed; but what if legitimate (eg, democratic) political institutions had no interest in reforming the law? What if, for instance, a country elected a president promising to withdraw from climate treaties,[69] or voted in a referendum to decrease national ambition on climate change mitigation?[70] Should scientific or international institutions be permitted to pre-empt democratic decision-making processes? Would they be able to do so – or would any attempt backfire by fuelling retaliatory politics? And would the end – addressing major planetary ecological issues – justify the anti-democratic means?

From an international law perspective, it can certainly be argued that international law pre-empts democratic decisions. The Vienna Convention on the Law of Treaties reflects in no uncertain terms the rule of general international law according to which a state 'may not invoke the provisions of its internal law as justification for its failure to perform' an international law obligation.[71] This rule applies just as well when the internal law at issue is a direct expression of the will of the people. While a state may be able to withdraw its consent to some norms of international law (for instance by withdrawing from a treaty), some other norms

[65] JHH Weiler, UR Haltern and FC Mayer, 'European Democracy and Its Critique' in J Hayward (ed), *The Crisis of Representation in Europe* (Abingdon-on-Thames, Routledge, 1995).

[66] Biermann (n 11) 52.

[67] ibid.

[68] Kim, Blanchard and Kotzé (n 1) 1.

[69] B Lefebvre and Z Colman, 'Trump Would Withdraw US from Paris Climate Treaty Again, Campaign Says' (28 June 2024) *Politico*, https://www.politico.com/news/2024/06/28/trump-paris-climate-treaty-withdrawal-again-00165903.

[70] D Graham, 'Swiss Press Say "Absurd" European Climate Ruling Could Harm Democracy' (10 April 2024) *Reuters*, https://www.reuters.com/sustainability/swiss-press-say-absurd-european-climate-ruling-could-harm-democracy-2024-04-10/.

[71] Vienna Convention on the Law of Treaties (adopted 23 May 1969, entered into force 27 January) 1115 UNTS 331; International Law Commission, *Draft Articles on Responsibility of States for Internationally Wrongful Acts, Yearbook of the International Law Commission 2001*, vol II, Part Two, Art 32.

cannot easily be avoided once they have emerged.[72] A state may be required to cooperate in good faith with a multilateral regime aimed at protecting global commons, especially when failure to do so would amount to free riding on the efforts of others.[73]

In practice, however, even the most ambitious international courts would be wise to refrain from directly opposing a direct expression of the will of the people. The question has arisen before the European Court of Human Rights in relation to referendums that, under some interpretations, might appear to be in tension with the European Convention on Human rights.[74] In particular, in *Verein Klimaseniorinnen Schweiz v Switzerland*, the Court found that Switzerland's action on climate change mitigation was insufficient to fulfil its obligation to protect human rights from the effects of climate change.[75] Central to the case was a national referendum, held on 13 June 2021, through which the Swiss people had rejected a statute that would have enhanced the state's climate action.[76] The national government had subsequently been unable to agree on alternative legislation with an equivalent level of ambition. During the proceedings before the European Court of Human Rights, the national government asserted that 'citizens had not rejected the idea of the necessity of combating global warming but rather the proposed means to do so'.[77] Emphasising this submission, the Court was careful to attribute the breach of Switzerland's obligation not to the referendum itself, but to 'a legislative lacuna' that the referendum had created.[78] Yet, it is unclear what the Court would be willing to do if a new statutory proposal by the Swiss government were again rejected by referendum.

[72] International Law Commission, *Draft Conclusions on Identification and Legal Consequences of Peremptory Norms of General International Law (Jus Cogens)* UN Doc A/77/10, Annex para (g), *Yearbook of the International Law Commission 2022*, vol II, Part Two; Vienna Convention on the Law of Treaties (n 71); *Barcelona Traction, Light and Power Company, Limited (Belgium v Spain)*, Judgment of 5 February 1970, [1970] ICJ Rep 3, para 33; *Responsibilities and Obligations of States with Respect to Activities in the Area, Advisory Opinion*, 1 February 2011, ITLOS Reports 10, para 180. Such is the case, most obviously, with a few peremptory norms of general international law (*jus cogens*), such as the prohibition of torture. In practice, however, the same applies to a broader body of obligations that a state owes to the international community as a whole (*erga omnes*), such as the prevention of global environmental harm.

[73] EJ Criddle and E Fox-Decent, 'Mandatory Multilateralism' (2019) 113 *American Journal of International Law* 272; *Request for an Advisory Opinion Submitted by the Commission of Small Island States on Climate Change and International Law, Advisory Opinion*, 20 May 2024, ITLOS Reports, paras 295, 441(3)(j), https://www.itlos.org/fileadmin/itlos/documents/cases/31/Advisory_Opinion/C31_Adv_Op_21.05.2024_orig.pdf.

[74] *A, B & C v Ireland*, Application no 25579/05, ECtHR, Judgment of 16 December 2010, (2010) 53 EHRR 13; F de Londras, 'When the European Court of Human Rights Decides not to Decide: The Cautionary Tale of A, B & C v Ireland and Referendum-Emergent Constitutional Provisions' in P Kapotas and V Tzevelekos (eds), *Building Consensus on European Consensus* (Cambridge, Cambridge University Press, 2019) 311.

[75] *Verein Klimaseniorinnen v Switzerland*, Application no 53600/20, ECtHR, Judgment of 9 April 2024, [2024] ECHR 304, https://hudoc.echr.coe.int/?i=001-233206.

[76] ibid paras 75, 92, 94.

[77] ibid 357.

[78] ibid 561–62.

This chapter can only scratch the surface of the many issues raised by the idea that a new legal paradigm is needed to address the Anthropocene. One of these central issues is that this new paradigm needs to be developed and adopted by some actors with the legitimacy to do so, and that this legitimacy is likely to arise from democratic processes, but that democratic processes in all countries around the world might not currently support such a new paradigm. The ability of the elected branches of government to produce such a new paradigm is limited by the will of the people, while the judiciary does not have a mandate to transform the law at its will.[79]

VI. Conclusion

One conclusion from the previous sections is that earth system law cannot be made by scientific, global, or national institutions alone. Rather, the making of earth system law should involve all three types of institutions: it should be a shared competence. Scientific institutions provide the necessary understanding of global, diffuse, and cumulative issues and the possible ways of addressing them. Global institutions are indispensable to addressing collective action problems by coordinating national action. National institutions, however, remain the essential basis for any legitimate, democratic, and effective law or governance.

Therefore, the competence for making earth system law must be a competence shared by these three types of institutions. In this regard, a parallel can be drawn with the principle of subsidiarity under European Union law. In areas of shared competence, Article 5(3) of the Treaty on European Union provides that

> the Union shall act only if and in so far as the objectives of the proposed action cannot be sufficiently achieved by the Member States … but can rather, by reason of the scale or effects of the proposed action, be better achieved at Union level.[80]

Similarly, scientific, global, and national institutions should understand the limits of their competence and the need to coordinate with other types of institutions in a harmonious, respectful, and mutually beneficial way.

Thus, each type of institution should limit its own action in order to respect the competence of other types of institutions. Scientific institutions should more clearly confine themselves to developing and circulating scientific findings – to the exclusion of scientists' policy recommendations – or else scientists' policy recommendations should be more clearly distinguished from scientific findings. Global institutions should continue to recognise the sovereignty of states in international

[79] LJ Kotzé and others, 'Courts, Climate Litigation and the Evolution of Earth System Law' (2024) 15 *Global Policy* 5.

[80] Consolidated Version of the Treaty on the European Union [2012] OJ C 326/13, Art 5(3).

responses to global environmental issues, a principle that should be limited only when justified, for instance, to coordinate national action aimed at addressing a collective action problem. And national institutions should recognise that democracy, while playing a fundamental role in legitimising law and governance, does not justify the short-sighted pursuance of the will of the majority (of voters) at the expense of the fundamental interests of national minorities, foreigners, ecosystems, and future generations.

14

Moving Images, Moving Society: Environmental Cinema and Earth System Law

BENJAMIN J RICHARDSON

I. Seeing is Believing

Have you ever considered how much you would know about the climate crisis, polluted oceans, or the loss of wildlife around the world, if there were not thousands of movies or television shows about such subjects? Telling stories is one of humankind's oldest pastimes, and with the invention and popularisation of photography in the mid-nineteenth century, then film from the early twentieth century onward, our visual culture has become one of our dominant means of storytelling.[1] Films dealing with environmental subjects, from erudite natural history documentaries to science-fiction thrillers, may help raise public awareness of nature conservation,[2] stimulate concern for the plight of endangered species,[3] and potentially change environmental practices.[4] The impact of any individual film on social change, including law reform, is usually impossible to measure or discern; yet, as a whole, the research canvassed later in this chapter suggests that the stories told in cinema influence public awareness and help forge solutions to environmental problems. Such influence depends not only on film's celluloid content but how it's produced and circulated.[5]

[1] J Kromm and SB Bakewell, *A History of Visual Culture: Western Civilization from the 18th to the 21st Century* (Oxford, Berg Publishers, 2010).

[2] K Hofman and K Hughes, 'Protecting the Great Barrier Reef: Analysing the Impact of a Conservation Documentary and Post-viewing Strategies on Long-term Conservation Behaviour' (2018) 24 *Environmental Education Research* 521, 521.

[3] JR O'Bryhim and ECM Parsons, 'Increased Knowledge about Sharks Increases Public Concern about Their Conservation' (2015) 56 *Marine Policy* 43.

[4] C Shreedhar and S Mourato, 'Experimental Evidence on the Impact of Biodiversity Conservation Videos on Charitable Donations' (2019) 158 *Ecological Economics* 180.

[5] P Smith, 'Introduction' in P Smith (ed), *The Historian and Film* (Cambridge, Cambridge University Press, 1976) 8.

This chapter examines environmental cinema as a potential agent of social change, and specifically its capacity to influence laws addressing our environmental problems from local to global scales; even on a planetary scale. The development of earth system law is postulated by this chapter as being aided by films with appropriate environmental content and mass distribution. By 'environmental cinema', I mean films, from major fiction features to short documentaries, that have the natural world as their principal subject.[6] A more extensive treatment of the subject-matter would unveil differences in the impact and role of different film genres, as well as furnish case studies on specific films; for the purpose of this introductory chapter on the subject however, such details of environmental cinema will be considered only lightly as illustrative examples.

At first glance, it might seem odd to write about environmental cinema in a book about earth system law, a concept I won't dwell on as it's generously discussed by others in this book as well as other researchers.[7] My contribution to this scholarship is shaped by concern that much environmental law literature, including in the earth system niche, dwells on its destination rather than the journey; it focuses on the planet we wish for, not the path to attaining it. Utopian dreaming, from nature's rights to the common heritage of humankind, inebriates many visions of better laws to govern the crisis of the Anthropocene.[8] Undoubtedly, we need revolutionary ideals for building earth system law or other radical mutations in how we govern our interactions with the natural world, as ideals can inspire and channel action.

Yet, how we might *reach* that destination is often downplayed, or examined through a narrow lens such as evaluation of the relative merits of different regulatory tools,[9] or the impact of test-case litigation,[10] or constitutional law reform,[11] among many other options. Recent, novel legal strategies, such as the convening of citizen assemblies – notably Scotland's Climate Assembly held from 2020 to 2022[12] – or raising complaints through international forums, such as that brought in 2019

[6] B McClanahan, A Brisman and N South, 'Green Criminology, Culture and Cinema' in N Rafter and M Brown (eds), *The Oxford Encyclopedia of Crime, Media and Popular Culture* (Oxford, Oxford University Press, 2018).

[7] LJ Kotzé and RE Kim, 'Earth System Law: The Juridical Dimensions of Earth System Governance' (2019) *Earth System Governance* 100003.

[8] K Baslar, *The Concept of the Common Heritage of Mankind in International Law* (Leiden, Nijhoff, 1998); J Jaria-Manzano and S Borrás (eds), *Research Handbook on Global Climate Constitutionalism* (Cheltenham, Edward Elgar Publishing, 2019); BJ Richardson, 'Imagined Utopias' in P Burdon and J Martel (eds), *Research Handbook of Law and the Anthropocene* (Abingdon-on-Thames, Routledge, 2023) 289.

[9] JL Huffman, 'The Past and Future of Environmental Law' (2000) 30 *Environmental Law* 23.

[10] See https://www.clientearth.org.

[11] DR Boyd, *The Rights of Nature: A Legal Revolution That Could Save the World* (Toronto, ECW Press, 2017).

[12] N Andrews, S Elstub, S McVean, and G Sandie, *Scotland's Climate Assembly Research Report – Process, Impact and Assembly member experience* (Edinburgh, Scottish Government Research, 2022).

by climate-impacted youth to a United Nations (UN) Committee,[13] and climate litigation in domestic courts, such as the *Sharma* case in Australia,[14] are also garnering attention as means of change.

Whilst the foregoing initiatives are valuable developments for researchers to consider, we should not lose sight of the underlying relationships between law and social change, as they can illuminate the actors, processes and contexts by which law reform might ensue. Commendably, a few earth system law specialists are exploring these relationships between legal and social change, such as Michael Leach's enquiries into how different subsystems of society (eg, the market, civil society and law) may interact to facilitate law reform.[15] There is also recent valuable research on strategies to give effect to new meta-norms, such as those relating to the rights of nature.[16] Insights from history, sociology, psychology, political science, the visual arts, and other disciplines may help legal scholars better understand how societies respond to their environmental problems, and illuminate opportunities for and barriers to change. One of these domains, cinema, has particular relevance in the quest for earth system law, along with environmental law reform generally.

The next section of this chapter explains the relevance of aesthetics and the arts to shaping humans' interactions with the natural world, as they are relevant to a background understanding of the salience of visual culture to humans' environmental behaviour. Thereafter, in section III, I examine environmental cinema itself in terms of how it may influence society and stimulate policy and legal changes. I also consider here some specific films and genres to illustrate the relevance of cinema to the journey to earth system law. The fourth section reflects on the social impact of some individual films and cinema generally in order to help appreciate how it may contribute to the journey to earth system law. In section V, I conclude this chapter with remarks on how teachers of environmental law can incorporate film into their classrooms in training and motivating the next generation of environmental law practitioners, scholars and activists.

II. Why Aesthetics Matter to Environmental Experiences and Action

I wish to step away briefly from cinema here to discuss the relevance of aesthetic experiences, and the arts, to people's interactions with nature, as cinema is not

[13] M Bryant, 'Young Climate Activists Vow to Keep Fighting despite UN Setback' (2021) *The Guardian* https://www.theguardian.com/environment/2021/oct/20/young-climate-activists-vow-to-keep-fighting-despite-un-setback.

[14] *Minister for the Environment v Sharma* [2022] FCAFC 35.

[15] MC Leach, 'Seeking "Systems" in Earth System Law: Boundaries, Identity, and Purpose in an Emergent Field' (2023) 15 *Earth System Governance* 100162.

[16] C Kauffman and P Martin, *The Politics of Rights of Nature: Strategies for Building a More Sustainable Future* (Cambridge MA, MIT Press, 2021).

just a conveyer of utilitarian or educational information but is also an art form and aesthetic experience of importance to understanding how cinema shapes public attitudes to nature and its legal governance. The aesthetic presentation of cinema has been recognised by researchers as crucial to the impact of film on audiences.[17]

Even with abundant scientific information about the planetary environmental crisis, from climate change to biodiversity loss, for many people the crisis is not yet palpable in their own, lived experiences. Despite the recent surge in forest fires, floods, droughts, storms and other palpitations of a distressed planet that some have personally suffered, for the vast majority these upheavals are encountered only vicariously via stories in newspapers, social media and other popular channels. (There is also the problem that the mainstream media can downplay or ignore climate change).[18] And many of the insidious environmental changes wrought by the Anthropocene are gestating too slowly to be perceptible even to those in their immediate vicinity, such as rising seas or acidifying oceans.

Sensory deficits of these temporally and spatially displaced impacts consequently may diminish the sense of urgency to act on climate change or other planetary crises that are central to the agenda of earth system law.[19] It reflects the proverbial phenomenon of 'out of sight, out of mind'. As Anthony Giddens explains in *The Politics of Climate Change*, 'since the dangers posed by global warming aren't tangible or visible in the course of day-to-day life … many will sit on their hands and do nothing of a concrete nature about them'.[20] In turn, the political will of governments (themselves also only bound to very brief political terms) to intervene lessens. This context is particularly relevant to earth system law, as its temporal and spatial scales of operation require lawmakers and other key stakeholders to address environmental changes on a scale often vastly beyond individuals' quotidian experiences.

Thus, we need other strategies to raise public awareness of environmental problems and motivate action beyond disseminating the 'facts and figures'.[21] Scientific evidence, economic calculations and ethical principles are crucial to guide earth system law but the emotional and sensory dimensions of people's experiences of the natural world also carry weight in building support for law reform. The aesthetic domain matters to how people experience, value and govern their interactions with the natural world, suggests the environmental aesthetics literature.[22]

[17] J Tarvainen, S Westman and P Oittinen, 'The Way Films Feel: Aesthetic Features and Mood in Film' (2015) 9(3) *Psychology of Aesthetics* 254; T Berliner, *Hollywood Aesthetic: Pleasure in American Cinema* (Oxford, Oxford University Press, 2017).

[18] K Pope and M Hertsgaard, 'Why Are the US News Media so Bad at Covering Climate Change?' (22 April 2019) *The Guardian*, https://www.theguardian.com/environment/2019/apr/22/why-is-the-us-news-media-so-bad-at-covering-climate-change.

[19] BJ Richardson, *Time and Environmental Law: Telling Nature's Time* (Cambridge, Cambridge University Press, 2017).

[20] A Giddens, *The Politics of Climate Change* (Cambridge, Polity Press, 2009) 2.

[21] M Miles, 'Representing Nature: Art and Climate Change' (2010) 17 *Cultural Geographies* 19.

[22] A Carlson, *Aesthetics and the Environment: The Appreciation of Nature, Art and Architecture* (Abingdon-on-Thames, Routledge, 2000).

Nature acquires aesthetic meaning through visual, acoustic and other sensory stimuli, while the anthropogenic impacts on it such as deforestation and pollution also have adverse aesthetic consequences, which can resonate more profoundly with some people than technical data about climate trends or biodiversity loss.[23] Our aesthetic valuation of the natural world via these sensory experiences can also occur via the arts, which have a long history of depicting and engaging with the natural world, such as landscape painting and wildlife photography. Visual representations of nature and its uses have been theorised as having significant cultural value.[24] The arts can have particular significance for engaging people aesthetically and emotionally in those realms of nature that are not directly experienced, such as remote wilderness areas, rare species, or ephemeral natural phenomena like the *aurora borealis*.

That some environmental aesthetic values have become objects of legal protection testifies to their cultural significance. Environmental laws have been adopted to protect natural beauty, such as England & Wales's Countryside and Rights of Way Act 2000 and the United States' Wild and Scenic Rivers Act of 1968, and to tackle pollution and other forms of environmental blight that spoil aesthetic appreciation of nature, such as New Zealand's Resource Management Act 1991. Similar objectives inform some international laws, such as in the World Heritage Convention of 1972[25] and the 1991 Madrid Protocol to the Antarctic Treaty of 1959 (Article 3(2)). However, the underpinning aesthetic standards for these and other laws have rarely been codified and there is limited aesthetic literacy among legal practitioners to implement them competently.

Earth system law, as presently understood, focuses on fundamental planetary-scale processes and tackling the roots of the socio-ecological crisis, rather than addressing nature's aesthetic values. Yet, just as landscape photography and painting helped win support for the creation of national parks from the late nineteenth century in Australia, the United States and other settler societies,[26] the aesthetic realm and its artistic expressions, including in cinema, can today help shift societal values and galvanise political support for the goals of earth system law. A seminal precedent was the repurposing by environmentalists of NASA's first images of Earth – the most revered being the iconic *Blue Marble* image taken by the Apollo 17 crew in 1972 at 45,000 km from Earth's surface. A mesmerising picture of a beautiful yet seemingly vulnerable planet, it was a beacon for the global environmental movement in the 1970s.[27] The image, of course, showed

[23] BJ Richardson, *The Art of Environmental Law: Governing with Aesthetics* (Oxford, Hart Publishing, 2019).

[24] SL Dobrin and S Morey (eds), *Ecosee: Image, Rhetoric, Nature* (New York, State University of New York Press, 2009).

[25] F Francioni (ed), *The 1972 World Heritage Convention: A Commentary* (Oxford, Oxford University Press, 2024).

[26] J Hore, *Visions of Nature: How Landscape Photography Shaped Settler Colonialism* (Oakland CA, University of California Press, 2022).

[27] R Kelsey, 'Reverse Shot: Earthrise and Blue Marble in the American Imagination' in EH Jazairy (ed), *Scales of the Earth* (Cambridge MA, Harvard University Press, 2011) 10.

a planet without borders or nation-states, unified spatially and timelessly in a manner congruent with earth system law.

The importance of such imagery has only grown since then, in our media-inebriated, digitally connected cultures, where the deployment of images, music and other creative expression has become an indispensable tool for social agitation on environmental issues. Environmental protest groups such as Extinction Rebellion and Just Stop Oil rely on artistic props such as costumes, stunts and street theatre to maximise their media attention.[28] Researchers such as James Jasper, Kevin DeLuca and William Mitchell have identified, with the rise of television, the internet and other media, the advent of a pictorial turn in politics where images have become crucial to political discourse.[29] Whilst image-based politics are invaluable for environmental activists to project a planet in distress to mass audiences, it has the downside of overly simplifying important messages, and they cannot in themselves furnish the basis for informed decision-making such as setting detailed standards to manage climate change or conserve biodiversity.

The foregoing remarks help situate environmental cinema within its wider aesthetic and social context. Through the arts, people can learn about and experience vicariously the aesthetic values of the natural world and the impacts of humankind, thereby cultivating deeper emotional connections to nature. The arts are also crucial to the political sphere, as imagery can stimulate public debate about seminal controversies and issues such as global warming, the rights of nature, and wilderness conservation.

III. Environmental Cinema

Film has enriched human culture for over a century, with its reach and influence having grown: from the first moving images in the 1890s, then the introduction of sound in the late 1920s, the mobilisation of film for government propaganda during the 1930s and 1940s, the emergence of television in the 1950s and use of film in corporate marketing, and finally, the digital and online revolution since the 1990s.[30] Like radio and the press, cinema is a mass medium but differs from them because it is a richer sensory medium that combines sound, images

[28] BJ Richardson, 'The Art of Disobedience: Climate Justice Activism' in D Brown, K Gwiazdon and L Westra (eds), *The Routledge Handbook of Applied Climate Change Ethics* (Abingdon-on-Thames, Routledge, 2023); TJ Demos, *Decolonizing Nature: Contemporary Art and the Politics of Ecology* (Berlin, Sternberg Press, 2016).

[29] WJT Mitchell, *Picture Theory: Essays on Verbal and Visual Representation* (Chicago IL, University of Chicago Press, 1995); JM Jasper, *The Art of Moral Protest: Culture, Biography, and Creativity in Social Movements* (Chicago IL, University of Chicago Press, 1999); K DeLuca, *Image Politics: The New Rhetoric of Environmental Activism* (Abingdon-on-Thames, Routledge, 2005).

[30] WW Dixon and GA Foster, *A Short History of Film*, 3rd edn (New Brunswick NJ, Rutgers University Press, 2018).

and narration, as well as having different modes of distribution and exhibition, such as picture houses and film festivals, that also help shape its reception and societal impact. The dominance of Hollywood studios such as Warner, Disney and Paramount in global feature film production and distribution – they hold the largest share of global box-office revenue – is a potential limiting factor to the types of environmental values expressed by the film industry and the industry's capacity to capture the diversity of human values and perspectives relevant to building earth system law. However, US dominance is waning, with rival filmmaking centres flourishing in the Global South, such as 'Nollywood' (Nigeria) and 'Bollywood' (India).

Whether as fiction features, documentaries or other cinematic genres, film has become a seminal part of the aesthetic landscape of environmental discourse. The growing societal debate and unease about the Anthropocene have stimulated numerous cinematic reflections, such as the Netflix-released film *Breaking Planetary Boundaries* (2021), narrated by David Attenborough and Johan Rockström. Film has become a powerful medium for conveying an increasingly hostile planet that threatens humanity itself, furnishing dramatising narratives and visually arresting accounts of industrial pollution, barren wastelands, shifting seas and dying wildlife. These offerings are often tied together by an underlying narrative of pending calamity but with the possibility of redemption if humankind can act urgently, by being more resourceful – harnessing new solution-enabling technologies from bio-genetics to geoengineering, repairing damage – or, as far-fetched as it seems, but shown in films such as *Avatar* (2009), by colonising other habitable planets. Such films use diverse cinematic techniques to tell their stories. Some rely heavily on aerial footage to convey the vastness of environmental change, such as deforested landscapes, huge mines gouged out of hillsides, scenes of immense crowds as a metonym for global population growth, and arresting imagery of devastation from fires or floods. Some films zoom-in on the plight of individuals or their local communities, taking a bottom-up approach to environmental permutations and impacts. And science fiction fantasies may rely on computer-generated imagery and 3D technology to jolt audiences.

Blockbusters such as *An Inconvenient Truth* (2006) and *Erin Brockovich* (2000), along with TV series such as David Attenborough's natural history epics, have attracted mass audiences and spawned considerable public interest. Illustratively, Attenborough's *Planet Earth III* series reached 10.6 million viewers in 2023,[31] whilst *Avatar* (2009) is the highest-grossing movie of all time. In recent years, environmental activists themselves have turned to making films as campaigning tools, such as *Wild Things* (2020), *I Am Greta* (2001) and *Franklin* (2022). Their circulation and impact have grown via dedicated eco-film festivals, online streaming,

[31] 'Planet Earth III Reaches 10.6 Million Viewers' (28 November 2023) *BBC*, https://www.bbc.co.uk/mediacentre/2023/planet-earth-iii-reaches-10-6-million-viewers.

and social media, supplementing the traditional venues of cinemas and home television. Concomitantly, lately a flurry of critical scholarship on environmental cinema has come to recognise is cultural salience in expressing, mediating or shaping public opinion, notably Robin Murray and Joseph Heumann's *Ecology and Popular Film*,[32] Willoquet-Maricondi's *Framing the World*,[33] Stephen Rust and others' *Ecocinema Theory and Practice*,[34] and Belinda Smaill's *Regarding Life: Animals and the Documentary Moving Image*.[35] Some researchers, such as Nadia Bozak, have even looked at the environmental footprint of the cinema industry itself.[36]

A complicated array of subfields or genres of environmental cinema now exist. No singular narrative or style connects them, and there are 'even contradictory themes of nature as power and nature as victim'.[37] Within fiction films, environmental issues have been explicitly addressed through genres such as adventure, animation, disaster and science fiction films, although sometimes environmental references may simply be quietly weaved into plots.[38] Climate change science fiction films with eschatological-type plots and dystopian futures have been stirring the public's imagination for at least two decades. Blockbusters include *The Day After Tomorrow* (2004), and *Snowpiercer* (2013), the latter depicting a failed climate geoengineering experiment that unintentionally created a frozen planet. Futuristic dystopias about the climate crisis, however, often get the science wrong and can be so unreal as to make audiences misunderstand the true nature of global warming. Another genre of environment-related films is the zombie apocalypse. Tales of human survival in the wake of apocalypse, such as in *28 Days Later* (2002) and its sequels, *28 Weeks Later* (2007) and *28 Years Later* (2025), can help convey the limits of human civilisation and that its survival depends ultimately on people accommodating themselves to the natural world rather than wanting to dominate it.

Some fiction films purport to be more subtle in their messages but just as impactful. The science fiction epic *Avatar* (2009) – whose success inspired the sequels *Avatar: The Way of Water* (2022) and *Avatar: Fire and Ash* (2025) – ostensibly concerns a conflict between a rapacious mining venture and an

[32] RL Murray and JK Heumann, *Ecology and Popular Film* (Albany NY, State University of New York Press, 2009).

[33] P Willoquet-Maricondi (ed), *Framing the World: Explorations in Ecocriticism and Film* (Charlottesville VA, University of Virginia Press, 2010).

[34] S Rust, S Monani and S Cubitt (eds), *Ecocinema Theory and Practice* (Abingdon-on-Thames, Routledge, 2013).

[35] B Smaill, *Regarding Life: Animals and the Documentary Moving Image* (Albany NY, State University of New York Press, 2016).

[36] N Bozak, *The Cinematic Footprint: Lights, Camera, Natural Resources* (New Brunswick NJ, Rutgers University Press, 2012).

[37] L Braudy, 'The Genre of Nature: Ceremonies of Innocence' in N Browne (ed), *Refiguring American Film Genres: Theory and History* (Oakland CA, University of California Press, 1998) 278, 296.

[38] A O'Brien, *Film and the Natural Environment: Elements and Atmospheres* (New York, Columbia University Press, 2017).

Indigenous tribe, but it has also been widely interpreted as about the political divisions in the United States between conservatives and liberals regarding environmental protection, even though the film does not explicitly state so.[39] Another example is *Don't Look Up* (2021), a comedy about how the insouciant media and struthious public ignore the threat of a life-extinguishing comet hurtling towards Earth; but at another level, it's a climate change allegory. A star-studded line-up, including Leonardo DiCaprio and Meryl Streep, contributed to its box-office success, and becoming Netflix's second most popular film debut to date.[40]

Some environmental fiction films are dramatised versions of true events, with one popular plot being the role of lawyers in obtaining environmental justice. *A Civil Action* (1998), starring John Travolta, is a true story of litigation against two corporations over the deaths of children caused by contaminated water that occurred in Massachusetts in the 1980s. *Erin Brockovich* (2000) stars Julia Roberts who plays a real-life heroine aided by a small-town law firm in uncovering contaminated drinking water in California and successfully taking on the heartless corporation responsible. A third American legal thriller that pitches the underdog against a corporate titan is *Dark Waters* (2019), that relives a case brought against the chemical manufacturer DuPont for unlawfully contaminating a town.

Documentary films are the most common cinema that explicitly engages with environmental subject-matter, and environmental activists use or make such films as tools of education and advocacy. Many documentaries use an expository style, of voice-over narration, sometimes supplemented with dialogue and interviews, often with academics or other experts such as ecologists, economists, historians or political analysts, as well as environmental activists and everyday persons from impacted communities. A major part of their gravitas lies in their pretence of objectivity, purporting to deal with real-life issues and problems.[41] The notion that any documentary can be strictly objective, without human judgement, is, however, dubious: every film involves human choices, from pointing the camera to editing the footage, and of course its accompanying narration.[42]

Until recent decades, environmental documentaries were predominantly natural history, educational works, showcasing the scientific and aesthetic values of nature rather than its degradation and damage.[43] These films have a

[39] 'The Politics of "Avatar:" Conservatives Attack Film's Political Message' (5 January 2010) *ABC News*, https://abcnews.go.com/Politics/Movies/politics-avatar-conservatives-attack-movies-political-messaging/story?id=9484885.

[40] KJ Yossman, 'Adam McKay's "Don't Look Up" smashes Netflix viewing records with over 150 million hours viewed' (6 January 2022) *Variety*, https://variety.com/2022/film/news/dont-look-up-netflix-weekly-viewing-records-1235147910/.

[41] C Plantinga, 'Moving Pictures and the Rhetoric of Nonfiction: Two Approaches' in D Bordwell and N Carroll (eds), *Post-Theory: Reconstructing Film Studies* (Madison WI, University of Wisconsin Press 1996) 307–24.

[42] B Nichols, *Introduction to Documentary* (Bloomington IN, Indiana University Press, 2010) xiii.

[43] F Schoog, 'Success–Collapse–Resilience: The Story of Homo Resiliens in Film Documentaries on the Anthropocene' (2022) 17 *Nature and Culture* 58.

long vintage, from the 1920s and 1930s which were, explains Gregg Mitman, a 'watershed in studies and discussions on the efficacy of visual education'.[44] Perhaps the first was the 1922-released *The Battle of the Ants*, a short, 12-minute silent film made in Britain by Geoffrey Barkas, showing two colonies of ants at a zoological gardens in conflict. It was one of 144 short black-and-white 'Secrets of Nature' productions of British Instructional Films about the nation's plants and animals, made between 1922 and 1933 for cinema release.[45] Natural history films grew considerably in the post-War era, as commercial giants got involved. In 1950 Walt Disney released the first of its 'True-Life Adventures' series, *Beaver Valley*, and others to follow including *The Living Desert* (1953) and *The Vanishing Prairie* (1954), the latter drawing attention to environmental loss caused by humans. Another pioneering film was the 1956 French production *The Silent World* (*Le monde du silence*), produced by Jacques Cousteau, featuring some of the first underwater cinematography of deep ocean life. In the 1960s and 1970s many of these films moved to the television screen and were shown in on-going series such as America's *Wild Kingdom* (1963–88), Australia's *In the Wild with Harry Butler* (1976–81), and Canada's *Untamed World* (1968–76). Whilst natural history documentaries can be very successful at reaching mass, mainstream audiences, where they emphasise a scientific understanding of a 'pristine' natural world, they problematically underplay environmental damage and loss, display anthropomorphism or disregard non-scientific environmental knowledge such as that of Indigenous peoples.[46]

In recent decades a vast array of environmental documentaries has been produced on themes that go beyond celebrating the aesthetic and scientific wonders of nature to examine critically its degradation by humankind, and reaching global audiences for distribution by Vimeo, Netflix and YouTube. The Dutch documentary *The Age of Man* (2015) offers a voice-over narration interspersed with interviewees consulted for their views of the Anthropocene, acknowledging humankind's responsibility but asking in an early scene: 'Are we responsible enough to manage this power?'. *The Anthropocene – The Age of Mankind* (2017) relies on interviews with scientists and other protagonists interspersed with footage of environmental change and degradation. Rahul Jain's *Invisible Demons* (2021) reveals the impacts of climate change and environmental degradation on the Indian mega-city of Delhi. The work of Canadian filmmaker and photographer Edward Burtynsky, who specialises in this genre, is featured in Jennifer Baichwal's *Manufactured Landscapes* (2006) on the effects of China's behemoth industrialisation. Another of his collaborations with Baichwal, *Anthropocene: The Human Epoch* (2018) offers an aestheticised portrayal of humanity's defacement of the planet, alternating panoramic drone footage and close-ups accompanied by sound

[44] G Mitman, 'Cinematic Nature: Hollywood Technology, Popular Culture, and the American Museum of Natural History' (1993) 84(4) *Isis* 637, 650.

[45] 'Secrets of Nature' https://secrets-of-nature.co.uk/films/615-2.

[46] MJ Williamson, 'Ethical Considerations in Natural History Film Production and the Need for Industry-Wide Best Practice' (2022) 34 *Global Ecology and Conservation* 01981.

effects, revealing horrific, disfigured landscapes in a variety of localities worldwide from a marble quarry in Italy to a vulture-filled landfill in Kenya. Whilst these films are visually frightening, they rarely engage explicitly with the political context of environmental destruction.

Some other documentaries seek to expose the corporate and political contexts of the environmental crisis, thus provoking debate about the adequacy of laws to govern it and the need for reforms that might dovetail with earth system law. Michael Moore's *Planet of the Humans* (2019) exposes the cosy partnerships between wealthy entrepreneurs and the green-tech revolution. *Climate Refugees* (2010) focuses on how global warming is precipitating millions of additional refugees displaced by rising seas and desiccated lands. Animal agriculture is critiqued in *Cowspiracy: The Sustainability Secret* (2014) as another major cause of climate change, from the land clearing for livestock to their methane emissions, and it seeks answers to why many environmental groups and regulators are ignoring or downplaying the impacts. Made by the same filmmakers, *Seaspiracy* (2021) presents a damning picture of the plight of our overfished oceans, and questions the 'sustainable' seafood sector, also unveiling dubious practices behind the labels issued by Dolphin Safe and the Marine Stewardship Council. The food economy is also vilified in the US documentary *Food Inc* (2008), which unveils problems including exploitative labour practices, animal cruelty, farm waste and unhealthy diets.

Based on Naomi Klein's book of the same name, *This Changes Everything* (2015) is among the more politically charged documentaries, featuring interviews from a variety of countries with people battling climate change, a crisis that the film postulates requires a radically different economic system. A more solutions-focused documentary is the French production *Tomorrow* (2015), which eschews doomsday narratives in favour of creative ways people can improve environmental outcomes in agriculture, energy and other sectors. Another feel-good documentary is *No Impact Man* (2009), which follows an American family's one-year experiment to live with zero impact on the environment, offering inspiration to environmentally concerned citizens. Even the eminent naturalist David Attenborough, now in his late 90s, has shifted his tone in series such *A Life on Our Planet* (2020) and *Breaking Boundaries: The Science of Our Planet* (2021) from showing pretty wildlife to offering more confronting and mournful reflections on a planet imperilled by humankind. Attenborough's new narrative shows how a better understanding of the planet could help humankind to save it.

IV. The Impact of Environmental Cinema

Environmental cinema matters because it facilitates the social change necessary for developing earth system law. The key principle it furnishes is that, just as earth system law is premised on viewing the Earth as a borderless, interrelated system, so too the process of social change to support law reform requires a transnational, shared cultural space for public dialogue and education – which film contributes to.

The contribution of environmental cinema aligns well with several of the themes of the Earth System Governance Network's Science and Implementation Plan, which also addresses processes for legal transformation, of law itself, and of society through law.[47] These include building vibrant civil societies, harnessing the mass media to challenge 'post-truth' misinformation, and fostering creative, interdisciplinary methods of education that utilise films and other popular culture materials. This requires, of course, that lawmakers support the film industry – especially, critical, independent filmmakers – and ensure open distribution of their work so that environmental cinema can play this role. Film censorship, and corporate domination of the film sector are challenges to this goal that the law can address.

Digging further into this subject, we can identify several ways in which film can dovetail with the agenda of earth system law. Foremostly, it is a transcultural mass medium, able to communicate across many societies through a universal, visual language. This capacity can help transcend the legal and spatial barriers to thinking on a planetary scale. Pietari Kääpä and Tommy Gustafsson consider how films dealing with global capitalism, environmental justice and sustainability have had a vital role in promoting transnational thinking.[48] Film production itself, explains Steven Rawle, has moved beyond national boundaries in becoming a truly transnational cultural field.[49] Film crews may work in multiple locations, bringing far-flung realms together into a narrative about the interconnected global impacts of climate change or plastic pollution, such as in *The Story of Plastic* (2019). And although the film industry has traditionally been dominated by the US, cinema has become much more open to communities around the world, with numerous environmental films coming from Global South filmmakers, such as *Temperature Rising* (2023) on climate justice activists in South Africa, or multinational collaborations such as *The Territory* (2022) about Amazonian Indigenous tribes fighting to save their homelands.

Further, as recognised by the Earth System Governance Science and Implementation Plan, film can aid democratic processes that are crucial to social and political transformation. This is largely owing to technological advances that have lowered the costs of film production as well as enabled global distribution through platforms such as Vimeo and YouTube, which have greatly assisted low-budget documentarians engaging with environmental issues who wish to reach wide audiences. Even students can now make their own environmental documentaries to aid their learning, as the final section of this chapter considers.[50]

[47] Earth System Governance Project, *Earth System Governance. Science and Implementation Plan of the Earth System Governance Project* (Utrecht, 2018), https://www.earthsystemgovernance.org/publication/earth-system-governance-science-and-implementation-plan/.

[48] P Kääpä and T Gustafsson (eds), *Transnational Ecocinema: Film Culture in an Era of Ecological Transformation* (Bristol, Intellect Books, 2013).

[49] S Rawle, *Transnational Cinema: An Introduction* (London, Bloomsbury Academic, 2018).

[50] H Harness and H Drossmann, 'The Environmental Education Through Filmmaking Project' (2011) 17(6) *Environmental Education Research* 829.

Also, film is a time-shifting mechanism, able to reshape human thinking across the enlarged temporal scales demanded of earth system thinking.[51] In engaging with the future, film can raise awareness of either a dystopian future we wish to avoid or a utopian world we hope to create. In this guise, film contributes to global narratives associated with earth system governance relating to promotion of sustainability, intergenerational equity and transnational thinking that require thinking in larger time-scales. Film has the potential to popularise and embed in mainstream culture the earth system sciences that deal with such themes, such as the time-frames modelled in climate science.

Cinema, though, has potential downsides that militate against some of these outcomes. It can be associated with nefarious propaganda, as was used systematically by Soviet Russia and Nazi Germany,[52] and now some contemporary authoritarian regimes such as in Russia and China. How one might neatly distinguish propaganda, with its pejorative connotations, from legitimate uses of film (and other media) designed for public education and information has vexed scholars.[53] This concern must at least be acknowledged, so that film audiences can be critically aware of how film can be manipulated for regressive purposes that undermine environmental goals, such as in corporate 'greenwashing' or government-sponsored, pro-development films. For example, many documentaries made by government-created, national film boards in Australia and Canada from the mid-1940s until late 1970s served such economic development purposes.[54]

A second potential downside of cinema is that increasing reliance on film, along with other electronic media, to mediate how people 'experience' nature, can contribute to the diminishment of their experiences in the natural world. Many now only observe wildlife outside its natural setting, in a motion picture or a zoo for instance.[55] This *ersatz* nature may not allow for the cultivation of deeper and more nuanced sensory connections to the natural world, especially to help overcome the 'othering' of nature that arises when it is viewed on a picture screen or in a zoo enclosure. Conversely, films that have critical, narrative content, such as documentaries exposing environmental crime and abuse, can help publicise problems and promote accountability; illustratively, the documentary *Blackfish* (2013) helped to end the cruel use of orcas as popular entertainment at SeaWorld.[56] So, the value and impact of environmental cinema can be highly varied and contextual.

[51] Richardson (n 19).

[52] R Taylor, *Film Propaganda: Soviet Russia and Nazi Germany* (London, Tauris, 1998).

[53] JAC Brown, *Techniques of Persuasion: From Propaganda to Brainwashing* (London, Penguin Books, 1963) 21.

[54] A Moran, *Projecting Australia: Government Film Since 1945* (Sydney, Currency Press, 1991); M Clemens, *Screening Nature and Nature: The Environmental Documentaries of the National Film Board, 1993-1974* (Athabasca, Athabasca University Press, 2022).

[55] R Louv, *Last Child in the Woods: Saving Our Children from Nature-Deficit Disorder* (London, Atlantic Books, 2010).

[56] L Thomas-Walters and D Veríssimo, 'Blackfish: How Captive Killer Whale Documentary Ended SeaWorld's Orca Breeding Programme' (21 June 2021) *The Conversation*, http://theconversation.com/blackfish-how-captive-killer-whale-documentary-ended-seaworlds-orca-breeding-programme-161775.

Thirdly, among potential downsides, not all environmental films have obvious governance content, and therefore may require audiences to make additional efforts to connect issues encountered on-screen and the real world of political and legal change. Popular films that explicitly address issues of environmental law, such as *A Civil Action* (1998) and *Erin Brockovich* (2001), tend to do so narrowly, such as dealing with tales about the pursuit of justice for individual victims of corporate pollution, rather than tackling the more complex agenda that earth system law challenges, such as problematising big business, the growth economy, and neoliberalism. Some more recent films, such as the documentary *I Am Greta* (2021), offer viewers a more critical insight into these issues relevant to that bigger agenda, and their critical impact is tied to how they are promoted and subject to critical reflection.[57] Thus, the impact of environmental cinema can depend not only on its celluloid content but also on the associated contexts in which film is distributed and reviewed.

To take films seriously as a means of moving society to shape the public's environmental knowledge and behaviour, we thus need to fully contextualise the wider domain of cinema. The film 'text' is where one will initially focus, analysing the subject-matter of the film, its cinematic techniques and other content-based features. Film theorist Thomas Elsaesser, however, rightly argues that films should also be analysed as an 'event', in which 'the actual film is only one piece' to consider along with its production and circulation.[58] This broader framework of enquiry enables one not only to assess the actual narratives and imagery in a film but also its wider institutional and cultural contexts. A film sponsored by a business corporation, for instance, might be tainted in the eyes of audiences as greenwashed marketing, or a government film might be tantamount to political propaganda. Independent, activist-made films no doubt also can carry their own agendas. The means by which a film is circulated and received, such as television, the internet, cinemas, and so on, as well as the country in which it is produced, also affect the type and size of audience reached, and how they react.

Few studies have examined the ability of films to move society.[59] My own research on the birth of environmental activism in Australia in the early 1970s has revealed the formative influence of film in shaping the politics and policies governing use of natural resources.[60] Films on climate change and other

[57] ED Ryalls and SR Mazzarella, 'Greta Thunberg: Climate Activism, Social Media, and the Greta Effect' in R Brinkmann (ed), *The Palgrave Handbook of Global Sustainability* (London, Palgrave Macmillan, 2023) 2491.

[58] T Elsaesser, 'Archives and Archaeologies: The Place of Non-Fiction Film in Contemporary Media' in V Hediger and P Vonderau (eds), *Films That Work* (Amsterdam, Amsterdam University Press, 2009) 19, 32.

[59] A Balmford and others, 'Hollywood, Climate Change, and the Public' (2004) 305(5691) *Science* 1713.

[60] BJ Richardson, 'Cinematic Activism and Tasmania's Lake Pedder: How Film Shaped Environmental History' (2025) 56(1) *Australian Historical Studies* 103.

environmental concerns have been studied for their influence on audiences.[61] Films about charismatic wildlife and scenic places have been found to trigger empathy and concern for their conservation.[62] A study of the impact on German audiences of the fantastical climate thriller *The Day After Tomorrow* (2004), based on polling 1,118 cinema visitors, showed that the movie 'did not lead to climate pessimism, but reinforced peoples' willingness to act, respectively to ask for political action. The film seems to have improved the public perception of science and the political role of scientists'.[63] Another study of this film's impact, from a survey of 529 US filmgoers, conducted by Yale University researchers, concluded that it significantly impacted 'climate change risk perceptions, conceptual models, behavioral intentions, and even voting intentions of moviegoers'.[64] But some commentators, such as Murray and Heumann, argue that the film's portrayal of global warming is so exaggerated and unrealistic, that the film is comical or risible rather than serious or informative.[65] Other research also suggests that mass media (cinema and other media) generally shapes public attitudes and resulting behaviours.[66]

Yet films individually vary dramatically in their affective capacity, depending on the subject-matter, cinematic techniques, and circulation. Various hypotheses have been suggested to decipher why some films are more impactful. Viewers may need sufficient film literacy to critically interpret cinema experiences.[67] It has also been hypothesised that film has a strong ability to tell stories, which resonates with audiences more than conveying facts and figures: the human brain more easily understands and recalls information presented as a story.[68] Use of comedy in film is another means to provoke heightened public attention.[69] Humour helps by 'getting people to "let their guard down"', thus overcoming audience resistance to an environmental message.[70] The relatability of characters in films is another

[61] ME Dunn, M Mills and D Veríssimo, 'Evaluating the Impact of the Documentary Series Blue Planet II on Viewers' Plastic Consumption Behaviors' (2020) 2 *Conservation Science and Practice* 1; A Franzen and S Mader, 'Can Climate Skeptics Be Convinced? The Effect of Nature Videos on Environmental Concern' (2020) 12 *Sustainability* 2972.

[62] Hofman and Hughes (n 2) 521.

[63] F Reusswig, J Schwarzkopf and P Pohlenz, 'Double Impact: The Climate Blockbuster *The Day After Tomorrow* and Its Impact on the German Cinema Public' (Potsdam, Potsdam Institute for Climate Impact Research, Report No 92, 2004) 'Abstract', p 3.

[64] A Leiserowitz, 'Before and After *The Day After Tomorrow*: A U.S. Study of Climate Change Risk Perception' (2004) 46 *Environment* 22, 34, https://climatecommunication.yale.edu/publications/before-and-after-the-day-after-tomorrow/.

[65] Murray and Heumann (n 32) 4–12.

[66] H Junsheng, et al, 'The Role of Mass Media in Communicating Climate Science: An Empirical Evidence' (2019) 238 *Journal of Cleaner Production* 117934, 1.

[67] Willoquet-Maricondi (n 33).

[68] MF Dahlstrom, 'Using Narratives and Storytelling to Communicate Science with Nonexpert Audiences' (2014) 111(Suppl 4) *Proceedings of the National Academy of Sciences* 13614.

[69] E Carroll-Monteil, 'Is Climate Change a Laughing Matter?' (2023) 29 *Environmental Education Research* 569.

[70] CM McCormack, JK Martin and KJH Williams, 'The Full Story: Understanding How Films Affect Environmental Change through the Lens of Narrative Persuasion' (2021) 3(6) *People and Nature* 1193.

emotional lever that can engage audiences.[71] Emphasising the story of individuals can help viewers empathise and draw comparisons between themselves and those featuring on screen. The timing of films' release also matters, such as before a political election. Such effects, however, may need to be reinforced by frequent references to the environmental issues on television or other viewing channels, as the spike in people's awareness created by a single film may be short-lived, suggest researchers.[72]

Thus far, we lack solid evidence that can disentangle cinema's wider impacts, including on law reform or government policy. Judgements can in most instances be made only in an anecdotal or contingent manner. Seasoned scholars suggest that 'an effective model for understanding *how* such films might persuade audiences to feel and act for the environment has not yet been developed'.[73] Jane Gaines explains that it is usually impossible to ascertain an individual film's impact empirically, given the difficulties of deciding what counts as a change or response, and ascertaining the relationship between cause and effect: 'we see very few examples of films that have been viewed widely let alone have sparked anything resembling a chain of social reactions'.[74] One instance where there *is* solid evidence is films that have led to an increase in visitors to the locations filmed, but that is merely as a form of tourism rather than necessarily involving any behavioural changes by audiences.[75] Advocating what he calls a 'coalition model', Whiteman suggests a better approach to understanding cinema's impact is to focus less on the effect of individual films and instead consider cinema's broader context of production and circulation, including how social movements use films as a campaigning tool.[76] Taking that cue, Caty Chattoo examined how documentaries on such diverse subjects as animal cruelty, racial injustice and privacy violations have disrupted cultural narratives and stimulated activists.[77] Films such as *The Corporation* (2003) and *Super Size Me* (2004) that were distributed in cinemas were major successes in shaping public discourse about corporate social responsibility.[78]

Networks are developing in the film industry for promoting awareness and dialogue on environmental problems. The Hollywood-based Climate Ambassadors

[71] R Gregg, 'Environmental Documentary Film: A Contemporary Tool for Social Movement' (MA Thesis, University of Montana, 2011) 66, 77.

[72] T Lowe, 'Does Tomorrow Ever Come? Disaster Narrative and Public Perceptions of Climate Change' (2006) 15 *Public Understanding of Science* 435.

[73] McCormack, Martin and Williams (n 70) 1193.

[74] J Gaines, 'Political Mimesis' in J Gaines and M Renov (eds), *Collecting Visible Evidence* (Minneapolis MN, University of Minnesota Press, 1999) 84, 86.

[75] N Tooke and M Baker, 'Seeing Is Believing: The Effect of Film on Visitor Numbers to Screened Locations' (1996) 17 *Tourism Management* 87.

[76] D Whiteman, 'Out of the Theaters and into the Streets: A Coalition Model of the Political Impact of Documentary Film and Video' (2004) 21 *Political Communication* 51.

[77] CB Chattoo, *Story Movements: How Documentaries Empower People and Inspire Social Change* (Oxford, Oxford University Press, 2020).

[78] E Bell, '*The Corporation* 10 Years On: An Interview and an Audience with Joel Bakan' (2015) 25(3) *Journal of Management Inquiry* 344.

Network's mission is to provide 'training and a community resource platform for entertainment industry professionals committed to changing the culture around climate change in the workplace'.[79] In Great Britain, the biennial Climate Crisis Film Festival promotes itself as 'pioneering, aspirational, grassroots and youth-led', with the focus on 'channelling constructive collection action and providing an intersectional analysis of climate, politics, economics and social justice'.[80] The inaugural Climate Crisis Film Festival was held online and in-person in Glasgow to coincide with the COP26 Climate Summit held there. There are also vast informal networks on social media for dissemination of and dialogue on environmental cinema that can reach mass audiences.

In conclusion at this juncture, whilst we cannot quantify cinema's precise impacts, we can reflect on the pathways and contexts by which it contributes to public discourse on the environment and its problems that may be relevant to earth system law thinking and making. It is most productive to focus on analysing how films engender public dialogue, by examining media coverage and wider debate associated with a movie rather than trying to quantify any specific, cause-and-effect impact on public policy or law. In this regard, film scholar James Monaco's advice is helpful: rather than seeking to decipher 'what caused what', we should seek to understand 'what is related to what', ascertaining how different phenomena 'relate to each other and the world around them'.[81]

But just because we cannot *quantify* the impact of cinema does not mean it lacks impact. I suggest three distinct realms in which environmental cinema can contribute to the processes that facilitate the reforms that earth system law seeks to drive. Most directly, films can furnish visual representation of natural places and accompanying narration, which can shape societal understandings of the environment and its uses, especially for people who cannot personally experience such places. Secondly, and obliquely, films can shape people's underlying values attached to nature, such as beliefs about its exploitation or conservation. In contrast to the first type of contribution, which conveys explicit factual information, the latter contribution is subtle and indirect, and is particularly mediated by how a film is curated, shown and interpreted. In this domain films can promote emotional connection to environmental causes. Thirdly, films can make a tertiary contribution, affecting the underlying legitimacy of those using or governing human impacts on the environment, from conservation to development purposes.

V. A Matter of Translation

There remains a difficulty of 'translating' societal shifts in understanding and activism engendered by cinema into legal standards and regulations. The difficulties of

[79] https://www.hollywoodclimatesummit.com/hcs-climate-ambassadors-network.
[80] https://www.climatecrisisff.co.uk/.
[81] J Monaco, *How to Read a Film* (Oxford, Oxford University Press, 2000) 231.

communicating the language of one societal domain, in this case popular culture and the entertainment sector, into legal norms and methods that inhabit another domain, have been theorised by sociologist Niklas Luhmann.[82] The increasing 'differentiation' of modern society into discrete subsystems of which the law is just one, operating with their own norms and logic,[83] makes it difficult, he argues, not only for other subsystems such as the realm of cinema to shape change in the legal system but also for the law in turn to shape other societal domains.[84] To put it another way, a film, for instance, about ocean pollution that shows the lethal impact on seabirds that ingest plastics will stir audiences' awareness that 'something must be done', but that empathy does not easily translate into a clear understanding of how to legally solve the problem in terms of who should be accountable and what regulations should be adopted.

I wish to close by suggesting what individual scholars of environmental law might do that is within their own power, and that's to make greater use of film in their own teaching. It is an important goal explicitly recognised in the Earth System Governance Science and Implementation Plan. In our digital era, film is a valuable teaching resource by which to engage university students. Law teaching has traditionally relied on printed texts such as court judgments, legislation and scholarly critiques in books and journals. But law is more than text; it is also about performance, from the drama in the courtroom or floor of parliament to the advocacy of street protesters. Traditionally, film has tended to be used in a minor, ad hoc way, such as designated 'background' watching or as a short diversion from the monotony of lecturing. Courses that embrace film as a core learning resource, however, have significant potential to innovatively engage students, in addition to offering courses that are explicitly devoted to the study of 'law-and-film', as a few law schools already do for students interested in media law, intellectual property and popular culture.[85] Carrie Menkel-Meadow and other legal scholars have researched how portrayals of lawyers and the legal system in film and television, arguing that they offer rich material for teachers to engage students and shift them from passive learning to active, critical reflection.[86]

One way to effectively use cinema is to have students watch an environmental film before a class, with the film providing a focal point for the theme

[82] N Luhmann, *Law as a Social System* (trans KA Ziegert, Oxford, Oxford University Press, 2004).

[83] N Luhmann, *The Differentiation of Society* (New York, Columbia University Press, 1982).

[84] H Willke, 'Societal Guidance Through Law?' in G Teubner (ed), *State, Law and Economy as Autopoietic Systems: Regulation and Autonomy in a New Perspective* (Milan, Giuffrè, 1992) 353, 354.

[85] For example, Osgoode Hall Law School in Toronto, Canada offers a course 'Law and Social Change: Documentary Film and Law', https://www.osgoode.yorku.ca/courses-and-seminars/law-social-change-documentary-film-and-law/.

[86] C Menkel-Meadow, 'The Sense and Sensibilities of Lawyers: Lawyering in Literature, Narratives, Film and Television and Ethical Choices Regarding Career and Craft' (1999) 31(1) *McGeorge Law Review* 1, 3; J Hermida, *Teaching Law and Criminal Justice through Popular Culture: A Deep Learning Approach in the Streaming Era* (Boca Raton FL, CRC Press, 2022); C Krueger and BJ Richardson, 'Fisk: Television legal dramas for educating lawyers', 28 January 2026, *Law Letter Journal* (The Law Society of Tasmania), https://www.lst.org.au/fisk-television-legal-dramas-for-educating-lawyers.

under discussion. Such an approach can also assist visual-dominant learners who are less engaged by the traditional 'chalk and talk' lecture. Students can watch law-related films for a variety of purposes, including to understand how environmental law is represented in films, the ways films engage with legal controversies, and the explicit use of film as a form of advocacy for the pursuit of environmental justice.

I follow this advice in my own teaching. For example, in my course on Corporate Social Responsibility I ask students to watch the documentary *Food, Inc.* (2008) to help inform class discussion about the environmental and social impacts of the corporate-dominated food industry, and then to compare how that industry is presently governed and the opportunities or barriers to law reform. In another course I teach, International Climate Change Law, I use the Canadian documentary *Rebellion: The Nature of Things* (2020), narrated by renowned environmentalist David Suzuki, to coax students to think about the strengths and weaknesses of civil disobedience in climate protests. The film helps students to visualise the tactics and effects of environmental protesting, and to consider their own lives and what they might personally do. I also teach a course on Law and Social Change, that covers topics beyond environmental law, where film is integrated into several topics as a learning resource for understanding the fundamental relationships between social changes and legal changes.

We should also consider how legal academics themselves might participate in films, either as expert interviewees in documentaries dealing with environmental law issues or even collaborating with cinematographers to make films. Illustratively, the University of British Columbia law academic Joel Bakan co-produced the documentary *The Corporation* (2003) and its sequel, *The New Corporation* (2020) – both seemingly influential on debates about corporate complicity in environmental degradation as well as the private sector's capacity to contribute to positive social change. Such collaborations also testify to the rich potential of transdisciplinary collaboration between humanities scholars and physical scientists, as recommended by the Earth System Governance: Science and Implementation Plan.

VI. Conclusion

Cinema has become pivotal for the cultural production and sharing of knowledge of humankind's environmental behaviours and impacts, from natural disasters to environmental crimes. Cinema can reflect the environmental outlooks of society, putting up a mirror to help audiences re-evaluate their own biases and behaviours. Furthermore, cinema can tell emotionally charged stories about the trials and tribulations of individuals' and communities' struggles, such as marginalised groups fighting environmental injustices, thereby fostering empathy and solidarity in audiences. We can also consider cinema as an agent of change, especially politically activist filmmaking, raising awareness of environmental problems such as plastic pollution or endangered species, stimulating wider public debate and pressure for legal accountability. Cinema is thus vital to the processes of social change to support the journey to earth system law, and, even more importantly, the journey of social transformation for sustainability that earth system law endeavours to facilitate.

Environmental cinema has also limitations. It is no panacea. A tension exists in framing environmental problems as cinematic spectacle, in which entertainment may be at the expense of education, information and social change. Environmental cinema itself can be embedded in big business, from Hollywood to Bollywood, as well as the cinema chains and online providers, and so its context in the capitalist system might be problematic. Changes in film technology and distribution have, however, made cinema a medium increasingly within the reach of grassroots communities and activists.[87]

In sum, then, this chapter has taken a novel approach to scholarly debates about earth system law by focusing not on the substantive content of such law but on the role of cinema in the processes of social transformation to underpin the development of the law. I have identified a number of opportunities for cinema to assist this transformation, yet also some risks and obstacles, given that film can be used equally by forces wishing to perpetuate the destructive status quo. For academics in law schools, such as myself, we can at least in one domain under our own control promote students' critical awareness of film as a potentially powerful aid to their learning and shaper of their future careers. This, in itself, should be valued as an important outcome – training more competent and empathetic lawyers, and hopefully nurturing earth system law itself.

[87] J Moncau and E Nikou, 'To Fight Invaders, Munduruku Women Wield Drone Cameras and Cellphones' (15 March 2022) *Mongabay*, https://news.mongabay.com/2022/03/to-fight-invaders-munduruku-women-wield-drone-cameras-and-cellphones/.

15

The United Times – A Chronopolitan Thought Experiment in Earth System Law

FREDERIC HANUSCH

I. Introduction

Immanuel Kant wrote *Perpetual Peace: A Philosophical Sketch* in 1795 in response to the turbulent political climate of his time and the aftermath of the French Revolution. The essay was a reflection on the possibility and principles of a lasting peace between hostile nations. Kant experienced firsthand the destructive consequences of war and the constant conflicts that plagued Europe. He was deeply troubled by the violent and unstable nature of international relations and sought to offer a philosophical examination of the conditions necessary to create a lasting peace.

The idea of cosmopolitanism underlying Kant's sketch can be traced back to Diogenes in the Ancient Greek period, later becoming popular within Stoicism, and then further developed until this day.[1] Consequently, a wide array of definitions and (critical) interpretations exists, but at the core of cosmopolitanism is the idea of 'world citizenship'. It is thus an idea of the spatial dissolution of boundaries where every human being should have the opportunities to gain the same quality of life irrespective of where they are born or live. Realising cosmopolitanism practically to even a limited degree took many attempts, including most prominently the foundation of the failed League of Nations, and later the United Nations (UN).

In this chapter, I posit that, similarly to the spatial conflicts observed by Kant, there exist widely unregulated *temporal conflicts* that require a juridical framework to be managed peacefully for the benefit of both people and the planet.[2] This also

[1] KA Appiah, *Cosmopolitanism: Ethics in a World of Strangers* (New York, WW Norton & Company, 2006).

[2] W Hope, 'Conflicting Temporalities: State, Nation, Economy and Democracy under Global Capitalism' (2009) 18 *Time and Society* 62; J Rifkin, *Time Wars: The Primary Conflict in Human History* (New York, Henry Holt & Co, 1987).

applies to earth system law. As suggested in the original paper that introduced the idea of earth system law, this juridical framework could be understood as a form of 'planetary earth law' that describes 'Earth-centered law for governance by and for all living beings from a planetary systems perspective'.[3] Thus, earth system law (and notably its planetary dimensions which I focus on in this chapter), is a comprehensive and yet at times highly idealistic and speculative approach to addressing the complex, multi-dimensional challenges of developing planetary politics with all living beings *across many timescales*.

Focusing on the broader theme of time and earth system law, this chapter first elaborates the need for temporal principles, ie why law must more comprehensively embrace temporality (section II), then surveys existing research on law and time to locate gaps (section III), develops a temporalised vision of earth system law with operational illustrations (section IV), advances the 'United Times' thought experiment and its charter as a design probe (section V), and concludes with implications for doctrine and future research (section VI).

II. The Need for Temporal Principles

To illustrate the necessity of temporal principles in earth system law, consider the issue of nuclear waste management. Most current legal regimes around the world typically address the immediate storage and safety of nuclear waste but hardly ever provide solutions for the long-term impacts of nuclear waste spanning thousands of years. A temporalised approach will involve creating legal frameworks that mandate the secure storage and monitoring of nuclear waste for periods far beyond the current century; possibly until a time when the waste is not harmful anymore, which might be hundreds of thousands of years into the future. This could involve not only physical containment strategies but also the development of communication methods to warn distant future societies about the dangers.

Similarly, coastal management provides a concrete example of why temporal legal principles are essential. Traditional coastal regulations might focus on immediate flood defences and zoning laws. However, with rising sea levels due to climate change, these measures are inadequate for an ever-changing planet. A temporalised, or future-oriented law, would require adaptive practices that plan for various sea-level rise scenarios over the coming centuries. This could include implementing buffer zones, restoring natural coastal barriers like mangrove forests, and constructing adaptable infrastructure that can be modified as conditions change.

To this end, several temporal questions arise, and most, if not all of these are relevant for the ongoing project of earth system law: Should we stabilise or reinvent the conditions of the geological epoch of the Holocene? To what extent

[3] LJ Kotzé and RE Kim, 'Earth System Law: The Juridical Dimensions of Earth System Governance' (2019) *Earth System Governance* 100003, 7.

does the (de)synchronisation of socio-economic demand and natural regeneration influence long-term prosperity? How can alternative futures be designed that counteract the ongoing and deepening 'Great-Again' retrotopias, such as those in the United States? Is it possible to avoid temporal violence between generations, such as those ignited by 'eternity costs' resulting from mining activities in the German Ruhr area? Can digitisation be used to preserve the diversity of planetary time? Is there a way to democratically represent all those future human and non-human generations possibly affected by our nuclear and other waste? Is it possible to harmonise an intentionally manipulated CO_2 cycle with exponential decarbonisation pathways? How can we create institutions with the capacity to attune contemporary political time with its stark focus on election cycles to the realities of planetary time and the development of life-sustaining resources over centuries? More pertinently, what forms of legislation enable the reconciliation of static legal frameworks with dynamic and expansive geological timescales of the earth system?

These questions clearly show the potential for temporal contestation to arise. Three historical phases set the scene for present temporal contestations emerging in particular from the activities of Western societies that need to be addressed by earth system law. First, the eighteenth century witnessed the rise of two competing time perspectives in the so-called 'Western' world. The first one is the result of a newly emerging historical consciousness separating a 'horizon of expectation' from a 'space of experience'.[4] Consequently, Western societies began to see the future as unconditioned and open to improvement and progress. Meanwhile, the detection of geological time led to another time perspective. The discovery of Earth's age by geologists, mineralogists, and palaeontologists laid the foundation for understanding the distinct history of the Earth and the resulting limited space for changing the future.[5] Right from the beginning, the two time perspectives proved incommensurable, because the historical consciousness perspective focuses on short-term human progress and change, whereas the geological time perspective stresses the slow, barely intentionally alterable processes of Earth's history.

Second, a manifestation phase of temporal contestation is situated in the 1950s. New evidence of Earth's time allows us to understand 'how the climate system operates, has operated and might be expected to operate in the future'; however, '[i]t has proved difficult to reconcile the timescales of past climate change with a human comprehension of how time passes'.[6] Such comprehension of time allowed for the development of a notion of a post-War future, building on a narrative of endless energy and resources. An extractivist futurism emerged, including the

[4] R Koselleck, *Futures Past: On the Semantics of Historical Time* (New York, Columbia University Press, 2004).

[5] C Caseldine, 'Conceptions of Time in (Paleo) Climate Science and Some Implications' (2012) 3 *Wiley Interdisciplinary Reviews: Climate Change* 329, 329–30.

[6] ibid 331, 335–36.

formation of an oil culture.[7] Although this futurism was based on geologically derived, and thus finite, resources (eg, fossil fuels and uranium), it was (and still is) fundamentally careless about the long-term impacts and secondary effects that the use of energy might have on future (non)-human generations. The deepening disconnect between geologic and societal timeframes resulted in the Great Acceleration, ie, the simultaneous and almost exponential increase of socio-economic activities that have increasingly destabilised the earth system.[8]

Third, since the 2000s, contestation has emerged around these two time perspectives. As long as human action did not substantially alter planetary processes, a disconnect between individual time perspectives and social conceptions of time on the one hand, and planetary times on the other, seemed largely irrelevant.[9] However, the ever-growing awareness that such separation of human histories from geological time is failing,[10] goes hand in hand with a temporal cleavage: 'The climate movement's reference to the scientific understanding of climate with its nonnegotiable timescales is at odds with populism's Great Again "retrotopias" referring to a romanticized fossil fuel past in which climate change is nonexistent'.[11] Despite such growing awareness, there are no institutions, legal, political or otherwise, that are capable of dealing with planetary times.[12]

In a planetary context, the need for a normative temporal foundation in the form of a novel planetary earth law principle called 'chronopolitanism' derives from the potential of time arrangements to modify not only the societal and political fabric, but also the capacity of the planet to sustain life. Going back to the first section of the chapter, should the idea of cosmopolitanism be complemented by that of a temporally-oriented principle of chronopolitanism?[13]

The basic idea of chronopolitanism is the timely dissolution of boundaries whereby every human and more-than-human being is afforded equivalent temporal standing irrespective of the temporal conditions into which they are born. In this vein, everyone should have the same opportunities to avoid suffering and be

[7] S Le Menager, *Living Oil: Petroleum Culture in the American Century* (Oxford, Oxford University Press, 2013); R Barrett and D Worden, *Oil Culture* (Minneapolis MN, University of Minnesota Press, 2014).

[8] W Steffen and others, 'Planetary Boundaries: Guiding Human Development on a Changing Planet' (2015) 347 *Science* 1259885.

[9] S Pahl, S Sheppard, C Boomsma and C Grove, 'Perceptions of Time in Relation to Climate Change' (2014) 5(3) *Wiley Interdisciplinary Reviews: Climate Change* 375.

[10] D Chakrabarty, 'The Climate of History: Four Theses' (2009) 35 *Critical Inquiry* 197.

[11] F Hanusch and S Meisch, 'The Temporal Cleavage: The Case of Populist Retrotopia vs. Climate Emergency' (2022) 31(5) *Environmental Politics* 883, 883.

[12] F Hanusch and F Biermann, 'Deep-Time Organizations: Learning Institutional Longevity from History' (2020) 7(1) *The Anthropocene Review* 19; F Hanusch, *The Politics of Deep Time* (Cambridge, Cambridge University Press, 2023).

[13] EF Cohen, '*Jus Tempus* in the Magna Carta: The Sovereignty of Time in Modern Politics and Citizenship' (2010) 43(3) *Political Science and Politics* 463; SB Cwerner, 'The Chronopolitan Ideal: Time, Belonging and Globalization' (2000) 9 *Time and Society* 331; H Dyke, *Time and Ethics: Essays at the Intersection* (Heidelberg, Springer Science & Business Media, 2003); JG Gunnell, *Political Philosophy and Time* (Middletown CT, Wesleyan University Press, 1968).

happy and thus gain the same quality of life irrespective of the temporal conditions into which they were, are, or will be born or live. Such a proposition is nested in proposals such as Arendt's[14] natality, Heidegger's[15] account of temporality and being-toward-death (*Sein zum Tode*) – where anxiety (*Angst*) discloses finitude and orients our understanding of time – and an as-yet-undefined association between generations through upholding the liberty to give birth.[16]

While we now know that planetary conditions can be shaped temporally, we barely know how to deal with this Promethean power, which is why *time* seems to be becoming dislodged as humankind acts as if we can establish temporal arrangements detached from Earth's temporalities. Given the historical phases of temporal contestations, from the eighteenth century's competing time perspectives to the Great Acceleration, and the recent recognition of the need to align human and planetary timescales, how can research on time and law inform and address these temporal conflicts?

III. Time and Legal Research

Since its beginning, the interdisciplinary study of time has been concerned with addressing a wide range of time-related topics.[17] The social sciences have been mostly excluded from time-relevant research and its concerns.[18] One of the few exceptions is the timescapes approach, which emphasises rhythmicity, timing, tempo and changes, as well as contingences for exploring environmental and socio-cultural phenomena.[19] Yet, the interdisciplinary study of time still lacks empirically translatable and widely applied integrative concepts to support a coherent investigative effort. In relation to timescapes, temporal design is defined as a way of 'highlighting the intersections of rhythms and the power relationships that are manifest and pacified through socially created hierarchies of time'.[20] Even though this concept of temporal design concentrates mainly on everyday life practices, the design perspective enables guidance for a

[14] H Arendt, *The Human Condition* (New York, Doubleday, 1958); O Marchart, 'Time for a New Beginning. Arendt, Benjamin, and the Messianic Conception of Political Temporality' (2006) 10 *Redescriptions: Political Thought and Conceptual History* 134, 136.

[15] M Heidegger, *Being and Time* (Oxford, Blackwell, 1962).

[16] A Shachar, *The Birthright Lottery: Citizenship and Global Inequality* (Cambridge MA, Harvard University Press, 2009).

[17] See, eg, JT Fraser, 'The Interdisciplinary Study of Time' (1967) 138 *Annals of the New York Academy of Sciences* 822.

[18] B Adam, *Time and Social Theory* (Cambridge, Polity Press, 1990).

[19] B Adam, *Timewatch: The Social Analysis of Time* (Cambridge, Polity Press, 1995); B Adam, *Timescapes of Modernity: The Environment and Invisible Hazards* (Abingdon-on-Thames, Routledge, 1998); B Adam and C Groves, *Future Matters: Action, Knowledge, Ethics* (Leiden, Brill, 2007).

[20] L Pschetz, *Temporal Design: Design for a Multi-Temporal World* (Doctoral Thesis, University of Dundee, 2014) 104, http://discovery.dundee.ac.uk/portal/files/6487763/PschetzThesisTemporalDesign.pdf.

societal time design, since it refers to invisible overall arrangements that are in need of associated temporal laws, which open up, cut, or even prevent possibilities for action; thereby, this perspective also includes an inherently political dimension.[21]

Looking at some research fields that are relevant for the present discussion, planetary change research often implicitly refers to time. In particular, the literature on so-called 'transformations towards sustainability' and the Anthropocene debate addresses various temporal elements: for example, the simultaneous efforts required due to temporal 'stop signs' based on planetary boundaries, such as net-zero emissions by 2050;[22] the non-linear dynamics of social realignments;[23] or sociotechnical transition pathways.[24] Here, it is implicitly assumed that a desirable social–natural order can be achieved through new circumstances of time.[25]

Societal and political research also addresses temporal considerations, such as election cycles or policy processes, but often without explicating and reflecting their genuine temporality, thus omitting to refer to the processes of change in their various forms, namely the phases of becoming, existing, and passing away, as well as the transience of things and the processes of change within ecosystems. Almost three decades ago, a review concluded that 'reflections on politics and time have remained unsystematic, implicit, and disperse, and our theoretical insights, conceptual tools, and empirical knowledge have remained severely limited'.[26] Specific, time-centred studies became more popular, particularly focusing on analysis of the European timescape.[27] However, these analyses primarily focus on the political system itself while a distinct connection between planetary times and politics remains, with few exceptions, missing.[28]

[21] L Burckhardt, 'Design ist unsichtbar' in H Höger (ed), *Design = unsichtbar* (Berlin, Cantz, 1995); K Krippendorff, *Die semantische Wende. Eine neue Grundlage für das Design* (Basel, Birkhäuser Verlag, 2013); C Mareis, *Theorien des Designs zur Einführung* (Hamburg, Junius Verlag, 2014).

[22] Steffen and others (n 8).

[23] D Messner, 'A Social Contract for Low Carbon and Sustainable Development: Reflections on Non-Linear Dynamics of Social Realignments and Technological Innovations in Transformation Processes' (2015) 98 *Technological Forecasting and Social Change* 260; GW Wallis, 'Chronopolitics: The Impact of Time Perspectives on the Dynamics of Change' (1970) 49(1) *Social Forces* 102.

[24] FW Geels, 'Technological Transitions as Evolutionary Reconfiguration Processes: A Multi-Level Perspective and a Case-Study' (2002) 31 *Research Policy* 1257; FW Geels and J Schot, 'Typology of Sociotechnical Transition Pathways' (2007) 36 *Research Policy* 399.

[25] K Kümmerer, 'The Ecological Impact of Time' (1996) 5 *Time and Society* 209; H Rau and R Edmondson, 'Time and Sustainability' in F Fahy and H Rau (eds), *Methods of Sustainability Research in the Social Sciences* (London, Sage, 2013); LA Reisch, *Time Policies for a Sustainable Society* (Heidelberg, Springer Science & Business Media, 2015).

[26] A Schedler and J Santiso, 'Democracy and Time: An Invitation' (1998) 19(1) *International Political Science Review* 5, 5.

[27] M Ekengren, *The Time of European Governance* (Manchester, Manchester University Press, 2002); KH Goetz and JH Meyer-Sahling, 'Political Time in the EU: Dimensions, Perspectives, Theories' (2009) 16 *Journal of European Public Policy* 180; KH Goetz, *The Oxford Handbook of Time and Politics* (Oxford, Oxford University Press, 2019).

[28] Hanusch (n 12).

This leads us to the question of how time is researched in law. Research on the interconnections between law and time exists, but not in the context of temporal conflicts regarding planetary times. In general terms, at least four research fields can be identified. The first is concerned with the philosophical and theoretical implications of time for law. This includes, eg, the extent to which legal norms are timeless or contextual, whether law can or should consider the passage of time, and whether legal decisions should be based on historical precedent and/or present circumstances.[29] Some explicit temporal law principles have been formulated, including *Ad tempus concessa post tempus censentur denegata* (What is granted for a time is considered denied after that time has passed); and *Ad tempus prohibitum post illud tempus censetur permissum* (What is prohibited for a time is considered permitted after that time has passed).

A second research field investigates legal history, namely how law changes over time. This includes the historical roots of legal concepts, institutions, and practices, and how they have evolved in response to changing social, economic, political and other conditions.[30]

A third research field is concerned with how law engages with and shapes the future. The challenge here is, for example, how legal institutions and practices, such as regulation, planning, and forecasting are to be used to manage future risks and uncertainties.[31] In this context the emphasis has been on future generations and specifically how law could embrace future generations as legal subjects, or at the very least, protect the interests of future generations in a more general sense. While it is encouraging that law increasingly focuses on future generations, it is also uncertain whether a focus on future generations might not ultimately detract from present efforts to enhance sustainability: 'the appeal to future generations obfuscates, rendering a series of critical boundaries diffuse, and, in doing so, abjures concrete urgent existing responsibilities towards those alive today in the same gesture that nominally assumes them for an abstract unformed future'.[32]

A fourth research field analyses the ways in which law constructs and regulates time. This includes how legal systems measure and mark time, how legal concepts such as 'past', 'present', and 'future' are used in legal reasoning, how sunset clauses divide the future from the past, and how legal institutions such as courts and legislatures manage the temporal dimensions of legal disputes.[33]

[29] T Chowdhury, *Time, Temporality and Legal Judgment* (Abingdon-on-Thames, Routledge, 2020).

[30] MD Dubber and C Tomlins (eds), *The Oxford Handbook of Legal History* (Oxford, Oxford University Press 2018).

[31] E Stokes, 'Beyond Evidence: Anticipatory Regimes in Law' (2021) 43 *Law and Policy* 73.

[32] S Humphreys, 'Against Future Generations' (2022) 33(4) *European Journal of International Law* 1061, 1061.

[33] A Wills, 'Old Crimes, New States and the Temporal Jurisdiction of the International Criminal Court' (2014) 12 *Journal of International Criminal Justice* 407; A Kouroutakis, *The Constitutional Value of Sunset Clauses: An Historical and Normative Analysis* (Abingdon-on-Thames, Routledge, 2016).

Two recent books particularly stand out as innovative examples of legal research specifically concerned with law, time and temporality. First, *Law and Time* addresses from an interdisciplinary perspective the concept of irreducible social time for law, which emerges from a continuous interweaving of social interactions that are both structured and contextual.[34] Within this framework, law plays a dual role: it serves as a pillar that maintains the status quo and stability, while subtly shaping new directions for social development. Time in this context is made in the same way as is the law with which it interacts. Second, *Time and Environmental Law* by Richardson (also in this book), considers 'both why environmental law is misaligned with nature's temporalities and how that dissonance can be overcome',[35] emphasising that 'the kernel of reform should be ecological restoration'.[36] Within this framework, not only should alignment of contemporary law with nature's past become possible, but also other temporal dimensions set in interaction with law.

The remainder of this chapter builds on but also aims to go beyond these approaches. It aims to elaborate a clearer *planetary perspective* in research on time and law that combines a broad perspective of time and its multiple dimensions with the vastness of the planetary processes it interacts with.

IV. Temporalising Earth System Law

Time has always been a central dimension for humankind and for our interactions with the Earth. Consequently, time has been a consistent theme of philosophy and the sciences, and specific issues such as social acceleration or future generations have recently gained greater attention in the humanities and social sciences. However, to investigate and direct the influence of time on planetary change, more temporal elements, ranging from rhythms to tempos, must be explored and integrated into the body of earth system law principles. This is necessary, since humankind seems increasingly able to manipulate temporal conditions extensively and thus to significantly influence planetary change, resulting in conflicts about how such investigations should be conducted. Law, as a social steering mechanism, is aptly positioned to govern how humans change temporal conditions and impact planetary health.

To make the idea of temporalising earth system law more concrete, let's consider the principle of intergenerational equity. This principle can be practically applied by integrating it into the legal requirements for environmental impact assessments (EIAs). Currently, EIAs often focus on the immediate and short-term impacts of

[34] S Beynon-Jones and E Grabham, *Law and Time* (Abingdon-on-Thames, Routledge, 2018).

[35] BJ Richardson, *Time and Environmental Law: Telling Nature's Time* (Cambridge, Cambridge University Press, 2017) 43.

[36] ibid 45.

proposed projects. A temporalised approach would require these assessments to also much more explicitly evaluate the proposal's long-term effects on future generations. For example, a new highway project would need to consider not only its immediate environmental footprint, but also its potential impact on future land use patterns, biodiversity, carbon emissions, and future lives over the coming centuries. Another example is the management of freshwater resources. Laws governing water use and distribution often fail to take account of the long-term functioning of aquifers and rivers. Properly temporalised legislation would enforce appropriate withdrawal rates by also considering projections of water availability and demand over the coming decades within the context of a changing climate. This could prevent the over-extraction of groundwater, which leads to issues like land subsidence and the depletion of water resources vital for future human and non-human generations.

If one reveals the dimension of time inscribed in planetary relationships, numerous possibilities for action open up. Humans can free themselves from their 'temporal immaturity', as it were, meaning that people can be temporally more literate due to their temporal capabilities. This could mean, for instance, developing long-term planning skills that span generations. This is not only an act of enlightenment but also permits the governability of planetary conditions in the first place. For example, by acknowledging and understanding the time-bound nature of environmental cycles, we can better manage planetary aspects and processes. To this end, we must learn to interpret and change the world in terms of time; for instance, by analysing historical data on deforestation trends, we can implement policies that not only address current forest preservation but also aim to restore ecosystems over the next several decades. Since this process cannot be value-free, it is necessary to offer orientation, for instance by applying the usufruct principle, which allows people to use and benefit from resources while ensuring their preservation for future generations. This could guide policies on resource management, encouraging individuals to act as caretakers of the planet for those who come after them. Considering that we cannot be separated from the circumstances into which we are ontologically 'thrown', opportunities for a good life must be made possible not only regardless of spatial circumstances such as birthplace or place of residence, but also regardless of temporal factors such as generation or societal times.

Planetary conditions can then be addressed more purposefully than before by democratically negotiated arrangements of the past, present and the future; or through deliberately initiated phases of rupture, evolution and conservation. Think of the establishment of the UN after World War II, which was a deliberate effort to create a global governance structure to prevent future conflicts. Similarly, the transition from fossil to renewable energy sources in various countries represents an evolution phase aimed at addressing climate change.

Much of the body of earth system law scholarship traditionally focuses on spatial dimensions and jurisdictional boundaries rather than the temporal dynamics of ecological and social systems.[37] The general view is that earth system law is 'informed by a planetary boundaries perspective that transcends geographic and jurisdictional boundaries'.[38] Even though the juridical treatment of the planetary boundaries might imply temporality, also because of its referencing of concepts such as climate tipping elements, it does not explicitly foreground how earth system law explicitly deals or should deal with temporal boundaries.[39] A temporalised vision of earth system law based on temporal boundaries might take its departure from a different angle, such as intergenerational freedom and equity metrics that inform the way we want to live with Earth's temporalities.

V. The United Times

Departing from the foregoing, this section develops a thought experiment that showcases an organisation which might inspire the formation of a temporalised form of earth system law. I call this hypothetical organisation, the United Times. As noted in the Introduction, assuming that the idea of cosmopolitanism materialised in the foundation of the UN to some extent at least, a thought experiment of creating a United Times might shed some light on the question how to deal with the temporal dimensions of earth system law. This thought experiment is essentially about an organisation, designed to deal with the challenges of temporality, which might never materialise in any future but which is worth thinking about because it could serve legal thought as a point of reference for a potentially more practical debate on how to temporalise earth system law.

Thought experiments as a method of legal theory can stimulate speculation about the construction of alternative legal frameworks, their possible implications, and potential changes in and of law more generally.[40] They might create imaginary scenarios to test the reasoning of various legal arguments in a controlled way or counterfactual manner. Traditional legal thought experiments include the trolley problem, the veil of ignorance, or the lifeboat scenario, often focusing on principles of justice, with specific examples in global environmental law including, for example, the tragedy of the commons or the spaceship Earth analogy. Currently, law's possible embrace of a planetary dimension is discussed with the '"question

[37] See, Kotzé, Angstadt and Kim, Chapter 2 in this book.

[38] Kotzé and Kim (n 3) 7; RE Kim, C Blanchard and LJ Kotzé, 'Law, Systems, and Planet Earth' (2022) 11 *Earth System Governance* 100127.

[39] See, eg D French and LJ Kotzé (eds), *Research Handbook on Law, Governance and Planetary Boundaries* (Cheltenham, Edward Elgar Publishing, 2021).

[40] G Domenech-Pascual, 'Thought Experiments in Law' [2021] (Special Issue: Experimental Legislation in Times of Crisis) *Law and Method* 1.

of possibilities" as a leitmotif', asking 'What could law become?'.[41] In conjunction with the speculative design of novel organisations, thought experiments can thus be seen as an enabler of future juridical circumstances and catalysts connecting law principles to real-world developments.[42]

Throughout history, humans have developed ever-more complex ways of both building and maintaining diverse relationships and influencing the planet. In recent decades this has led to the emergence of new challenges and opportunities with which juridical thinking and action continue to grapple. The advent of the Anthropocene debate suggests that humankind has acquired the ability to alter the world in ways that will affect many generations to come – indeed, it has already begun to do so. But these interventions on planetary change occur to a large degree unintentionally and are driven by Holocene institutions that were established to address challenges that arose in previous centuries and that were perceived to be of a smaller temporal and spatial scale.[43] In the words of British author George Monbiot: 'It is a world of our making, but not of our choice'.[44]

The United Times would serve as a complementary institution to the UN, specifically designed to address temporal politics. For instance, the United Times could facilitate cooperation on long-term projects such as the Great Green Wall initiative in Africa, which aims to combat desertification and create livelihoods. By providing a temporal framework, the United Times would ensure that such projects are planned and executed with a long-term vision, securing benefits for both present and future generations. The United Times would also address the rapid occupation of Low Earth Orbit. While current space law focuses on immediate launch rights, the United Times could establish 'orbital decay quotas' to ensure that present-day commercial satellite expansion does not permanently obstruct space access. By auditing the long-term debris footprint of megaconstellations, it would force a reconciliation between the nanosecond speeds of digital telecommunications and the multi-century 'cleansing' rhythms of the exosphere. This would involve mandate-based life-cycle assessments to prevent the atmospheric equivalent of a 'temporal enclosure'.

Based on the notion of a world of many worlds,[45] let us imagine for a second that there is an international organisation named the United Times: What would

[41] L Mai, 'The "Question of Possibilities" as a Leitmotif for Re-imagining Law for the "Anthropocene"' (2022) 13 *Global Policy* 49, 49.

[42] L Barendregt and NS Vaage, 'Speculative Design as Thought Experiment' (2021) 7 *She Ji: The Journal of Design, Economics, and Innovation* 374; M Blythe and E Encinas, 'Research Fiction and Thought Experiments in Design' (2018) 12(1) *Foundations and Trends in Human–Computer Interaction* 1.

[43] LJ Kotzé and RE Kim, 'Exploring the Analytical, Normative and Transformative Dimensions of Earth System Law' (2021) 50(6) *Environmental Policy and Law* 457.

[44] G Monbiot, 'Lost in the 21st Century' (3 February 2015), https://www.monbiot.com/2015/02/03/lost-in-the-21st-century/.

[45] M de la Cadena and M Blaser, *A World of Many Worlds* (Durham NC, Duke University Press, 2018).

be its portfolio? Essentially, it will have to organise time based on a United Times Charter (not unlike the UN), which might in its core read as follows:

Preamble

We, the earthlings and temporal community of the world, united in our commitment to address the temporal challenges in the planetary age and foster a harmonious relationship between more-than-human societies and the Earth, hereby establish the United Times. As a planetary organisation, the United Times seeks to promote the peaceful coexistence of diverse temporal perspectives, uphold intergenerational freedom, and create a liveable future for earthlings who are part of the planet. We adopt this Charter to serve as the foundation of our collective temporal endeavour.

Chapter I: Purposes and Principles

Article 1. The United Times is established as a planetary organisation to address the temporal challenges in the planetary age and to facilitate cooperation and collaboration among all earthlings in the past, present and future.

Article 2. The United Times shall seek to promote peaceful temporal coexistence, recognising the importance of balancing short-term interests with long-term habitability of the planet.

Chapter II: Structure and Organisation

Article 3. The United Times shall consist of three main bodies, a Secretariat, a General Assembly and an International Court of Temporal Justice.

Article 4. The three principal organs of the Secretariat are: the Observation Department, the Strategic Orientation Department, and the Implementation Department.

Article 5. The General Assembly, composed of representatives from the temporal community, shall serve as the supreme deliberative body of the United Times.

Article 6. The International Court of Temporal Justice shall adjudicate temporal disputes and interpret the provisions of this Charter and related agreements.

Chapter III: Functions and Powers

Article 7. The United Times shall conduct research, analysis, and assessment of temporal challenges and opportunities, facilitating evidence-based policymaking.

Article 8. The United Times shall develop an annual agenda, setting priorities for addressing critical temporal issues and guiding its activities.

Article 9. The United Times shall promote public participation in temporal decision-making through dialogues, consultations, and engagement with citizens and stakeholders.

Article 10. The United Times may provide technical assistance and cooperation in addressing temporal challenges.

Chapter IV: Final Provisions

Article 11. This Charter, including its preamble, shall be deposited with the Secretary-General of the United Times.

In accordance with the United Times Charter, the United Times executive-like Secretariat has three departments: (i) Observation, (ii) Strategic Orientation, and (iii) Implementation. The Observation Department observes the manifold functions of temporal elements in areas such as demography (eg, measuring the impact of temporal violence among generations); land use (eg, does (de)synchronisation between social and natural times affect wealth?); urbanisation (eg, do monocentric and polycentric agglomerations have similar mobility rhythms?); technology (eg, under what circumstances does artificial intelligence compress, stretch, or standardise subjective vs world time); and energy (eg, what tempos and sequences enable or hinder a transformation towards renewables?). The head of this department collates these findings in a 'Yearly Time Outlook' that presents the status quo in each area and analyses the dynamic interplay of the detected temporal functions, ranging from temporal data collection to temporal impact assessments.

The Strategic Orientation Department delves into ethical considerations of temporal decision-making. It develops strategic orientation on desirable forms of temporal development, such as considering how actions taken in the present influence the future, and how future possibilities can shape present decisions. Temporal development could be translated into a metric of temporal development, which measures the extent to which laws must ensure equitable opportunities and quality of life across different generations. The head of the Department is an advocate of chronopolitanism. They advise their staff on how to develop codes of conduct and guidelines which ensure that earthlings have the same opportunities to achieve a given quality of life irrespective of the temporal conditions into which they were, are, or will be born and live. The Department's main priority is to define at what point temporal self-rule by individuals and society has to end, since the natural rhythms of planetary systems are (deeply) influenced and disrupted.

The Department of Implementation determines how the foregoing strategic orientations can be implemented under the current temporal circumstances, ranging from our deep-time interactions with geological processes to the nanosecond temporality of algorithms, considering evidence-based risk and opportunity assessments. Therefore, it develops policy proposals and initiates citizen and stakeholder dialogues. This department could, for example, initiate a project with legislators and politicians to work on the constitutional changes necessary to enable law-making that addresses the intertwining of different timescales, especially regarding short-term interests and long-term needs within the contexts of climate change and nuclear waste.

The United Times also has a legislature-like body, a General Assembly. It represents all the different temporal elements, such as the past, the present and the future, as well as flexibility, tempo or synchronisation of societal and environmental actions across time. These temporal elements are then discussed and elaborated upon to determine what needs to be done to address the challenges of the planetary age.

Lastly, the International Court of Temporal Justice is a specialised judicial body to adjudicate temporal disputes and interpret and apply the provisions of the United Times Charter and related agreements. Composed of temporal law experts, this court operates independently and impartially to ensure a fair resolution of temporal disputes between members. Its primary role is to interpret and apply the temporal principle of chronopolitanism and guide members in managing complex temporal interactions. For example, the International Court of Temporal Justice might hear a landmark case dealing with the question of whether deep-time reparations, which aim to compensate for the degradation of fertile land, are an appropriate way to address injustices in the use of planetary resources by different communities from different generations.

While admittedly situated at the very far end of an imaginary spectrum, this thought experiment demonstrates the tangible character of time, influencing and connecting our lives and the Earth in multiple ways. Even though the United Times, or anything even closely resembling it, is far from realisation, time's influences are real, and its functions could be designed in a more desirable way by ending our collective temporal ignorance, including law's ignorance of time, as I have argued above. A temporalised view on earth system law would include considerations that legally address the genuinely temporal nature of our planetary condition. This could include planning and building major infrastructures that connect and last across various timeframes, or coastal management plans that consider sea-level rise, and corresponding settlement structures, which might be thought of in a much more adaptive and forward-looking way than at present.

Furthermore, the lens of a United Times can stimulate thought on what might co-develop with a temporalised form of earth system law. This includes the need for temporal maturity to ensure planetary habitability. Temporal maturity in this sense means that people are temporally literate due to their temporal capabilities. Temporal maturity would allow people, for example, to proactively compress, bypass, stretch, terminate, standardise, diversify, or synchronise time by using resources such as deadlines, windows of opportunity, time budgets, urgency, phases, or buffers. For instance, for urban planning in the planetary age, temporal maturity could enable the development of flexible zoning laws that can be adapted over time. A city could implement phases of development with specific deadlines and buffers to take into account changing population needs and planetary conditions. Planners might use time budgets to allocate periods for construction and green space development, synchronise infrastructure projects to minimise disruption, or create windows of opportunity to encourage investment during economically advantageous times. And earth system law could regulate all the legal aspects related to the foregoing.

Less legalistically, but not less importantly, temporal maturity and literacy must be cultivated in social life, including, for example, time as an object of learning, from kindergarten to adulthood – lifelong learning. This education should emphasise explicitly the relationship between human activities and the temporal dynamics of planetary change. In kindergarten, children could be introduced to the basic concepts of Earth time through storytelling and activities that highlight natural cycles. They could learn about the seasons, the day-night cycle, and the idea of growth over time through interactive play and observation, such as planting seeds and observing their growth. Lifelong learning opportunities, at the other end of the spectrum, such as community workshops and online courses, could provide adults with the tools to enhance their temporal literacy in the context of planetary health, fostering a deeper respect for the rhythms of Earth.

The features of a chronopolitical time design must also be deliberated. Just as there is spatial design in architecture, we can think of a time design for our interactions with planetary change. Can we identify similar principles for designing temporal arrangements, akin to Vitruvius' principles of architecture: firmness, commodity, and delight?[46] These timeless architectural principles ensure stability, functionality, and aesthetic pleasure, and similarly, principles for time design, such as reflexivity, anticipation and adaptability, could guide chronopolitan deliberation. For example, certain time designs might be imbalanced towards conservation, while others might be too present-oriented. Others might require revision to ensure that the synchronisation of social and planetary rhythms does not lead to a catastrophe of resonance where perfectly aligned but harmful activities accelerate environmental degradation, trigger climate crises, or cause ecological collapses. Given the specific context, a range of temporal elements would have to be arranged in a harmonious or disharmonious way and may include: horizon (short-term vs long-term), tempo (slow vs fast), sequence (sequentially vs simultaneously), volume (high vs low), timing (early vs late), rhythm (regular vs irregular), and cyclic vs linear time arrangements.

VI. Conclusion

This chapter proposed the thought experiment of a United Times as a starting point to explore temporal principles of earth system law to address the divide between societal and planetary times and resulting temporal conflicts. It has been shown that the temporal idea of chronopolitanism can accompany the spatial idea of cosmopolitanism. The impact of a complementary institution such as the United Times on planetary politics could address temporal conflicts that are overlooked by spatially-oriented frameworks. The thought experiment of a United Times could guide us to envision alternative institutions that might pave the way to formulate, eventually in future research, genuine temporal laws, or to temporalise existing ones in the same way as Kant's *Perpetual Peace: A Philosophical Sketch* did with its preliminary laws (reducing the chance of war) and definitive laws (the foundation on which to build peace) that were the theoretical foundation for the UN Charter.

[46] M Vitruvius Pollio, *The Ten Books on Architecture* (trans MH Morgan, Cambridge MA, Harvard University Press, 1914) Book I, Chapter 3 ('*firmitas, utilitas, venustas*').

As we continue to explore the potential of temporalised visions of earth system law, it is crucial to engage in empirical research and pilot projects that test these concepts in real-world scenarios. For example, implementing pilot projects in cities prone to climate change impacts could provide valuable insights into the effectiveness of temporal politics in urban planning and disaster management. Moreover, the United Times thought experiment suggests that earth system law scholars should include temporal dimensions more explicitly in their analyses of existing (and future) legal frameworks. By translating and operationalising temporal principles such as chronopolitanism, the research agenda of earth system law could better foresee and accommodate the long-term impacts on planetary change. Temporalised legal frameworks could also ensure future-oriented regulations on nuclear waste management by demanding long-term monitoring, repeated public consultations between generations, and secure containment that has to span many thousands of years. Similarly, laws governing deep-sea infrastructures and extraction could mandate staged authorisations and long-horizon monitoring, recognising recovery times that exceed ordinary regulatory and political cycles. Such a focus on the genuine temporalities of earth system law could mitigate temporal conflicts and provide prospects to formulate laws that are more resilient to changing and yet-unknown future challenges.

INDEX

www.ingramcontent.com/pod-product-compliance
Ingram Content Group UK Ltd.
Pitfield, Milton Keynes, MK11 3LW, UK
UKHW021910150926
475560UK00003B/288

9 781509 994663